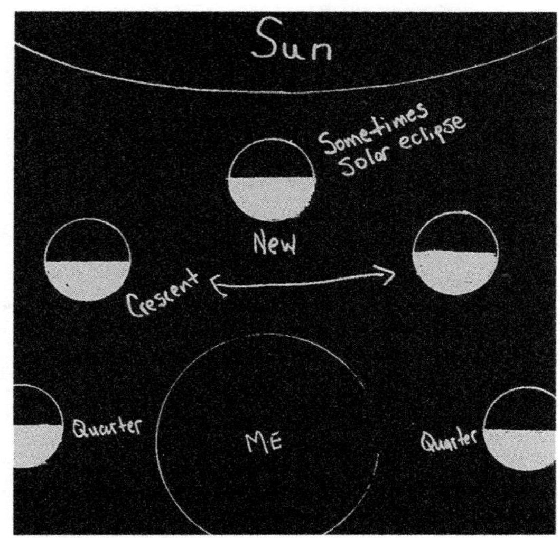

PERFORMANCE

Volume 2 ▪ Middle School

STANDARDS

NEW STANDARDS™

English Language Arts

Mathematics

Science

Applied Learning

Support for the development of the New Standards performance standards was provided by:

The Pew Charitable Trusts,
John D. and Catherine T. MacArthur Foundation,
William T. Grant Foundation,
and the
New Standards partners.

Reprinted 2001, 2005

Designed by Harcourt Brace Educational Measurement.

Printed in the United States of America.

ISBN 1-889630-52-7

TABLE OF CONTENTS

INTRODUCTION

ABOUT NEW STANDARDS

New Standards is a joint project of the Learning Research and Development Center (LRDC) at the University of Pittsburgh and the National Center on Education and the Economy (NCEE). Since it began in 1991, New Standards has led the nation in standards-based reform efforts. Heading a consortium of 26 states and six school districts, New Standards developed the *New Standards™ Performance Standards*, a set of internationally competitive performance standards in English language arts, mathematics, science and applied learning at the 4th, 8th and 10th grade levels.

New Standards also pioneered standards-based performance assessment, developing the *New Standards™ Reference Examinations* and a portfolio assessment system to measure student achievement against the performance standards.

New Standards was founded by Lauren Resnick, Director of the Learning Research and Development Center , and Marc Tucker, President of the National Center on Education and the Economy. Its Governing Board, during the initial years, included chief state school officers, governors and their representatives, and others representing the diversity of the partnership, whose jurisdictions accounted for nearly half the nation's student population.

Today the New Standards program, led by Phil Daro, is managed by the NCEE. The research and development team is located in the Office of the President of the University of California and in the NCEE branch office in Fort Worth, Texas. Other New Standards staff members are based at the LRDC and the NCEE as well as the American Association for the Advancement of Science, the National Council of Teachers of English, and the University of California Office of the President. Technical studies are based at the LRDC and Northwestern University, with an advisory committee of leading psychometricians from across the nation.

The **performance standards** are derived from the national content standards developed by professional organizations, e.g., the National Council of Teachers of Mathematics, and consist of two parts:

Performance descriptions—descriptions of what students should know and the ways they should demonstrate the knowledge and skills they have acquired in the four areas assessed by New Standards—English Language arts, mathematics, science, and applied learning—at elementary, middle, and high school levels.

Work samples and commentaries—samples of student work that illustrate standard-setting performances, each accompanied by commentary that shows how the performance descriptions are reflected in the work sample.

The performance standards were endorsed unanimously by the New Standards Governing Board in June 1996 as the basis for the New Standards assessment system—consisting of an on-demand examination and a portfolio system.

The on-demand examination, called the **reference examination** because it provides a point of reference to national standards, is currently available in English language arts and mathematics at grade levels 4, 8, and 10. It assesses those aspects of the performance standards that can be assessed in a limited time frame under standardized conditions. In English language arts, this means reading short passages and answering questions, writing first drafts and editing. In mathematics, this means short exercises or problems that take 5 to 15 minutes, and longer problems that take up to 45 minutes. The reference examination stops short of being able to accommodate longer pieces of work—reading several books, writing with revision, conducting investigations in mathematics and science and completing projects in applied learning—that are required by New Standards performance standards and by the national content standards from which they are derived.

The **portfolio system** complements the reference examination. It provides evidence of the achievement of the performance standards that depend on extended pieces of work (especially those that show revision) and accumulation of evidence over time. During development, 3,000 teachers and almost 60,000 students participated in a field trial of the portfolio system.

The New Standards Portfolio Systems is available in English language arts, mathematics and science at the elementary, middle and high school levels.

The portfolio system includes:

- A black-line master book with teacher and student instructions and masters of all the entry slips that are needed for students to identify their work, samples of student work and scoring profiles.
- Student accordion folders with legal-size folders for each of the exhibits required by the New Standards Portfolio System. Instructions for assembling exhibits are printed directly on the folders so that links to the performance standards are easily seen.

PRIMARY LITERACY STANDARDS

In 1999 New Standards developed **primary literacy standards**, released in 1999 under the title *Reading and Writing Grade by Grade*. Teachers and schools across the country had expressed a need for more guidance on what learning is needed by students before they enter 4th grade, particularly in the critical area of literacy. At the same time, the nation, as seen in statements by the President and many governors, voiced a new commitment to ensuring that all children learn to read by the end of 3rd grade. New Standards responded by bringing together 22 of the nation's top experts on literacy including some of the best-known advocates of the phonics approach as well as the whole-language approach. Five of them had served on the National Research Council's Committee on the Prevention of Reading Difficulties in Young Children, which published an influential report on early literacy in 1998.

The New Standards Primary Literacy Standards offer a unique set of grade-by-grade expectations in reading and writing for students in kindergarten through 3rd grade. They state what primary-grades students should know and be able to do, and how well they should be able to perform. They offer examples of that student performance taken from real classrooms. The Primary Literacy Standards challenge traditional classroom practice by giving equal weight to the teaching of reading and writing, linking the skills in one to skills in the other.

The New Standards Primary Literacy Standards give teachers and parents examples of the kind of reading and writing that children should be able to do in kindergarten through 3rd grade. Drawn from real classrooms, these work samples include a CD-ROM of recordings of children reading specially identified books that allow adults to rate student progress against the standards.

ABOUT THE PERFORMANCE STANDARDS

We have adopted the distinction between content standards and performance standards that is articulated in *Promises to Keep: Creating High Standards for American Students* (1993), a report commissioned by the National Education Goals Panel. Content standards specify "what students should know and be able to do"; performance standards go the next step to specify "how good is good enough."

These standards are designed to make content standards operational by answering the question: how good is good enough?

Where do the performance standards come from?

These performance standards are built directly upon the consensus content standards developed by the national professional organizations for the disciplines. The Mathematics performance standards are based directly on the content standards produced by the National Council of Teachers of Mathematics (1989). (See "Introduction to the Mathematics performance standards," page 52.) Similarly, the performance standards for English Language Arts were developed in concert with the content standards produced by the National Council of Teachers of English and the International Reading Association (1996). (See "Introduction to the English Language Arts performance standards," page 20.)

The Science performance standards are built upon the National Research Council's *National Science Education Standards* (1996) and the American Association for the Advancement of Science's Project 2061 *Benchmarks for Science Literacy* (1993). (See "Introduction to the Science performance standards," page 90.)

The case of the Applied Learning performance standards is a little different. Applied Learning focuses on connecting the work students do in school with the demands of the twenty-first century workplace. As a newer focus of study, Applied Learning does not have a distinct professional constituency producing content standards on which performance standards can be built. However, the Secretary's Commission on Achieving Necessary Skills (SCANS) laid a foundation for the field in its report, *Learning a Living: A Blueprint for High Performance* (1992) which defined "Workplace Know-how." We worked from this foundation and from comparable international work to produce our own "Framework for Applied Learning" (New Standards, 1994). The Applied Learning performance standards have been built upon this framework. (See "Introduction to the Applied Learning performance standards," page 112.)

STANDARDS FOR STANDARDS

In recent years several reports on standards development have established "standards for standards," that is, guidelines for developing standards and criteria for judging their quality. These include the review criteria identified in *Promises to Keep*, the American Federation of Teachers' "Criteria for High Quality Standards," published in *Making Standards Matter* (1995), and the "Principles for Education Standards" developed by the Business Task Force on Student Standards and published in *The Challenge of Change* (1995). We drew from the criteria and principles advocated in these documents in establishing the "standards" we have tried to achieve in the New Standards performance standards.

Standards should establish high standards for all students.

The New Standards partnership has resolved to abolish the practice of expecting less from poor and minority children and children whose first language is not English. These performance standards are intended to help bring all students to high levels of performance.

Much of the onus for making this goal a reality rests on the ways the standards are implemented. The New Standards partners have adopted a Social Compact, which says in part, "Specifically, we pledge to do everything in our power to ensure all students a fair shot at reaching the new performance standards...This means they will be taught a curriculum that will prepare them for the assessments, that their teachers will have the preparation to enable them to teach it well, and there will be...the resources the students and their teachers need to succeed."

There are ways in which the design of the standards themselves can also contribute to the goal of bringing all students to high levels of performance, especially by being clear about what is expected. We have worked to make the expectations included in these performance standards as clear as possible. For some standards it has been possible to do this in the performance descriptions. For example, the Reading standard includes expectations for students to read widely and to read quality materials. Instead of simply exhorting them to do this, we have given more explicit direction by specifying that students should be expected to read at least twenty-five books each year and that those books should be of the quality and complexity illustrated in the sample reading list provided for each grade level. In Mathematics, we have gone beyond simply listing problem solving among our expectations for students. We set out just what we mean by problem solving and what things we expect students to be able to do in problem solving and mathematical reasoning. In addition, by providing numerous examples we have indicated the level of difficulty of the problems students are expected to solve.

The inclusion of work samples and commentaries to illustrate the meaning of the standards is intended to help make the standards clearer. Most of the standards are hard to pin down precisely in words alone. In the Writing standard, for example, the work samples show the expected qualities of writing for the various kinds of writing required and the commentaries explain how these qualities are demonstrated in the work samples. The work samples and commentaries are an integral part of the performance standards.

The work samples will help teachers, students, and parents to picture work that meets standards and to establish goals to reach for. Students need to know what work that meets standards looks like if they are to strive to produce work of the same quality. They also need to see themselves reflected in the work samples if they are to believe that they too are capable of producing such work. We have included work samples drawn from a diverse range of students and from students studying in a wide variety of settings.

Standards should be rigorous and world class.

Is what we expect of our students as rigorous and demanding as what is expected of young people in other countries—especially those countries whose young people consistently perform as well as or better than ours?

That is the question we are trying to answer when we talk about developing world class standards.

Through successive drafts of these performance standards, we compared our work with the national and local curricula of other countries, with textbooks, assessments, and examinations from other countries and, where possible, with work produced by students in other countries. Ultimately, it is the work students produce that will show us whether claims for world class standards can be supported.

We shared the *Consultation Draft* with researchers in other countries and asked them to review it in terms of their own country's standards and in light of what is considered world class in their field. Included among these countries were Australia, Belgium, Canada, the Czech Republic, Denmark, England and Wales, Finland, France, Germany, Japan, the Netherlands, New Zealand, Norway, Poland, Scotland, Singapore, Sweden, and Switzerland. We asked these reviewers to tell us whether each standard is at least as demanding as its counterparts abroad and whether the set of standards represents an appropriately thorough coverage of the subject areas. We also shared the *Consultation Draft* with recognized experts in the field of international comparisons of education, each of whom is familiar with the education systems of several countries.

Our reviewers provided a wealth of constructive responses to the *Consultation Draft*. Most confined their responses to the English Language Arts, Mathematics, and Science standards, though several commended the inclusion of standards for Applied Learning. The reviewers supported the approach we adopted to "concretize" the performance standards through the inclusion of work samples (similar approaches are being used in some other countries, notably England and Wales and Australia). Some of the reviewers were tentative in their response to the question of whether these performance standards are at least as demanding as their counterparts, noting the difficulty of drawing comparisons in the absence of assessment information, but offered comparative comments in terms of the areas covered by the standards. Some provided a detailed analysis of the performance descriptions together with the work samples and commentaries in terms of the expectations of students at comparable grade levels in other countries.

The reviews confirmed the conclusion we had drawn from our earlier analyses of the curricula, textbooks, and examinations of other countries: while the structure of curricula differs from country to country, the expectations contained in these performance standards represent a thorough coverage of the subject areas. No reviewer identified a case of significant omission. In some cases, reviewers noted that the range of expectations may be greater in the New Standards performance standards than in other countries; for example, few countries expect young people to integrate their learning to the extent required by the standards for investigation in New Standards Mathematics. At the same time, a recent study prepared for the Organisation for Economic Co-operation and Development reports that many countries are moving towards expecting students to engage in practical work of the kind required by the New Standards Science standards (Black and Atkin, 1996). The reviews also suggest that these performance standards contain expectations that are at least as rigorous as, and are in some cases more rigorous than, the demands made of students in other countries. None of the reviewers identified standards for which the expectations expressed in the standards were less demanding than those for students in other countries.

We will continue to monitor the rigor and coverage of the New Standards performance standards and assessments in relation to the expectations of students in other countries. In addition to the continued collection and review of materials from other countries, our efforts will include a review of the New Standards performance standards by the Third International Mathematics and Science Study, collaboration with the Council for Basic Education's plan to collect samples of student work from around the world, continued review of the American Federation of Teachers' series, *Defining World Class Standards,* and collaborative efforts with visiting scholars at the Learning Research and Development Center.

Standards should be useful, developing what is needed for citizenship, employment, and life-long learning.

We believe that the core disciplines provide the strongest foundation for learning what is needed for citizenship, employment, and life-long learning. Thus, we have established explicit standards in the core areas of English Language Arts, Mathematics, and Science. But there is more. In particular, it is critical for young people to achieve high standards in Applied Learning—the fourth area we are working on.

Applied Learning focuses on the capabilities people need to be productive members of society, as individuals who apply the knowledge gained in school and elsewhere to analyze problems and propose solutions, to communicate effectively and coordinate action with others, and to use the tools of the information age workplace.

Applied Learning is not about "job skills" for students who are judged incapable of, or indifferent to, the challenges and opportunities of academic learning. They are the abilities all young people will need, both in the workplace and in their role as citizens. They are the thinking and reasoning abilities demanded both by colleges and by the growing number of high performance workplaces, those that expect people at every level of the organization to take responsibility for the quality of products and services. Some of these abilities are familiar; they have long been recognized goals of schooling, though they have not necessarily been translated clearly into expectations for student performance. Others break new ground; they are the kinds of abilities we now understand will be needed by everyone in the near future. All are skills attuned to the real world of responsible citizenship and dignified work that values and cultivates mind and spirit.

Many reviewers of drafts of these performance standards noted the absence of standards for the core area of social studies, including history, geography, and civics. At the time we began our work, national content standards for those areas were only in early stages of development; we resolved to focus our resources on the four areas we have worked on. As consensus builds around content standards in this additional area, we will examine the possibilities for expanding the New Standards system to include it.

Standards should be important and focused, parsimonious while including those elements that represent the most important knowledge and skills within the discipline.

As anyone who has been involved in a standards development effort knows, it is easier to add to standards than it is to limit what they cover. It is especially easier to resolve disagreements about the most important things to cover by including everything than it is to resolve the disagreements themselves. We have tried not to take the easier route. We adopted the principle of parsimony as a goal and have tried to practice it. At the same time, we have been concerned not to confuse parsimony with brevity. The performance descriptions are intended to make

STANDARDS FOR STANDARDS

explicit what it is that students should know and the ways they should demonstrate the knowledge and skills they have acquired. For example, the standards relating to conceptual understanding in Mathematics spell out the expectations of students in some detail.

The approach we have adopted distinguishes between standards as a means of organizing the knowledge and skills of a subject area and as a reference point for assessment, on the one hand, and the curriculum designed to enable students to achieve the standards, on the other. The standards are intended to focus attention on what is important but not to imply that the standards themselves should provide the organizing structure for the curriculum. In English Language Arts, for example, we have established a separate standard for conventions, grammar, and usage. This does not imply that conventions, grammar, and usage should be taught in isolation from other elements of English Language Arts. In fact, all of the work samples included in this book to illustrate the Conventions standard also illustrate parts of the Writing standard. What we are saying is that the work students do should be designed to help them achieve the Conventions standard. This means that conventions, grammar, and usage should not only be among the things assessed but should also be a focus for explicit reporting of student achievement.

Standards should be manageable given the constraints of time.

This criterion follows very closely on the last one, but focuses particularly on making sure that standards are "doable." One of the important features of our standards development effort is the high level of interaction among the people working on the different subject areas. We view the standards for the four areas as a set at each grade level; our publication of the standards by grade level reflects this orientation. This orientation has allowed us to limit the incidence of duplication across subject areas and to recognize and use opportunities for forging stronger connections among subject areas through the work that students do. A key to ensuring the standards are manageable is making the most of opportunities for student work to do "double" and even "triple duty." Most of the work samples included in this book demonstrate the way a single activity can generate work that allows students to demonstrate their achievement in relation to several standards within a subject area. Several of the work samples show how a single activity can allow students to demonstrate their achievement in relation to standards in more than one subject area. (See, for example, "A New Look on a Budget," page 82.)

Standards should be adaptable, permitting flexibility in implementation needed for local control, state and regional variation, and differing individual interests and cultural traditions.

These standards are intended for use in widely differing settings. One approach to tackling the need for flexibility to accommodate local control, state and regional variation, and differing individual interests and cultural traditions, is to make the standards general and to leave the job of translating the standards into more specific statements to the people who use them. We have not adopted that approach. These standards need to be specific enough to guide the New Standards assessment system; we have tried to make them specific enough to do so. We have also tried to achieve the degree of specificity necessary to do this without unduly limiting the kinds of flexibility outlined above. Most of the standards are expressed in a way that leaves plenty of room for local decisions about the actual tasks and activities through which the standards may be achieved.

However, the specificity needed for standards intended to guide an assessment system does place some limits on flexibility. To tackle these apparently contradictory demands on the standards, we have adopted the notion of "substitution." This means that when users of these standards identify elements in the standards that are inconsistent with decisions made at the local level, they can substitute their own. An example of this is the Reading standard in English Language Arts. The Reading standard includes the requirement that students should read the equivalent of twenty-five books each year and specifies that they should read material of the quality and complexity illustrated in the sample reading list. We have included the reading list so as to be clear about the quality of reading material we are talking about at each grade level. But we do not claim that the titles on this list are the only ones that would be appropriate. Thus, users who have established their own reading lists and are satisfied with them can replace the lists provided with their own. There is, however, one important proviso: substitution only works when what is substituted is comparable with the material it replaces both in terms of the quality and the quantity of expectation.

Standards should be clear and usable.

Making standards sufficiently clear so that parents, teachers, and students can understand what they mean and what the standards require of them is essential to the purpose for establishing standards in the first place. It is also a challenge because while all of these groups need to understand what the standards are, the kinds of information they need are different. The most obvious difference is between the way in which the standards need to be presented to elementary school students so that they know what they should be striving to achieve and the way in which those same standards need to be presented to teachers so that they can help their students get there. If the standards were written only in a form that elementary school students could access, we would have to leave out information teachers need to do their job.

These standards are being presented in several formats. This version of the standards is written primarily for teachers. It includes technical language about the subject matter of the standards and terms that educators use to describe differences in the quality of work students produce. It could be described as a technical document. That does not mean that parents and students should not have access to it. We have tried to make the standards clear and to avoid jargon, but they do include language that may be difficult for students to comprehend and more detail than some parents may want to deal with.

The standards are also included in the portfolio materials provided for student use. In these materials, the standards are set out in the form of guides to help students select work to include in their portfolios.

A less technical version of the standards is in preparation. It is being written with parents and the community in general in mind. The standards will be the same but they will be explained in more generally accessible language.

Standards should be reflective of broad consensus, resulting from an iterative process of comment, feedback, and revision including educators and the general public.

This publication is the result of progressive revisions to drafts over a period of eighteen months. Early drafts were revised in response to comment and feedback from reviewers nominated by the New Standards partners and the New Standards advisory committees for each of the subject areas, as well as other educators.

The *Consultation Draft,* published in November 1995, was circulated widely for comment. Some 1,500 individuals and organizations were invited to review the *Draft.* The reviewers included nominees of professional associations representing a wide range of interests in education, subject experts in the relevant fields, experienced teachers, business and industry groups, and community organizations. In addition, we held a series of face-to-face consultations to obtain responses and suggestions. These included detailed discussions with members of key groups and organizations and a series of meetings at which we invited people with relevant experience and expertise to provide detailed critique of the *Consultation Draft.* We also received numerous responses from people who purchased the *Consultation Draft* and who took the trouble to complete and return the response form that was included with each copy.

The process of revision of the performance standards was further informed by a series of independently-conducted focus group meetings with parents and other members of the community in several regions of the country and with teachers who were using the *Consultation Draft.*

The reviewers provided very supportive and constructive commentary on the *Consultation Draft,* both at the broad level of presentation and formatting of the performance standards and at the detailed level of suggestions for refinements to the performance descriptions for some of the standards. These comments have significantly informed the revisions made to the standards in the preparation of this publication.

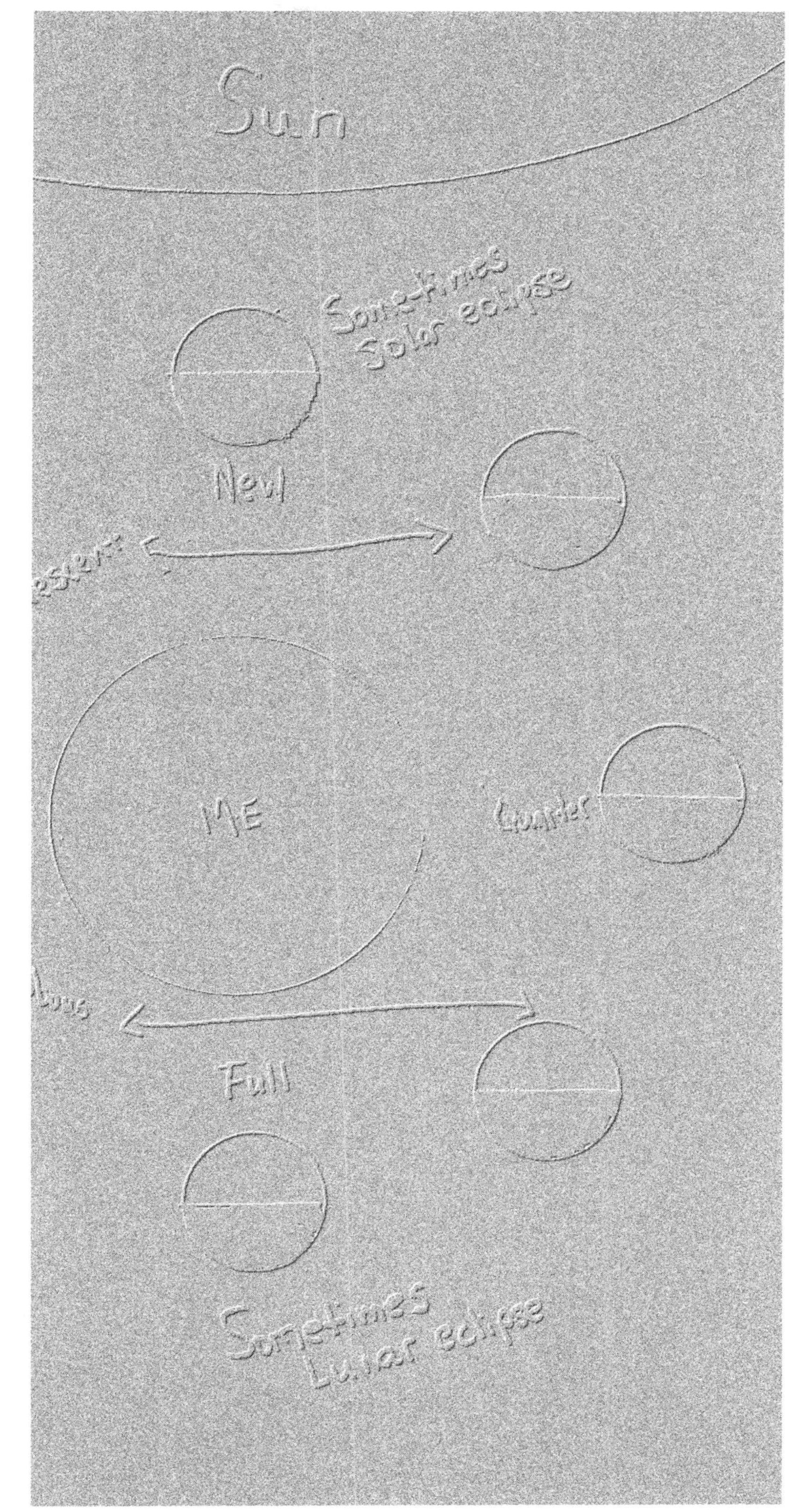

HOW TO READ THESE PERFORMANCE STANDARDS

The standards for middle school are set out in an overview on page 19. The overview provides the names of the standards for each of the four areas: English Language Arts, Mathematics, Science, and Applied Learning. To help you navigate your way through the book, a different color is used for each area.

Middle school level means the end of eighth grade.

The standards for middle school are set at the level of achievement expected of students at approximately the end of eighth grade. Some students will achieve this level of performance earlier than the end of eighth grade. Some students will reach it later than the end of eighth grade. What is important is that students have the opportunity to meet the standards. (See "Deciding what constitutes a standard-setting performance," page 12.)

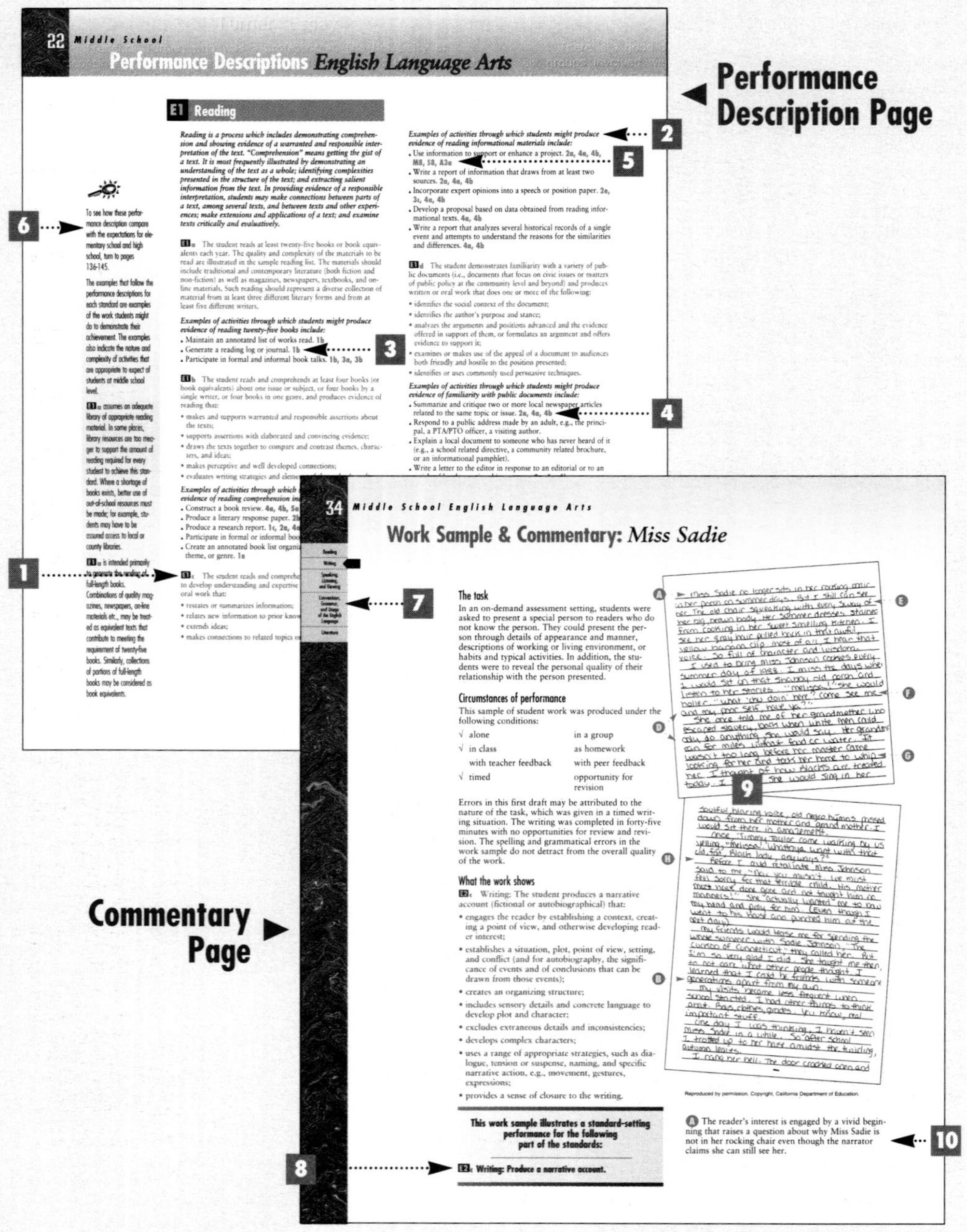

Each standard is identified by a symbol.

Turn to the performance descriptions for English Language Arts on pages 22-26. There are five standards for English Language Arts, each identified by a symbol. The symbol for the Reading standard is E1. This symbol appears throughout the book wherever there is a reference to this standard.

1 Most standards are made up of several parts.

Most of the standards are made up of several parts, for example, the Reading standard has five parts. Each part is identified by a lower case letter; for example, the part of the Reading standard that refers to reading informational materials is E1c. These symbols are used throughout the book wherever there is a reference to the relevant part of a standard.

Performance descriptions tell what students are expected to know and be able to do.

Each part of a standard has a performance description. The performance description is a narrative description of what students are expected to know and be able to do. It is shown in color.

2 Examples are the kinds of work students might do to demonstrate their achievement of the standards.

Immediately following the performance descriptions for the standard are examples of the kinds of work students might do to demonstrate their achievement. The examples also indicate the nature and complexity of activities that are appropriate to expect of students at the grade level. However, we use the word "example" deliberately. The examples are intended only to show the kinds of work that students might do and to stimulate ideas for further kinds of work. None of the activities shown in the examples is necessarily required to meet the standard.

3 Cross-references highlight the links between the examples and the performance descriptions.

The symbols that follow each example show the part or parts of the standard to which the example relates.

4 Cross-references also highlight links among the standards.

Often the examples that go with the English Language Arts performance descriptions include cross-references to other parts of the English Language Arts standards.

5 Cross-references also highlight opportunities for connecting activities across subject areas.

Some cross-references shown following the examples identify parts of standards in other subject areas. These cross-references highlight examples for which the same activity may enable students to demonstrate their achievement in more than one subject matter.

Some cross-references are to Applied Learning.

Some of the cross-references are to Applied Learning. Applied Learning is not a subject area in its own right. Applied Learning activities are expected to draw on subject matter from English language arts, mathematics, science, or other subjects. Generally, they will take place as part of studies within one or more subjects. The cross-references show activities that may provide a vehicle for students to demonstrate achievement of standards within one or more subject areas as well as standards for Applied Learning.

Some cross-references also show the possibilities for using work from Mathematics or Science to demonstrate their achievement of English Language Arts standards, and vice versa.

We have not tried to highlight every possible cross-reference, only to give an indication of the possibilities. The potential of these examples for realizing the possibilities of enabling students to demonstrate their achievement in more than one subject area depends to a large extent on the specific tasks that are presented to students.

6 Margin notes draw attention to particular aspects of the standards.

The notes in the margin draw attention to particular aspects of the standards, such as the resources to which students need access in order to meet the requirements of the standards.

Comparing the grade levels.

Each page showing performance descriptions has a note in the margin that directs attention to the Appendices which show the performance descriptions at each of the three grade levels: elementary, middle, and high school.

Work samples and commentaries.

Work samples and commentaries appear on the pages immediately following the performance descriptions.

7 Standards are highlighted in the bar at the side of the page.

The bar along the side of the pages showing student work highlights the standards that are illustrated by each work sample.

8 The box at the bottom of the page shows what is illustrated in the work sample.

The shaded box at the bottom of the page lists the parts of the standards that are illustrated in the work sample.

9 Work samples illustrate standard-setting performances.

Each work sample is a genuine piece of student work. We have selected it because it illustrates a standard-setting performance for one or more parts of the standards. (See "Not all performance standards are the same," page 10.)

10 The commentary explains why the work illustrates a standard-setting performance.

The commentary that goes with each work sample identifies the features of the work sample that illustrate the relevant parts of the standards. The commentary explains the task on which the student worked and the circumstances under which the work was completed. It draws attention to the qualities of the work with direct reference to the performance descriptions for the relevant standards.

The commentary also notes our reservations about the work.

The commentary also draws attention to any reservations we have about the student work. (See "Genuine student work," page 12.)

Performance Standards = performance descriptions + work samples + commentaries on the work samples.

Performance standards are, therefore, made up of a combination of performance descriptions, work samples, and commentaries on the work samples:

- The performance descriptions tell what students should know and the ways they should demonstrate the knowledge and skills they have acquired.
- The work samples show work that illustrates standard-setting performances in relation to parts of the standards.
- The commentaries explain why the work is standard-setting with reference to the relevant performance description or descriptions.

Each of these is an essential component of a performance standard.

Most work samples illustrate a standard-setting performance for parts of more than one standard.

Most work samples illustrate the quality of work expected for parts of more than one standard. For example, some of the work samples selected to illustrate parts of E2, Writing, also illustrate a standard-setting performance for one or both parts of E4, Conventions, Grammar, and Usage of the English Language, or for part of E5, Literature, or, possibly, all of these.

"Using the Library Reference Computers" (see page 27) is an example of a work sample that illustrates parts of more than one standard in English Language Arts.

A work sample may illustrate standards from more than one subject area.

Similarly, a work sample may illustrate parts of standards in more than one subject area. For example, a project completed for M8, Putting Mathematics to Work, might also illustrate the report writing part of E2, Writing. It might also qualify as a project within the requirements of A1, Problem Solving.

"A New Look on a Budget" (see page 82) is an example of a work sample that illustrates parts of standards from more than one subject area.

NOT ALL PERFORMANCE STANDARDS ARE THE SAME

As you read these performance standards, you will notice that the standards are not all the same. The most obvious difference is in the way in which the performance descriptions for the standards are written. We did not impose a single style on the way in which the standards were written although we probably intended to do so when we began work. The reason we abandoned the idea of a single style is that during the course of the development process, it became increasingly apparent that the various standards are different in nature and have different purposes that lend themselves to different kinds of presentation. But the style we have adopted for each standard is not entirely idiosyncratic. There are some patterns that help make sense of the different styles and of the nature and purposes of the standards for which those styles have been used.

The first distinction that most people notice is the difference between the way the performance descriptions for the Mathematics and Science standards are written, on the one hand, and the way the performance descriptions for the English Language Arts and Applied Learning standards are written, on the other. But closer inspection reveals that the differences among the standards do not fall out as neatly as that division would suggest. Each subject area includes different styles of standards and the styles apply across subject areas.

We have identified four categories or kinds of standards, distinguished by their relationship to products of student learning and by the range of evidence required to demonstrate achievement of the standards. The distinctions are broad rather than neat, and we have sought only to define them generally rather than precisely. These differences among the standards have consequences for what it means to "meet a standard" and, therefore, for the ways in which we can use samples of student work to illustrate standard-setting performances.

Standards that describe a piece of work or a performance

One kind of standard is characterized by E2, Writing. Each part of this standard literally describes a piece of work that students are expected to produce and the knowledge and skills that should be evident in that work. For this kind of standard there is a one to one relationship between each part of the standard and a piece of work.

Standards that fit this category generally are the parts of E1, E2, E3, E5b, M8, S8, A1, A2, and A5.

Standards of this kind have several features:

• A single piece of work can meet the standard. In fact all of the requirements of the standard usually must be evident in a single piece of work for it to be judged as meeting the standard.

• The qualities that must be evident in a piece of work for it to meet the standard can be stated explicitly and are listed in bullet points as part of the performance description. These qualities can be thought of as assessment criteria or as a rubric for work that meets the standard.

Work samples and commentaries to illustrate standard-setting performances for standards of this kind include: "Miss Sadie," page 34, "A New Look on a Budget," page 82, "Paper Towels," page 110, and "Career Day," page 130.

Standards that describe conceptual understanding

A second kind of standard is characterized by M1, Number and Operation Concepts. This standard describes conceptual understanding.

Standards that fit this category are E5a, M1, M2, M3, M4, S1, S2, S3, and S4.

These standards have several features:

• The standard is made up of a number of distinct parts. It is most unlikely that any single piece of work will demonstrate all parts of the standard. In fact, it is common for a single piece of work to relate only to some aspects of one part of the standard. Thus, the standard can usually only be met by multiple pieces of work.

• Conceptual understanding is developmental. Any one piece of work may contain elements of conceptual understanding that are below what is expected for the grade level and elements that either meet or exceed what is expected for the grade level. Judging whether the work is "good enough" often means making an on-balance judgment. The developmental nature of conceptual understanding makes it difficult to specify in more than general terms the qualities that need to be present in a piece of work for it to be judged as "good enough." These expectations need to be defined concept by concept.

In M1, M2, M3, and M4, the expectations have been defined more closely through progressive drafts of these performance standards.

S1, S2, S3, and S4 are derived from the *National Science Education Standards* and the *Benchmarks for Science Literacy,* each of which contains detailed explication of the concepts and the expectations of students for conceptual understanding at different grade levels.

Work samples and commentaries to illustrate standard-setting performances for standards of this kind include: "Dart Board," page 61, and "Buoyancy," page 100.

Standards that describe skills and tools

The third kind of standard is made up of the standards that describe skills and tools, such as analytical skills. It is characterized by S6, Scientific Tools and Technologies.

Standards that fit this category generally are E4, M5, M6, M7, S5, S6, S7, A3, and A4.

These standards have several features:

• As with the standards that describe conceptual understanding, it is most unlikely that any single piece of work will demonstrate all parts of the standard. In fact, it is common for a single piece of work to relate only to some aspects of one part of the standard. Thus, the standard can only be met by multiple pieces of evidence.

• Also, like conceptual understanding, use of skills and tools is developmental. Any one piece of work may contain evidence of use of skills and tools that is below what is expected for the grade level and evidence of use that either meets or exceeds what is expected for the grade level. Deciding whether the work is "good enough" often means making an on-balance judgment.

• What distinguishes these standards from the other kinds is the body of evidence needed to demonstrate that the standard has been met. Here, sufficiency refers not only to the idea of coverage but also to a notion of consistency of application. We want to be confident that the work in question is representative of a body of work.

Ideally, work that provides evidence for these standards also provides evidence for other standards. This is the case for all of the work samples in this book that illustrate parts of these standards.

Work samples and commentaries to illustrate standard-setting performances for standards of this kind include: "Points and Segments," page 68, "Discovering Density," page 101, and "Video 2," page 117.

Standards that describe an accomplishment based on effort

The fourth category is closely related to the first, standards that describe a piece of work or a performance; it could be regarded as a sub-category of those standards. It is characterized by E1a, Read at least twenty-five books or book equivalents each year.

This part of the Reading standard is designed to encourage and reward effort. It is designed on principles similar to those that apply to the merit badges that have long formed a part of the system of encouragement and rewards for young people in community youth organizations like the Boy Scouts of America and the Girl Scouts of the U.S.A. The twenty-five book requirement is designed to encourage students to develop a habit of reading by requiring that they read a lot. The requirement is challenging, especially since the reading is expected to be of the quality of the materials included in the sample reading list, but it is also confined. This part of the standard is not made more complex by requirements for evidence of depth of reading and comprehension. The message is, if you invest the effort, you will meet the requirement.

An example of a work sample and commentary to illustrate a standard-setting performance for this part of the Reading standard is "Reading Log," page 48.

The differences among standards described here have implications for their assessment. (See "How the assessments are connected to the performance standards," page 14.)

THE WORK SAMPLES

The work samples and commentaries form an essential element of the performance standards because they give concrete meaning to the words in the performance descriptions and show the level of performance expected by the standards.

Genuine student work

In all cases, the work samples are genuine student work. While they illustrate standard-setting performances for parts of the standards, many samples are not "perfect" in every respect. Some, for example, include spelling errors, clumsy grammatical constructions, or errors of calculation. We think it is important that the standards be illustrated by means of authentic work samples and accordingly have made no attempt to "doctor" the work in order to correct these imperfections: the work has been included "warts and all." Where errors occur, we have included a note drawing attention to the nature of the mistakes and commenting on their significance in the context of the work. In some cases, for example, the work was produced as a first draft only (in which case it would be expected that the errors would be corrected in work presented as finished work), or there is evidence in the rest of the work to suggest that an error was a slip rather than an error in conceptual understanding.

In other words, we have tried to adopt reasonable expectations for correctness, but not to overlook errors where they arise. We have also resolved to apply those expectations consistently to all the work samples. We have paid attention to spelling, for example, not only in the work samples included to illustrate the English Language Arts standards, but also in those samples included to illustrate standards in the other subject areas. Similarly, we reviewed all work samples for accuracy in relation to mathematical and scientific content.

Work produced by a diverse range of students

The work samples in this book were produced by a diverse range of students in a wide variety of settings. The work comes from places as different from one another as rural communities in Vermont and Iowa, urban communities in Fort Worth, Pittsburgh, San Diego, and New York City, and suburban communities in Washington, California, and Colorado. It comes from students with a wide range of cultural backgrounds, some of whom have a first language other than English. And it comes from students studying in regular programs and from students studying in special education programs. Some of the work was produced under examination conditions in timed settings; most of it was produced in the context of on-going class work and extended projects. Most of the work was produced in school, but some samples were produced through out-of-school programs, such as 4-H and a community youth program.

What unites the work samples is that they all help to illustrate the performance standards by demonstrating standard-setting performances for parts of one or more of the standards.

Deciding what constitutes a standard-setting performance

The work samples published in this book were selected from a much wider range of samples. The samples came from students working on producing New Standards portfolios, from students' work on New Standards reference examinations, from other work produced by students in the classrooms of schools of the states and urban school districts that form the New Standards partnership, and from work produced by students in schools that are involved in related programs.

The collections of student work were reviewed through a variety of strategies to tap the judgment of teachers and subject experts about the "level of performance" at which each of the standards for middle school should be set. We define the middle school level as being the expectations for student performance at approximately the end of eighth grade. We used grade level as our reference point because it is in common use and most people understand it. However, "at approximately the end of eighth grade" begs some questions. Do we mean the level at which our eighth graders currently perform? Or, do we mean the level at which our eighth graders might perform if expectations for their performance were higher and the programs through which they learn were designed to help them meet those higher expectations? And, do we mean the level at which the highest-achieving eighth graders perform or the level at which most eighth graders perform?

We established our expectations in terms of what we should expect of students who work hard in a good program; that is, our expectations assume that students will have tried hard to achieve the standards and they will have studied in a program designed to help them to do so. These performance standards are founded on a firm belief that the great majority of students can achieve them, providing they work hard, they study a curriculum designed to help them achieve the standards that is taught by teachers who are prepared to teach it well, and they have adequate resources to succeed.

Some of the work samples included in this book were also included in the *Consultation Draft*; some appeared in earlier drafts as well. The appropriateness of these work samples as illustrating standard-setting performances has been the subject of extensive review, through discussions among our subject advisory committees and through round table discussions among experienced teachers and subject experts. Some of the work samples included in earlier drafts did not pass the scrutiny of these reviews and are not included in this book. Many of the new work samples were identified in the course of meetings set up to score portfolios produced through the New Standards portfolio field trial in 1995-96; others were identified in the process of scoring tasks on New Standards reference examinations. These scoring meetings involve multiple scoring and discussion of samples among experienced teachers and subject experts. Cross-referencing the selection of work samples to illustrate the performance standards with the scoring of work produced through the two elements of the New Standards assessment system is critical to ensuring the development of coherence among all the parts of the system.

We used this process of progressive iterations of review of work samples, both in relation to the performance descriptions and in relation to our definition of middle school level, to arrive at agreement about the meaning of middle school level.

Inevitably, agreement about what work constitutes a standard-setting performance was easiest to achieve for those parts of the standards that relate to familiar kinds of expectations for student work. The parts of the Writing standard that refer to familiar and often-practiced kinds of writing such as narrative account are good examples of this. Not only did we have access to a wide range of samples from which to choose, but teachers and experts in the field have a long tradition of discussion and assessment of the features of good writing for a narrative account. Work samples to illustrate some other parts of the standards are much harder to find; for example, work samples to illustrate the investigations and projects standards in Mathematics and Science and work samples to illustrate each of the Applied Learning standards. Overall, we had access to relatively few work samples for Science and Applied Learning, since work on these areas within the New Standards system is at an early stage by comparison with the work in English Language Arts and Mathematics.

The comprehensiveness of the work samples

This book contains thirty-five samples of student work and more are contained in the videotape that accompanies the book. We have sought to include work samples that illustrate standard-setting performances for each of the standards and for as many of the parts of the standards as possible. The range of work samples has been expanded considerably over progressive drafts of the standards. But the collection is still not comprehensive. We have included work samples to illustrate only some parts of the conceptual understanding standards in Mathematics and Science, for example, and work samples to illustrate only some of the kinds of projects and investigations included in those standards.

Limiting the number of samples was a deliberate decision. We decided that we would make best use of a print format by seeking to illustrate as many parts of the standards as possible but restricting the overall number of work samples to a manageable number. We also decided to restrict the work samples to samples that illustrate standard-setting performances in relation to parts of the standards, rather than include work samples that illustrate performances that are not of sufficient quality or that exceed expectations for the standards. (With regard to the latter point, collections of work samples that illustrate performances at a range of performance levels do exist within the New Standards system, as part of the Released Tasks and scoring guides for the reference examinations and in the example portfolios; see page 16.)

It is arguable whether any given collection of work samples, regardless of how large, would be adequate for illustrating every part of the standards. Similarly, it is arguable whether any such collection could also demonstrate the range of ways that students might produce work that illustrates standard-setting performances and illustrate the standards more fully by including work that demonstrates a range of levels of performance. To be really useful, such a collection would also need to be capable of being updated to include more effective illustrations of the standards as work that serves the purpose becomes available—a need that we have already noted exists in relation to some of the standards. A publication format that could perform all of those functions presents a tall order, indeed. However, electronic formats hold the promise of making it possible to build a collection of this sort and to make it easily accessible. We hope to make use of the potential of electronic formats in the future.

HOW WILL THE PERFORMANCE STANDARDS BE USED?

The primary audience for these performance standards is teachers. We hope that teachers will use the standards to:

- Help students and parents understand what work that meets standards looks like;
- Inform discussions with their colleagues as they plan programs to help students learn to high standards;
- Challenge assumptions about what we can expect from students;
- Communicate the meaning of high standards to district administrators, school board members, and the public so they can work together to build learning environments that challenge all students.

New Standards will use the performance standards to provide:

- The basis of design specifications for the New Standards assessment system;
- The basis for reporting student scores on assessments within the New Standards system; and
- The basis for linking the New Standards assessment system with the standards and assessment systems of the members of the New Standards partnership.

Assessment based on standards

Performance standards define a student's academic responsibilities and, by implication, the teaching responsibilities of the school. How do we determine whether students have lived up to their academic responsibilities? We assess their work—is it "good enough" by comparison with the standards.

Assessment that serves the purpose of telling us how well students are performing by comparison with standards (standards-referenced assessment) differs from assessment designed to compare students to average performances (norm-referenced assessment). New Standards assessments are standards-referenced assessments. They start with performance standards and they take seriously the type, quality, and balance of performances spelled out by the standards. Assessment systems of this kind look a lot like a sampling of questions and assignments from a standards-based curriculum.

Common examples of standards-referenced examinations are the Advanced Placement (AP) exams of the College Board. The Scholastic Achievement Test (SAT), also from the College Board, is a contrasting example of a norm-referenced test. The AP exams look like the work (type, quality, and balance) students do in the AP courses whereas the SAT looks very different from the work students do in their college preparatory courses. Other well established standards-based examinations include licensure exams for many occupations such as pilots, architects, and electricians.

Unlike the AP or licensure exams, with explicit courses of study that have been debated and agreed upon in an open, public forum (e.g., the College Board, the state bar association or the board of realtors), many individual teacher's grades are based solely on their experience as students and teachers. Unless they participate in an external program like the AP or the International Baccalaureate, teachers rarely have the opportunity to see or discuss an end-of-course examination with others who teach the same course, no less to apply common criteria for marking. Even in the case of high school courses with departmental final examinations, the majority of the feedback to students throughout the school year is based on their individual teacher's judgment. And in the vast majority of the instances, especially in the elementary and middle school years, the individual teacher's standards apply almost exclusively.

It can be argued that the teacher, the person closest to the student's work, is in the best position to assess the student's accomplishment. However, the problem with an assessment system based on individual teacher judgment is that students in different classes, with different teachers, in different schools, work to widely varying standards. There is no common reference for teachers, students, or the public to compare performance across individuals or classrooms. This leads to wide variation in expectation and opportunity. Students get good grades one year for trying hard, then fail the following year for being too far below the average on a test.

New Standards has designed an assessment system that provides a common reference point for students, parents, teachers, and the public who want to judge student performance on the quality and quantity of student work that is expected at a particular level. The New Standards assessment system is based on these performance standards. It has three parts: reference examinations, portfolios, and teacher assessment. While each part of the system can be used independently, the most complete picture of performance referenced to the performance standards comes from using all three.

How the assessments are connected to the performance standards

The performance standards define a domain of expected student performances. Take the Reading standard as an example (see page 22). This standard begins with a definition of reading that describes what we expect students to *be able to do* at approximately the end of eighth grade. The performance descriptions go on to spell out expectations for what students *will accomplish* in terms of the quantity, quality, range, and concentration of their reading. Furthermore, students are expected to *put their reading to work* and the standards say so; students have to produce work based on their reading of specific types of text.

We assess the different elements of the domain defined by a standard by using assessment methods appropriate to the expected performances.

In the English Language Arts reference examination students read a selection of grade-level appropriate passages. The passages include both literary and informational selections. Students answer two types of questions about the passages. One type of question assesses "understanding of the text as a whole" as described in the definition in the Reading standard. These are straightforward questions about the gist of the text. Some of these questions ask students to write a few sentences; some are multiple choice. The second type of question about the same passages asks students to analyze the text, draw reasonable conclusions, and make interpretations—behaviors that characterize what competent readers do.

To demonstrate their achievement of the Reading standard students must also show what they have accomplished—just as people do when they apply for a job. Assessing actual accomplishments means evaluating a selection of student work according to criteria derived directly from the performance descriptions for the standards. New Standards portfolios are organized around "exhibits," each focused on an area of performance. The reading exhibit in the English Language Arts portfolio requires that students include at least four pieces of work that demonstrate their accomplishments in responding to literary and informational texts of appropriate complexity and in interpreting public documents and functional documents. The portfolio includes criteria for judging the entries in this exhibit. These criteria are drawn directly from the relevant performance descriptions. The criteria can be used by the student for self-assessment, by the teacher for feedback and grading, and by independent external scorers to report on achievement of standards to the public.

A further requirement of the reading exhibit in the portfolio, again based directly on the performance standards, is certification of what the student has read. The first part of the Reading standard (E1a) requires that students read at least twenty-five books or book equivalents each year. The reading must include a range of literary forms and works from several writers. Students are also required to read in depth (E1b). The appropriate assessor for these requirements is the teacher or another adult close to the student who can verify the student's claims for meeting this requirement. This component of the system for assessing achievement of the Reading standard is designed to work like a merit badge in the style of the awards developed by the Girl Scouts of the U.S.A. and the Boy Scouts of America.

In summary, students' achievement of the Reading standard is assessed through a combination of methods:

• The reference examination provides evidence of comprehension, analysis, and interpretation of literary and informational texts, related to the Reading standard as a whole and particularly to E1c. (These parts of the reference examination also provide evidence of the first part of the Literature standard, E5a.)

• The reading exhibit for the portfolio provides evidence of working with literary and informational texts, related to E1b, E1c, E1d, and E1e. (Entries included in this exhibit also demonstrate accomplishment in relation to E5a and may be used to fulfill part of the requirements of the writing exhibit.)

• Teacher assessment, in the form of certification included in the reading exhibit, provides verification of students' claims regarding the twenty-five requirement, related to E1a and E1b.

This example of how reading is assessed in the New Standards system illustrates several important points. First, the assessment methods and instruments suit the part of the standard to be assessed. Second, the criteria for judging achievement of the standard are drawn as directly as possible from the performance descriptions of the relevant standard. Third, comprehensive assessment of student achievement of the performance standards requires an appropriate combination of external on-demand assessments like the reference examination, externally-set auditable criteria like the portfolio, and teacher assessment.

The assessments are built on the basic principle that students who work hard in a good program should be able to achieve the performance standards. Students who do what is asked of them, read what they are assigned, do their homework, study for examinations, participate in class, and so on, have a right to expect all this work to pay off in learning. If it does not, there is something wrong with the program.

These standards expect students to work hard. For example, the Science standards include an expectation that every student will complete one science investigation in each of the years leading up to graduation chosen from the following: experiment, fieldwork, design, or secondary research. This requirement is demanding for all students, but doable. Most current college bound students are not asked do this much, let alone students who are not intending to go to college. This is not because these students are not capable of doing the work, but because their programs are not organized to give them the opportunity. However, virtually any student who works hard in a good program can produce investigations such as those identified above that meet standards for quality. By setting expectations like this, standards are raised for all students.

Raising standards for all students has important implications for the quality of curriculum and instruction. Indeed, one of the most important reasons for setting high standards is to challenge the system to perform for the students. Appropriate assessments based on these high standards can give the system feedback on how well it is doing and what it has to do next.

HOW WILL THE PERFORMANCE STANDARDS BE USED?

The reference examinations

Mathematics

The Mathematics reference examinations are targeted for grades 4, 8, and 10. Each examination consists of extended response and short answer items. Student responses are scored both holistically and dimensionally.

Students receive three scores for the Mathematics reference examination: one for understanding of mathematical concepts, one for mathematical skills, and one for problem solving and reasoning and mathematical communication.

Standards defining mathematics scores

SCORE	STANDARDS INCLUDED IN SCORE
Conceptual Understanding	M1, M2, M3, M4
Mathematical Skills	M6
Problem Solving and Reasoning/ Mathematical Communication	M5, M7

English Language Arts

The English Language Arts reference examinations are targeted for grades 4, 8, and 10. Each examination includes open-ended responses, short answer responses, essay questions, and multiple choice items. The student responses are scored holistically on two of these forms; the multiple choice responses are scanned.

Students receive four scores for the English Language Arts reference examination: one for writing, one for reading for basic understanding, one for interpretation and analysis of reading, and one for conventions, grammar, and usage of the English language.

Standards defining English Language Arts scores

SCORE	STANDARDS INCLUDED IN SCORE
Reading: Basic Understanding	E1
Reading: Inference and Analysis	E1
Writing	E2
Writing Conventions	E4

The criteria for scoring each task, for example, the writing sample or responses to the reading questions, are defined by rubrics for each score level (usually 0 to 5) and by anchor examples of student performance at each level. Trained scorers use these rubrics and anchor examples to score responses with high reliability.

Released Tasks from the reference examinations, complete with anchor examples and rubrics, are available to assist teachers and students to prepare for the examinations. The Released Tasks also include examples of student responses scored at each of the performance levels.

Each student's level of performance on the reference examination is determined by decision rules for profiles of scores on sets of items or tasks. These rules were established by panels of judges based on the stated expectations of the performance standards, with allowance made for the usual effects of the test-taking situation.

Levels of performance

For each standards-based score, there are five levels of student performance:

H—Achieved the Standard with Honors means that in addition to meeting the standards, a number of the student's responses exceeded the basic criteria for meeting the standard or displayed features characteristic of advanced knowledge and skill.

S—Achieved the Standard means that the student's performances met the standards as set out in the New Standards performance standards.

N—Nearly Achieved the Standard means that the student's performances almost but did not quite meet the performance standards.

B—Below the Standard means that the student's performances clearly did not meet the performance standards.

L—Little Evidence of Achievement means that the student's performances demonstrated little or none of the knowledge and skill expected by the performance standards.

The portfolio system

The portfolio system complements the reference examination by requiring selections of student work that provide evidence of achievement of the performance standards. The portfolios are organized into exhibits; each focuses on an area of performance and includes clear criteria for assessment. The structure and content of the exhibits parallel the structure of the performance standards. Each exhibit is composed of one or more entries; the entry slips tell students exactly what is required and how it will be assessed. The criteria come directly from the performance descriptions for the standards. For example, the middle school Mathematics portfolio has five exhibits drawn directly from the performance standards as is shown in the chart on the next page.

Mathematics portfolio

EXHIBIT	ENTRIES	STANDARD	EXHIBIT REQUIREMENTS
Conceptual Understanding	• Number and Operations • Geometry and Measurement • Functions and Algebra • Probability and Statistics	M1 M2 M3 M4	To demonstrate conceptual understanding, students are required to provide evidence that they can use the concept to solve problems, represent it in multiple ways (through numbers, graphs, symbols, diagrams, or words, as appropriate), and explain it to someone else. The student must include at least two problems, and may include a third if necessary, to provide evidence of all three ways of demonstrating conceptual understanding (using, representing, and explaining).
Problem Solving	• Four problems	M5	The student must include four problems which, taken together, show the full range of problem solving required by the performance standard, including formulation, implementation, and conclusion. Problem solving is defined as using mathematical concepts and skills to solve non-routine, usually realistic, problems that challenge the student to organize the steps to follow for a solution.
Skills and Communication	• Skills • Communication Entries submitted for the other three exhibits are cited as evidence. A few additional pieces of work may be included here to fill important gaps.	M6 M7	Entry slips list skills from M6 (e.g., compute accurately with rational numbers, use equations, formulas, and simple algebraic notation, use geometric shapes and terms correctly) and M7 (e.g., present mathematical procedures and results clearly, systematically, and correctly; use mathematical language and representations with accuracy: numerical tables and equations, formulas, functions, algebraic equations, charts, graphs, and diagrams).
Project	• At least one large scale project each year	M8	This exhibit requires students to put their mathematics to work. Entry slips state criteria, from M8, for assessing the following kinds of projects: data study, mathematical model of a physical system, design of a physical structure, management and planning analysis, pure mathematics investigation, and history of a mathematical idea.
Work in Progress	• No entries submitted		Students keep sample work during the year as candidates for selecting as entries.

Portfolios put the standards directly in the hands of students. They help students manage their responsibility for producing work that achieves the performance standards. They also provide a focus for conversations among teachers and students about how the students' work shows evidence of meeting the performance standards and about the further work students need to do to meet the standards.

The portfolio system includes exhibit instructions and entry slips for students, and materials for teachers, including scoring materials. The scoring materials include procedures, criteria, and example exhibits of student work.

Linking the New Standards system with partners' standards and assessment systems

"Linking" is the process of establishing the extent and degree of match between the New Standards system and those of the New Standards partners. It is an essential step in the process of enabling our partners to make decisions about their use of the New Standards system, either in part or as a whole.

Linking is crucial for assuring that student work is assessed according to the same standards that guided its production.

The performance standards provide the initial point of reference for the linking process. While comprehensive linking of assessment systems requires the further step of linking scores on performances, linking standards is a necessary first step and provides a good indication of the potential for linking New Standards with partners' systems.

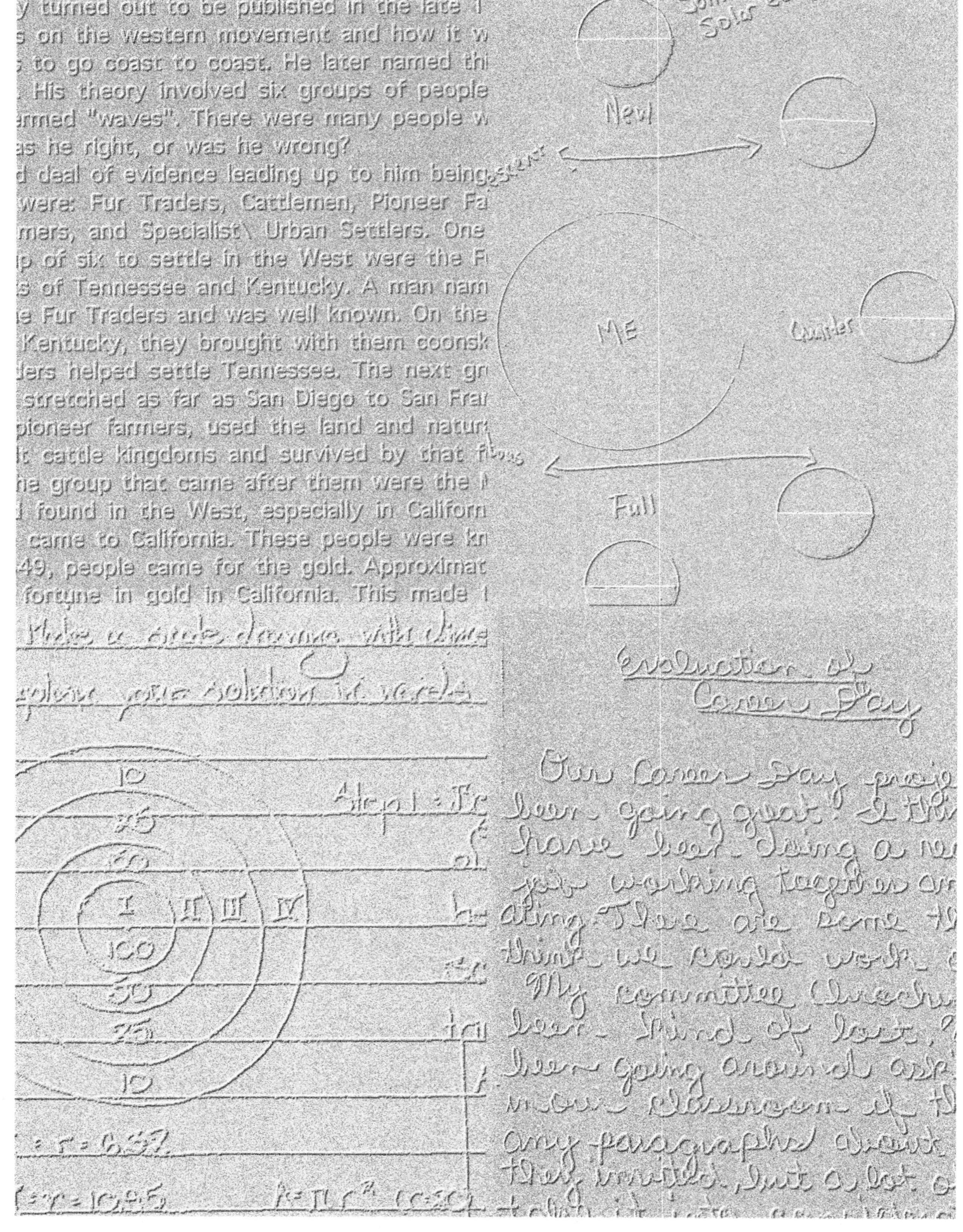

y turned out to be published in the late 1
s on the western movement and how it w
s to go coast to coast. He later named thi
His theory involved six groups of people
rmed "waves". There were many people w
as he right, or was he wrong?
d deal of evidence leading up to him being
were: Fur Traders, Cattlemen, Pioneer Fa
mers, and Specialist\ Urban Settlers. One
p of six to settle in the West were the F
s of Tennessee and Kentucky. A man nam
e Fur Traders and was well known. On the
Kentucky, they brought with them coonsk
ders helped settle Tennessee. The next gr
stretched as far as San Diego to San Fra
pioneer farmers, used the land and natur
t cattle kingdoms and survived by that f
he group that came after them were the
found in the West, especially in Californ
came to California. These people were kn
49, people came for the gold. Approximat
fortune in gold in California. This made
New
ME
Quarter
Full
Evaluation of
Career Day
Our Career Day proj
been going great! I thi
have been doing a ne
job working together an
along. There are some th
think we could work
My committee (brochu
been kind of lost,
been going around ask
in our classroom if th
any paragraphs about
they wrote, but a lot o

OVERVIEW OF THE PERFORMANCE STANDARDS

The middle school standards are set at a level of performance approximately equivalent to the end of eighth grade. It is expected that some students might achieve this level earlier and others later than this grade. (See "Deciding what constitutes a standard-setting performance," page 12.)

E English Language Arts

- E1 Reading
- E2 Writing
- E3 Speaking, Listening, and Viewing
- E4 Conventions, Grammar, and Usage of the English Language
- E5 Literature

M Mathematics

- M1 Number and Operation Concepts
- M2 Geometry and Measurement Concepts
- M3 Function and Algebra Concepts
- M4 Statistics and Probability Concepts
- M5 Problem Solving and Mathematical Reasoning
- M6 Mathematical Skills and Tools
- M7 Mathematical Communication
- M8 Putting Mathematics to Work

S Science

- S1 Physical Sciences Concepts
- S2 Life Sciences Concepts
- S3 Earth and Space Sciences Concepts
- S4 Scientific Connections and Applications
- S5 Scientific Thinking
- S6 Scientific Tools and Technologies
- S7 Scientific Communication
- S8 Scientific Investigation

A Applied Learning

- A1 Problem Solving
- A2 Communication Tools and Techniques
- A3 Information Tools and Techniques
- A4 Learning and Self-management Tools and Techniques
- A5 Tools and Techniques for Working With Others

Introduction to the performance standards for *English Language Arts*

The performance standards for English Language Arts define high standards of literacy for American students. The standards focus on what is central to the domain; they are built around reading, writing, speaking, listening, and viewing; and they acknowledge the importance of conventions, literature, public discourse, and functional documents. The standards were developed with the help of classroom teachers and content experts in concert with both the National Council of Teachers of English and the International Reading Association.

The performance standards represent a balanced view of what students should know and the ways they should demonstrate the knowledge and skills they have acquired in this domain. Students are expected to read both literature and informational texts. They are required to produce writing that is traditionally associated with the classroom, including narratives and reports, and they are also expected to exhibit increasing expertise in producing and critiquing public and functional documents. In addition, students are expected to become proficient speakers, to hone their listening skills, and to develop a critical awareness of viewing patterns and the influence of media on their lives. The work that students produce in both written and spoken formats is expected to be of high quality in terms of rhetorical structures as well as the conventions of the English language.

The five standards for English Language Arts are as follows:

- **E1 Reading;**
- **E2 Writing;**
- **E3 Speaking, Listening, and Viewing;**
- **E4 Conventions, Grammar, and Usage of the English Language;**
- **E5 Literature.**

At the high school level, two additional standards are added:

- **E6 Public Documents;**
- **E7 Functional Documents.**

The expansion of literacy at the high school level reflects the growing need for students to understand the range of materials they must deal with throughout their lives. Both public documents and functional documents are introduced in the Reading standard at the middle school level, where students are required to demonstrate a familiarity with these kinds of texts. It is important that the middle school standard anticipates the advanced degree of understanding expected at the high school level where students are expected both to critique and produce materials of these kinds.

The first part of the Reading standard, E1 a, requires students to read a wide range of materials by a range of authors on different subjects. The requirement here is fairly simple: read twenty-five books of the quality illustrated in the sample reading list. Too often students are not given the opportunity to read full-length books because of curricular restraints, a lack of resources, or a lack of access to books. The missed opportunity results in a tremendous loss of potential literacy skills that can only be developed when students become habitual readers. The requirement to read twenty-five books a year provides all students the opportunity to become habitual readers and represents a realistic and worthwhile goal that can be reached if students simply invest the effort. The sample reading list is included to provide an indication of the quality and complexity of the materials students are expected to read. Any or all of the specific works on the list may be substituted with other works providing the works that are substituted are of comparable quality and complexity to those that are replaced.

The second part of the Reading standard, E1 b, requires students to "go deep" in at least one area of interest. We know that students who read regularly tend to read what interests them; note the trends in the work sample, "Reading Log," page 48. This part of the Reading standard is intended to encourage all students to do what good readers do and pursue themes, authors, and genres that are of interest to them.

The third part of the Reading standard, E1 c, requires students to work with informational materials in order to develop understanding and expertise about the topics they investigate. This area of informational materials is of great importance, and for too long it has been neglected in the school curriculum. Its inclusion as a separate part of the Reading standard indicates our desire that more attention be given to reading a broad range of materials written for a variety of audiences and purposes.

The fourth and fifth parts of the Reading standard, E1 d and E1 e, require students to demonstrate a familiarity with both public and functional documents. The category of public documents includes speeches, editorials, political advertisements, and other materials that engage a current issue. The category of functional documents consists of what is written or spoken in an attempt to get something done, whether that be a memorandum making a request of someone else, a computer reference manual, or a set of instructions that tell someone how to assemble something or how to carry out a procedure. Familiarity with these kinds of documents in middle school prepares students for a more sophisticated treatment of them in high school.

The Writing standard, E2, requires students to demonstrate accomplishment in four types of writing. Each of these writing types is defined by a distinct set of criteria, though there is clearly some overlap. The use of criteria specific to the writing types is meant to ensure that students become familiar with the strategies that characterize specific writing forms and to encourage students to use these criteria when they review and revise their work. All of the commentaries on the work samples related to the Writing standard use the language of these criteria and make explicit how the student work sample illustrates an accomplished example. The types of writing included in this standard are all forms of writing commonly produced both in and out of school.

The Speaking, Listening, and Viewing standard, E3, is the only standard that has changed dramatically from previous drafts of these performance standards. The primary change is that the speaking and listening parts of the standard now revolve around a variety of social situations: one-to-one interaction, group discussion, and oral presentation, and that the viewing part of the standard now asks for evidence of an awareness of media influences. The attention to viewing represents a growing awareness that the media play an integral part in most students' lives and that students require increasingly sophisticated tools for dealing with media influences.

The Conventions, Grammar, and Usage of the English Language standard, E4, is listed as a separate standard even though the parts of the standard are always assessed in either a written or spoken context. The first part of the standard indicates the expectation that students should be able to represent themselves appropriately using standard English. The second part of the standard reflects the understanding that high quality work most often comes about as a result of a sustained effort represented by numerous drafts of a particular piece of work. In classrooms where high quality work is consistently produced, the revision process is most often an integral part of the curriculum.

The Literature standard, E5, like the Conventions standard, is listed separately even though it could easily be broken into two pieces and placed respectively within the Reading and Writing standards. However, for many people who go through school, the study of literature is the only situation in which they have the chance to explore the big ideas and the themes that emerge from social and political conflict, both in their own writing and in the writing of others. An understanding of these ideas and themes is integral for students who will one day be responsible for the negotiation of meaning important to a democracy. The first part of the Literature standard asks students to explore and critique the writing of others with these kinds of critical skills in mind. The second part of the standard asks students to produce literature with the hope that doing this will help students better understand the world that shapes both their literature and the literature of professional writers.

Turner Essay

Frederick Turner, who was a profe
Wisconsin as well as Harvard, believed i
the frontier. At first this was only an
hypothesis and theory turned out to be
Turner wrote a thesis on the western m
for the United States to go coast to co
the Manifest Destiny. His theory involve
settled in what he termed "waves". Ther
his point of view. Was he right, or was
There is a good deal of evidence l
six groups involved were: Fur Traders,
Miners, Equipped Farmers, and Specialist
first among the group of six to settle in
They discovered parts of Tennessee and
Boone was among the Fur Traders and w
from Tennessee and Kentucky, they bro
leather. The Fur Traders helped settle T
the Cattleman. They stretched as far as
Cattlemen, like the pioneer farmers, us
to survive. They built cattle kingdoms a
food, and warmth. The group that came
was a rumor of gold found in the West
Thousands of people came to California.
49ers because in 1849, people came fo

E1 Reading

To see how these performance description compare with the expectations for elementary school and high school, turn to pages 136-145.

The examples that follow the performance descriptions for each standard are examples of the work students might do to demonstrate their achievement. The examples also indicate the nature and complexity of activities that are appropriate to expect of students at middle school level.

E1 a assumes an adequate library of appropriate reading material. In some places, library resources are too meager to support the amount of reading required for every student to achieve this standard. Where a shortage of books exists, better use of out-of-school resources must be made; for example, students may have to be assured access to local or county libraries.

E1 a is intended primarily to generate the reading of full-length books. Combinations of quality magazines, newspapers, on-line materials etc., may be treated as equivalent texts that contribute to meeting the requirement of twenty-five books. Similarly, collections of portions of full-length books may be considered as book equivalents.

Reading is a process which includes demonstrating comprehension and showing evidence of a warranted and responsible interpretation of the text. "Comprehension" means getting the gist of a text. It is most frequently illustrated by demonstrating an understanding of the text as a whole; identifying complexities presented in the structure of the text; and extracting salient information from the text. In providing evidence of a responsible interpretation, students may make connections between parts of a text, among several texts, and between texts and other experiences; make extensions and applications of a text; and examine texts critically and evaluatively.

E1 a The student reads at least twenty-five books or book equivalents each year. The quality and complexity of the materials to be read are illustrated in the sample reading list. The materials should include traditional and contemporary literature (both fiction and non-fiction) as well as magazines, newspapers, textbooks, and on-line materials. Such reading should represent a diverse collection of material from at least three different literary forms and from at least five different writers.

Examples of activities through which students might produce evidence of reading twenty-five books include:

- Maintain an annotated list of works read. **1b**
- Generate a reading log or journal. **1b**
- Participate in formal and informal book talks. **1b, 3a, 3b**

E1 b The student reads and comprehends at least four books (or book equivalents) about one issue or subject, or four books by a single writer, or four books in one genre, and produces evidence of reading that:

- makes and supports warranted and responsible assertions about the texts;
- supports assertions with elaborated and convincing evidence;
- draws the texts together to compare and contrast themes, characters, and ideas;
- makes perceptive and well developed connections;
- evaluates writing strategies and elements of the author's craft.

Examples of activities through which students might produce evidence of reading comprehension include:

- Construct a book review. **4a, 4b, 5a**
- Produce a literary response paper. **2b, 4a, 4b, 5a**
- Produce a research report. **1c, 2a, 4a, 4b, 5a**
- Participate in formal or informal book talk. **1a, 1c, 3a, 3b**
- Create an annotated book list organized according to author, theme, or genre. **1a**

E1 c The student reads and comprehends informational materials to develop understanding and expertise and produces written or oral work that:

- restates or summarizes information;
- relates new information to prior knowledge and experience;
- extends ideas;
- makes connections to related topics or information.

Examples of activities through which students might produce evidence of reading informational materials include:

- Use information to support or enhance a project. **2a, 4a, 4b, M8, S8, A3a**
- Write a report of information that draws from at least two sources. **2a, 4a, 4b**
- Incorporate expert opinions into a speech or position paper. **2e, 3c, 4a, 4b**
- Develop a proposal based on data obtained from reading informational texts. **4a, 4b**
- Write a report that analyzes several historical records of a single event and attempts to understand the reasons for the similarities and differences. **4a, 4b**

E1 d The student demonstrates familiarity with a variety of public documents (i.e., documents that focus on civic issues or matters of public policy at the community level and beyond) and produces written or oral work that does one or more of the following:

- identifies the social context of the document;
- identifies the author's purpose and stance;
- analyzes the arguments and positions advanced and the evidence offered in support of them, or formulates an argument and offers evidence to support it;
- examines or makes use of the appeal of a document to audiences both friendly and hostile to the position presented;
- identifies or uses commonly used persuasive techniques.

Examples of activities through which students might produce evidence of familiarity with public documents include:

- Summarize and critique two or more local newspaper articles related to the same topic or issue. **2a, 4a, 4b**
- Respond to a public address made by an adult, e.g., the principal, a PTA/PTO officer, a visiting author.
- Explain a local document to someone who has never heard of it (e.g., a school related directive, a community related brochure, or an informational pamphlet).
- Write a letter to the editor in response to an editorial or to an article of local or national importance. **2e, 4a, 4b**

E1 e The student demonstrates familiarity with a variety of functional documents (i.e., documents that exist in order to get things done) and produces written or oral work that does one or more of the following:

- identifies the institutional context of the document;
- identifies the sequence of activities needed to carry out a procedure;
- analyzes or uses the formatting techniques used to make a document user-friendly;
- identifies any information that is either extraneous or missing in terms of audience and purpose or makes effective use of relevant information.

Examples of activities through which students might produce evidence of familiarity with functional documents include:

- Write a memo or conduct a briefing on procedures to be followed in a given situation. **2d, 3c, 4a, 4b**
- Produce a manual setting out school rules. **2d, 4a, 4b, A1a**
- Revise a set of instructions to improve their clarity. **2d, 4a, 4b**

This is a sample reading list from which the students and teachers could select. This list is not exclusive. Acceptable titles also appear on lists produced by organizations such as the National Council of Teachers of English and the American Library Association. Substitutions might also be made from lists approved locally.

Fiction

Anaya, *Bless Me, Ultima;*
Armstrong, *Sounder;*
Bonham, *Durango Street;*
Cohen, *Tell Us Your Secret;*
Collier, *My Brother Sam Is Dead;*
Cormier, *I Am the Cheese;*
Danziger, *The Cat Ate My Gymsuit;*
Fast, *April Morning;*
Gaines, *A Gathering of Old Men;*
Goldman, *The Princess Bride;*
Greene, *Summer of My German Soldier;*
Hansen, *Which Way Freedom;*
Hinton, *The Outsiders;*
Holman, *Slake's Limbo;*
London, *The Call of the Wild;*
Mathis, *Listen for the Fig Tree;*
Mohr, *Nilda;*
Neufeld, *Lisa, Bright and Dark;*
O'Brien, *Z for Zachariah;*
Schaefer, *Shane;*
Stevenson, *Treasure Island;*
Voigt, *Dicey's Song;*
Walker, *To Hell With Dying;*
Walter, *Because We Are;*
Zindel, *The Pigman.*

Non-Fiction

Amory, *The Cat Who Came for Christmas;*
Berck, *No Place to Be: Voices of Homeless Children;*
Frank, *The Diary of a Young Girl;*
George, *The Talking Earth;*
Gilbreth, *Cheaper by the Dozen;*
Haskins, *Outward Dreams;*
Hautzig, *Endless Steppe: A Girl in Exile;*
Herriott, *All Creatures Great and Small;*
Lester, *To Be a Slave;*
Meyers, *Pearson, a Harbor Seal Pup;*
Reiss, *The Upstairs Room;*
Soto, *Living Up the Street;*
White, *Ryan White: My Own Story;*
Yates, *Amos Fortune, Free Man.*

Poetry

Adams, *Poetry of Earth and Sky;*
Eliot, *Old Possum's Book of Practical Cats;*
Frost, *You Come Too;*
Greenfield, *Night on Neighborhood Street;*
Livingston, *Cat Poems.*

Drama

Blinn, *Brian's Song;*
Davis, *Escape to Freedom;*
Gibson, *The Miracle Worker;*
Lawrence and Lee, *Inherit the Wind;*
Osborn, *On Borrowed Time;*
Shakespeare, *A Midsummer Night's Dream;*
Stone, *Metamora, or, the Last of the Wampanoags.*

Folklore/Mythology

Blair, *Tall Tale America;*
Bruchac, *The First Strawberries: A Cherokee Story;*
Bryan, *Beat the Story-Drum, Pum-Pum;*
D'Aulaire, *Norse Gods and Giants;*
Gallico, *The Snow Goose;*
Lee, *Toad Is the Uncle of Heaven: A Vietnamese Folk Tale;*
Pyle, *Merry Adventures of Robin Hood.*

Modern Fantasy and Science Fiction

Babbitt, *Tuck Everlasting;*
Bradbury, *Dandelion Wine;*
Cooper, *The Grey King;*
Hamilton, *The Magical Adventures of Pretty Pearl;*
L'Engle, *A Wrinkle in Time;*
Tolkien, *The Hobbit;*
Yep, *Dragon of the Lost Sea.*

Magazines/Periodicals

Calliope (world history);
Cobblestone (American history);
Faces (anthropology);
Junior Scholastic (Scholastic);
Odyssey (science);
Science World (Scholastic);
Scope (Scholastic);
World (National Geographic);.

Other

Computer manuals; instructions; contracts. See also the reading lists included in award books corresponding to reading provided by the Girl Scouts of the U.S.A. and the Boy Scouts of America.

E1 b is intended to encourage students to invest themselves thoroughly in an area that interests them. Such an investment will generate reading from an array of resources, giving students more experience of reading as well as increased understanding of a subject. **E1 b** is not intended to be a cursory experience of doing research on a topic which often requires little more than scanning materials, copying directly from references, and inserting transitional phrases and paragraphs. The challenge with the depth requirement is to encourage a complex understanding developed and enhanced through reading.

Much writing can be classified as belonging to the public arena. New Standards, however, defines public documents to mean those pieces of text that are concerned with public policy, that address controversial issues confronting the public, or that arise in response to controversial issues or public policy. At the middle school level (**E1 d**), the issues students write about come primarily from the school or local community.

Functional writing is writing that exists in order to get things done. Functional writing is ordinarily considered technical writing and, as such, is often not part of the typical English curriculum. New Standards requires students to demonstrate proficiency with functional writing because such writing is of increasing importance to the complex literacy of our culture. Functional documents are included in **E1 e**.

E2 Writing

Writing is a process through which a writer shapes language to communicate effectively. Writing often develops through a series of initial plans and multiple drafts and through access to informed feedback and response. Purpose, audience, and context contribute to the form and substance of writing as well as to its style, tone, and stance.

To see how these performance descriptions compare with the expectations for elementary school and high school, turn to pages 136-145.

The examples that follow the performance descriptions for each standard are examples of the work students might do to demonstrate their achievement. The examples also indicate the nature and complexity of activities that are appropriate to expect of students at middle school level.

The cross-references that follow the examples highlight examples for which the same activity, and possibly even the same piece of work, may enable students to demonstrate their achievement in relation to more than one standard. In some cases, the cross-references highlight examples of activities through which students might demonstrate their achievement in relation to standards for more than one subject matter.

E2 b is meant to expand the repertoire of responses students traditionally write when they respond to literature. This type of response requires an understanding of writing strategies.

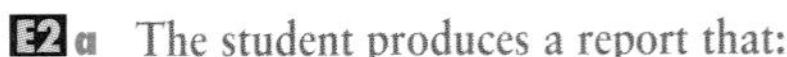

E2 a The student produces a report that:

- engages the reader by establishing a context, creating a persona, and otherwise developing reader interest;
- develops a controlling idea that conveys a perspective on the subject;
- creates an organizing structure appropriate to purpose, audience, and context;
- includes appropriate facts and details;
- excludes extraneous and inappropriate information;
- uses a range of appropriate strategies, such as providing facts and details, describing or analyzing the subject, narrating a relevant anecdote, comparing and contrasting, naming, and explaining benefits or limitations;
- provides a sense of closure to the writing.

Examples of reports include:

- An I-search essay (an essay that details a student's search for information as well as the information itself; I-search papers are developed through a variety of means, e.g., interviews and observation, as well as traditional library research). **1c, 4a, 4b**
- A saturation report (a report that recounts substantial information on a topic gathered by a student over a period of time). **1c, 4a, 4b**
- A report produced as part of studies in subjects such as science, social studies, and mathematics. **1c, 4a, 4b, M7a, M7b, M7c, S7a, S7b, S7c**

E2 b The student produces a response to literature that:

- engages the reader through establishing a context, creating a persona, and otherwise developing reader interest;
- advances a judgment that is interpretive, analytic, evaluative, or reflective;
- supports a judgment through references to the text, references to other works, authors, or non-print media, or references to personal knowledge;
- demonstrates an understanding of the literary work;
- anticipates and answers a reader's questions;
- provides a sense of closure to the writing.

Examples of responses to literature include:

- A literary analysis. **1b, 4a, 4b, 5a**
- A book or movie review. **1b, 3d, 4a, 4b, 5a**
- A literary response paper. **1b, 4a, 4b, 5a**
- A comparison of a piece of literature with its media presentation. **1b, 3d, 4a, 4b, 5a**

E2 c The student produces a narrative account (fictional or autobiographical) that:

- engages the reader by establishing a context, creating a point of view, and otherwise developing reader interest;
- establishes a situation, plot, point of view, setting, and conflict (and for autobiography, the significance of events and of conclusions that can be drawn from those events);
- creates an organizing structure;
- includes sensory details and concrete language to develop plot and character;
- excludes extraneous details and inconsistencies;
- develops complex characters;
- uses a range of appropriate strategies, such as dialogue, tension or suspense, naming, and specific narrative action, e.g., movement, gestures, expressions;
- provides a sense of closure to the writing.

Examples of narrative accounts include:

- A biographical account. **4a, 4b**
- A fiction or non-fiction story. **4a, 4b, 5b**
- A personal narrative. **4a, 4b, 5b**
- A historical account. **1c, 4a, 4b**
- A detailed travel diary. **4a, 4b**
- A news account of an event, fiction or non-fiction. **4a, 4b**

E2 d The student produces a narrative procedure that:

- engages the reader by establishing a context, creating a persona, and otherwise developing reader interest;
- provides a guide to action for a relatively complicated procedure in order to anticipate a reader's needs; creates expectations through predictable structures, e.g., headings; and provides transitions between steps;
- makes use of appropriate writing strategies such as creating a visual hierarchy and using white space and graphics as appropriate;
- includes relevant information;
- excludes extraneous information;
- anticipates problems, mistakes, and misunderstandings that might arise for the reader;
- provides a sense of closure to the writing.

Examples of narrative procedures include:

- A set of rules for organizing a class meeting. **4a, 4b**
- A set of instructions for playing computer games. **4a, 4b**
- A set of instructions for using media technology. **4a, 4b**
- An explanation of a mathematical procedure. **4a, 4b, M7c, M7e**
- A project manual. **4a, 4b, A1a**

E2 e The student produces a persuasive essay that:

- engages the reader by establishing a context, creating a persona, and otherwise developing reader interest;
- develops a controlling idea that makes a clear and knowledgeable judgment;
- creates and organizes a structure that is appropriate to the needs, values, and interests of a specified audience, and arranges details, reasons, examples, and anecdotes effectively and persuasively;
- includes appropriate information and arguments;
- excludes information and arguments that are irrelevant;
- anticipates and addresses reader concerns and counter-arguments;
- supports arguments with detailed evidence, citing sources of information as appropriate;
- provides a sense of closure to the writing.

Examples of persuasive essays include:

- A position paper. **4a, 4b**
- An evaluation of a product or policy. **4a, 4b, A1a**
- An editorial on a current issue that uses reasoned arguments to support an opinion. **4a, 4b**
- A speech for a candidate running for school or public office. **4a, 4b**

E3 Speaking, Listening, and Viewing

Speaking, listening, and viewing are fundamental processes which people use to express, explore, and learn about ideas. The functions of speaking, listening, and viewing include gathering and sharing information; persuading others; expressing and understanding ideas; coordinating activities with others; and selecting and critically analyzing messages. The contexts of these communication functions include one-to-one conferences, small group interactions, large audiences and meetings, and interactions with broadcast media.

E3 a The student participates in one-to-one conferences with a teacher, paraprofessional, or adult volunteer, in which the student:

- initiates new topics in addition to responding to adult-initiated topics;
- asks relevant questions;
- responds to questions with appropriate elaboration;
- uses language cues to indicate different levels of certainty or hypothesizing, e.g., "what if...," "very likely...," "I'm unsure whether...";
- confirms understanding by paraphrasing the adult's directions or suggestions.

Examples of one-to-one interactions include:

- Book talks with a teacher or parent. **1a, 1b, 1c, 5a**
- Analytical discussion of a movie or television program with a teacher or parent. **3d**
- Student-teacher conferences regarding a draft of an essay, the student's progress on a mathematics assignment, or the status of a science project. **4b**
- Interviews with teachers or adults. **2a**
- Discussion with a teacher or parent about a portfolio of work. **4b**

E3 b The student participates in group meetings, in which the student:

- displays appropriate turn-taking behaviors;
- actively solicits another person's comment or opinion;
- offers own opinion forcefully without dominating;
- responds appropriately to comments and questions;
- volunteers contributions and responds when directly solicited by teacher or discussion leader;
- gives reasons in support of opinions expressed;
- clarifies, illustrates, or expands on a response when asked to do so; asks classmates for similar expansions;
- employs a group decision-making technique such as brainstorming or a problem-solving sequence (e.g., recognize problem, define problem, identify possible solutions, select optimal solution, implement solution, evaluate solution).

Examples of activities involving group meetings include:

- Create a plan for a group project (e.g., organize a presentation to be made to the class; plan a science project).
- Develop and negotiate a class rubric.
- Engage in classroom town meetings.
- Take part in book talks with other students. **1a, 1b, 1c, 5a**
- Work as part of a group to solve a complex mathematical task.
- Role-play to better understand a certain historical event. **1c**
- Participate in peer writing response groups. **4b**

E3 c The student prepares and delivers an individual presentation in which the student:

- shapes information to achieve a particular purpose and to appeal to the interests and background knowledge of audience members;
- shapes content and organization according to criteria for importance and impact rather than according to availability of information in resource materials;
- uses notes or other memory aids to structure the presentation;
- develops several main points relating to a single thesis;
- engages the audience with appropriate verbal cues and eye contact;
- projects a sense of individuality and personality in selecting and organizing content, and in delivery.

Examples of presentations include:

- A presentation of project plans or a report for an Applied Learning project. **4a, 4b, A2a**
- A report that analyzes several historical records of a single event and attempts to understand the reasons for the similarities and differences. **1c, 4a, 4b**
- A report that presents data collected to prove/disprove a particular hypothesis, along with an appropriate conclusion. **1c, 4a, 4b**
- A talk that outlines a plan of action for implementing a new school policy and the reasoning supporting the selected plan over other options. **4a, 4b**
- A report that analyzes a trend running through several literary works. **1b, 4a, 4b, 5a**

E3 d The student makes informed judgments about television, radio, and film productions; that is, the student:

- demonstrates an awareness of the presence of the media in the daily lives of most people;
- evaluates the role of the media in focusing attention and in forming opinion;
- judges the extent to which the media are a source of entertainment as well as a source of information;
- defines the role of advertising as part of media presentation.

Examples of activities through which students might produce evidence of making informed judgments about television, radio, and film productions include:

- Present a paper or report on reasons for selecting one media choice over another. **1c, 2a, 3c**
- Prepare a report on the benefits obtained (including information learned) from media exposure. **1c, 2a, 4a, 4b**
- Summarize patterns of media exposure in writing or in an oral report. **1c, 2a, 3c, 4a, 4b**
- Describe the appeal of particularly memorable commercials. **2a, 3c**
- Analyze the appeal of popular television shows and films for particular audiences. **2a, 4a, 4b**
- Explain the use of "propaganda techniques" (e.g., bandwagon, glittering generalities, celebrity) in television commercials. **2a, 4a, 4b**

Samples of student work that illustrate standard-setting performances for these standards can be found on pages 27-50.

For samples of student work that illustrate standard-setting performances for E3 a and E3 b refer to the videotape accompanying this book.

The work students produce to meet the English Language Arts standards does not all have to come from an English class. Students should be encouraged to use work from subjects in addition to English to demonstrate their accomplishments. The work samples include some examples of work produced in other classes that meet requirements of these standards. See page 32 and page 82.

To see how these performance descriptions compare with the expectations for elementary school and high school, turn to pages 136-145.

The examples that follow the performance descriptions for each standard are examples of the work students might do to demonstrate their achievement. The examples also indicate the nature and complexity of activities that are appropriate to expect of students at middle school level.

The cross-references that follow the examples highlight examples for which the same activity, and possibly even the same piece of work, may enable students to demonstrate their achievement in relation to more than one standard. In some cases, the cross-references highlight examples of activities through which students might demonstrate their achievement in relation to standards for more than one subject matter.

These standards allow for oral performances of student work where ever appropriate.

E4 Conventions, Grammar, and Usage of the English Language

Having control of the conventions and grammar of the English language means having the ability to represent oneself appropriately with regard to current standards of correctness (e.g., spelling, punctuation, paragraphing, capitalization, subject-verb agreement). Usage involves the appropriate application of conventions and grammar in both written and spoken formats.

E4 a The student demonstrates an understanding of the rules of the English language in written and oral work, and selects the structures and features of language appropriate to the purpose, audience, and context of the work. The student demonstrates control of:

- grammar;
- paragraph structure;
- punctuation;
- sentence construction;
- spelling;
- usage.

Examples of activities through which students might demonstrate an understanding of the rules of the English language include:

- Demonstrate in a piece of writing the ability to manage the conventions, grammar, and usage of English so that they aid rather than interfere with reading. **1d, 1e, 2a, 2b, 2c, 2d, 2e, 5a, 5b**
- Proofread acceptably the student's own writing or the writing of others, using dictionaries and other resources, including the teacher or peers as appropriate. **1d, 1e, 2a, 2b, 2c, 2d, 2e, 5a, 5b**
- Observe conventions of language during formal oral presentations. **3c**
- Revising a piece of writing by combining sentences. **1d, 1e, 2a, 2b, 2c, 2d, 2e, 5a, 5b**

E4 b The student analyzes and subsequently revises work to clarify it or make it more effective in communicating the intended message or thought. The student's revisions should be made in light of the purposes, audiences, and contexts that apply to the work. Strategies for revising include:

- adding or deleting details;
- adding or deleting explanations;
- clarifying difficult passages;
- rearranging words, sentences, and paragraphs to improve or clarify meaning;
- sharpening the focus;
- reconsidering the organizational structure.

Examples of activities through which students might provide evidence of analyzing and revising work include:

- Incorporate into revised drafts, as appropriate, suggestions taken from critiques made by peers and teachers. **1d, 1e, 2a, 2b, 2c, 2d, 2e, 3c, 3d, 5a, 5b**
- Produce a series of distinctly different drafts that result in a polished piece of writing or presentation. **1d, 1e, 2a, 2b, 2c, 2d, 2e, 3c, 3d, 5a, 5b**
- Describe the reasons for stylistic choices made as a writer or presenter. **1d, 1e, 2a, 2b, 2c, 2d, 2e, 3c, 3d, 5a, 5b**
- Critique the writing or oral presentation of a peer.

E5 Literature

Literature consists of poetry, fiction, non-fiction, and essays as distinguished from instructional, expository, or journalistic writing.

E5 a The student responds to non-fiction, fiction, poetry, and drama using interpretive, critical, and evaluative processes; that is, the student:

- identifies recurring themes across works;
- interprets the impact of authors' decisions regarding word choice, content, and literary elements;
- identifies the characteristics of literary forms and genres;
- evaluates literary merit;
- identifies the effect of point of view;
- analyzes the reasons for a character's actions, taking into account the situation and basic motivation of the character;
- makes inferences and draws conclusions about fictional and non-fictional contexts, events, characters, settings, and themes;
- identifies stereotypical characters as opposed to fully developed characters;
- identifies the effect of literary devices such as figurative language, allusion, diction, dialogue, and description.

Examples of responding to literature include:

- Analyze stereotypical characters in a popular television production. **3d**
- Examine themes in the work (fiction or non-fiction) of one popular young-adult author. **1b, 2b, 4a, 4b**
- Evaluate the effect of literary devices in a number of poems by one author or poems on a common topic. **1b, 2b, 4a, 4b**
- Compare the literary merits of two or more short stories, biographies of one individual, novels, or plays. **1b, 2b, 4a, 4b**
- Write or perform a skit. **1b, 2b, 4a, 4b, 5b**
- Write a parody. **2b, 4a, 4b**
- Speculate about point of view in a work read by the class. **3b**

E5 b The student produces work in at least one literary genre that follows the conventions of the genre.

Examples of literary genres include:

- A personal essay. **4a, 4b**
- A short story. **2c, 4a, 4b**
- A short play. **4a, 4b**
- A poem. **4a, 4b**
- A vignette. **4a, 4b**

Work Sample & Commentary: *Using the Library Reference Computers*

The task

Students were asked to write a set of instructions for a familiar procedure. They were encouraged to find situations beyond the classroom where a set of instructions was needed. The students were asked to pay particular attention to the audience and purpose of their work. The final version of the following work sample that came from this assignment is being used currently in a library to guide students in their research.

Circumstances of performance

This sample of student work was produced under the following conditions:

	alone	√	in a group
√	in class	√	as homework
√	with teacher feedback	√	with peer feedback
	timed	√	opportunity for revision

What the work shows

E2 d Writing: Produce a narrative procedure that:

- engages the reader by establishing a context, creating a persona, and otherwise developing reader interest;
- provides a guide to action for a relatively complicated procedure in order to anticipate a reader's needs; creates expectations through predictable structures, e.g., headings; and provides smooth transitions between steps;
- makes use of appropriate writing strategies such as creating a visual hierarchy and using white space and graphics as appropriate;
- includes relevant information;
- excludes extraneous information;
- anticipates problems, mistakes, and misunderstandings that might arise for the reader;
- provides a sense of closure to the writing.

This work sample illustrates a standard-setting performance for the following parts of the standards:

E2 d Writing: Produce a narrative procedure.

E4 a Conventions: Demonstrate an understanding of the rules of the English language.

E4 b Conventions: Analyze and subsequently revise written work.

Final Draft

(A) **Using the Library Reference Computers To Find Books For Your Research**

Usually the computer is already turned on for you. On the screen there is a big, light green rectangle that reads *inquired by* and *subject, author,* and *title* in that order. In the bottom right-hand corner there are four arrows that move the cursor or marker up, down, right, and left (exactly like the arrow points). The cursor is a bright blue line that highlights the title of the folder as you move the arrows. (B) Use the up and down arrows to move the cursor to the folder you choose. Then press enter.

(F) **Working in Your Chosen Folder**

(G) The following directions will help you find books after you have chosen a folder:

(C) **Title**

After you choose the Title folder, type the title of the book. If the book you are looking for is in the library, the screen will bring up the author's name, short summary, call number, number of pages, and tell you if it is available or not. **Example:** Say you are looking for **The Game**, a book by **R. L. Stine.** Type the title and the screen will show you if the book is in our library and if it is available.

Author

After you choose the Author folder, type the author's name and the screen will show you all the books we have by that author. If you see the book you want in the list, move the

(A) The guide engages the reader by establishing a simple context in the title, i.e., how to use reference computers to conduct research for school tasks.

The creation of the persona of a helpful, non-critical guide who has personal knowledge of the procedure being described lends credibility to the instructions.

(B) The guide anticipates the reader's needs by describing what is on the computer screen and by explaining where to find the arrows that move the cursor, what the cursor looks like, and how to select a folder.

(C) White space and headings are incorporated as guides to the procedure. In addition, single words are used to provide transitions.

The guide includes information relevant to a particular type of computer in a specific library.

(D) Problems that the reader might encounter are anticipated in the section on "Helpful Tips."

For a further sample of work that illustrates a standard-setting performance for narrative procedure, see "A New Look on a Budget," page 82.

Using the Library Reference Computers

Reading
Writing E2
Speaking, Listening, and Viewing
Conventions, Grammar, and Usage of the English Language E4
Literature

E4a Conventions, Grammar, and Usage of the English Language: The student demonstrates an understanding of the rules of the English language in written and oral work, and selects the structures and features of language appropriate to the purpose, audience, and context of the written or oral work. The student demonstrates control of:

- grammar;
- paragraph structure;
- punctuation;
- sentence construction;
- spelling;
- usage.

This guide provides evidence that the students managed effectively the conventions of English through almost error free writing.

cursor to that title and press enter. The screen will then show you a call number, a short summary, number of pages title, and subject.
Example: Say you are looking for a book by **Christopher Pike**, but you do not know the title. Type his name into the computer and the screen will show you all the books by him that are available in the library.

Subject

After you have chosen the Subject folder, type the subject that interests you. Look through the list of books under that subject (use the arrows to move through the list). If you find a book you want, press enter again and the screen will show you the call number, short summary, number of pages, title, and author's name.
Example: Say you are looking for Texas History. Type that in and the screen will show you a long list of different topics on that subject. Of course, you can narrow down your topic. The Alamo or Sam Houston or Ranching will have fewer entries than Texas History, but the entries will be more specific.

D

Helpful Tips

E

•To get out of a folder, press escape.

•If you get in a mess, just ask anyone in the library for help. You will not get in trouble since you are just learning and how else would you learn? Usually pressing escape several times will get you out of your mess and back to the first screen.

•If you cannot find books on your subject, try the magazine index. (There is a set of directions for that index also.)

Using the Library Reference Computers

E4b Conventions, Grammar, and Usage of the English Language: The student analyzes and subsequently revises work to clarify it or make it more effective in communicating the intended message or thought. The student's revisions should be made in light of the purposes, audiences, and contexts that apply to the work. Strategies for revising include:

- adding or deleting details;
- adding or deleting explanations;
- clarifying difficult passages;
- rearranging words, sentences, and paragraphs to improve or clarify meaning;
- sharpening the focus;
- reconsidering the organizational structure.

E The students added information in the writing process, e.g., the early draft has one helpful tip while the final draft includes three tips.

F The students deleted selected passages, e.g., the section titled "How to use the Reference Computers" in the early draft was compressed into the section titled "Working in Your Chosen Folder."

G The students clarified a number of passages, e.g., "The following directions will help you find your book" became "The following directions will help you find books after you have chosen a folder."

A H The students sharpened the focus, e.g., the change of title from "Getting Started" to "Using the Library Reference Computers To Find Books For Your Research" makes the piece specific rather than general.

Early Draft

H → **Getting Started**

Usually the computer is already turned on for you. On the screen there is a big, light green rectangle that says inquired by and subject, author, and title in that order. In the bottom right hand corner there are four arrows that go up, down, right, left use the up and down arrows to move the cursor to go to the folder you want. The cursor is bright blue line that high lights the title of the folder as you move the arrows.

F → **How to use the Reference Computers**

At the reference computer there are three different folders you can choose from (author, title and subject) to help you find the book you are looking for. G → The following directions will help you find your book:

Title
On the reference computer screen go to the folder that says "Inquired by Title" and press enter. Next type the title of the book into th computer. If we have the book you're looking for in our library it will give you the authors name, short summary, call number, number of pages, and tell you if it is available or not.
Example: Say your looking for **The Game** a book by **R.L. Stine**. Type the title and it will show you if the book is in our library

and if it's available.

Author:
On the reference computer screen go to the folder that says "Inquire by Author" and press enter. After you do that, type the authors name and the screen will show you all the books we have by that author. If they have the book you want go to the title and press enter again. When you finish that, you will see on the screen call number, a short summary, number of pages, title, and subject.
Example: For instance say your looking for a book by **Christopher Pike**, but you don't know the title. Type his name into the computer and it will show you all the books we have by him in our library.

Subject
On the reference computer screen go to the folder that says "Inquired by Subject" and press enter. Next type the subject you are looking for. If it lists the book you want, press enter and it will show you all the books we have on that subject. If it has the book you want, press enter again and it will show you the call number, short summary, number of pages, title, and authors name.
Example: Say you're looking for the subject *Texas History*, it will show a long list of different topics on that subject.

A Helpful Tip
E → • To get out of a folder press the escape key (esc). In the upper left hand corner.

Work Sample & Commentary: *Turner Essay*

The task

Students were asked to evaluate Turner's Frontier Hypothesis and compare his theory of the westward movement in America with what the students were learning in class about the actual events. The students were asked to discuss ways in which Turner was both right and wrong, and whether or not his hypothesis was an accurate one.

Circumstances of performance

This sample of student work was produced under the following conditions:

√ alone	in a group
√ in class	√ as homework
√ with teacher feedback	√ with peer feedback
timed	√ opportunity for revision

The few mistakes in the piece seem to represent slips rather than errors (e.g., using the word "seeked" instead of "sought").

What the work shows

E1c Reading: The student reads and comprehends informational materials to develop understanding and expertise and produces written or oral work that:

- restates or summarizes information;
- relates new information to prior knowledge and experience;
- extends ideas;
- makes connections to related topics or information.

Information from a variety of sources is organized and restated in a manner appropriate for an informational piece of writing.

(A) The student produced evidence from various sources to support a possible criticism of the theory being discussed.

(B) The student used evidence from a variety of sources to make a judgment about the theory of manifest destiny.

This work sample illustrates a standard-setting performance for the following parts of the standards:

E1c Reading: Read and comprehend informational materials.

E2a Writing: Produce a report.

April 26,1996

Turner Essay

(D) → Frederick Turner, who was a professor at The University of
Wisconsin as well as Harvard, believed in a theory. This theory was about
the frontier. At first this was only an assignment; however, his
hypothesis and theory turned out to be published in the late 1800's.
Turner wrote a thesis on the western movement and how it was "destiny"
for the United States to go coast to coast. He later named this ~~destiny~~
the Manifest Destiny. His theory involved six groups of people who
settled in what he termed "waves". There were many people who opposed
(E) → his point of view. Was he right, or was he wrong?
There is a good deal of evidence leading up to him being right. The
six groups involved were: Fur Traders, Cattlemen, Pioneer Farmers,
Miners, Equipped Farmers, and Specialist\ Urban Settlers. One of the
first among the group of six to settle in the West were the Fur Traders.
They discovered parts of Tennessee and Kentucky. A man named Daniel
Boone was among the Fur Traders and was well known. On the way back
from Tennessee and Kentucky, they brought with them coonskins and
leather. The Fur Traders helped settle Tennessee. The next group were
the Cattleman. They stretched as far as San Diego to San Francisco. The
Cattlemen, like the pioneer farmers, used the land and natural resources
to survive. They built cattle kingdoms and survived by that for shelter,
food, and warmth. The group that came after them were the Miners. There
was a rumor of gold found in the West, especially in California.
(F) → Thousands of people came to California. These people were known as the
49ers because in 1849, people came for the gold. Approximately 80,000
people seeked their fortune in gold in California. This made the territory
eligible for statehood, and later on, California became a state. Miners
were usually ahead of the settlers, and were nomadic. They built "boom
towns," and moved when an opportunity came up. A short while after,
Pioneer Farmers came. The Pioneer Farmers followed the trails to the
West, and there they cut down trees to build roads, farms, grow crops,
etc. They wanted to find rich fertile land for their crops. They eventually
got to California where the land was rich. As the Pioneer Farmers moved
further west, the Equipped Farmers followed. The Equipped Farmers
followed the Oregon trail and ended up forming a town at the end of the
trail called Oregon City. They built better roads and turnpikes. They also

(C) Ideas that emerged from the theory of manifest destiny are related to modern day circumstances.

E2a Writing: The student produces a report that:

- engages the reader by establishing a context, creating a persona, and otherwise developing reader interest;
- develops a controlling idea that conveys a perspective on the subject;
- creates an organizing structure appropriate to purpose, audience, and context;
- includes appropriate facts and details;
- excludes extraneous and inappropriate information;
- uses a range of appropriate strategies, such as providing facts and details, describing or analyzing the subject, narrating a relevant anecdote, comparing and contrasting, naming, and explaining benefits or limitations;
- provides a sense of closure to the writing.

(D) The essay establishes in the opening paragraph the information that is to be presented in the body of the work, generating an interest in the material in the body of the essay that helps maintain the reader's interest throughout.

Turner Essay

E The controlling idea of the essay is established in the form of a question regarding the accuracy of a particular theory.

The student worked within an appropriate structure for an informational piece of writing by presenting the information that serves as the basis for later judgments.

F The essay includes an appropriate amount of information on each of the groups mentioned in Turner's theory, but not so much that the reader becomes bogged down in extraneous details.

A B The student analyzed the two possible answers to the initial question asked in the essay: "Was he [Turner] right, or was he wrong?"

G The essay closes appropriately with a restatement of the original question and a brief summary of the findings.

sold tools and utensils to miners in the West. The last group of people to settle the West were the Specialist/Urban Settlers. They were inspired to start new settlements and become friends with the Indians as well as learn some of their culture. A man named Jason Lee was a Specialist who educated whites and Indians The Specialists were different because they were already wealthy and had another job then working the land. They established towns and communities and settled in Ohio. They also opened shops, schools, churches, etc. As you can see Turner was right that these six groups came in waves, first starting with the Fur Traders and ending with the Specialist.

Was he wrong? There is not as much evidence, but there is enough to question whether he was right or wrong in his theory. For example, one major group he left out were the Mormons. The Mormons followed the Oregon trail to Utah. To get to Utah they probably went on the California Trail which is connected to the Oregon Trail. The Mormons were very religious and believed in the practice of having more than one wife. The Mormons also had the most successful businesses in the West. Other reasons why he could be wrong are because people went to the West for opportunities. For example, a man named Nathan Hammond went to the West to become wealthy, find bigger land, and a better job. Otto and Anna Schippen moved to the West because their life consisted of moving around. Each place was a new adventure. However, Matthew and Patrice Reynolds moved for better jobs and to sell land. This proved that he could be wrong because it was not all "destiny."

I feel he was able to make a correct hypothesis because his findings all tie in — the six groups went West in waves and it appears it was destiny for them to go. One could say it was correct because he gathered all the facts, made generalizations, and from that, was able to draw a conclusion resulting in a correct hypothesis.

If I could ask Frederick Turner questions about his theory, I would first ask him one obvious question: What made you get so interested in the Western Movement? I would also ask him: How did he get all of his information and form a hypothesis?

Turner displayed many characteristics on the groups of people involved in this. For example, he spoke about Daniel Boone and his leather products as well as his coonskin hats. He explained thoroughly who these people were, what they wanted, and how they would achieve it. This can relate to computer technology because each year we are exploring more and more areas and finding out newer things just like the pioneers. We've come very far; from the first computer to America On Line, Cyberspace, and the World Wide Web. This could also relate to the space program because each year we are finding and learning more things about space and the planets. We have landed on the moon, and now Russia and the United States are teaming up together to build a space station so they can explore further galaxies. That is just like when the trails and towns were built.

In conclusion, what started to be an assignment turned out to be published in a book, and become a well known part of history. Turner's theory opened up everybody into learning about Westward Movement. The main question is, do you think he was right or wrong?

Work Sample & Commentary: *Interview With the Vet*

The task

As an Applied Learning project students on an English/history team decided to design and publish a series of magazines organized around historical themes. The magazines were then distributed to middle school students who could not afford to buy magazines of this kind. The article here was one of many produced by the students that was subsequently published.

This piece of work was completed as part of an Applied Learning project. See page 125 for commentary on the project as a whole.

Circumstances of performance

This sample of student work was produced under the following conditions:

√ alone	in a group
√ in class	√ as homework
√ with teacher feedback	√ with peer feedback
timed	√ opportunity for revision

Although a single student took the responsibility for this particular article, the decisions as to topics, as well as the compilation of written articles into magazines, were handled by the class as a whole.

The error in the transition from page one to page two occurred during the process of setting up the page layout.

Interview With the Vet

It was a silent night in 1968. The day was rather hot, with some steamy wetness in the tropical Vietnamese climate. The night was a pretty normal one for twenty-one year old Corporal. Fransisco "Frank" ________. Patrolling had been rather uneventful, and the quiet night air was relaxing for the members of ________'s group. Men silently prowled the grounds amidst the looming compound in Da Nang, Vietnam, watching intently for any signs of disturbance. Cpl. ________ stood still, relaxed, taking it easy after a lonely, difficult day at work. But, how could you ever say that war was easy? The seemingly unnecessary and costly Vietnam War had been going on for several years, and Frank was there to do his job for right now. However, right then, Frank began to get some of his soldiers instinct for danger. He saw that the other soldiers on the patrol had also begun to look up with alertness. The night had grown deathly quiet in a normally noisy part of the land.

Just as Frank decided that it had definitely grown too quiet, whistling mortar shells and booming gunfire shattered the peaceful calm of the compound with shrieking and deafening noises. Everything seemed to be raining down from the pitch black sky, sending with it shards of powder, metal and debris. In the few seconds that all this occurred, Frank suddenly felt a searing, intense pain in his gut, near his stomach. He leaped to the ground for safety as emergency teams got him to the hospital. As he was rushed there, he got scared at the thought of a bullet hitting him. When he entered the

Frank ________ as a young soldier in Vietnam in 1968.

emergency room, the medics immediately began looking for the bullet hole, except it was never found. The sudden event had scared Frank so immensely that he had formed a huge ulcer in the pit of his stomach fear gripping him from the real world.

Mr. ________, now age forty-nine, looks back on that incident with a chuckle because he remembers how one of his first encounters scared him thoroughly. Although many followed after that one in that foreign land, he looks back saying, "It scared the heck outta me...I'll never forget that night." That night was one of a lifetime for Frank while he served in the U.S. Marine Corps during the Vietnam War.

Although there were a few good times and a duty to finish out, Mr. ________ never quite got over the fact that this political war was fought for the wrong reasons. In his opinion and other's view on this war, "Everyone was out to profit or gain from this war. Generals got promoted, business boomed for the defense industry, new jobs were made in Vietnam and America alike. I really think that the basic effort of this whole operation was a wasted one." Vietnam was remembered to many as an unnecessary, cruel war that ruined two countries.

But how did this affair start? Well, you could say that it began with the end of World War II. During the reconstruction period after World War II, President Truman and other leaders of America, one of the most powerful nations during that time, wanted to have capitalism, which is when most property is owned privately by people or corporations. Communism was

A The reader's interest is engaged by a brief story that introduces the subject of the article.

B The article makes a transition from the opening story that took place in Vietnam to the present day interview that identifies the controlling idea for the article: a soldier remembering what war was like.

The structure of the article replicates the organizing structure often found in human interest articles in newspapers and magazines. The structure is appropriate here considering that the article is written within this genre.

The student stayed within the genre of a human interest article throughout, focusing on what the war was like primarily through the eyes of the article's subject, as opposed to dealing with the war in broad generalizations. As a result, the information included was appropriate.

What the work shows

E2 a Writing: The student produces a report that:

- engages the reader by establishing a context, creating a persona, and otherwise developing reader interest;
- develops a controlling idea that conveys a perspective on the subject;
- creates an organizing structure appropriate to purpose, audience, and context;
- includes appropriate facts and details;
- excludes extraneous and inappropriate information;
- uses a range of appropriate strategies, such as providing facts and details, describing or analyzing the subject, narrating a relevant anecdote, comparing and contrasting, naming, and explaining benefits or limitations;
- provides a sense of closure to the writing.

This work sample illustrates a standard-setting performance for the following part of the standards:

E2 a Writing: Produce a report.

Interview With the Vet

The article includes a number of strategies appropriate to this genre. For example, the article begins with an engaging anecdote before moving on to less interesting facts and details, allowing those details to gain significance for the reader.

C A sense of closure is produced by ending on an uplifting note appropriate for human interest articles.

...porations. Communism, a system where all businesses and properties are owned by the government. was also and idea spreading quickly. In an effort to prevent communism from taking over the foreign policies of that era, Truman and his colleagues promised to help any country trying to resist communism. In short, throughout the years of Eisenhower, Kennedy, Johnson, and Nixon, many efforts were made for the prevention it spreading through Vietnam.

Born in Big Spring, Texas, 250 miles west of Fort Worth, Fransisco ______ was born to a Hispanic family, who also had roots in the border city of Presidio, where his father worked for the Air Force. Frank went through high school in Big Spring and graduated there. After graduation, he joined the Marine Corps and fought in Vietnam. His jobs there consisted of being an administrative clerk, and translator, the only one in his unit. Returning from Vietnam, he began attending ______ County Junior College and earned an associate degree in general business. Soon after, he met and married his wife, Elizabeth. They have two daughters, who are adults now. Their eldest had a son, Frank's first grandson.

I had wondered, however, if he had ever had any trouble with his race, a rather controversial issue in the world, then and now. He explained, "In getting my education in the schools, I had little problem getting to where I eventually got. If I did, I probably ignored it. I mean, that's what you have to do. When I was in the boot and infantry camps, and even on the battleground, there were mainly blacks, whites, and I was the only Hispanic there. The people there in my unit didn't

Frank with the kids in the orphanage

bother me much; we were too busy working on a job that we had to do. I had a goal to accomplish, and I really didn't let any racism get in my way."

Basically, Frank was not quite satisfied with his one degree and started pursuing another one recently. He is currently attending ______ University to earn a Bachelor's degree in business. He is, however, already a successful man, working for ______ at its Fort Worth plant. Although he only had one degree, he worked himself up from the bottom several steps to become

steps to become an English supervisor in the plant. With even more education, he will work his way up in the business world. It just goes to show what one can accomplish with a sufficient education. In addition to his hard work at ______, he is in the Army Reserve with the rank of Sergeant Major and is a member of the Vietnam Veterans Association.

Mr. ______ turned out to be a very successful and well-grounded individual despite the effect the war had on him. He did have a suggestion for minorities or anyone else willing to join efforts in the military, though. He pointedly stated, "Get the best education you can while you are at it. Goofing off is never going to get you anywhere. If you do your best, never hesitate on being the leader. Lead you own crowd if you have to. The leaders of this day and age always get the best jobs in the military. Only the smart, intelligent and hardest workers get promoted to the senior stage. Always keep a positive outlook on the world, because war in one of the most negative things you'll mess with. It can really test you because it is never what you think it is. Just keep that positive outlook on life."

Work Sample & Commentary: *Miss Sadie*

The task

In an on-demand assessment setting, students were asked to present a special person to readers who do not know the person. They could present the person through details of appearance and manner, descriptions of working or living environment, or habits and typical activities. In addition, the students were to reveal the personal quality of their relationship with the person presented.

Circumstances of performance

This sample of student work was produced under the following conditions:

√ alone	in a group
√ in class	as homework
with teacher feedback	with peer feedback
√ timed	opportunity for revision

Errors in this first draft may be attributed to the nature of the task, which was given in a timed writing situation. The writing was completed in forty-five minutes with no opportunities for review and revision. The spelling and grammatical errors in the work sample do not detract from the overall quality of the work.

What the work shows

E2 Writing: The student produces a narrative account (fictional or autobiographical) that:

- engages the reader by establishing a context, creating a point of view, and otherwise developing reader interest;
- establishes a situation, plot, point of view, setting, and conflict (and for autobiography, the significance of events and of conclusions that can be drawn from those events);
- creates an organizing structure;
- includes sensory details and concrete language to develop plot and character;
- excludes extraneous details and inconsistencies;
- develops complex characters;
- uses a range of appropriate strategies, such as dialogue, tension or suspense, naming, and specific narrative action, e.g., movement, gestures, expressions;
- provides a sense of closure to the writing.

This work sample illustrates a standard-setting performance for the following part of the standards:

E2 Writing: Produce a narrative account.

(A) Miss Sadie no longer sits in her rocking chair
on her porch on summer days. But I still can see (E)
her. The old chair squeaking with every sway of
her big, brown body. Her summer dresses stained
from cooking in her sweet smelling kitchen. I
see her gray hair pulled back in that awful,
yellow banana clip. Most of all, I hear that
voice. So full of character and wisdom.
I used to bring Miss Johnson cookies every
summer day of 1988. I miss the days when
I would sit on that shabby old porch and
listen to her stories. "Melissa!" she would
holler. "What 'chu doin' here? Come see me (F)
and my poor self, have ya?" (D)
She once told me of her grandmother who
escaped slavery, back when white men could
only do anything, she would say. Her grandma
ran for miles without food or water. It
wasn't too long before her master came
looking for her and took her home to whip (G)
her. I thought of how Blacks are treated
today. I sighed. She would sing in her

soulful, blaring voice, old negro hymns passed
down from her mother and grand mother. I
would sit there in amazement.
Once, Jimmy Taylor came walking by us
yelling, "Melissa!. Whattaya want with that
old, fat, Black lady, anyways?" (H)
Before I could retaliate, Miss Johnson
said to me, "Now you musn't. We must
feel sorry for that terrible child. His mother
must have done gone and not taught him no
manners!" She actually wanted me to bow
my head and pray for him. (Even though I
went to his house and punched him out the
next day.)
My friends would tease me for spending the
whole summer with Sadie Johnson, "The
Cuckoo of Connecticut," they called her. But
I'm so very glad I did. She taught me then,
to not care what other people thought. I
learned that I could be friends with someone
(B) generations apart from my own.
My visits became less frequent when
school started. I had other things to think
about. Boys, clothes, grades. You know, real
important stuff.
One day I was thinking, I haven't seen
Miss Sadie in a while. So after school
I trotted up to her house amidst the twirling,
autumn leaves.
I rang her bell. The door cracked open and

(A) The reader's interest is engaged by a vivid beginning that raises a question about why Miss Sadie is not in her rocking chair even though the narrator claims she can still see her.

Miss Sadie

The reader is further engaged by the creation of a persona that can handle an emotional issue, that is, the loss of a valued friend, without becoming overly sentimental.

B The significance of the events of the summer are established.

A **C** The student created an organizing structure by effectively completing the circle begun in the first paragraph: from "Miss Sadie no longer sits in her rocking chair on her porch on summer days. But I still can see her," to "Because Miss Sadie no longer sits in her rocking chair on her porch on summer days. I'm glad that I can still see her."

D Sensory details are included that draw the reader into the situations being described.

The character of Miss Sadie is developed through dialogue, description, short anecdotes, and a recounting of certain events, so that when the final meeting between the persona and Miss Sadie occurs, the reader has a clear understanding of its significance.

The student used a wide range of strategies to present the character of Miss Sadie, including:

E vivid imagery;

F dialect;

G accounts of ancestors; and

H the ability to understand and forgive rude behavior.

the women adjusted her glasses. "May I help you?"

"Miss Sadie, it's me, Melissa."

"I-I," she'd stuttered. "I don't remember," she said and shut the door. I heard crying. I rang the door again and she screamed, "Please leave!" in a scared, confused voice.

I went home bewildered and my mother told me to stop bothering Miss Sadie. I said I wasn't bothering her. Mama said, "Miss Johnson has a disease. Alzheimer's disease. It makes her forget things... people, family even. and so, I don't want you over there anymore, you hear?"

Then, I didn't realize or comprehend, how someone so special to you could forget your own existence when you'd shared a summer so special and vivid in your mind.

That christmas I went to bring Miss Johnson cookies. She wasn't there. I learned from a family member that she was in the hospital and that she'd die very soon. As the woman, a daughter maybe, spoke, my heart broke.

"Well, you make sure she gets these cookies," I said, my voice cracking and tears welling in my eyes.

Today, I've learned to love old people. For their innocence, for their knowledge. I've learne to always treat people with kindness, no matter how cruel they may seem. But mainly I've learned, that you must cherish the time spent with a person. And memories are very valuable. Because Miss Sadie no longer sits in her rocking chair on her porch on summer days. I'm glad that I can still see her. **C**

Work Sample & Commentary: *A Geographical Report*

Reading E1
Writing E2
Speaking, Listening, and Viewing
Conventions, Grammar, and Usage of the English Language E4
Literature

The task

Students in a science class were asked to define an interesting question that could be answered through scientific research. The students were required to conduct a review of the research and to produce a report of information. The teacher encouraged the use of illustrations to clarify key points and the inclusion of a complete bibliography.

This report was selected also to illustrate a standard-setting performance for parts of the Science standards at the high school level. (See *New Standards Performance Standards* Volume 3.) Thus, the report not only illustrates standards in more than one subject area but also illustrates achievement of standards at different grade levels.

Circumstances of performance

This sample of student work was produced under the following conditions:

√ alone	in a group
√ in class	√ as homework
√ with teacher feedback	√ with peer feedback
timed	√ opportunity for revision

This work sample represents a substantial project carried out over a period of several months.

What the work shows

E1 c Reading: The student reads and comprehends informational materials to develop understanding and expertise and produces written or oral work that:

- restates or summarizes information;
- relates new information to prior knowledge and experience;
- extends ideas;
- makes connections to related topics or information.

(A) Information acquired through a number of interviews is restated and summarized clearly.

(B) The report relates new information to prior knowledge. In the section titled "Protection Techniques" the information presented earlier in the report regarding the ecological value of vernal pools leads to the judgments here that more education is needed and that preserves for the vernal pools should be established.

This work sample illustrates a standard-setting performance for the following parts of the standards:

E1 c Reading: Read and comprehend informational materials.

E2 a Writing: Produce a report.

E4 a Conventions: Demonstrate an understanding of the rules of the English language.

A GEOGRAPHICAL CONFLICT

(E) My report is on a very rare and unique wetland that many people do not even know exists. They occur only in a few places around the world.

My topic is created by a specific geographical condition. Vernal pools in San Diego occur only on the local mesas and terraces, where soil conditions allow, but these are the ideal place for much of the city's urban and agricultural development. Is it possible to find a balance between the two conflicting purposes of expansion and preservation?

(G) This raises an interesting question; how can you establish vernal pools being thought of as a geographical asset?

METHODS

To answer my question I had to get information on vernal pools: what they are, where they are, and how they are a sensitive natural habitat. Then I needed to examine how city expansion is affecting vernal pools, and if it is apt to continue. I needed to know what the City thinks about the problem and what they are planning to do.

(F) First I looked for any information available on vernal pools at public libraries, but I couldn't find what I was looking for. The topic is apparently too obscure. Next I went to a university library that had an environmental department, to get as much information as possible (University of San Diego).

(J) I also interviewed several authorities in the field: the district representative for the U.S. Army Corps of Engineers, the federal agency responsible for the protection of wetlands; a senior environmental planner with the City of San Diego, who wrote the City's Resource Protection Ordinance

3

(RPO); the Station botanist at Miramar Naval Air Station, who is in charge of their vernal pool management plan on the land that has the largest number of pools remaining in the City of San Diego; a biologist working for RECON (Regional Environmental Consultants), a firm which is mapping the vernal pools for the City of Hemet, (another city in San Diego County facing the same issues); and finally a geographer working for SANDAG (San Diego Association of Governments), a regional organization that gathers, records, and analyzes data associated with regional planning and environmental issues. They answered many questions and offered their own ideas and information, including additional articles on my subject. I looked at several maps and photos of vernal pool locations, and charts of changing land use.

(A) To decide how much education may be needed about vernal pools, I made a questionnaire, and surveyed two classrooms of elementary students, and a group of forty-two adults, trying to cover most age groups.

WHAT VERNAL POOLS ARE

Vernal pools are a unique and rare form of wetland. Wetlands are areas that are covered or soaked by water enough to support plants that grow only in moist ground. Some examples of wetlands are bogs, swamps, marshes, and edges of lakes and streams. These are what people think of when they hear "wetland". But vernal pools are different than these other types of wetlands. They are located on dry and flat places. No one would expect to find a wetland in such a dry area!

San Diego vernal pools are surrounded by small mounds called "mima mounds". The name mima mounds comes from the Mima Prairie near Olympia, Washington. People don't know for sure how mima mounds are formed. Some

4

A Geographical Report

E1 Reading
E2 Writing
Speaking, Listening, and Viewing
E4 Conventions, Grammar, and Usage of the English Language
Literature

think that they were formed by gophers piling up the earth. Others think that ice wedges from glaciers caused the upheaval, or maybe the wind pushed loose dirt, catching in clumps of shrubs. Mounds can be found on prairies or terraces with a hardpan or clay layer underneath.

K → Vernal pools are depressions between the mima mounds. In winter the pools are filled by rain storms. In spring the pools look their best, when plants are in full splendor. By summer the pools are dry and look only like a dry pothole. (See illustration of pool cycles and typical cross section.) A vernal pool does not dry by soaking into the ground; the layer of clay or rock underneath the pool prevents the water from soaking through. Instead they dry out from evaporation, or use by the plants. The mima mounds are not impervious so one pool tends to drain into another. Therefore, the pools have to be on flat land; the pools cannot be on a slope or the water would run off, and the pools would not be filled.

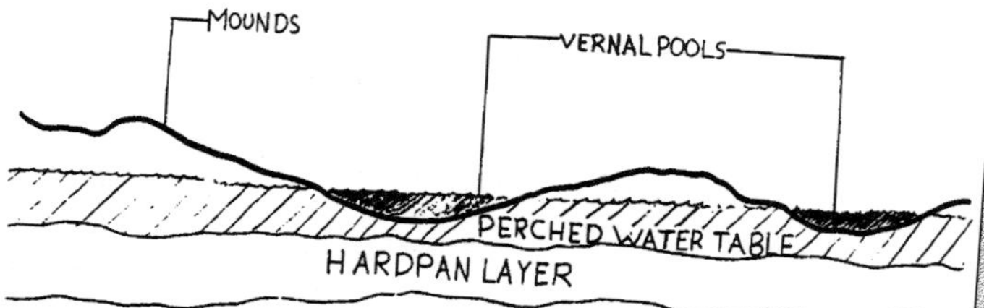

MOUNDS
VERNAL POOLS
PERCHED WATER TABLE
HARDPAN LAYER

TYPICAL CROSS SECTION OF VERNAL POOL

5

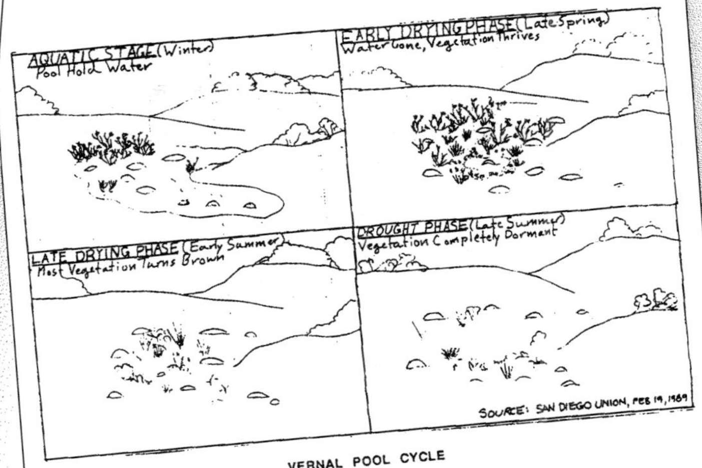

AQUATIC STAGE (Winter) Pool Hold Water
EARLY DRYING PHASE (Late Spring) Water Gone, Vegetation Thrives
LATE DRYING PHASE (Early Summer) Most Vegetation Turns Brown
DROUGHT PHASE (Late Summer) Vegetation Completely Dormant
SOURCE: SAN DIEGO UNION, FEB 19, 1989

VERNAL POOL CYCLE

WHY VERNAL POOLS ARE SO IMPORTANT

Vernal pools are a very rare, specific habitat. Hardly any are left, so we don't have many to lose. There used to be vernal pools on many of the mesas and terraces of San Diego County, and the Central Valley of California. Now there are almost no vernal pools in the Central Valley, and an estimated 97% have been lost in San Diego County. An estimated 80% of the remaining pools in San Diego are located on Miramar Naval Air Station. (See map, next page.)

6

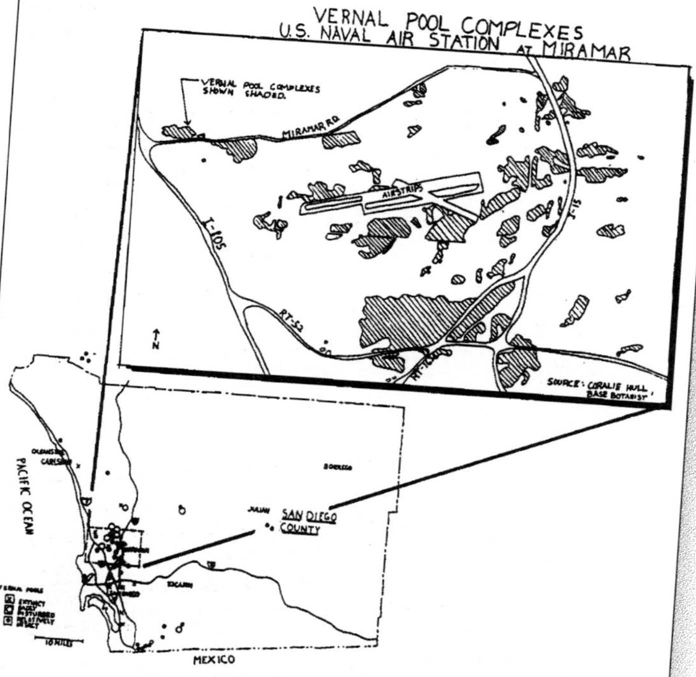

VERNAL POOL COMPLEXES
U.S. NAVAL AIR STATION AT MIRAMAR
VERNAL POOL COMPLEXES SHOWN SHADED
MIRAMAR RD.
AIRSTRIPS
I-805
I-15
SOURCE: CORALIE HULL BASE BOTANIST
PACIFIC OCEAN
SAN DIEGO COUNTY
MEXICO

VERNAL POOL DISTRIBUTION, SAN DIEGO COUNTY

7

It does not take much to disturb a vernal pool. Even grazing or off road vehicle use in the summer, when pool species are dormant and people could think they are just a dry hole, can damage them. Most are disturbed by grading and flattening of their habitat, or by breakup of the impervious layer. With just flat land there would be no depressions for vernal pools to form; what would form would be "vernal mud". With no impervious layer the water would just sink into the ground, and would be there only for a short period of time, not enough for wetland plants.

The mima mounds have to be protected too. If the watershed for the pools is changed, the condition of the pools changes. If there isn't enough water from runoff, then all plant or animal life in them disappears, because they need enough moisture at the right time, to live. If there is too much water, then the pool may turn into another kind of wetland, such as a bog.

Although people have begun to study them, there is still a lot to learn. One thing scientists know is that they are a part of a larger environment. Many animals travel from other areas to feed on plants or animals , or drink from the vernal pools. For example, water fowl from many other places will stop at the pools to eat the fairy shrimp and snack on the plants.

Vernal pools have a large assortment of rare and exotic flora and fauna (plants and animals). Five of them are on the federal list of endangered species, and one more is a candidate for listing. The plants and animals in vernal pools are unusual because they have only developed recently compared to other changes in evolution. As scientists study the pools more intently they are finding more and more unknown species. There are temporary pools in other places around the world, but California's vernal pools are different because of their long drought phase, which causes the plants and animals to adapt to the climate. They go into a dormant phase. For example, fairy shrimp

8

A Geographical Report

lay eggs before the drought which hatch when it gets moist enough to be active. Some plants, in a short period of time, develop seeds; others appear to die out, but quickly sprout again from the rain. Many of these species cannot survive outside vernal pools, and some are "endemic" (species found only in a very restricted geographical area).

B PROTECTION TECHNIQUES

The first step is to try to keep development away from vernal pools. But to do this you first need to know where the pools are. Thanks to regional mapping efforts, existing vernal pools have been fairly well identified in San Diego County.

There are already laws against disturbances of vernal pools. You could go to jail or get fined a large sum of money for disturbing a wetland. The U.S. Fish and Wildlife Service protects the listed endangered species present, and the U.S. Army Corps of Engineers makes sure you don't fill any kind of wetland habitat, including vernal pools. The local office of the U.S. Army Corps of Engineers has submitted a proposal to Washington for a stricter permit process for vernal pools.

When possible the vernal pools should be part of a large preserve of open space. That way the pools would not be isolated islands, but part of their natural communities, and would be protected by a buffer of distance. Fences should not be put directly around the vernal pools unless it cannot be avoided, because it would keep some animals out, such as rabbits which spread plant seeds around when they eat them.

It is important to educate people about vernal pools so they know how important they are and what they look like, and so they know how to preserve

9

them. To see how much education may be needed in San Diego, I surveyed ninety-two people (forty-two adults and fifty elementary students to try to cover all age groups). I asked them if they had heard of vernal pools, and if they knew what they were. About 21% thought they had heard of them, but only 7% really knew what they were. (See pie chart.) I found that much education is needed.

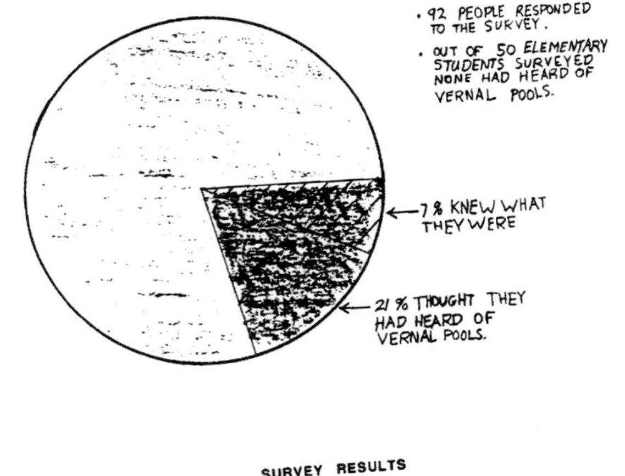
• 92 PEOPLE RESPONDED TO THE SURVEY.
• OUT OF 50 ELEMENTARY STUDENTS SURVEYED NONE HAD HEARD OF VERNAL POOLS.
7% KNEW WHAT THEY WERE
21% THOUGHT THEY HAD HEARD OF VERNAL POOLS.

SURVEY RESULTS

At N.A.S. Miramar the Station botanist has been putting articles dealing with vernal pools in almost every issue of the base newspaper. Now most people on the base know about vernal pools, and know how valuable they are.

10

C The student extended ideas by speculating about the topic of a possible nature center in the section titled "Recognizing An Asset."

D The student made connections by reflecting on the implications inherent in the information gathered, particularly in the "Conclusion."

E2 a Writing: The student produces a report that:

- engages the reader by establishing a context, creating a persona, and otherwise developing reader interest;
- develops a controlling idea that conveys a perspective on the subject;
- creates an organizing structure appropriate to purpose, audience, and context;
- includes appropriate facts and details;
- excludes extraneous and inappropriate information;
- uses a range of appropriate strategies, such as providing facts and details, describing or analyzing the subject, narrating a relevant anecdote, comparing and contrasting, naming, and explaining benefits or limitations;
- provides a sense of closure to the writing.

E G The student established a context by identifying the subject of the report as "a very rare and unique wetland" and by posing a significant question: "how can you establish vernal pools being thought of as a geographical asset?"

F The report successfully engages the reader by creating, in the section on "Methods," the authoritative persona of a reasonable, intelligent individual who takes logical steps to find information, by referring to "public libraries," "a university library," "several authorities in the field," "several maps and photos," "charts of changing land use," and developing "a questionnaire" which "surveyed two classrooms... and a group of forty-two adults."

G H The student developed a controlling idea by posing a question, "how can you establish vernal pools...?" The student used the researched information to conclude that "A balance between expansion and preservation will not come easily, but...will shift toward long-term vernal pool preservation."

The organizing structure divides the report into appropriate sections.

The report includes appropriate facts and details within each section, including graphics and illustrations where appropriate.

I The student used a range of appropriate strategies, including adequate illustrations and diagrams. He also argued persuasively for the benefits of educating the public about vernal pool preservation in the section titled "Recognizing An Asset."

A Geographical Report

E1 Reading
E2 Writing
Speaking, Listening, and Viewing
E4 Conventions, Grammar, and Usage of the English Language
Literature

C → RECOGNIZING AN ASSET

Education is a key to preserving vernal pools. Vernal pools are very unique and we do not have many to lose. Making new ones does not work. Studies done at the University of California, Santa Barbara, have shown that after five years their complexity goes down.

First, vernal pools must be protected. There could be different ranges of accessibility, from remote (available to research only), somewhat accessible (good for guided seasonal visits), to readily accessible (which may have to be protected by fencing or supervision). The most accessible ones would be a great educational opportunity for the general public. The pools closer to development could be developed into nature centers, with raised boardwalks to protect the habitat, as is done over the hot springs in Yellowstone. (See illustration.)

I →

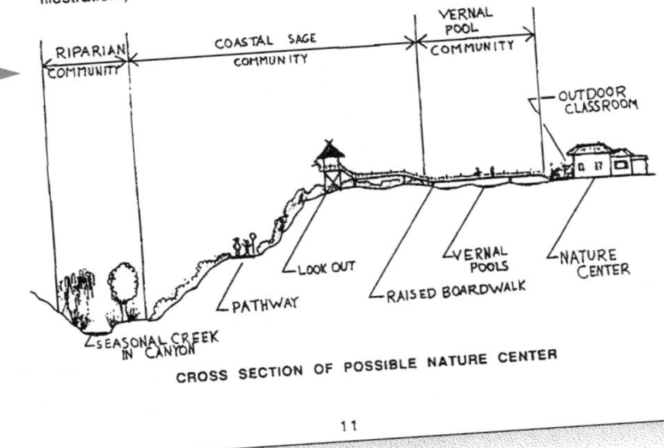

CROSS SECTION OF POSSIBLE NATURE CENTER

11

Interpretive signs and docents could provide information. Being very unique, vernal pools would make interesting learning centers. People would learn how the plants and animals adapt to the seasonal changes. This would teach people the importance of vernal pools, how complex they are, how to identify them, and how to preserve them when wet or dry. A park in the Sacramento area has an adjacent vernal pool with hiking trails around it; and it seems to work there because the people there know how important and delicate it is.

Ecotourism, a popular concept now, would be another idea. San Diego is a place where tourists already come. The very climate and geography that brings people here is what created vernal pools. Ecotourism would be easy to add to the other attractions, and would indirectly benefit the city. A tour company might be authorized to place advertisements to bring people to learn the importance of vernal pools and their ecosystem. With many people outside San Diego knowing about vernal pools and concerned about their well-being, there would be widespread support for vernal pool protection.

D → CONCLUSION

The problem of endangering vernal pools will not go away, because the City will need more land to develop. However, vernal pools remain a rare and unique wetland, and need protection. Even though there are laws made to protect them, pools are still being lost. Education is needed. Widespread education showing how important vernal pools are, and how easy they are to disturb, will create widespread support for protection.

H → A balance between expansion and preservation will not come easily, but if the public views vernal pools as a geographical asset, the balance will shift toward long-term vernal pool preservation.

12

BIBLIOGRAPHY

Ashworth, William. "Vernal Pool". The Encyclopedia of Environmental Studies, 1991, p. 412.

Barbour, Michael G. and Major, Jack, ed. Terrestrial Vegetation of California. New York: John Wiley and Sons, 1977.

Baskin, Yvonne. "California's Ephemeral Vernal Pools May be a Good Model for Speciation". BioScience, vol. 44 no. 6, June 1994, pp. 384-388.

City of San Diego Mima Mound-Vernal Pool Guidelines. July 20, 1993.

City of San Diego Municipal Code, Section 101.0462. "Resource Protection Ordinance".

Franklin, Jerry F., and Dyrness, C.T.. "Natural Vegetation of Oregon and Washington". Portland, Oregon: Pacific Northwest Forest and Range Experiment Station (General Technical Report PNW-8), 1973.

Hutchison, Steven M. "A Phenomenon of Spring: Vernal Pools". Environment Southwest, no. 480, Winter 1978.

Jenny, Hans. "The Soil Resource: Origin and Behavior". New York; Springer, 1980, pp. 228-231, 280-282, 356.

Martin, Glen. "Spring Fever". Discover, vol. 11 no. 3, March 1990, pp. 70-74.

Osment, Noel. "Dwindling Treasures: Unique Desert / Marsh Habitats Vanishing Fast". San Diego Union, February 19, 1989.

"Regulatory Permit Program". U.S. Army Corps of Engineers, Los Angeles District (SPL PAM 1130-2-1), Nov., 1993.

SANDAG. "A Look at San Diego's Future". INFO, January-February, 1994.

SANDAG. "Land Use in the San Diego Region". INFO, January-February, 1993.

White, Scott D. "Vernal Pools in the San Jacinto Valley". Fremontia, vol. 22 no. 4, October 1994, pp. 17-19.

Zedler, Paul H.. "The Ecology of Southern California Vernal Pools: A Community Profile". U.S.D.I. Fish and Wildlife Service, Washington D.C. (Biological Report 85 (7.11)), May 1987.

13

E4a Conventions, Grammar, and Usage of the English Language: The student demonstrates an understanding of the rules of the English language in written and oral work, and selects the structures and features of language appropriate to the purpose, audience, and context of the work. The student demonstrates control of:

- grammar;
- paragraph structure;
- punctuation;
- sentence construction;
- spelling;
- usage.

The student managed the conventions, grammar, and usage of English so that they aid rather than interfere with reading.

J K The student managed a variety of sentence constructions, e.g., paragraph three in "Methods"; and paragraph structures, e.g., paragraph three in "What Vernal Pools Are."

Work Sample & Commentary: *Analysis of* The Old Man and the Sea

The task

During a unit on literature, students were asked to write a critical analysis on a work of their choice.

Circumstances of performance

This sample of student work was produced under the following conditions:

√	alone		in a group
√	in class		as homework
	with teacher feedback		with peer feedback
	timed	√	opportunity for revision

What the work shows

E2b Writing: The student produces a response to literature that:

- engages the reader through establishing a context, creating a persona, and otherwise developing reader interest;
- advances a judgment that is interpretive, analytic, evaluative, or reflective;
- supports a judgment through references to the text, references to other works, authors, or non-print media, or references to personal knowledge;
- demonstrates an understanding of the literary work;
- anticipates and answers a reader's questions;
- provides a sense of closure to the writing.

A The essay engages the reader through a brief summary of the plot in the first paragraph.

B The final sentence of the first paragraph establishes a context by incorporating a quotation into the guiding statement or thesis.

C The essay advances an interpretive judgment, i.e., "Santiago does not let the loss of his friend or the defeat that others see him suffering keep him off the sea…and prepares to catch the biggest fish of his life."

D Assertions about the piece are supported through references to the text.

This work sample illustrates a standard-setting performance for the following parts of the standards:

E2b Writing: Produce a response to literature.

E4a Conventions: Demonstrate an understanding of the rules of the English language.

ANALYSIS OF THE OLD MAN AND THE SEA

In the book The Old Man and the Sea, Ernest Hemingway tells the story of an old Cuban fisherman named Santiago who, considered by the villagers to be the worst type of unlucky, is still determined to win a battle against a giant Marlin off the coast of Cuba. Santiago succeeds, but his successes do not come without great hardship and struggle. He spends three days being dragged in his skiff by the enormous marlin with minimal food and water, all the while enduring acute physical pain, tiredness, and an unending loneliness due to the absence of his young friend, Manolin. It is only after Santiago's prize fish is completely devoured by sharks that he returns home to the village scorners and the safety of Manolin's trust. As his suffering and loss compound, ~~we~~ can see that Hemingway's quote "a man can be destroyed but not defeated" offers a key insight into Santiago's life.

As the story begins, we learn that Santiago has gone eighty-four days straight without catching a fish. Young Manolin's parents will no longer allow the two to fish together, for they do not want their son being exposed any more to this type of failure. Santiago and Manolin are deeply saddened by this news, but Santiago does not let the loss of his friend or the defeat that others see him suffering keep him off the sea. Rather, with bright and shining eyes he thinks "maybe today. Every day is a new day" (pg. 32), and prepares to catch the biggest fish of his life. This shows that even though almost all of Santiago's acquaintances feel that his fishing career is over, he sees it about to reach its all time high. Though he knows he is physically older and weaker than most of his fellow fisherman, he refuses to let their opinions and stereotypes destroy his confidence and determination.

As the story progresses, Hemingway pre ·ents an even more vivid picture of Santiago refusing to be destroyed by the forces that threaten to defeat him. Even after he accomplishes the difficult task of hooking the giant Marlin, he finds his skiff being dragged by the fish for over two days. Living in the small boat is no easy task for Santiago, and soon injury and suffering seem to take over his entire body. His back is sore from sitting so long against the stiff wood, his face is cut from fishing hooks, his shoulders ache, and his eyes have trouble focusing. Most difficult to endure though is the terrible condition in which he finds his hands. The left one is weakened from a period of being tightly cramped, and both are extremely mutilated from the burn of the moving fishing line. It would have been so much easier for Santiago to simply give up and release the fish, yet he knows that if he endures a little longer, victory will be his. Even when it seems he has no effort left, Santiago promises himself "I'll try it again." (pg. 93) This is Santiago's real inner determination coming through. He has encountered so many obstacles during the past few days, yet he will not let them defeat his dream of killing the fish. There is no outside force promising a splendid reward if he succeeds, only those that threaten to ridicule him if he is destroyed. Santiago is working solely on his own desire to fulfill his dream and prove to himself that, although his struggles may cost him his life, he can accomplish even the seemingly impossible.

Analysis of The Old Man and the Sea

E The student demonstrated an understanding of the literary work by making evaluative judgments that connected Santiago's dreams of lions to his victory over tremendous odds.

F The material is organized logically by using two key elements of the quotation from the thesis statement as devices to guide the structure, i.e., "destroyed" but "not defeated" are the elements which are repeated in each paragraph; the concluding paragraph returns to the quotation in the guiding statement.

E4a Conventions, Grammar, and Usage of the English Language: The student demonstrates an understanding of the rules of the English language in written and oral work, and selects the structures and features of language appropriate to the purpose, audience, and context of the work. The student demonstrates control of:

- grammar;
- paragraph structure;
- punctuation;
- sentence construction;
- spelling;
- usage.

The student managed the conventions, grammar, and usage of English so that they aid rather than interfere with reading.

The student managed a variety of sentence constructions and paragraph structures, e.g., see paragraph three for use of detail to develop the paragraph.

After three long days and nights, Santiago's determination pays off, and at last he
manages to catch and kill the Marlin. It is only a very short time that he has to relish in
his triumph though, for a few hours later vicious sharks begin to destroy the carcass of
the great fish. For hours, Santiago manages to ward them off, but this time it is not he
who wins the final battle. Spirits low and pain at an all time high, Santiago returns to the
village, towing behind him only the bare skeleton of a treasure that once was. It seems as
though Santiago is ready to just curl up and die, and indeed he has reason to feel this
way. Yet as he rests alone and talks with Manolin, we see a hint of Santiago's
determination, that has characterized his personality throughout the entire story, begin to
shine through. Upon reaching home, he begins to make plans with Manolin about future
adventures they will have together. Hemingway tells us that Santiago, in his youth, had
loved to watch the majestic lions along his home on a white sand beach in Africa, and he
still returns to those dreams when searching for contentment. That night, as Santiago
drifts off to sleep, Hemingway tells us that he was indeed "dreaming about the lions."
(pg. 127) This is perhaps the truest test of how much courage and determination a person
has. If even when thev have suffered the biggest defeat of their life, they are able to look
to the future and realize the wonderful things they still posses. Though the forces of
nature and time destroyed Santiago's prize fish, he refuses to let that fact ruin the rest of
his life. No one can take away his love for Manolin or memories of what once was, and
because of this, no one can ever truly defeat Santiago.

In conclusion, throughout the entire story <u>The Old Man and the Sea</u>, Santiago
refuses to surrender to the forces working against him. He ignores the comments of those
who think he is unlucky, endures great physical pain, and rises up from the depths of
sorrow over the lost Marlin to find happiness in what he does possess. Hemingway's
quote "a man can be destroyed but not defeated" truly does display the amount of
determination that Santiago shows throughout his life.

Work Sample & Commentary: *Lena and Chayim*

Reading
Writing E2
Speaking, Listening, and Viewing
Conventions, Grammar, and Usage of the English Language E4
Literature

The task

Students were asked to write a story about someone who meant something to them. The students read a number of narratives to help them become familiar with the various elements that create a narrative and to learn how different writers work to achieve different effects according to the purpose of the story. The student who wrote this story preceded it with a note labeled "Author's Note." The note reads: "Everything in the story you are about to read is true! There are no falsities whatsoever! All the characters were real people! Thank You."

Circumstances of performance

This sample of student work was produced under the following conditions:

√ alone	in a group
√ in class	√ as homework
√ with teacher feedback	√ with peer feedback
timed	√ opportunity for revision

What the work shows

E2 c Writing: The student produces a narrative account (fictional or autobiographical) that:

- engages the reader by establishing a context, creating a point of view, and otherwise developing reader interest;
- establishes a situation, plot, point of view, setting, and conflict (and for autobiography, the significance of events and of conclusions that can be drawn from those events);
- creates an organizing structure;
- includes sensory details and concrete language to develop plot and character;
- excludes extraneous details and inconsistencies;
- develops complex characters;
- uses a range of appropriate strategies, such as dialogue, tension or suspense, naming, and specific narrative action, e.g., movement, gestures, expressions;
- provides a sense of closure to the writing.

This work sample illustrates a standard-setting performance for the following parts of the standards:

E2 c Writing: Produce a narrative account.

E4 a Conventions: Demonstrate an understanding of the rules of the English language.

Lena and Chayim

With a loud bump and thud against the dock, a huge ship filled with immigrants seeking hope and prosperity in America, landed in New York harbor. As the boat doors were opened, a heavy flow of people streamed out. They looked tired and rumpled from their long journey from Europe and their eyes, accustomed to the darkness of the ship, squinted into the blinding sunlight. Dragging bags, boxes and baskets, these bedraggled humans made their way into the main building on Ellis Island. Among these newcomers was Lena, a young Polish Jew, and her husband, Chayim.

Lena was beautiful with deepset blue eyes, and long flowing black hair. She had high cheekbones and stood almost six feet tall. Chayim was rather plain. These two young people had not married by choice but had been forced to wed. While still in Poland, Lena had been deeply in love with a young man called Jacob. He was sought out by all the young women in the village, for he was handsome and sang very well. He, however, only liked Lena and would have married her at once but the choice belonged to their parents so Jacob and Lena were forced to go their separate ways. For a while, Lena was very unhappy but soon she forgot about Jacob and went on with her life.

Now, as Lena walked closer and closer to the main inspection building on Ellis Island, her heart was filled with dread. Should she or Chayim show any signs of illness, mental or physical, they might be detained and then (the immigrant's nightmare), DEPORTED! (E) Once inside the building, Lena and the others were ushered up the stairs and into the dreaded Registration Room. If a person had any trouble walking up the stairs, they would be taken aside and examined for tuberculosis, pneumonia, consumption or other breathing disorders. Neither Lena nor Chayim encountered any trouble.

Now the immigrants walked into the Registration Room, filling all the hard wooden benches that filled the entire room. It was here that many of them would wait for days, even weeks, before being examined and questioned by officials. Luck smiled upon Lena and Chayim and they only waited a few hours. When their names were called though, they had much trouble with the questions they were asked. Lena did not speak a word of English; Yiddish was her native tongue. They did not know what to do until a young official approached them. His name was Fiorello LaGuardia and he spoke Yiddish with great ease. Translating questions and answers, he helped Lena and Chayim with their passage to America.

Before leaving the island, Lena sat down to a meal in the large Ellis Island dining room. The foods on her plate were all American and she, like many others, were greatly puzzled over them. One of the most fascinating things set before Lena was a long, yellow crescent. She watched as people all around her pick it up and eat it as it was. However, the person sitting next to her removed the outer part first and then bit in. Lena did the same. DELICIOUS!

Lena and Chayim were among the many immigrants to have friends or relatives already in New York. Their friends had found them a coldwater flat on the Lower East Side of Manhattan. Living conditions were terrible! The apartment had no running

The work creates an omniscient point of view for the voice of the narrator and then maintains that voice consistently throughout the story.

The student established a plot sequence that followed the timeline of Lena's entry into America and her first ten years or so of trying to deal with life in a new country.

The organizing structure centers on the difficulties experienced by the main character. These difficulties build to the tragedy of Charlie's death in ways that make Lena's reaction understandable and Charlie's dramatic recovery that much more welcome.

(A) The student used language in a mature fashion, bringing to life the various characters and developing the plot at the same time. The short paragraph describing Charlie's death is a good example of the student's capacity to do both.

(B) By giving brief glimpses of certain events and more extended versions of others, the student created differing effects to communicate different messages. The selection of information serves to create the desired effects.

(C) The story creates the various characters and identifies the complex nature of each character. In the case of Chayim, for example, the story identifies Chayim's frustration at not being able to make a living in his new country, and then identifies the series of events that caused him to start drinking heavily and to eventually alienate himself from his family.

Lena and Chayim

water or private bathroom. It was freezing in the winter and swelteringly hot in the
summer. But what could they do? There was no where else to go.

After a while, Chayim bought a small sewing machine. He had been a tailor in
B the old country and a very reputable one at that. He had been rich and people had sought
him out far and wide to do custom tailoring for them. Now he could work again.
Chayim's hope dwindled when he saw that the type of work he was getting was not what
he had expected. Few people had enough money to buy new clothes and called upon him
only for patching and mending. Soon Chayim realized that he would have to find better
F work. Lena was pregnant and they simply did not have enough money to support a child.

Eventually Lena gave birth to twins, a boy and a girl. Chayim was almost in
despair. He took a job in a factory, working sixteen hours a day, six days a week. A year
later, both twins died of the measles.

Lena would not be beaten. She had heard of a man, Samuel Gompers, who
believed strongly in unionism and convinced Chayim they should both attend the
meetings he led. Soon, Lena and Chayim believed in unionism too.

Lena gave birth to another child, a boy and happiness again found the lonely
couple. Their happiness could not last. This child too died from the measles within a
year. Chayim mourned over the third lost child and forgot about unionism. He began to
drink heavily. Lena, though saddened was determined not to let life strike her down. She
C began to take in sewing because Chayim was no use any more.

Soon Lena had another child. She called him Yeshayahu, meaning "God will
save him." Later on she changed the boys name to English and he became "Charlie."
Her whole life now centered around this new son. He was her pride and joy. She ignored
Chayim more and more. As a result, Chayim grew jealous of his son and often beat the
young boy. Lena spoke out against Chayim and put a stop to these beatings but now a
D terrible hate grew between husband and wife. Chayim barely spoke to Charlie except to
say such things as, "Charlie, take this dime and go out and buy me a bucket of beer. I'm
expecting company." It was terrible.

Lena still loved Charlie. She catered to his every whim and babied him
incredibly. She also decided that Charlie would grow up to love music. She took him to
free band concerts and sang him old Yiddish lullabies. Her plan worked. Charlie's hero
was John Philip Sousa, the composer of the United States National Anthem.

The winter of 1901 came in cold and angry. Wind howled bitterly and their was
ice and snow everywhere. It seemed as if there would be no end. Lena took in no more
sewing because none of the neighbors wanted to walk outside to bring it to her. She had
also borne another son and things looked grimmer than ever.

One day Lena saw eight-year-old Charlie sitting near the stove. He had on a thin
shirt and was shivering terribly. She brushed her hand against his head and felt that it
was burning with fever. Lena immediately put down her newborn son and went out to
seek the neighbors help. She needed money for the doctor.

The doctor arrived at the house very quickly. Charlie had a high fever and was
shivering more than ever. He was stricken with pneumonia. The doctor sponged him
A down with cold water to lessen the fever. Instead it rose! Suddenly the shivering
stopped. Charlie's face became sheet white. The doctor checked unsuccessfully for a
pulse. Charlie was dead.

Lena was horrified. She was angry. She began screaming and beating the doctor.
The neighbors heard her cries and came to help the poor doctor. It took three men to get
Lena away from him. They had to restrain her so the body could be taken away. One
woman took the baby away to care for it. Then they took her shoes and money and
locked her in the apartment. They were afraid she might do something violent. Lena
screamed and cried out for hours and finally fell asleep from exhaustion.

Lena awakened at the crack of dawn. She had to see Charlie, she had to. Lena
climbed out the window and out onto the fire escape. She reached the street below and
ran ten blocks through the snow to the funeral parlor. Lena at last reached her
destination. She was barefoot and unkempt and had the appearance of someone gone
mad.

She opened Charlie's coffin. His thin body was enveloped in a prayer shawl. As
Lena gazed into the coffin, Charlie sat up! He told Lena he was thirsty and wanted some
milk. Now, this is a very strange occurrence. It happens maybe once in 50 years. If
Lena had been in any other state of mind at the time, she might have passed out on the
floor. But she didn't. She was in *such* a crazed state that she couldn't have cared less
Charlie had started to fly. She acted as though his awakening were a normal occurrence.

"Yes my child, I'll get you some milk." she said.

For the second time that morning Lena went out into the cold winter weather.
She ran about looking desperately for an opened store. There were none. Finally Lena
came across a store with steel cans of milk displayed in front. She pried one opened
(only in such a crazed state could she have done this) and poured the contents of it into a
ladle used for serving customers. Then she carefully made her way back to Charlie,
careful not to spill a drop of milk.

When Lena returned, Charlie was crying for her to come back and an old
watchman (having recovered from an earlier fainting spell when Charlie awakened) was
doing his best to comfort the little boy. Lena gave Charlie the milk and carried him back
home. She had regained control of life at last.

Chayim died soon after of a liver illness at the age of 41. Lena was consoled by
friends who told her that her first love Jacob was living in the area. He too was mourning
the loss of his spouse. Lena and Jacob met and found that they were still very much in
G love. They married and (here is the most annoying last line of a story ever but I have to
say/write/type it) lived happily ever after.

D The student used dialogue sparingly, but where it is used it serves as a strategy to tell the reader something about the character.

E A The student used suspense as an effective strategy, allowing it to create reader anticipation both in the introduction when Lena and Chayim are first trying to enter the country and then towards the end when Charlie dies.

F The use of tension as a strategy between the moments of anticipation where things suddenly look brighter for Lena and Chayim, and the events that serve to squelch the anticipation, such as the births and deaths of three children, serve to make the story interesting.

G The story ends in the fashion of many stories with a "happily ever after" conclusion. Although the ending is a bit dissatisfying for a story of this caliber, the parenthetical note in the last sentence showing that the student recognized this fact, combined with the preface to the piece that declares the truthfulness of the events being recounted, indicates that the choice for an ending was a conscious one. The clear indication that the student understood the implications for such a simplistic ending and yet chose it nevertheless, suggests that the ending functions just as the student intended.

E4a Conventions, Grammar, and Usage of the English Language: The student demonstrates an understanding of the rules of the English language in written and oral work, and selects the structures and features of language appropriate to the purpose, audience, and context of the work. The student demonstrates control of:

- grammar;
- paragraph structure;
- punctuation;
- sentence construction;
- spelling;
- usage.

The student demonstrated through virtually error free writing the ability to manage the conventions of grammar and usage. The student managed a variety of sentence constructions, appropriate punctuation, and complex syntax. This is evident throughout the work.

Work Sample & Commentary: *Conformity in Numbers*

The task

Students were asked to write an essay to persuade an audience one way or another on an issue of current significance in the news.

Circumstances of performance

This sample of student work was produced under the following conditions:

√ alone	in a group
√ in class	√ as homework
with teacher feedback	√ with peer feedback
timed	√ opportunity for revision

What the work shows

E1 d Reading: The student demonstrates familiarity with a variety of public documents (i.e., documents that focus on civic issues or matters of public policy at the community level and beyond) and produces written or oral work that does one or more of the following:

- identifies the social context of the document;
- identifies the author's purpose and stance;
- analyzes the arguments and positions advanced and the evidence offered in support of them, or formulates an argument and offers evidence to support it;
- examines or makes use of the appeal of a document to audiences both friendly and hostile to the position presented;
- identifies or uses commonly used persuasive techniques.

The student responded to a matter of public policy that may affect her directly, and yet did so in a manner that engages the issue rather than attacks it irresponsibly.

The essay analyzes the major argument for advocating school uniforms and identifies some of the possible problems with the argument.

Conformity in Numbers

(A) Robots. Bleak, perfunctory masses. I feel this is what children will become if forced to wear school uniforms. The idea of school uniforms becoming mandatory in public schools is hardly engaging to me. In fact, I am against the idea, full force. They (B) will stifle creativity, but hardly eliminate any the threat of violence that has aroused in the education populous.

School uniforms are barricades, invisible prisons. Children should be nurtured to be different, not mechanically the same. They do not operate on the same level, nor should they have to. Uniforms will make them appear similar, to a dangerous point. Children will not see themselves as "special," but no better than anyone else. They will be without motivation or reason to go beyond what is expected. We will live in a world where we are no better than our comrades. We will become statistics, not judged as individuals, but as numbers. Nameless, faceless, black and white ideas. Not existing together but as one. Children will stop being children. Instead, they will become monotonous automans, working for nothing. There will be nothing to strive for.

(C) Again, uniforms will hardly eliminate violence. If people are attacked for jackets, and the school they attend forces mandatory uniforms, other possessions will become target. How are we to know if clothes are motivation for killing? Does drab garb eliminate the hate and animosity people feel towards one another? Is it jealousy of clothes or what they portray? Clothes are material, inanimate. They do not have feelings. On the other hand, the people inside them do. We can not suppress emotion, whether it be good or bad. Uniforms can not, either.

(D) I hate to think that we have so lost touch with our children as not to see that it isn't uniforms they need, but love and support. Uniforms will not eliminate the threat of violence. They will only stifle creativity, leaving us barren and vacant. They will confine us into becoming the same. They should not be mandatory in public schools.

This work sample illustrates a standard-setting performance for the following parts of the standards:

E1 d Reading: Demonstrate a familiarity with public documents.

E2 e Writing: Produce a persuasive essay.

Conformity in Numbers

E2e Writing: The student produces a persuasive essay that:

- engages the reader by establishing a context, creating a persona, and otherwise developing reader interest;
- develops a controlling idea that makes a clear and knowledgeable judgment;
- creates an organizing structure that is appropriate to the needs, values, and interests of a specified audience, and arranges details, reasons, examples, and anecdotes effectively and persuasively;
- includes appropriate information and arguments and excludes information and arguments that are irrelevant;
- anticipates and addresses reader concerns and counter-arguments;
- supports arguments with detailed evidence, citing sources of information as appropriate;
- provides a sense of closure to the writing.

(A) A bleak context is established in the opening sentence that serves to emphasize the negative judgment.

(B) The controlling idea for the argument is established in a thesis statement at the end of the first paragraph.

The essay holds to the structure of the argument identified in the thesis statement, dealing first with the idea of stifled creativity and then with the idea that uniforms do not properly address the issue of violence.

(C) The essay deals directly with the traditional arguments given in support of school uniform policies, particularly in dealing with the issue of violence.

(D) The strong conclusion reiterates the point made in the opening regarding school uniforms, but in a more forceful manner that takes into consideration the argument presented.

Work Sample & Commentary: *The Carnival Is Almost Here*

The task

For an Applied Learning project students planned a school carnival and used the proceeds to buy food for a homeless shelter. The project was initiated by a proposal from a student. As the actual event drew near the students recognized the need for a number of documents to help manage the event. The flier included here was produced to provide some last minute details so that the event would flow as smoothly as possible.

Circumstances of performance

This sample of student work was produced under the following conditions:

	alone	√	in a group
√	in class		as homework
	with teacher feedback	√	with peer feedback
	timed	√	opportunity for revision

What the work shows

E1 e Reading: The student demonstrates familiarity with a variety of functional documents (i.e., documents that exist in order to get things done) and produces written or oral work that does one or more of the following:

- identifies the institutional context of the document;
- identifies the sequence of activities needed to carry out a procedure;
- analyzes or uses the formatting techniques used to make a document user-friendly;
- identifies any information that is either extraneous or missing in terms of audience and purpose or makes effective use of relevant information.

A The work identifies the context of the flier clearly and concisely, so that readers will know immediately its purpose.

The students attempted to make the document readable by numbering the points to be made, listing the points in a logical order so that similar points are grouped together, and including a border so that the flier stands out from other papers and can be recognized easily.

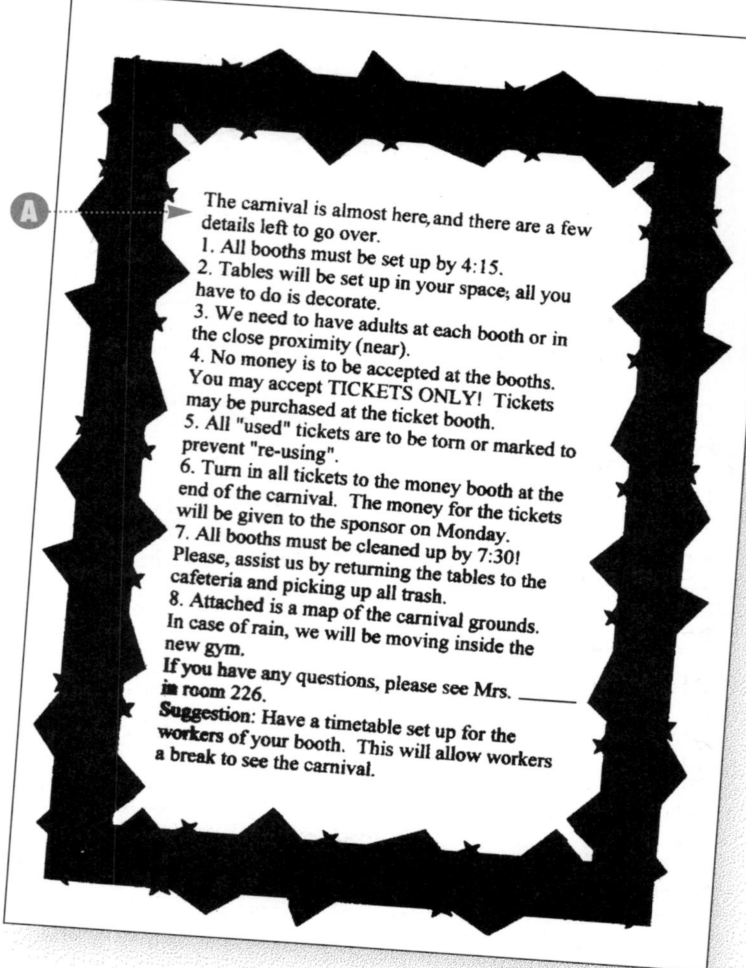

A ▸ The carnival is almost here, and there are a few details left to go over.
1. All booths must be set up by 4:15.
2. Tables will be set up in your space; all you have to do is decorate.
3. We need to have adults at each booth or in the close proximity (near).
4. No money is to be accepted at the booths. You may accept TICKETS ONLY! Tickets may be purchased at the ticket booth.
5. All "used" tickets are to be torn or marked to prevent "re-using".
6. Turn in all tickets to the money booth at the end of the carnival. The money for the tickets will be given to the sponsor on Monday.
7. All booths must be cleaned up by 7:30! Please, assist us by returning the tables to the cafeteria and picking up all trash.
8. Attached is a map of the carnival grounds. In case of rain, we will be moving inside the new gym.

If you have any questions, please see Mrs. _____ **in room** 226.

Suggestion: Have a timetable set up for the **workers** of your booth. This will allow workers **a break** to see the carnival.

The flier points out that those participating in the carnival will need to be aware of a number of procedures integral to doing their jobs. The procedures are succinct and to the point, providing an appropriate amount of information so that the participants should have no trouble following them.

This work sample illustrates a standard-setting performance for the following part of the standards:

E1 e Reading: Demonstrate familiarity with functional documents.

Work Sample & Commentary: *Sunset on the Water*

The task

Students were asked to write poems that served as a reflection of a time or place that held special meaning to them. The assignment came during an intensive unit on poetry in which students read a great deal of poetry, studied the various elements of poetry, and were given numerous opportunities to try their hands at writing poems.

Circumstances of performance

This sample of student work was produced under the following conditions:

√ alone	in a group
√ in class	√ as homework
√ with teacher feedback	√ with peer feedback
timed	√ opportunity for revision

Sunset On The Water

As I turned to face the ocean
my limbs became tensely packed with excitement.
I slowly surveyed everything around me before running down to the lapping water.
It was calling out to me -- reaching -- wanting to be free of its shores,
wondering what my life was like.
(A) The water is a great friend that I would be calling out for too,
if it were not there.
What would I do without it?
What would happen to my paradise?

Mother nature is my best friend at times.
I think that is what makes the beach a place of solitude,
where I can think my thoughts out loud,
(B) until it seems that I am speaking them,
and the only other sound being the rippling waves
harmonizing with the music of my words.
As all of this happens, I feel numb while the sun warms my back.
I especially love this place because
this is where I can come and blow off steam,
I can swim to my heart's desire,
or I can watch the sun set on the water.
(C) I weave that moment into my mind --
that moment where I step out of my picture --
where as I once again am cut off from my favorite place in the world,
to be left alone with only an image
(D) until I could once again see the glorious sight of the beach
and my friend welcoming me there.

November 9, 1995

What the work shows

E5 b Literature: The student produces work in at least one literary genre that follows the conventions of the genre.

A sunset on a beach provides the focal point for the poetic reflection.

(A) The personification of the water as a close friend serves to show the significance of the image of the ocean for the poet, whether she is physically near the ocean or merely visiting it in her mind.

(B) The poem appeals to the senses of hearing and touch in the descriptions of the physical sensations of the beach during the day.

(C) The images of the poem combine effectively to evoke a feeling of oneness between the words in the poem and the sights and sounds of the beach. The combination of words and images is particularly evocative considering that the persona of the poem is trying to capture an image and "weave that moment into my mind."

(D) The poem concludes by a return of the persona to the present, away from the water and the beach, but with the image of the welcoming ocean firmly embedded in memory. The conclusion allows the reader to relate to the feelings of the poet by sharing the feeling of being absent from someone or something and looking forward to the time when a reunion can take place.

This work sample illustrates a standard-setting performance for the following part of the standards:

E5 b Literature: Produce work in at least one literary genre that follows the conventions of the genre.

Work Sample & Commentary: *Reading Log*

The task

Students were asked to keep a reading log of the materials they read throughout the course of one year. The students' logs were to consist of three parts: a log listing the books read with brief annotations; a log listing the articles and informational materials read with brief annotations; and a two week log that went into depth in terms of a detailed description of the reading students did during those two weeks. The log of books read is included, as is one page from the five page log of articles and informational materials.

Circumstances of performance

This sample of student work was produced under the following conditions:

√ alone	in a group
√ in class	√ as homework
with teacher feedback	with peer feedback
timed	opportunity for revision

What the work shows

E1 a Reading: The student reads at least twenty-five books or book equivalents each year. The quality and complexity of the materials to be read are illustrated in the sample reading list. The materials should include traditional and contemporary literature (both fiction and non-fiction) as well as magazines, newspapers, textbooks, and on-line materials. Such reading should represent a diverse collection of material from at least three different literary forms and from at least five different writers.

The reading log provides evidence that the student met the goal of reading twenty-five books of the quality of literature appropriate for the middle school standard. The reading log also shows the variety of texts he engaged in from fiction, classic literature, and informational materials.

Mrs. ________
April 22, 1996

Annotated Book List

1. 4/29: Great Expectations, by Charles Dickens - A story about a young boy named Pip who lives with his older sister and her husband. Throughout the entire book, you watch Pip grow in his way towards his expectations of becoming a true gentleman.

2. 3/15: To Kill a Mockingbird, by Harper Lee - Tells the story of a white girls accusation of a black man raping her and is told through the eyes of a girl named Scout. Describes the racial tensions in a quiet, southern Alabama town named Maycomb.

3. 2/12: Gulliver's Travels, by Jonathan Swift - A classic work of literature, this story tells of the imaginary adventures of a man called Gulliver during his voyages away from his mother country, England. He encounters the most astonishing things in his travels.

4. 12/29: The Mysterious Island, by Jules Verne - Although not a very well known piece of literature, this book is very well written, describing the adventures of a party of men on a deserted island. In this story, you know what really happened to Captain Nemo.

5. 9/23: Treasure Island, by Robert Louis Stevenson - This story describes the happenings and adventure of a young boy named Jim Hawkins. With pirate fights, and buried treasure, it proves to be an excellent source of entertainment for any type of reader.

6. 10/15: Kidnapped, by Robert Louis Stevenson - The tale of the Jacobite rebellion in the highlands of Scotland, it contains a patriotic spirit that only Stevenson himself could only capture, writing of his homeland. This is sometimes considered his best work.

7. 1/14: Weir of Hermiston, by Robert Louis Stevenson - Left unfinished by Stevenson when he died, this novel is about an austere Scottish judge, and his son, and contains some of Stevenson's most brilliant dialogue passages in all of the books he wrote.

8. 1/31: Black Arrow, by Robert Louis Stevenson - The story is an exciting adventure story in which the hero, Richard Shelton, is fighting for the Yorkist cause in England's War of the Roses. Set in medieval times, it clearly defines Stevenson's variety of style.

9. 8/12: The Master of Ballantrae, by Robert Louis Stevenson - This novel tells of the lifelong feud between the Master Ballantrae and his younger brother Henry. This novel in particular underlines Stevenson's preoccupation with destiny and fate.

10. 9/5: The Strange Case of Dr. Jekyll and Mr. Hyde, by Robert Louis Stevenson - A chilling tale about how a doctor creates a separate personality, evil in instinct and repulsive in appearance, through the use of a special drug he discovers.

This work sample illustrates a standard-setting performance for the following parts of the standards:

E1 a Reading: Read at least twenty-five books or book equivalents each year.

E1 b Reading: Read and comprehend at least four books about one issue or subject, or four books by a single writer, or four books in one genre.

Reading Log

11. 6/9: Op-Center, by Tom Clancy - This thriller is all about the Op-Center, the beating heart of defense, intelligence, and crisis management technology. It's run by a crack team of operatives both within its own walls and out in the field.

12. 4/30: Debt of Honor, by Tom Clancy - A story of a purely hypothetical situation, in which the United States, and the former Soviet Union destroy their last nuclear missiles. In the ensuing era of peace, Japan invades and occupy the Marinas islands.

13. 6/26: Sum of All Fears, by Tom Clancy - Another "what if?" story about how a crude, Israeli nuclear aerial bomb could somehow turn up into the hands of some terrorists, and be set off inside the supposed safety of the United States of America.

14. 8/29: The Hunt For Red October, by Tom Clancy - The story of a defecting Russian submarine captain, who is commanding a nuclear missile submarine equipped with the latest stealthy modes of transporting itself across the Atlantic undetected.

15. 5/31: Clash of Steel, by L.H. Burruss - A fictional story of how the Soviet Union has re-invaded Afghanistan. The Kremlin is in chaos, and the United States must send a special force of men to stop the flow of tanks and men into the potential war zone.

16. 7/1: Rock of Refuge, by John Haworth - A sequel to his first book titled, Heart of Stone, this story is about Henry Stanwick, a reluctant rescuer and spy in the middle of a plot by opposing forces to save the world and its inhabitants.

17. 8/12: Never Sniff a Gift Fish, by Patrick F. McManus - A humorous book about the life of the perfect hunter/fisher/outdoorsman. It brings important rules to mind whenever out camping, along with a very sorely needed dictionary of the camper's dictionary.

18. 5/26: The Sea Wolf, by Jack London - This story is about a man named Van Weyden who finds himself aboard the seal-hunting schooner, the *Ghost*. Captain Wolf Larsen is the most vicious man on the seas, and his nickname, The Sea Wolf, fits him perfectly.

19. 11/5: The Trumpeter of Krakow, by Eric P. Kelly - A story that is derived from the legendary tale of young boy in Poland in the fifteenth century. It describes the world at that time through the unbiased account of the boy, named Joseph Charnetski.

20. 12/7: Escape From Warsaw, by Ian Serraillier - The setting for this story is in Warsaw, of course, during the second World War. The Balicki family is torn apart by Hitler's ruling of his conquered lands. The family must make plans to survive and re-unite.

21. 10/24: A Flock of Ships, by Brian Callison - This novel is about a convoy during World War II. It is an intriguing mystery of that balances the members of the ship with the enemy's cunning, and clever planning. This story has a very surprising conclusion!

22. 7/17: The Arabian Nights, These tales weren't really written by one specific man, because the book doesn't list any names for an author; it only lists some illustrator's names. These are the tales of a desperate princess trying to preserve her life before her execution.

23. 3/12: The Lord of the Flies, by William Golding - This story is quite adventurous, with the entire story-line based upon a group of boys who have crashed upon a desert island from flying away from England during the second World War.

24. 2/23: Crooked House, by Agatha Christie - This mysterious murder case is about a wealthy patriarch named Aristide Leonides and how his family is thrown into turmoil and dark doubts of one another once their ancestor is killed.

25. 4/24: Combat and Survival, This is the first two books in a long series of volumes of books that train the average citizen in how to survive the harsh outdoors, and hand-to-hand combat. There's also a special part about weapons and special forces.

26. 3/31: The Complete Sherlock Holmes, by Sir Arthur Conan Doyle, this 1,122 page book contained everything that Sir Arthur Conan Doyle wrote about the legendary Sherlock Holmes, with all four novels, all fifty-six adventures, and numerous short stories.

27. 11/29: The Count of Monte Cristo, by Alexandre Dumas - This thrilling adventure story is about a dashing young hero, named Edmond Dantes, who is betrayed by his enemies, and thrown into a secret dungeon. Eventually, he escapes, and gets revenge.

E1 b **Reading: The student reads and comprehends at least four books (or book equivalents) about one issue or subject, or four books by a single writer, or four books in one genre, and produces evidence of reading that:**

- **makes and supports warranted and responsible assertions about the texts;**
- **supports assertions with elaborated and convincing evidence;**
- **draws the texts together to compare and contrast themes, characters, and ideas;**
- **makes perceptive and well developed connections;**
- **evaluates writing strategies and elements of the author's craft.**

The reading log shows evidence that the student read in depth at least four books from one author or at least four texts in one genre. He fulfilled the requirement by reading more than four books by Robert Louis Stevenson as well as four books by Tom Clancy.

Mrs. ________
April 25, 1996

Annotated Reading Log
4/18 - 4/26

1. 4/18: Doctor No, Ch. 1,2,3,4, and 5, by Ian Fleming - This novel is about the British Secret Service agent, James Bond; code number 007. He's sent to Jamaica to investigate two recent murders, but ends up discovering a formidable enemy named Dr. No.

2. 4/18: "Newsfronts: Automobiles", by Dan McCosh - This article out of the March issue of Popular Science was all about concept cars. The one car that was investigated in this report was the Synergy 2010 concept car, by the design team at Ford Motor Co.

3. 4/18: "Newsfronts: Motorcycles" Popular Science, by Dan McCosh - This article was all about the new motorcycle cruiser wars between Harley-Davidson, Yamaha, and numerous other motorcycle companies over engine emission sounds. Unusual story!

4. 4/18: "Newsfronts: BMW 5-Series: Going Soft" Popular Science, by Dan McCosh - This articles was about the brand new, re-styled 5-series sedans from BMW. Tells about a better engine, stiffer chassis and suspension, plus side-impact air bags.

5. 4/18: "Home Technology: Environment" Popular Science, by Judith Anne Gunther - This article was about energy efficient houses constructed to provide energy efficient housing for people who were displaced or made homeless by Hurricane Andrew.

6. 4/18: "Home Technology: Lighting" Popular Science, by Judith Anne Gunther - The article was all about how researchers found a way to dim compact fluorescent lamps, some of which are already on the market. The "switch is an element called solium.

7. 4/18: "Home Technology: Pests" Popular Science, by Judith Anne Gunther - The article was about explaining why cockroaches are so attracted to the sticky bug traps that will kill them. It's because of a chemical called supellapyrone

8. 4/18: "Home Technology: Heating and Cooling" Popular Science, by Judith Anne Gunther - This article was over how you could use a special aerosol apparatus that seals the leaks in your home's attics, basements, and crawl spaces. Saves gob's of money.

9. 4/18: "Home Technology: Pipe Protection" Popular Science, by Judith Anne Gunther - The article was about how you could be able to tell that your pipes were frozen before they burst and fill your basement full of water. The answer is to install a cheap sensor.

10. 4/18: "What's New: Beam Us Up" Popular Science, by Mariette Dichristina & Suzanne Kantra Kirschner - The caption says that a new device called the Tri-corder Mark I detects the strength of electromagnetic radiation, and monitors weathers predictions.

Reading Log

Mrs. ________
Jan. 31, 1996

____

____

Reading Log Over The Black Arrow
by: Robert Louis Stevenson

1/31: Began the story today. First thing I need to say about this book is the
amount of difficulty it takes to read it unless you come from the times way back
when. The author Stevenson did an excellent job of transporting the reader back to
the times of when Richard III was the ruling king over England, and at the time
when the War of the Roses was being fought between the York's and the Lancaster's.
The book that I read was a collection of all of the great works by Stevenson, and was
also unabridged, so it led to an almost impossible story to write a book log on. The
characters in the story talk in a tongue that consists of words not used in today's
modern language. Words and phrases like nay, ye, praised be the saints!, bill (in this
book the word is not a notice for payments wanted, but is used in the same
concordance as the word sword), and many more. Well the story starts out with a
chapter named John Amend-All. A possible hero? Or villain? Who knows? Anyway
the beginning chapter starts out very ponderously, even though a battle is about to
be fought between the York's and the Lancaster's. A messenger is telling the
occupants of a village to prepare to battle. A certain Sir Daniel is sending for all of
the able men in the village to gather up their arms and march towards his army to
reinforce it. The leader/governor of the village is Sir Oliver Oates, a friend of Sir
Daniel's. The messenger having delivered his message to the villagers, sends some
sealed orders to Sir Oliver from Sir Daniel that is not to be opened unless by Sir
Oliver himself. Just as the messenger boy is preparing to leave young Master
Richard Shelton is seen approaching. The villagers flock around his horse and ask
him questions about his guardian, Sir Daniel. Evidently Sir Daniel is not much of a
very loyal leader, switching sides from York to Lancaster and back over the course of
events that happen to befall him. Richard is evidently very aware of this fact, and
blushes. Right then and there, Richard is saved from being publicly embarrassed
when Bennet Hatch when the latter rides up and bluntly orders the villagers off to
the rendezvous point. Hatch and Richard ride off to the house of an old shrew, or
soldier. The shrew's name is Nick Appleyard, and he is evidently a former archer in
that once served in a former war. Young Master Dick and Bennet Hatch watch the
old archer tend his garden and sing a tune. Apparently, Sir Daniel wants Appleyard
to keep watch over the village. Appleyard isn't pleased with the order and is even in
a worse temper when he finds out that he will only receive six other men to help in
his task. Bennet Hatch and Appleyard talk about the times when Harry the Fifth was
ruler of England, and when Appleyard was serving as an archer in his army. The two
men converse about when the king used to reward his soldiers money for long shots
or difficult feats. The discussion turns towards a good target for a long shot. They
think that the edge of the forest would make a nice target shot from Appleyard's
field. Just as they're speaking, Appleyard stares intently at the forest tree-line. He is
apparently worried about something, for he suddenly becomes very still, and turns
into a composed, cautious man. He looks pretty frightened, and seems to quiver
with trembling limbs. What in the world could he be worried about?

*1. *Analyze the reasons for a character's actions, taking into account the situation and motivation of the character.*
I predict that it must be something or some act that Appleyard committed earlier.
Probably something wild and crazy act when he was much younger, and full of energy.
Bennet Hatch evidently isn't very worried, for he asks old Appleyard what's bothering him.
Appleyard simply replies, " The birds Master Hatch." And sure enough, over the top of
the forest tree-line, where it ran down in a tongue among the meadows, and ended in a
pair of goodly green elms, about a bow-shot from the field where they were standing, a
flight of birds was skimming to and fro, clearly in evident disorder. What caused them to
fly away so suddenly? That is probably what mad old Appleyard so concerned. But
Bennet Hatch scoffs at his notion. How could there be any chance of an enemy soldier
being anywhere near old Appleyard's garden? Even so, Appleyard feels very unsecured,
and proceeds to defend his cautious actions by berating Hatch and himself about how they
are serving under Sir Daniel, and just that fact could easily make them hated and killed.
Suddenly, an arrow sang in the air, like a huge hornet; it struck old Appleyard between the
shoulder-blades, and pierced him clean through, and he fell forward on his face among the
cabbages in his garden. Hatch, with a broken cry, leapt into the air; then, stooping double,
he ran for the cover of the house. In the meanwhile, Master Dick Shelton had dropped
behind a lilac, and had his steel crossbow bent and shouldered, covering the point of the
forest. Not a leaf stirred. The sheep were patiently browsing; the birds had settled but
there lay the old archer/shrew, with a cloth-yard arrow standing in his back; and there was
hatch holding onto the gable, and Dick crouching and ready to fire behind the lilac bush.
Cautiously, Bennet Hatch peers from his hiding place behind the stone walls of old
Appleyard's house. He asks Dick if anything is moving in the woods far off in the
distance. Dick replies that nothing has happened, and Hatch murmurs that he really hates
to see the old archer on his face. Carefully turning the archer over, he finds out that old
Appleyard isn't quite dead, and is just going through the motions of dying. His face is all
ugly and full of pain as he gasps to Hatch to pull out the shaft in his back. Bennet Hatch
cannot do it, so he calls to Dick who promptly comes over, and with a considerable heave,
pulls out the arrow from old Appleyard's back. A gush of blood flows out, and the old
archer scrambles half upon his feet, calling once towards God, and then falls dead amongst
his garden. Dick and Bennet pray quietly for his spirit, but keep their eyes open in case.
*2. *Make connections to real life, school and other books:*
Of course, violence occurs all the time in real life, with the exception that different kinds
of weapons are used instead of arrows, and swords. Today the crimes are committed with
pistols, rifles, knives, etc., and are really easy to receive. And they're committed over the
dumbest reasons like an insult, a misunderstood comment, etc. Back then when Richard
the III was ruling England, deaths were carried out in different fashions like wars, and
duels. The ways and reasons for killing people has really evolved over the ages.
(Continuing from before the question:) Dick picks up the arrow he pulled from
Appleyard's back, and is quite surprised to see that it is not an ordinary arrow, but a black
colored one. Moreover, it has writing on it. The black arrow reads, "*Appulyarid for Jon Amend-All*". For some reason Hatch is worried about the arrow, and immediately tells
Dick to help him place old Appleyard's body into his house. After they put the body in the
house, they await the arrival of Sir Oliver, (also a priest) at old Appleyard's house.

* 4. Make interences about a certain character

2/09: As Bennet Hatch and Dick Shelton await Sir Oliver arrive, you get a sample of
just why people might be out to kill Sir Daniel and his fellow followers. What I mean is
that you're able to see how greedy and uncaring Hatch acts towards old Appleyard's old
property and timeless death. Here's what happened: While Bennet and Dick are waiting
impatiently for Sir Oliver to arrive, Bennet goes over to the wall, and eyes Appleyard's
amoury of arrows, weapons, and defensive armor, and states aloud that he just might take
a look through the dead man's personal artifacts, and even might take a few of them with
him when he leaves. Can you imagine the rage you would feel if you suddenly were killed
and just a few minutes later a man comes by and begins to sort through your personal
items and taking a few of them out for himself! Apparently, Hatch is sort of embarrassed,
because he tries to make and excuse for himself that he is just sort of an heir to old
Appleyard's surviving estate and items. He especially seems very interested in an old chest
of Appleyard's, believing that the old archer probably stores all of his gold in it. But Dick
is pretty firm on letting the old archer's items alone. He tells Hatch to respect old
Appleyard's stone-blind eyes, and asks him if he would rob the man before his body. No!
It's just not right. Hatch made several signs of the cross; but by this time his natural
complexion had returned, and he was not going to be easily dashed by any purpose. This
really tells you a lot about this man Bennet Hatch. He apparently didn't and still doesn't
care much about the old archer, Appleyard. The old shrew's only importance to Hatch
was his experience and leadership. Besides that, Hatch probably doesn't care much for the
old archer. This probably accounts for why Bennet was so fast to "recovering" from his
"traumatic" experience, and so eager to pick the pockets of the old archer. This tells me a
lot about how bad the company of Sir Daniel can possibly be. Anyway, it would have
gone hard, with especially with the chest had the gate not opened. Presently afterwards
the door of the house opened and admitted a tall, portly, ruddy, black-eyed man of near
fifty, in a surplice and black robe. This apparently is the Sir Oliver that Bennet and Hatch
have been waiting for. After Sir Oliver is made aware of the situation and the untimely
death of old Appleyard, he is quite shocked and uncomprehending. The three of them
decide to ride forth for the jack-men should be at the church by now. So they rode
forward down the road, with the wind after them. They had passed three of the scattered
houses when they saw the church before them. Ten or dozen horses were clustered
around the church, but the meadows were behind it. Apparently, Sir Oliver feels pretty
satisfied at the turnout to the messengers, and feels that Sir Daniel will probably pleased.
Suddenly, a man was seen slipping through the churchyard among the yew trees. Men
pursue him, and Dick fires a crossbow quarrel after him, but the man is lucky and dodges
both. A man brings a letter to Dick that was pinned to the church's door. It is written in a
very crude manner, like the person who wrote it wasn't very well educated. It reads: 'I
had four blak arrows under my belt, Four for the greefs that I have felt, Four for the
nomber of ill menne That have opressid me now and then. One is gone; one is wele sped;
Old Apulyaird is ded. One is for Maister Bennet Hatch, That burned Grimstone, walls and
thatch. One for Sir Oliver Oates, That cut Sir Harry Shelton's throat. Sir Daniel, ye shull
have the fourt; We shall think it fair sport. Ye shull each have your own part, A blak
arrow in each blak hart. Get ye to your knees for to pray: Ye are ded theeves, by yea and
nay!' 'Jon Amend-All of the Green Wood, And his jolly fellowship. 'Item, we have mo

y turned out to be published in the late 1
s on the western movement and how it w
s to go coast to coast. He later named thi
. His theory involved six groups of people
ermed "waves". There were many people w
as he right, or was he wrong?
d deal of evidence leading up to him being
were: Fur Traders, Cattlemen, Pioneer Fa
mers, and Specialist\ Urban Settlers. One
p of six to settle in the West were the F
s of Tennessee and Kentucky. A man nam
e Fur Traders and was well known. On the
Kentucky, they brought with them coonsk
ders helped settle Tennessee. The next gr
stretched as far as San Diego to San Fran
pioneer farmers, used the land and natur
lt cattle kingdoms and survived by that f
he group that came after them were the M
d found in the West, especially in Californ
came to California. These people were kn
49, people came for the gold. Approximat
fortune in gold in California. This made t

Evaluation of Career Day

Introduction to the performance standards for *Mathematics*

Building directly on the National Council of Teachers of Mathematics (NCTM) Curriculum Standards, the Mathematics performance standards present a balance of conceptual understanding, skills, and problem solving.

The first four standards are the important conceptual areas of mathematics:

- **M1 Number and Operation Concepts;**
- **M2 Geometry and Measurement Concepts;**
- **M3 Function and Algebra Concepts;**
- **M4 Statistics and Probability Concepts.**

These conceptual understanding standards delineate the important mathematical content for students to learn. To demonstrate understanding in these areas, students need to provide evidence that they have used the concepts in a variety of ways that go beyond recall. Specifically, students show progressively deeper understanding as they use a concept in a range of concrete situations and simple problems, then in conjunction with other concepts in complex problems; as they represent the concept in multiple ways (through numbers, graphs, symbols, diagrams, or words, as appropriate) and explain the concept to another person.

This is not a hard and fast progression, but the concepts included in the first four standards have been carefully selected as those for which the student should demonstrate a robust understanding. These standards make explicit that students should be able to demonstrate understanding of a mathematical concept by using it to solve problems, representing it in multiple ways (through numbers, graphs, symbols, diagrams, or words, as appropriate), and explaining it to someone else. All three ways of demonstrating understanding—use, represent, and explain—are required to meet the conceptual understanding standards.

Complementing the conceptual understanding standards, M5-M8 focus on areas of the mathematics curriculum that need particular attention and a new or renewed emphasis:

- **M5 Problem Solving and Mathematical Reasoning;**
- **M6 Mathematical Skills and Tools;**
- **M7 Mathematical Communication;**
- **M8 Putting Mathematics to Work.**

Establishing separate standards for these areas is a mechanism for highlighting the importance of these areas, but does not imply that they are independent of conceptual understanding. As the work samples that follow illustrate, good work usually provides evidence of both.

Like conceptual understanding, the definition of problem solving is demanding and explicit. Students use mathematical concepts and skills to solve non-routine problems that do not lay out specific and detailed steps to follow; and solve problems that make demands on all three aspects of the solution process—formulation, implementation, and conclusion. These are defined in M5, Problem Solving and Mathematical Reasoning.

The importance of skills has not diminished with the availability of calculators and computers. Rather, the need for mental computation, estimation, and interpretation has increased. The skills in M6, Mathematical Skills and Tools, need to be considered in light of the means of assessment. Some skills are so basic and important that students should be able to demonstrate fluency, accurately and automatically; it is reasonable to assess them in an on-demand setting, such as the New Standards reference examination. There are other skills for which students need only demonstrate familiarity rather than fluency. In using and applying such skills they might refer to notes, books, or other students, or they might need to take time out to reconstruct a method they have seen before. It is reasonable to find evidence of these skills in situations where students have ample time, such as in a New Standards portfolio. As the margin note by the examples that follow the performance descriptions indicates, many of the examples are performances that would be expected when students have ample time and access to tools, feedback from peers and the teacher, and an opportunity for revision. This is true for all of the standards, but especially important to recognize with respect to M6.

M7 includes two aspects of mathematical communication—using the language of mathematics and communicating about mathematics. Both are important. Communicating about mathematics is about ideas and logical explanation. The travelogue approach adopted by many students in the course of describing their problem solving is not what is intended.

M8 is the requirement that students put many concepts and skills to work in a large-scale project or investigation, at least once each year, beginning in the fourth grade. The types of projects are specified; for each, the student identifies, with the teacher, a clear purpose for the project, what will be accomplished, and how the project involves putting mathematics to work; develops a question and a plan; writes a detailed description of how the project was carried out, including mathematical analysis of the results; and produces a report that includes acknowledgment of assistance received from parents, peers, and teachers.

The examples

The purpose of the examples listed under the performance descriptions is to show what students might do or might have done in achieving the standards, but these examples are not intended as the only ways to demonstrate achievement of the standard. They are meant to illustrate good tasks and they begin to answer the question, "How good is good enough?" "Good enough" means being able to solve problems like these.

Each standard contains several parts. The examples below are cross-referenced to show a rough correspondence between the parts of the standard and the examples. These are not precise matches, and students may successfully accomplish the task using concepts and skills different from those the task designer intended, but the cross-references highlight examples for which a single activity or project may allow students to demonstrate accomplishment of several parts of one or more standards.

The purpose of the samples of student work is to help to explain what the standards mean and to elaborate the meaning of a "standard-setting performance." Few pieces of work are so all-encompassing as to qualify for the statement, "meets the standard." Rather, each piece of work shows evidence of meeting the requirements of a selected part or parts of a standard. Further, most of these pieces of work provide evidence related to parts of more than one standard. It is essential to look at the commentary to understand just how the work sample helps to illuminate features of the standards.

Resources

We recognize that some of the standards presuppose resources that are not currently available to all students. The New Standards partners have adopted a Social Compact, which says, in part, "Specifically, we pledge to do everything in our power to ensure all students a fair shot at reaching the new performance standards...This means that they will be taught a curriculum that will prepare them for the assessments, that their teachers will have the preparation to enable them to teach it well, and there will be an equitable distribution of the resources the students and their teachers need to succeed."

The NCTM standards make explicit the need for calculators of increasing sophistication from elementary to high school and ready access to computers. Although a recent National Center for Education Statistics survey confirmed that most schools do not have the facilities to make full use of computers and video, the New Standards partners have made a commitment to create the learning environments where students can develop the knowledge and skills that are delineated here. Thus, M6, Mathematical Skills and Tools, assumes that students have access to computational tools at the level spelled out by NCTM. This is not because we think that all schools *are* currently equipped to provide the experiences that would enable students to meet these performance standards, but rather that we think that all schools *should be* equipped to provide these experiences. Indeed, we hope that making these requirements explicit will help those who allocate resources to understand the consequences of their actions in terms of student performance.

The middle school performance standards are set at a level of performance that is approximately equivalent to the end of eighth grade. It is expected, however, that some students might achieve this level earlier and others later than this grade. Some students will take a course in algebra before high school; their preparation, particularly in M3, Function and Algebra Concepts, should surpass the level of the middle school standards.

M1 Number and Operation Concepts

To see how these performance descriptions compare with the expectations for elementary school and high school, turn to pages 146-157.

The examples that follow the performance descriptions for each standard are examples of the work students might do to demonstrate their achievement. The examples also indicate the nature and complexity of activities that are appropriate to expect of students at the middle school level. Depending on the nature of the task, the work might be done in class, for homework, or over an extended period.

The cross-references that follow the examples highlight examples for which the same activity, and possibly even the same piece of work, may enable students to demonstrate their achievement in relation to more than one standard. In some cases, the cross-references highlight examples of activities through which students might demonstrate their achievement in relation to standards for more than one subject matter.

The student demonstrates understanding of a mathematical concept by using it to solve problems, by representing it in multiple ways (through numbers, graphs, symbols, diagrams, or words, as appropriate), and by explaining it to someone else. All three ways of demonstrating understanding—use, represent, and explain—are required to meet the conceptual understanding standards.

The student produces evidence that demonstrates understanding of number and operation concepts; that is, the student:

M1 a Consistently and accurately adds, subtracts, multiplies, and divides rational numbers using appropriate methods (e.g., the student can add $\frac{1}{2} + \frac{5}{6}$ mentally or on paper but may opt to add $\frac{13}{24} + \frac{57}{68}$ on a calculator) and raises rational numbers to whole number powers. (Students should have facility with the different kinds and forms of rational numbers, i.e., integers, both whole numbers and negative integers; and other positive and negative rationals, written as decimals, as percents, or as proper, improper, or mixed fractions. Irrational numbers, i.e., those that cannot be written as a ratio of two integers, are not required content but are suitable for introduction, especially since the student should be familiar with the irrational number π.)

M1 b Uses and understands the inverse relationships between addition and subtraction, multiplication and division, and exponentiation and root-extraction (e.g., squares and square roots, cubes and cube roots); uses the inverse operation to determine unknown quantities in equations.

M1 c Consistently and accurately applies and converts the different kinds and forms of rational numbers.

M1 d Is familiar with characteristics of numbers (e.g., divisibility, prime factorization) and with properties of operations (e.g., commutativity and associativity), short of formal statements.

M1 e Interprets percent as part of 100 and as a means of comparing quantities of different sizes or changing sizes.

M1 f Uses ratios and rates to express "part-to-part" and "whole-to-whole" relationships, and reasons proportionally to solve problems involving equivalent fractions, equal ratios, or constant rates, recognizing the multiplicative nature of these problems in the constant factor of change.

M1 g Orders numbers with the $>$ and $<$ relationships and by location on a number line; estimates and compares rational numbers using sense of the magnitudes and relative magnitudes of numbers and of base-ten place values (e.g., recognizes relationships to "benchmark" numbers $\frac{1}{2}$ and 1 to conclude that the sum $\frac{1}{2} + \frac{5}{6}$ must be between 1 and $1\frac{1}{2}$ (likewise, $\frac{13}{24} + \frac{57}{68}$)).

Examples of activities through which students might demonstrate understanding of number and operation concepts include:

- Sara placed one number on each side of two disks. She said that if she flipped the disks and added the two numbers facing up, the sum was always one of the following numbers: 1, .23, .87, .1. What numbers could Sara have placed on each face of the two disks? (Balanced Assessment) **1a, 5a, 5b**
- How can you compute a 15%, 10%, or 20% tip, other than by multiplying an amount by 0.15, 0.1, or 0.2 on paper? **1a, 1c, 1e**
- Mrs. Brown wrote a number on the chalkboard and said, "I know that to be sure I find all the factor pairs for this number I must check each number from 1 to 29." What numbers could Mrs. Brown have written? What is the smallest number Mrs. Brown could have written? What is the largest number Mrs. Brown could have written? (Middle Grades Mathematics Project: Factors and Multiples) **1b, 1d**
- Burger Jack's ads claim that their $\frac{1}{2}$-pound burger contains 50% more beef than Winnie's $\frac{1}{3}$-pound burger. Is their claim true? **1c, 1e**
- The members of the school marching band wanted to arrange themselves into rows with exactly the same number of band members in each row. They tried rows of two, three, and four, but there was always one band member left over. Finally, they were able to arrange themselves into rows with exactly five in each row. What is the least number of members in the marching band? (Creative Problem Solving in Mathematics) **1d**
- Is the sum of two consecutive integers odd or even? Always? How about the product of two consecutive numbers? Why? What can you say about three consecutive numbers? **1d**
- Find the last two digits of 6^{1000}. (NCTM, Mathematics Teaching in the Middle School) **1d**
- If, in a school of 1,000 lockers, one student opens every locker, another student closes every other locker (2nd, 4th, 6th, etc.), a third student changes every third locker (opens closed lockers and closes open lockers), and so on, until the thousandth student changes the thousandth locker, which lockers are open? Why? **1d, 5a, 5b, 5c**
- A certain clock gains one minute of time every hour. If the clock shows the correct time now, when will it show the correct time again? (Creative Problem Solving in Mathematics) **1f, 2h**
- How much space would a million shoe boxes fill? How large would a pile of a million pennies be? How about a million sheets of notebook paper? **1g**
- How small would a millionth of a sheet of notebook paper be? **1g**

M2 Geometry and Measurement Concepts

The student demonstrates understanding of a mathematical concept by using it to solve problems, by representing it in multiple ways (through numbers, graphs, symbols, diagrams, or words, as appropriate), and by explaining it to someone else. All three ways of demonstrating understanding—use, represent, and explain—are required to meet this standard.

The student produces evidence that demonstrates understanding of geometry and measurement concepts in the following areas; that is, the student:

M2 a Is familiar with assorted two- and three-dimensional objects, including squares, triangles, other polygons, circles, cubes, rectangular prisms, pyramids, spheres, and cylinders.

M2 b Identifies similar and congruent shapes and uses transformations in the coordinate plane, i.e., translations, rotations, and reflections.

M2 c Identifies three dimensional shapes from two dimensional perspectives; draws two dimensional sketches of three dimensional objects that preserve significant features.

M2 d Determines and understands length, area, and volume (as well as the differences among these measurements), including perimeter and surface area; uses units, square units, and cubic units of measure correctly; computes areas of rectangles, triangles, and circles; computes volumes of prisms.

M2 e Recognizes similarity and rotational and bilateral symmetry in two- and three-dimensional figures.

M2 f Analyzes and generalizes geometric patterns, such as tessellations and sequences of shapes.

M2 g Measures angles, weights, capacities, times, and temperatures using appropriate units.

M2 h Chooses appropriate units of measure and converts with ease between like units, e.g., inches and miles, within a customary or metric system. (Conversions between customary and metric are not required.)

M2 i Reasons proportionally in situations with similar figures.

M2 j Reasons proportionally with measurements to interpret maps and to make smaller and larger scale drawings.

M2 k Models situations geometrically to formulate and solve problems.

Examples of activities through which students might demonstrate understanding of geometry and measurement concepts include:

- Jan says rectangles and rhombi are completely different. Joan says they are almost exactly the same. Explain and illustrate why both students are partially correct. Compare and contrast the two figures. (College Preparatory Mathematics, "Rhombus and Rectangle") Can you think of a special shape that is both a rectangle and a rhombus? **2a**
- Jamaal installed two sprinkler heads to water a square patch of lawn twelve feet on a side. He placed the sprinkler heads in the middle of two opposite edges of the lawn. If the spray pattern of each sprinkler is semi-circular and just reaches the two nearest corners, what percentage of the lawn is not watered by the two sprinkler heads? (College Preparatory Mathematics, "Watering the Lawn") **2a, 2d**
- Examine logos of businesses in the yellow pages for rotational and bilateral symmetry. **2b, 2e**
- From square grid paper, cut "jackets" for "space food packages," which are actually blocks of cubes (same size as the squares of the grid); each cube contains one day's supply of food pellets, and each square of "material" costs $1. For different space armor jackets cut from the grid paper, find the number of days the food supply will last (the volume of the package). Also find the cost of the jacket (the surface area) and the dimensions of the package. (Middle Grades Mathematics Project: Mouse and Elephant: Measuring Growth) **2c**
- A rectangular garden has two semicircular flower beds on opposite ends. Find the area of the entire figure. (College Preparatory Mathematics, "The Garden") **2d**

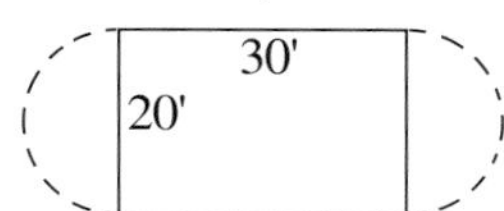

- Investigate the area around your school and neighborhood to describe the size of an acre and a square mile. **2d**
- Domino's Pizza is offering a free 16" pizza to the first student who can tell them the greatest number of 1" x 2" x ⅜" dominoes it will take to fill their take-out shop. The dimensions of the take-out shop are 10' x 11' x 8'. How many is it? (College Preparatory Mathematics, "The Domino Effect") **2d, 2h, 1f**
- Display data from a survey with an accurately drawn and divided pie chart: the angles should be accurately computed and measured so that the regions of the circle are proportional to the percentages of the survey results. **2g, 1f, 6g**
- Stand nine feet from a friend and hold a one-foot ruler vertically in front of yourself. Line up the top of the ruler with the top of your friend and the bottom of the ruler with the feet of your friend. If the ruler is two feet from your eyes, how tall is your friend? (Middle Grades Mathematics Project: Similarity and Equivalent Fractions) Measure the actual distance from your eyes to the top of the ruler. According to the relationships of your similar triangles, how tall is your friend? Measure your friend's height. Was your calculation accurate? **2i**
- Construct an enlargement of some simple geometric shape by a scale factor of 3 by utilizing grid paper and also by measuring from a projection point. **2j**
- Make a two-dimensional, cardboard or paper replica of yourself using measurements of lengths and widths of body parts that are half those of your own body. (UCSMP, Transition Mathematics) **2j**
- Create a poster by enlarging, to scale, a favorite cartoon panel. **2j**
- Make a scale drawing of your bedroom. **2j**

Samples of student work that illustrate standard-setting performances for these standards can be found on pages 60-88.

M3 Function and Algebra Concepts

This standard describes the foundation expected of middle school students in preparation for high school mathematics. Some students will take a course in algebra before high school, and their understanding of functions and algebra should surpass what is described below.

The student demonstrates understanding of a mathematical concept by using it to solve problems, by representing it in multiple ways (through numbers, graphs, symbols, diagrams, or words, as appropriate), and by explaining it to someone else. All three ways of demonstrating understanding—use, represent, and explain—are required to meet this standard.

The student produces evidence that demonstrates understanding of function and algebra concepts; that is, the student:

M3 a Discovers, describes, and generalizes patterns, including linear, exponential, and simple quadratic relationships, i.e., those of the form $f(n)=n^2$ or $f(n)=cn^2$, for constant c, including $A=\pi r^2$, and represents them with variables and expressions.

M3 b Represents relationships with tables, graphs in the coordinate plane, and verbal or symbolic rules.

M3 c Analyzes tables, graphs, and rules to determine functional relationships.

M3 d Finds solutions for unknown quantities in linear equations and in simple equations and inequalities.

Examples of activities through which students might demonstrate understanding of function and algebra concepts include:

- Graph and explain the growth of population over time of a colony of organisms that doubles once a day. **3a**
- Use diagrams, tables, graphs, words, and formulas to show the relationships between the length of the sides of a square and its perimeter and area. **3a, 3b**
- A ball is dropped from a height of sixteen feet. At its first bounce, the ball reaches a peak of eight feet. Each successive time the ball bounces, it reaches a peak height that is half that of the previous bounce. How many times will the ball bounce until it bounces to a peak height of one foot? Make a table that shows the peak bounce height of the ball for the number of bounces. Make a graph and write an algebraic expression that show the relationship between the number of bounces and the peak height of the ball. (Balanced Assessment) **3b**
- Examine areas that can be enclosed by 24 feet of fencing and figure out the maximum area. **3b**
- Your principal wants to hire you to work for her for ten days. She will pay you either $6.00 each day for all ten days; or $1.00 the first day, $2.00 the second day, $3.00 the third day, and so on; or $0.10 the first day and each day thereafter twice the amount of the day before. Under which arrangement would you earn the most money? Under which arrangement would you earn the least money? (NCTM, Mathematics Teaching in the Middle School) **3c**
- Investigate the following situation: Bricklayers use the rule $N=7 \cdot L \cdot H$ to determine the number N of bricks needed to build a wall L feet long and H feet high. Examine a brick wall or portion of a brick wall to see whether this seems to be true. If it works, why? If not, what would be a better formula? (UCSMP, Transition Mathematics) **3c**
- When inquiring about the dimensions of a lot, you are told, "I can't remember. It's shaped like a rectangle, and I know that they needed ninety meters of fencing to enclose it. Oh, yes! The crew putting up the fence remarked that the lot is exactly twice as long as it is wide." What are the dimensions of the lot? (Creative Problem Solving in Mathematics) **3d**

To see how these performance descriptions compare with the expectations for elementary school and high school, turn to pages 146-157.

The examples that follow the performance descriptions for each standard are examples of the work students might do to demonstrate their achievement. The examples also indicate the nature and complexity of activities that are appropriate to expect of students at the elementary level. Depending on the nature of the task, the work might be done in class, for homework, or over an extended period.

The cross-references that follow the examples highlight examples for which the same activity, and possibly even the same piece of work, may enable students to demonstrate their achievement in relation to more than one standard. In some cases, the cross-references highlight examples of activities through which students might demonstrate their achievement in relation to standards for more than one subject matter.

M4 Statistics and Probability Concepts

The student demonstrates understanding of a mathematical concept by using it to solve problems, by representing it in multiple ways (through numbers, graphs, symbols, diagrams, or words, as appropriate), and by explaining it to someone else. All three ways of demonstrating understanding—use, represent, and explain—are required to meet this standard.

The student produces evidence that demonstrates understanding of statistics and probability concepts; that is, the student:

M4 a Collects data, organizes data, and displays data with tables, charts, and graphs that are appropriate, i.e, consistent with the nature of the data.

M4 b Analyzes data with respect to characteristics of frequency and distribution, including mode and range.

M4 c Analyzes appropriately central tendencies of data by considering mean and median.

M4 d Makes conclusions and recommendations based on data analysis.

M4 e Critiques the conclusions and recommendations of others' statistics.

M4 f Considers the effects of missing or incorrect information.

M4 g Formulates hypotheses to answer a question and uses data to test hypotheses.

M4 h Represents and determines probability as a fraction of a set of equally likely outcomes; recognizes equally likely outcomes and constructs sample spaces (including those described by numerical combinations and permutations).

M4 i Makes predictions based on experimental or theoretical probabilities.

M4 j Predicts the result of a series of trials once the probability for one trial is known.

Examples of activities through which students might demonstrate understanding of statistics and probability concepts include:

- From a sample news headline, an article, and a table of data, select and construct appropriate graphs or other visual representations of the data. Decide whether or not the headline seems appropriate. Write a letter to the editor. (Balanced Assessment) **4a, 4d, 4e, 7e**
- In a game to see who could best guess when 30 seconds had passed, the actual times (measured by a stopwatch) of Gilligan's guesses were 31, 25, 32, 27, and 28 seconds; Skipper's guesses were 37, 19, 40, 36, and 22 seconds; Ginger's guesses were 32, 38, 24, 32, and 32 seconds. Who do you think is best at estimating 30 seconds? Why? (Balanced Assessment) **4b, 4c**
- When tossing two fair numbered cubes and finding the sum of the two numbers turned up, if the sum is seven, then Keisha gets seven points, but if the sum is not seven, then Shawna gets one point. Is the game fair or not? Explain your reasoning to Keisha and Shawna. (Balanced Assessment) **4h**
- Decide whether it is most advantageous to use three tetrahedra, two cubes, or one dodecahedron to arrive at a specific number (like 10) when rolling polyhedral dice. **4h, 1g**
- Lottery players often say, "Well, my numbers have to come up sometime!" Analyze a state lottery game to see how many number combinations there are and how many weeks, months, or years it will take for all of them to be drawn. **4h, 4j**
- A poll was taken of 40 students on their favorite school lunch. The results show hamburgers and fries, 14; pizza and salad, 13; spaghetti and salad, 8; hot dogs and beans, 5; liver and spinach, 0. Assuming this is an accurate sample, if a student is chosen at random, what is the probability that he or she favors each lunch offering? If there are 400 students in the school, how many prefer hamburgers? Hot dogs? Liver? (Middle Grades Mathematics Project: Probability) **4i**

M5 Problem Solving and Mathematical Reasoning

The student demonstrates problem solving by using mathematical concepts and skills to solve non-routine problems that do not lay out specific and detailed steps to follow, and solves problems that make demands on all three aspects of the solution process—formulation, implementation, and conclusion.

Formulation

M5 a The student participates in the formulation of problems; that is, given the basic statement of a problem situation, the student:

- formulates and solves a variety of meaningful problems;
- extracts pertinent information from situations and figures out what additional information is needed.

Implementation

M5 b The student makes the basic choices involved in planning and carrying out a solution; that is, the student:

- uses and invents a variety of approaches and understands and evaluates those of others;
- invokes problem solving strategies, such as illustrating with sense-making sketches to clarify situations or organizing information in a table;
- determines, where helpful, how to break a problem into simpler parts;
- solves for unknown or undecided quantities using algebra, graphing, sound reasoning, and other strategies;
- integrates concepts and techniques from different areas of mathematics;
- works effectively in teams when the nature of the task or the allotted time makes this an appropriate strategy.

Conclusion

M5 c The student provides closure to the solution process through summary statements and general conclusions; that is, the student:

- verifies and interprets results with respect to the original problem situation;
- generalizes solutions and strategies to new problem situations.

Mathematical reasoning

M5 d The student demonstrates mathematical reasoning by generalizing patterns, making conjectures and explaining why they seem true, and by making sensible, justifiable statements; that is, the student:

- formulates conjectures and argues why they must be or seem true;
- makes sensible, reasonable estimates;
- makes justified, logical statements.

Examples of activities through which students might demonstrate problem solving and mathematical reasoning include:

- Aaron's Pizzeria will pay you $75 if you and a partner can eat his 26" diameter pizza in one hour. To practice for this eating event, you and your friend go to Round Label Pizza. How many of Round Label's 12" diameter pizzas would the two of you need to eat to equal the amount of pizza you hope to eat at Aaron's? (College Preparatory Mathematics, "Pizza Problem") **5a, 5b, 2d**
- Design a carnival game in which paper "parachutes" are dropped onto a target of five concentric rings, for which a player scores five points for landing in the center, four points in the next ring, three in the next, two in the next, and one point for landing in the outer ring. Experiment and create rules for the game so that it is fun, makes a profit, and people feel they have a chance of winning. (Balanced Assessment) **5a, 5b, 4a, 8d**
- Your rich uncle has just died and has left you $1 billion. If you accept the money, you must count it for eight hours a day at the rate of $1 per second. When you are finished counting, the $1 billion is yours, and then you may start to spend it. Should you accept your uncle's offer? Why or why not? How long will it take to count the money? (College Preparatory Mathematics, "Big Bucks") **5a, 5b, 5c, 1f, 1g**
- Starting with the numbers from 1 to 36, find out all you can about writing them as sums of consecutive whole numbers. What kinds of numbers can be written as the sum of two consecutive whole numbers; of three consecutive whole numbers; of four consecutive whole numbers? Which numbers cannot be written as the sum of consecutive whole numbers? What patterns do you notice? Why do you think they occur? (Balanced Assessment) **5b, 5c, 5d, 1d**
- A diagonal of the 3 x 5 grid rectangle passes through seven of the squares. In the 4 x 4 grid rectangle, the diagonal passes through only four squares. Come up with at least two conjectures about grid rectangles, diagonals, and the squares they pass through. (College Preparatory Mathematics, "On Grids") **5d, 1d**

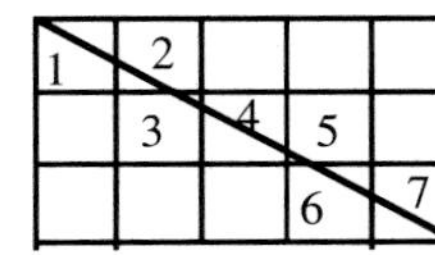

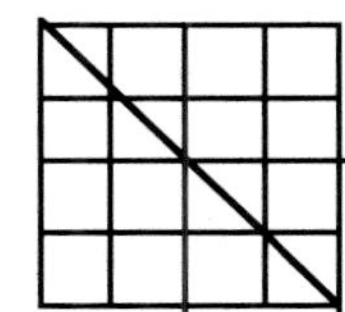

Samples of student work that illustrate standard-setting performances for these standards can be found on pages 60-88.

To see how these performance descriptions compare with the expectations for elementary school and high school, turn to pages 146-157.

The examples that follow the performance descriptions for each standard are examples of the work students might do to demonstrate their achievement. The examples also indicate the nature and complexity of activities that are appropriate to expect of students at the elementary level. Depending on the nature of the task, the work might be done in class, for homework, or over an extended period.

The cross-references that follow the examples highlight examples for which the same activity, and possibly even the same piece of work, may enable students to demonstrate their achievement in relation to more than one standard. In some cases, the cross-references highlight examples of activities through which students might demonstrate their achievement in relation to standards for more than one subject matter.

M6 Mathematical Skills and Tools

The student demonstrates fluency with basic and important skills by using these skills accurately and automatically, and demonstrates practical competence and persistence with other skills by using them effectively to accomplish a task (perhaps referring to notes, or books, perhaps working to reconstruct a method); that is, the student:

M6 a Computes accurately with arithmetic operations on rational numbers.

M6 b Knows and uses the correct order of operations for arithmetic computations.

M6 c Estimates numerically and spatially.

M6 d Measures length, area, volume, weight, time, and temperature accurately.

M6 e Refers to geometric shapes and terms correctly.

M6 f Uses equations, formulas, and simple algebraic notation appropriately.

M6 g Reads and organizes data on charts and graphs, including scatter plots, bar, line, and circle graphs, and Venn diagrams; calculates mean and median.

M6 h Uses recall, mental computations, pencil and paper, measuring devices, mathematics texts, manipulatives, calculators, computers, and advice from peers, as appropriate, to achieve solutions.

Examples of activities through which students might demonstrate facility with mathematical skills and tools include:

- How (many ways) can you use four 4s to create an expression that has a value equal to 1? (e.g., $1 = (4+4-4) \div 4 = 4 - \sqrt{4} - 4 \div 4 = (4+4)^{(4-4)} = \ldots$) (Creative Problem Solving in Mathematics) **6b, 6h**
- Figure out how long it would take to say your name a million times; how long it would take to count to a million. **6c, 1f, 1g, 5a, 5b, 5c**
- Accurately describe a geometric design on a 10 x 10 grid to a friend by telephone. (Balanced Assessment) **6e, 7c**
- Use the formula $A=\frac{1}{2}bh$ for areas of triangles measured with customary and metric rulers. **6f**
- Analyze advertisements for different music clubs and decide which offers best value for money. **6g**

M7 Mathematical Communication

The student uses the language of mathematics, its symbols, notation, graphs, and expressions, to communicate through reading, writing, speaking, and listening, and communicates about mathematics by describing mathematical ideas and concepts and explaining reasoning and results; that is, the student:

M7 a Uses mathematical language and representations with appropriate accuracy, including numerical tables and equations, simple algebraic equations and formulas, charts, graphs, and diagrams.

M7 b Organizes work, explains facets of a solution orally and in writing, labels drawings, and uses other techniques to make meaning clear to the audience.

M7 c Uses mathematical language to make complex situations easier to understand.

M7 d Exhibits developing reasoning abilities by justifying statements and defending work.

M7 e Shows understanding of concepts by explaining ideas not only to teachers and assessors but to fellow students or younger children.

M7 f Comprehends mathematics from reading assignments and from other sources.

Examples of activities through which students might demonstrate facility with mathematical communication include:

- Use diagrams, tables, graphs, words, and formulas to show the relationship of the length of the sides of a square to its perimeter and area. **7a**
- Use box-and-whiskers plots, stem-and-leaf plots, and bar graphs to compare characteristics of the boys and girls in the class; compare the kinds of information provided by the different displays. **7a, 7b**
- Use symbols and a Cartesian map to explain to another student how to get from your home to school. **7c**
- Make the following conjectures: What happens to the area of a square when you double its perimeter? What happens to the area when you triple its perimeter? Investigate to see if this is true and, if so, explain why. What does doubling the circumference of a circle do to its area? Explain. **7d, 2d, 3b**
- Your fifth grade cousin is convinced that the probability of rolling a 12 on two numbered cubes is $\frac{1}{11}$. Explain to your cousin why this is incorrect, and convince your cousin of the actual probability of getting 12. **7e, 4h**

M8 Putting Mathematics to Work

The student conducts at least one large scale investigation or project each year drawn from the following kinds and, over the course of middle school, conducts investigations or projects drawn from three of the kinds.

A single investigation or project may draw on more than one kind.

M8 a Data study based on civic, economic, or social issues, in which the student:

- selects an issue to investigate;
- makes a hypothesis on an expected finding, if appropriate;
- gathers data;
- analyzes the data using concepts from Standard 4, e.g., considering mean and median, and the frequency and distribution of the data;
- shows how the study's results compare with the hypothesis;
- uses pertinent statistics to summarize;
- prepares a presentation or report that includes the question investigated, a detailed description of how the project was carried out, and an explanation of the findings.

M8 b Mathematical model of physical phenomena, often used in science studies, in which the student:

- carries out a study of a physical system using a mathematical representation of the structure;
- uses understanding from Standard 3, particularly with respect to the determination of the function governing behavior in the model;
- generalizes about the structure with a rule, i.e., a function, that clearly applies to the phenomenon and goes beyond statistical analysis of a pattern of numbers generated by the situation;
- prepares a presentation or report that includes the question investigated, a detailed description of how the project was carried out, and an explanation of the findings.

M8 c Design of a physical structure, in which the student:

- generates a plan to build something of value, not necessarily monetary value;
- uses mathematics from Standard 2 to make the design realistic or appropriate, e.g., areas and volumes in general and of specific geometric shapes;
- summarizes the important features of the structure;
- prepares a presentation or report that includes the question investigated, a detailed description of how the project was carried out, and an explanation of the findings.

M8 d Management and planning, in which the student:

- determines the needs of the event to be managed or planned, e.g., cost, supply, scheduling;
- notes any constraints that will affect the plan;
- determines a plan;
- uses concepts from any of Standards 1 to 4, depending on the nature of the project;
- considers the possibility of a more efficient solution;
- prepares a presentation or report that includes the question investigated, a detailed description of how the project was carried out, and an explanation of the plan.

M8 e Pure mathematics investigation, in which the student:

- extends or "plays with," as with mathematical puzzles, some mathematical feature, e.g., properties and patterns in numbers;
- uses concepts from any of Standards 1 to 4, e.g., an investigation of Pascal's triangle would have roots in Standard 1 but could tie in concepts from geometry, algebra, and probability; investigations of derivations of geometric formulas would be rooted in Standard 2 but could require algebra;
- determines and expresses generalizations from patterns;
- makes conjectures on apparent properties and argues, short of formal proof, why they seem true;
- prepares a presentation or report that includes the question investigated, a detailed description of how the project was carried out, and an explanation of the findings.

Examples of investigations or projects include:

- Gather and analyze data from the neighborhood and compare the data with published statistics for the city, state, or nation. **8a, 4a, 4b, 4c, 4d**
- Compare the growth of a set of plants under a variety of conditions, e.g., amount of water, fertilizer, duration and exposure to sunlight. **8b, 3b, S2a, S3d**
- Design and equip a recreational area on one acre with a limited budget. **8c, 1a, 2a, 2d, 2h, 2j, A1a**
- Analyze and concoct games of chance for a school carnival. **8d, 4h, 4i, A1c**
- Discover relationships among, and properties of, the numbers in Pascal's triangle. Read to find more relationships and properties. **8e, 1e, 4h, 7f**

Samples of student work that illustrate standard-setting performances for these standards can be found on pages 60-88.

Work Sample & Commentary: *Pieces of String*

The quotations from the Mathematics performance descriptions in this commentary are excerpted. The complete performance descriptions are shown on pages 54-59.

The task

Students were assigned the following task:

A length of string that is 180 cm long is cut into 3 pieces. The second piece is 25% longer than the first and the third piece is 25% shorter than the first. How long is each piece?

Circumstances of performance

This sample of student work was produced under the following conditions:

√ alone	in a group
in class	as homework
with teacher feedback	with peer feedback
timed	opportunity for revision

What the work shows

First, the work does *not* show a standard approach that a student of algebra might take. Let x represent the length of the middle piece of string. Then $1.25x + x + .75x = 180$ cm. Therefore, $3x = 180$ cm, and $x = 60$ cm. So the longest piece is $1.25x = 1.25 \cdot 60 = 75$ cm and the shortest piece is $.75x = .75 \cdot 60 = 45$ cm. The student, instead, employed her understanding of the percent concept and proportional reasoning to achieve a solution.

M1 a Number and Operation Concepts: The student consistently and accurately adds, subtracts, multiplies, and divides rational numbers using appropriate methods....

M1 e Number and Operation Concepts: The student interprets percent as part of 100 and as a means of comparing quantities of different sizes....

M1 f Number and Operation Concepts: The student...reasons proportionally to solve problems involving equivalent fractions, equal ratios, or constant rates, recognizing the multiplicative nature of these problems in the constant factor of change.

This work sample illustrates a standard-setting performance for the following parts of the standards:

M1 a Number and Operation Concepts: Consistently and accurately add, subtract, multiply, and divide rational numbers.

M1 e Number and Operation Concepts: Interpret percent as part of 100.

M1 f Number and Operation Concepts: Reason proportionally to solve problems involving equivalent fractions, equal ratios, or constant rates.

M5 b Problem Solving and Mathematical Reasoning: Implementation.

A length of string that is 180 cm long is cut into 3 pieces. The second piece is 25% longer than the first and the third piece is 25% shorter than the first. How long is each Piece ?

(A) Since the first peice was what the percentages were based on, I decided to use 100 to represent that peice. It said that the second peice was 25% longer than the first, so I found 25% of 100 (25) and added it to 100. The answer was 125. Now, the third peice is supposed to be 25% *shorter* than the first. So, I subtracted 25 from 100 and got 75.

(B) Now I know what the string peices measure on scale. I added up the peices, and got 300. I know that 100 (the first peice of string) is 1/3 of 300, so the real first peice of string must be 1/3 of 180. 180/3= 60. So the first string peice is 60 cm. Now all I have to do is find 25% of 60. 60/100x25= 15. For the second peice of string I will add 15 cm to the first, and for the third peice of string, I will subtract 15 from the first.

60+15= 75   60-15= 45

1st peice= 60 cm, 2nd peice= 75 cm, 3rd peice= 45 cm

(C) 1st (A) / 100 + 2nd / 125 + 3rd / 75 = 300

100 = 1/3 300   Piece 1 = 60 cm   15 + 60 = 75
                                     60 - 15 = 45

(E) A = 1/3 180   60/100 25 = 15

180/3 = 60   15 = 25% · 60

(D) 1st / 60 cm   2nd / 75 cm   3rd / 45 cm

(A) The decision to consider a piece of length 100 suggests that the student realized she could use her understanding of percents to solve this problem. This made it easy, initially, to consider the comparable pieces 25% longer and shorter.

(B) (C) The student determined that her 100 unit piece of string must have been the middle piece of a string of length 300.

(C) (D) The student's notation could be confusing. Her sketches of the pieces of string might appear to be "bars" from common fraction notation. A puzzled reader could initially wonder, "What does she mean, '2nd over 125'?"

(B) (E) The student recognized that the measurements of the pieces of the 180 cm string were proportional to those of the 300 unit string she concocted. To find the length A of the middle piece of the 180 cm string, she examined the proportional relationship 300:180 = 100:A and recognized the constant factor of change, ⅓. The student captured the essence of proportional reasoning in the statement, "I know that 100...is ⅓ of 300, so the real first peice [sic] of string must be ⅓ of 180."

M5 b Problem Solving and Mathematical Reasoning: Implementation. The student...invents... approaches....

As noted above, a standard solution to this problem would have used algebra.

Work Sample & Commentary: *Dart Board*

The task

Students were asked to respond to the following task:

Design a dart board that has four regions with the following features:

score value	*probability %*
100 points	10%
50 points	20%
25 points	30%
10 points	40%

The dart board may be any shape (circle, square, etc.) and must have an area between 1,000 sq. cm and 3,000 sq. cm. Assume the probability is proportional to the area of the region. Make a scale drawing with dimensions and explain your solution in words.

The task calls for the student to set up a total area that satisfies given constraints. Then the student must partition this area correctly into regions of sizes proportional to the given percentages. The scale drawing requires understanding of appropriate measurement and proportional reasoning. A firm grasp of area measurement is needed for a successful solution.

Design a dartboard that has four regions
with the following features:
score value — Probability %
100 points — 10%
50 points — 20%
25 points — 30%
10 points — 40%
The dartboard may be any shape (circle, square, etc), and must have an area between 1000 sq. cm. and 3000 sq. cm. Assume the probability is proportional to the area of the region. Make a scale drawing with dimensions and explain your solution in words.

Step 1: Begin by finding the dimension of the circle to find the area between 1000 sq. cm. and 3000 sq. cm. I shall use trial and error.

$A = \pi r^2$ (r = 10)
$= 3.14 \times (10)^2$
$= 3.14 \times 100$
$= 314$ = too small

$A = \pi r^2$ (r = 20)
$= 3.14 (20)^2$
$= 3.14 \times 400$
$= 1256$: falls in place of 1000 and 3000

B

I: r = 6.32
II: r = 10.95
III: r = 15.49
IV: r = 20

Probability, while mentioned, is not actually called for by the task. The assumption that equates the probability of hitting a region with the area of the region presumes that darts would always land on the board and that players' aim at the target would be ineffective.

Nevertheless, the task lends itself to a wide variety of solutions. Some approaches are quite involved and complex, calling for considerable care, thought, and skill. This student response exemplifies such an approach. Other satisfactory solutions might be insightful, yet less complicated. An example would be a choice of dart board as a 100 cm x 20 cm rectangle, divided along the length in 10, 20, 30, and 40 cm segments.

Circumstances of performance

This sample of student work was produced under the following conditions:

√ alone	in a group
√ in class	√ as homework
with teacher feedback	with peer feedback
timed	opportunity for revision

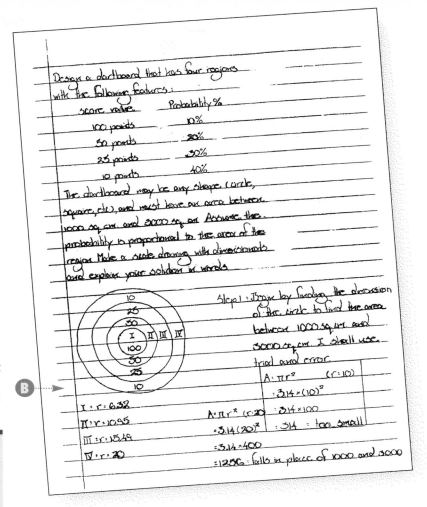

This work sample illustrates a standard-setting performance for the following parts of the standards:

M1 a Number and Operation Concepts: Consistently and accurately multiply and divide rational numbers.

M1 b Number and Operation Concepts: Use and understand the inverse relationships between multiplication and division, and exponentiation and root-extraction.

M1 e Number and Operation Concepts: Interpret percent as part of 100.

M1 f Number and Operation Concepts: Reason proportionally.

M2 a Geometry and Measurement Concepts: Be familiar with assorted two- and three-dimensional objects.

M2 d Geometry and Measurement Concepts: Determine and understand length, area, and volume.

M5 b Problem Solving and Mathematical Reasoning: Implementation.

M6 a Mathematical Skills and Tools: Compute accurately with arithmetic operations on rational numbers.

M6 f Mathematical Skills and Tools: Use equations, formulas, and simple algebraic notation appropriately.

M7 b Mathematical Communication: Organize work, explain a solution orally and in writing, and use other techniques to make meaning clear to the audience.

The quotations from the Mathematics performance descriptions in this commentary are excerpted. The complete performance descriptions are shown on pages 54-59.

Dart Board

Number and Operation Concepts M1
Geometry & Measurement Concepts M2
Function & Algebra Concepts
Statistics & Probability Concepts
Problem Solving & Mathematical Reasoning M5
Mathematical Skills & Tools M6
Mathematical Communication M7
Putting Mathematics to Work

What the work shows

M1a Number and Operation Concepts: The student consistently and accurately…multiplies and divides rational numbers….

M1b Number and Operation Concepts: The student uses and understands the inverse relationships between…multiplication and division, and exponentiation and root-extraction…; uses the inverse operation to determine unknown quantities in equations.

M1e Number and Operation Concepts: The student interprets percent as part of 100….

M1f Number and Operation Concepts: The student…reasons proportionally….

A Here, as in subsequent steps, the student appropriately applied the usual area formula for circles. She substituted correctly, taking care to recognize that the area of the circle in her formula is the cumulative area of the regions at each step. Then she correctly used the area formula to determine the appropriate radius.

Step 2: To find the dimension of region one which is 10%, I shall multiply the total area of the circle (1256 sq. cm.) with 10% and then divide it with 3.14 and find the square root.
example: 1256 × 0.1 = A: 125.6
125.6 ÷ 3.14 = 40
√40 r = 6.32

Step 3 To find the dimension of region two, I shall add region one (10%) with region two (20%) and come out with 30% and I will use the formula that I used with Step 2. After I find the dimension I will subtract the area of region one from this area because I only want to know the area for 20%, not 30%.
example: 1256 × 0.3 = A: 376.8
376.8 ÷ 3.14 = 120
√120 = r = 10.95
376.8 − 125.6 = ~~A = 2~~
A = 251.2

M2a Geometry and Measurement Concepts: The student is familiar with assorted two- and three-dimensional objects, including…circles….

M2d Geometry and Measurement Concepts: The student determines and understands…area…; computes areas of…circles….

The student exhibited command of the concept of area throughout the work. She recognized the areas of the rings as the differences of areas of concentric circles. Accordingly, she computed the areas of the inner circles and subtracted them from the areas of the outer circles.

B The dart board sketch is not a scale drawing. A well executed diagram would have provided strong evidence of proportional reasoning, part of **M2**. Still, concentric circles are appropriate for the dart board design and the board fits the constraints posed by the task.

The cm unit is nowhere given as the unit of measure for the radius in the student's solution. This is a fairly minor omission in the context of such an involved problem.

M5b Problem Solving and Mathematical Reasoning: Implementation. The student…

- determines, where helpful, how to break a problem into simpler parts;
- solves for unknown or undecided quantities using algebra, graphing, sound reasoning, and other strategies;
- integrates concepts and techniques from different areas of mathematics….

A The student broke the task into smaller, more manageable pieces: Steps 1 through 5.

B The student determined a dart board radius of 20 cm, which satisfied the constraints of the problem.

Dart Board

M6 a Mathematical Skills and Tools: The student computes accurately with arithmetic operations on rational numbers.

M6 f Mathematical Skills and Tools: The student uses equations, formulas, and simple algebraic notation appropriately.

The computations and notation are correct. This is evident throughout the work.

M7 b Mathematical Communication: The student organizes work, explains facets of a solution orally and in writing, labels drawings, and uses other techniques to make meaning clear to the audience.

The response is well organized and easy to follow.

C Here, as elsewhere, the prose makes clear to the reader the means by which the student built on the previous steps to determine the radius of the next dart board circle.

Step 4: To find the dimension of region three, I shall add 30% (region #1 and #2) with region three which is 30% and come out with 60%. I will then use the same set up from Step 2 and subtract the area of region #1 and #2 with the area of region three.

example: 1256 × 0.6 = A = 753.6
753.6 ÷ 3.14 = 240
$\sqrt{240}$ = r = 15.49
753.6 - 376.8 = A = 376.8

Step 5: For region four, I know that the area is 1256 because when you add all three regions together it becomes r = 20 and the area of the whole circle is 1256. All I have to do now is subtract the area of region #1, #2, and #3 (753.6) from 1256 and get an answer of 502.4 which is 40% of the total area.

Work Sample & Commentary: *Science Fair*

Number and Operation Concepts M1
Geometry & Measurement Concepts
Function & Algebra Concepts
Statistics & Probability Concepts
Problem Solving & Mathematical Reasoning M5
Mathematical Skills & Tools M6
Mathematical Communication
Putting Mathematics to Work

The quotations from the Mathematics performance descriptions in this commentary are excerpted. The complete performance descriptions are shown on pages 54-59.

The task

The context of this task is a science fair with three attending middle schools of different populations. The student must consider the numbers of students as fractions and percents of the total. The student also must appropriately divide among the schools both the area in which the fair will be conducted and the cost of the fair.

Circumstances of performance

This sample of student work was produced under the following conditions:

√ alone	in a group
√ in class	as homework
with teacher feedback	with peer feedback
√ timed	opportunity for revision

This is a Released Task from the New Standards reference examination. Students were expected to need no more than fifteen minutes to solve it.

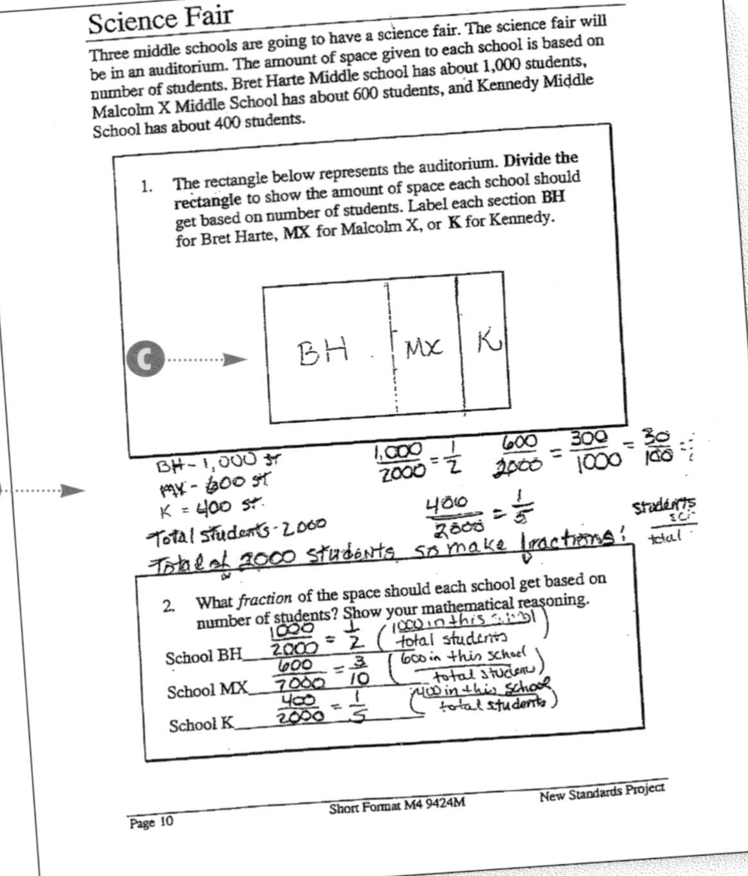

Science Fair

Three middle schools are going to have a science fair. The science fair will be in an auditorium. The amount of space given to each school is based on number of students. Bret Harte Middle school has about 1,000 students, Malcolm X Middle School has about 600 students, and Kennedy Middle School has about 400 students.

1. The rectangle below represents the auditorium. **Divide the rectangle** to show the amount of space each school should get based on number of students. Label each section **BH** for Bret Harte, **MX** for Malcolm X, or **K** for Kennedy.

BH | MX | K

BH - 1,000 st
MX - 600 st
K = 400 st
Total students - 2000
Total of 2000 students so make fractions!

1,000/2000 = 1/2 600/2000 = 300/1000 = 30/100
400/2000 = 1/5

2. What *fraction* of the space should each school get based on number of students? Show your mathematical reasoning.

School BH 1000/2000 = 1/2 (1000 in this school / total students)
School MX 600/2000 = 3/10 (600 in this school / total students)
School K 400/2000 = 1/5 (400 in this school / total students)

Page 10 Short Format M4 9424M New Standards Project

What the work shows

M1 a Number and Operations Concepts: The student…adds, subtracts, multiplies, and divides rational numbers….

A The student made appropriate computations and accurately divided the cost of the science fair proportionally, according to the approximate populations given at the beginning of the task.

M1 c Number and Operations Concepts: The student…applies and converts the different kinds and forms of rational numbers.

B The work makes clear the relationship between fractions and quotients, that "$3/10 = 3 \div 10$," etc. He converted the fractions into percentages.

M1 f Number and Operations Concepts: The student…reasons proportionally to solve problems involving equivalent fractions….

C The rectangle is not divided precisely in 5:3:2 ratio, but it is very nearly so. The partitions are drawn sufficiently for the given task. The school populations were approximations anyway ("about 1,000 students," etc.).

D In part two, the student exhibited understanding of some fundamental concepts of fractions. He used fractions to express a part/whole relationship where the whole is not a single item but a set (of 2,000 students). He determined the whole given the parts. He used equivalent fractions and simplified here, as appropriate.

A The student accurately divided the cost of the science fair proportionally, according to the approximate populations given at the beginning of the task.

This work sample illustrates a standard-setting performance for the following parts of the standards:

- **M1 a Number and Operation Concepts: Add, subtract, multiply, and divide rational numbers.**
- **M1 c Number and Operation Concepts: Apply and convert the different kinds and forms of rational numbers.**
- **M1 f Number and Operation Concepts: Reason proportionally to solve problems involving equivalent fractions.**
- **M5 c Problem Solving and Mathematical Reasoning: Conclusion.**
- **M6 a Mathematical Skills and Tools: Compute accurately with arithmetic operations on rational numbers.**

Science Fair

M5c Problem Solving and Mathematical Reasoning: Conclusion. The student verifies and interprets results with respect to the original problem situation....

B The "check" that the three percentages computed must add up to 100%, the total, is more convincing evidence of understanding of percent than the actual rote computations performed by the student to obtain 50%, 30%, and 20%.

A The student checked that the charges computed for each school indeed add up to the $300 cost of the fair.

M6a Mathematical Skills and Tools: The student computes accurately with arithmetic operations on rational numbers.

A **B**

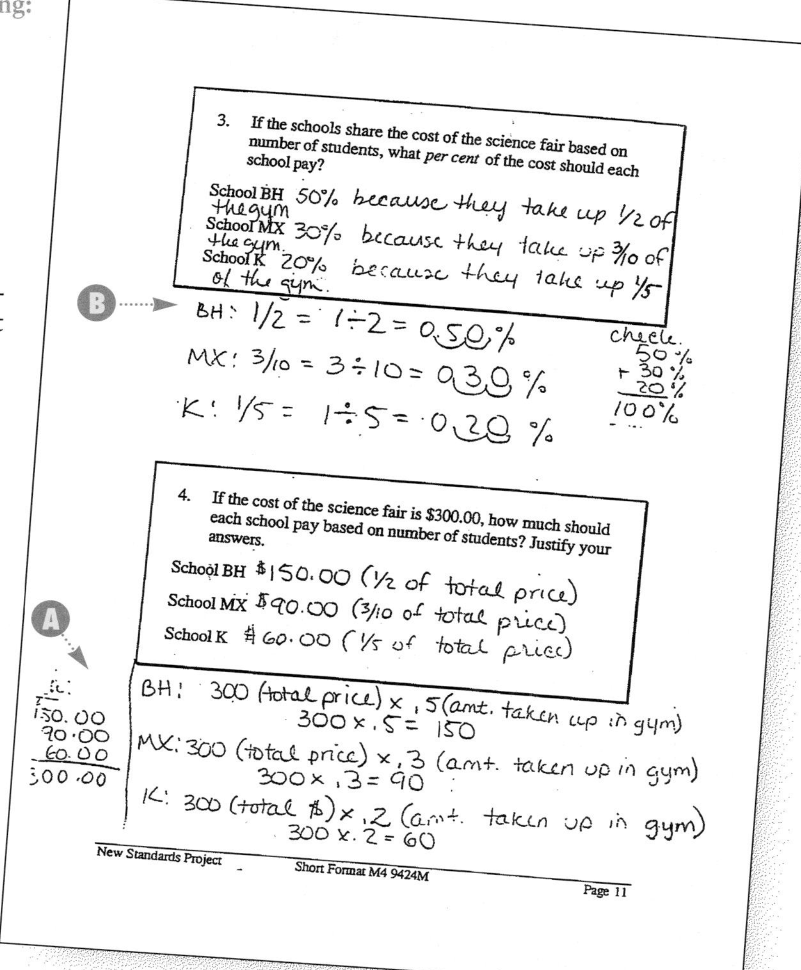

3. If the schools share the cost of the science fair based on number of students, what *per cent* of the cost should each school pay?

School BH 50% because they take up 1/2 of the gym

School MX 30% because they take up 3/10 of the gym.

School K 20% because they take up 1/5 of the gym.

B → BH: 1/2 = 1÷2 = 0.50.%

MX: 3/10 = 3÷10 = 0.30 %

K: 1/5 = 1÷5 = 0.20 %

check. 50% + 30% + 20% = 100%

4. If the cost of the science fair is $300.00, how much should each school pay based on number of students? Justify your answers.

School BH $150.00 (1/2 of total price)

School MX $90.00 (3/10 of total price)

School K $60.00 (1/5 of total price)

A → 150.00 + 90.00 + 60.00 = 300.00

BH: 300 (total price) x .5 (amt. taken up in gym) 300 x .5 = 150

MX: 300 (total price) x .3 (amt. taken up in gym) 300 x .3 = 90

K: 300 (total $) x .2 (amt. taken up in gym) 300 x .2 = 60

New Standards Project Short Format M4 9424M Page 11

Work Sample & Commentary: *Cubes*

Number and Operation Concepts
Geometry & Measurement Concepts M2
Function & Algebra Concepts
Statistics & Probability Concepts
Problem Solving & Mathematical Reasoning
Mathematical Skills & Tools M6
Mathematical Communication M7
Putting Mathematics to Work

The quotations from the Mathematics performance descriptions in this commentary are excerpted. The complete performance descriptions are shown on pages 54-59.

The task

Students were given a three-part question about volumes and surface areas of cubes.

Circumstances of performance

This sample of student work was produced under the following conditions:

√ alone	in a group
√ in class	as homework
with teacher feedback	with peer feedback
√ timed	opportunity for revision

This is a Released Task from the New Standards reference examination. Students were expected to need no more than fifteen minutes to solve it.

What the work shows

M2d Geometry and Measurement Concepts: The student determines and understands length, area, and volume (as well as the differences among these measurements), including perimeter and surface area; uses units, square units, and cubic units of measure correctly; computes areas of rectangles, triangles, and circles; computes volumes of prisms.

A Work on the first question illustrates understanding of volume.

B Work on the second question illustrates understanding of surface area. Equals signs (=) are used a little carelessly, though. Colons (:) or arrows (→) would be more appropriate links; or equals signs could have been retained while clarifying just what is equal or the same. For example, "Area of 1 side = 9 sq. cm."

Cubes

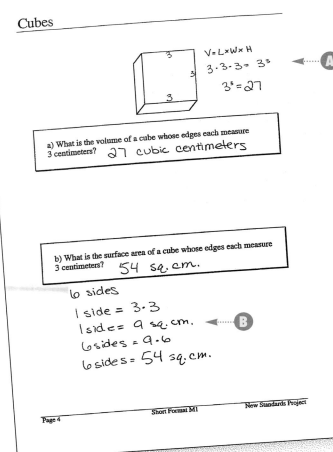

V = L × W × H
3·3·3 = 3³
3³ = 27 — A

a) What is the volume of a cube whose edges each measure 3 centimeters? 27 cubic centimeters

b) What is the surface area of a cube whose edges each measure 3 centimeters? 54 sq. cm.

6 sides
1 side = 3·3
1 side = 9 sq. cm. — B
6 sides = 9·6
6 sides = 54 sq. cm.

Page 4 Short Format M1 New Standards Project

This work sample illustrates a standard-setting performance for the following parts of the standards:

M2d Geometry and Measurement Concepts: Determine and understand length, area, and volume.

M6f Mathematical Skills and Tools: Use formulas appropriately.

M7b Mathematical Communication: Organize work, explain a solution orally and in writing, and use other techniques to make meaning clear to the audience.

Cubes

M6 f Mathematical Skills and Tools: The student uses…formulas…appropriately.

A B C

M7 b Mathematical Communication: The student organizes work, explains facets of a solution orally and in writing, labels drawings, and uses other techniques to make meaning clear to the audience.

A The explanation of the answer "27 cubic centimeters" is very clear and concise. A minor observation is that the student labeled three edges of the cube "3," but she did so in only two of its three dimensions.

C Several examples are given to counter Eddie's claim, not just one example. Not only is Eddie's claim not true for all cubes, it is false for most cubes.

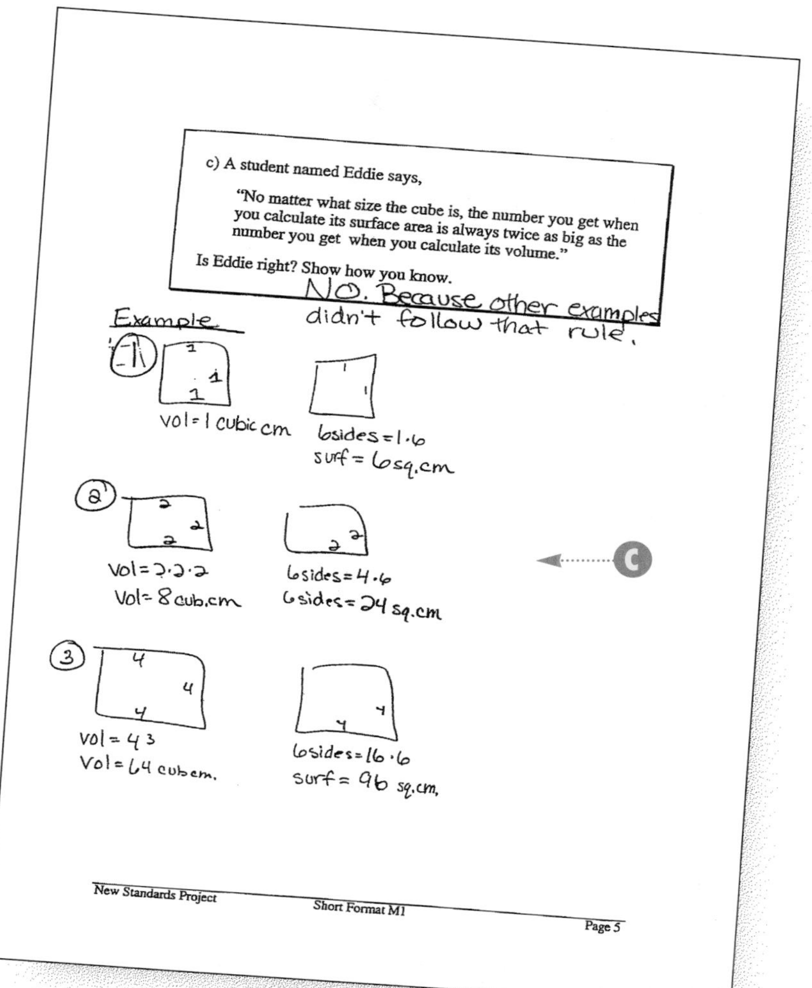

c) A student named Eddie says,

"No matter what size the cube is, the number you get when you calculate its surface area is always twice as big as the number you get when you calculate its volume."

Is Eddie right? Show how you know.

NO. Because other examples didn't follow that rule.

Example

1) Vol = 1 cubic cm; 6 sides = 1·6; surf = 6 sq.cm

2) Vol = 2·2·2; Vol = 8 cub.cm; 6 sides = 4·6; 6 sides = 24 sq.cm

3) Vol = 4³; Vol = 64 cub.cm.; 6 sides = 16·6; surf = 96 sq.cm.

New Standards Project Short Format M1 Page 5

Work Sample & Commentary: *Points and Segments*

The quotations from the Mathematics performance descriptions in this commentary are excerpted. The complete performance descriptions are shown on pages 54-59.

The task

Students were given the following task:

Connect all points with segments.

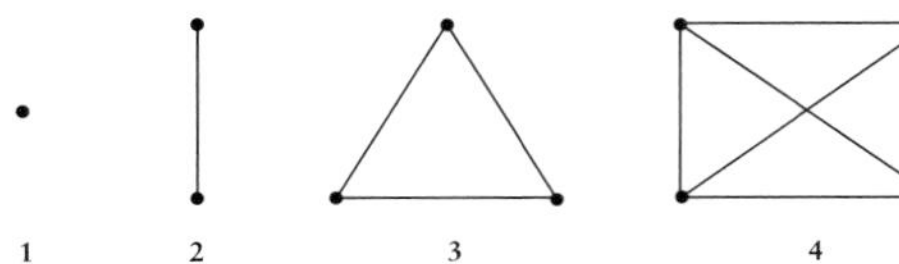

How many segments are needed to connect:
5 points? 6 points? 8 points? 10 points? 30 points? 100 points? n points?

Students were then cued on how they might proceed:

Make drawings for some of the above. Hints: Make a table. Look for patterns.

The task called for students to explore a relationship (between numbers of points and connecting segments) and to recognize a pattern and generalize it. More specifically, in asking how many segments are needed to connect 100 points, then n points, the task invites a closed-form generalization, such as $\frac{n(n-1)}{2}$, instead of an open-ended form, such as 1+2+3+4+...+(n-1). The open-ended form is not well-suited for finding solutions with large values of n.

Other manifestations of this problem are the popular "handshake problem" often posed to elementary school children (see *New Standards Performance Standards*, Volume 1) as well as the common formula for high school students new to the method of proof-by-induction, $1+2+3+4+...+(n-1) = \frac{n(n-1)}{2}$ [or $\frac{n^2-n}{2}$].

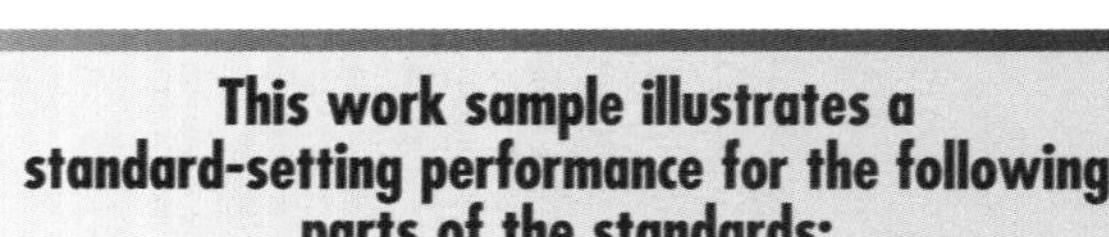

This work sample illustrates a standard-setting performance for the following parts of the standards:

M3 a Function and Algebra Concepts: Discover, describe, and generalize patterns, and represent them with variables and expressions.

M3 b Function and Algebra Concepts: Represent relationships.

M5 b Problem Solving and Mathematical Reasoning: Implementation.

M5 d Problem Solving and Mathematical Reasoning: Mathematical reasoning.

M7 a Mathematical Communication: Use mathematical language and representations with appropriate accuracy.

M7 b Mathematical Communication: Organize work, explain a solution orally and in writing, and use other techniques to make meaning clear to the audience.

P.O.W. Points + Segments

Connect all points with segments.

How many segments are needed to connect: 5 points, 6 points, 8 points, 10 points, 30 points, 100 points, n points?

Make drawings for some of the above. Hints: Make a table. Look for patterns.

points	lines
1	0
2	1
3	3
4	6
5	

This is what I did to solve this problem: First I made the 5 point figure and I systematically connected all the points together. I got 10 segments like this then I took the outside makes 5 point A and since it was

G

Circumstances of performance

This sample of student work was produced under the following conditions:

√ alone	in a group
√ in class	√ as homework
with teacher feedback	with peer feedback
timed	opportunity for revision

What the work shows

This student's work provides clear evidence for the strategies he used to tackle the problem and for the development of the solution in stages. This response provides particularly strong evidence for the standards cited because the student's approach seems too unusual to have come from a teacher-led discussion of the problem.

M3 a Function and Algebra Concepts: The student discovers, describes, and generalizes patterns..., and represents them with variables and expressions.

A The first two terms are n+(n-3), the same quantity as the first two terms of the more "classic" (n-1)+(n-2)+...+3+2+1.

M3 b Function and Algebra Concepts: The student represents relationships with tables,...and verbal or symbolic rules.

B The student succeeded in expressing the number of segments as a function of the number of points. Parentheses are repeatedly used incorrectly here,

Points and Segments

already connected to B and E. I made two more lines that connected it to C and D. Then B is connected to A and C so 2 lines connect it to D and E. Then C is now connected to all but E so you draw one line and now all are connected together. 3+2+2+1=10. I used this same method to connect the 6 point figure. I came up with 6+3+3+2+1=15 segments. I did it for 8 points and got 8+5+5+4+3+2+1=28 segments. For 10 points it was 10+7+7+6+5+4+3+2+1= 45 segments. I saw a pattern, it was always (n points ×1)+(n-3)×2)+(n-4)+(n-5)+b-6) and so on until you had n- the number right before n. So for 30 it would be 30+27+27+26+25 and so on down to +1=435. I knew there had to be an easier formula so I made a chart that looked like this

A

C

n points	2	3	4	5	6	7	8	9	10	30
lines	1	3	6	10	15	21	28	36	45	435

100	n

D

I tried many different things to find the relationship between the top number and the one below it but with no success. Then I tried dividing the bottom number by the top number and it made a pattern. 1÷2=.5 3÷3=1 6÷4=1.5 10÷5=2 15÷6=2.5 21÷7=3 28÷8=3.5 36÷9=4

E

Each time it went up by ½. Then I said what can I do to the top number to get the number to multiply it by. Then I found this ((n÷2)-.5)×n as the formula and it worked. So for 100 points it would be 100÷2=50 50-.5=49.5 49.5×100=4,950. Shortened it would be like this (100÷2)-.5)×100 = the bottom number

B

of lines n×(n÷2)-.5) = line segments

F

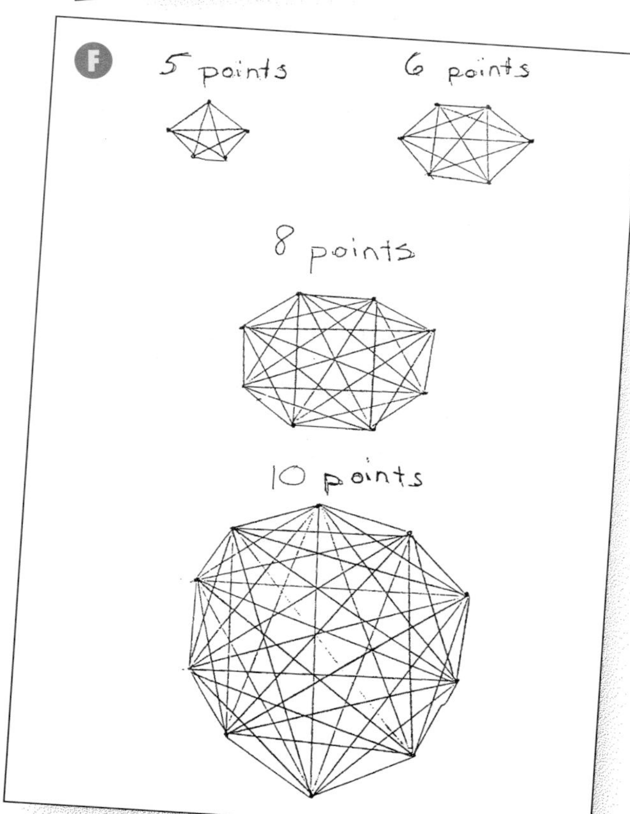

which does not detract from this solution, but is worthy of correction for clearer communication.

C

M5b Problem Solving and Mathematical Reasoning: Implementation. The student...

- uses and invents a variety of approaches....
- invokes problem solving strategies, such as illustrating with sense-making sketches to clarify situations or organizing information in a table....

C D

M5d Problem Solving and Mathematical Reasoning: Mathematical reasoning. The student...

- formulates conjectures...
- makes justified, logical statements.

E The recognition, here, of the recurring increase of ½ in the fraction s/n (where s is the number of segments) is powerful. The student went beyond the recognition of simple quadratic functions such as $f(n)=n^2$ or $f(n)=cn^2$ and "reduced" a quadratic pattern to a linear pattern. The work does not communicate well the reasoning used to conclude that $s = ((n÷2) - .5) \times n$. The student's phrase, "Then I found this," leaves the reader to wonder, "How?"

M7a Mathematical Communication: The student uses mathematical language and representations with appropriate accuracy, including numerical tables...and diagrams.

C F

M7b Mathematical Communication: The student organizes work, explains facets of a solution orally and in writing, labels drawings, and uses other techniques to make meaning clear to the audience.

G Giving the points alphabetical names is central to the clarity of the student's explanation.

Work Sample & Commentary: *Locker Lunacy*

The quotations from the Mathematics performance descriptions in this commentary are excerpted. The complete performance descriptions are shown on pages 54-59.

The task

The student is called on to analyze a scenario in which school lockers are alternately opened and closed in a particular manner. The task calls for evidence from M5, as the student determines how to describe the situation mathematically and achieve a solution. That solution should provide the student ample opportunity to show prowess in M7, since this problem lends itself to features that illustrate this standard—appropriate mathematical language, well-organized work and ideas, clarity, assorted mathematical representations, etc.

As part of the problem conclusion, if not earlier in the student's work, the reflective question "Why?" should come to mind upon discovery that only those lockers whose numbers are perfect squares of natural numbers are open in the end. The student who investigates the reason for this will realize the relationship between the factors that divide those perfect squares and the procedure by which lockers were opened and closed. This will demonstrate considerable achievement under M1.

Finally, the "Extra!" section of the prompt leads students to generalize and "find a rule for any number," providing an opportunity to show evidence under M3.

Locker Lunacy!

In a school with 100 students, there are 100 lockers, numbered 1 through 100. One day, one student walks down the hall and opens all the lockers. Then, a 2nd student closes all the lockers with even numbers. Then, a 3rd student changes the position of all the lockers with numbers that are multiples of 3. ("Changing the position" means that a closed locker is opened and an open locker is closed.) If this pattern continues for all 100 students, which lockers will remain open after the 100th student walks down the hall? A

Explain your strategies clearly, using appropriate mathematical representation and mathematical language.

Extra! What if there were 500 students and 500 lockers? 1000? Can you find a rule for any number of students and lockers? Explain why your rule works.

B

This work sample illustrates a standard-setting performance for the following parts of the standards:

M1 d Number and Operation Concepts: Be familiar with characteristics of numbers.

M3 a Function and Algebra Concepts: Discover, describe, and generalize patterns.

M3 c Function and Algebra Concepts: Analyze tables to determine functional relationships.

M5 b Problem Solving and Mathematical Reasoning: Implementation.

M5 c Problem Solving and Mathematical Reasoning: Conclusion.

M5 d Problem Solving and Mathematical Reasoning: Mathematical reasoning.

M6 f Mathematical Skills and Tools: Use equations, formulas, and simple algebraic notation appropriately.

M6 g Mathematical Skills and Tools: Read and organize data on charts.

M6 h Mathematical Skills and Tools: Use calculators, as appropriate, to achieve solutions.

M7 a Mathematical Communication: Use mathematical language and representations with appropriate accuracy.

M7 b Mathematical Communication: Organize work, explain a solution in writing, and use other techniques to make meaning clear to the audience.

M7 c Mathematical Communication: Use mathematical language to make complex situations easier to understand.

Circumstances of performance

This sample of student work was produced under the following conditions:

√ alone	in a group
√ in class	√ as homework
with teacher feedback	with peer feedback
timed	√ opportunity for revision

Locker Lunacy

What the work shows

The student analyzed the locker scenario successfully, studying the factors ("only after a long while of experimenting") of natural numbers and how those divisors could correspond to the opening and closing of lockers. As he writes about this, he carefully explains the correspondence to the reader and attempts to justify his work, going beyond the level required by the task prompt.

In attempting to generalize the locker results for larger, then arbitrary, numbers of students and lockers, the student created a large table of values and inferred from there the desired relationship. Troubled in his attempt to write a symbolic rule for the *number* of lockers that would remain open (a more significant result than that which was sought, it seems, by the prompt), he overcame the problem by developing his own rendition of the classic greatest-integer function.

This work sample shows strength across several standards, most thoroughly in relation to M5 and M7. The student took an apparently unfamiliar situation (becoming more difficult as "the locker problem" continues its spread across middle grade classrooms) and determined a mathematical context and approach that yielded a solution. He used appropriate representations, organization, and reasoning both to attain and to explain his solution.

A B Observe that the prompt asks "Which lockers will remain open?" rather than "How many lockers?" which is the more-involved question the student answered in the work that follows. The "Extra!" section asks for some generalization, but it still does not pose the question of "How many?"

M1 d Number and Operation Concepts: The student is familiar with characteristics of numbers (e.g., divisibility, prime factorization)....

C D The student analyzed the parity of the numbers of factors and how that determines a locker's final position, explaining why locker numbers with even numbers of factors end up closed and why those with odd numbers of factors remain open. He went on to determine that it is only the perfect squares that have odd numbers of factors. Here ("...because they have the same number of factors as their square root and another factor—itself"), though, there is a flaw in his logic. It is true that squares of prime numbers have just one more factor than their square roots, and it seems he saw this in 4, 9, and 25 (2^2, 3^2, and 5^2) and made too strong a claim. Observe that he did recognize that 16 (4^2) gives a different result and he attempted to account for this ("8 is also here to be multiplied by 2"). However, instead of concluding that extra factors exist for squares of composite numbers, he only recognized that they exist for squares of square numbers.

Locker Lunacy

The pattern that they are referring to is that the first person opens lockers with multiples of 1, the second switches multiples of 2, the third switches multiples of 3 and so on. How many lockers will be open after the 100th person?

First, I realized that prime numbers were going to be closed at the end, because they (C) only have two factors: 1 and itself. That got me thinking about factors. I then gave the factors of 1 through ten:

Number	Factors	Odd or Even # of Factors
1	1	Odd (1)
2	1,2	Even (2)
3	1,3	Even (2)
4	1,2,4	Odd (3)
5	1,5	Even (2)
6	1,2,3,6	Even (4)
7	1,7	Even (2)
8	1,2,4,8	Even (4)
9	1,3,9	Odd (3)
10	1,2,5,10	Even (4)

When a number has and even number of factors, it will always be closed in the end. This

D A fundamental idea underlying the locker problem—that square numbers have an odd number of factors, whereas other natural numbers have even numbers of factors—is just an extension of a common occurrence in classrooms when factorization is taught. "Pairing" of factors is often done by teachers and students to check for missing numbers in a factorization. For example, the factors of 63 are 1, 3, 7, 9, 21, and 63; they can be paired as 1 x 63, 3 x 21, and 7 x 9, with all pairs giving product 63. Perfect squares, though, have a "twist": the factors of 36 are 1, 2, 3, 4, 6, 9, 12, 18, 36; 1 x 36, 2 x 18, 3 x 12, and 4 x 9 are all paired, leaving 6 by itself ($6^2 = 36$).

Locker Lunacy

M3a Function and Algebra Concepts: The student discovers, describes, and generalizes patterns...and represents them with variables and expressions.

M3c Function and Algebra Concepts: The student analyzes tables...to determine functional relationships.

E The student created his own version of the "greatest integer function," often symbolized [x], which returns the largest integer less than or equal to the real number x. Presumably unacquainted with this function, he created it for himself with his rule of computing the square root and subtracting the remainder, $L = \sqrt{t} - r$. Each variable is defined and explained well.

The work demonstrates understanding of concepts of irrational numbers that surpasses the demand of **M1**, which focuses on proficiency with the rationals in the middle school. Notice that the student recognized that, except for square numbers, the written decimal forms of his square roots are only approximations of the numbers' actual values ("the square root is ≈ 22.36068").

M5b Problem Solving and Mathematical Reasoning: Implementation. The student...invokes problem solving strategies, such as...organizing information in a table....

F The student noticed early in the problem the need to examine the numbers of factors of the natural numbers and to think about the implications of the factorization on whether or not the corresponding locker would be open or closed in the end. This is astute, particularly so early in the problem. More commonly, students notice experimentally that those lockers whose numbers are perfect squares (of natural numbers) remain open when all is done. It is only on reflection (asking "Why?") that they reason and realize the relationship between the perfect squares and their odd numbers of factors.

G

M5c Problem Solving and Mathematical Reasoning: Conclusion. The student...generalizes solutions and strategies to new problem situations.

H The student tackled the related question of "How many open lockers?" This is no more complicated for the 100 locker scenario, but it is considerably more involved for a generalization to n lockers.

M5d Problem Solving and Mathematical Reasoning: Mathematical reasoning. The student...

- formulates conjectures and argues why they must be or seem true...
- makes justified, logical statements.

D

is because when there are 2 factors, the lockers is opened and closed, and all even numbers are divisible by 2. With an odd number of factors, the result will be open because the pattern is open, close, open. **D** → Squares have odd numbers of factors because they have the same number of factors as their square root and another factor—itself. This works for square roots that have an even number of factors. If the square root is also a square, there is another factor. Ex.:

4 —— factors are 1,2,4 Odd
16 —— factors are 1,2,4,8,16 Odd
↑ 8 is also here to be multiplied by 2.

J → There are 10 squares in 100: 1,4,9,16,25,36,49, 64,81, and 100, so there will be 10 open lockers in the end. I then tried to find a formula for how many open lockers there would be for any number of lockers. **H** → I made a chart that shows a number and its square. I made markings for the 100 marks. From my chart, you can see the number of squares in multiples of 100 specifically or any other number.

M6f Mathematical Skills and Tools: The student uses equations, formulas, and simple algebraic notation appropriately.

I

M6g Mathematical Skills and Tools: The student reads and organizes data on charts....

F **G**

M6h Mathematical Skills and Tools: The student uses...calculators,...as appropriate, to achieve solutions.

I

M7a Mathematical Communication: The student uses mathematical language and representations with appropriate accuracy, including numerical tables....

F **G**

Locker Lunacy

M7 b Mathematical Communication: The student organizes work, explains facets of a solution…in writing, labels drawings, and uses other techniques to make meaning clear to the audience.

J The answer to the task's primary question ("Which lockers will remain open?") deserves more prominent placement so as not to be overlooked by the reader. Despite this minor point, the entire piece of work is clear and well organized.

M7 c Mathematical Communication: The student uses mathematical language to make complex situations easier to understand.

K The student used examples to clarify confusion that might arise from the function he created. Observe that he provided examples to illustrate both of the cited cases, with remainder and without remainder. Of course, the latter could be subsumed in the former by saying, "with remainder of zero."

L No apology necessary!

G

x	x^2	x	x^2
1	1	26 –700	676
2	4	27	729
3	9	28 –800	784
4	16	29	841
5	25	30 –900	900
6	36	31 –1000	961
7	49	32	1024
8	64	33 –1100	1089
9	81	34 –1200	1156
10 –100	100	35	1225
11	121	36 –1300	1296
12	144	37 –1400	1369
13	169	38 –1500	1444
14 –200	196	39	1521
15	225	40 –1600	1600
16	256	41 –1700	1681
17 –300	289	42 –1800	1764
18	324	43 –1900	1849
19 –400	361	44 –2000	1936
20	400	45 –2100	2025
21	441	46 –2200	2116
22 –500	484	47 –2300	2209
23	529	48 –2400	2304
24 –600	576	49	2401
25	625	50 –2500	2500

I used so many examples to get my point across.

From the chart we see that there are 10 squares in 100, 14 in 200, 17 in 300, 19 in 400, 22 in 500, 31 in 1000, etc. I then tried to find a rule. I saw that there were 10 in 100, and 10^2 was 100. The same went for 400, 900, 1600, and 2500. This was not true for the other numbers, but it was almost true. In 500, the square root is ≈22.36068. In 1100, it is ≈33.166248.

E If I drop the remainder, I get the number of open lockers or squares. I then devised a formula:

$L=\sqrt{x}-r$

Here, L is the number of open lockers at the end. x is the number of total lockers. r is the remainder of $\sqrt{x}$. All you have to do is find the square root of x, and

K if there is a remainder, drop it. Ex:

700: $L=\sqrt{x}-r$
$L=\sqrt{700}-r$
$L\approx 26.457513-r$
$L\approx 26.457513-.457513$
$L=26$ open lockers

900: $L=\sqrt{x}-r$
$L=\sqrt{900}-r$
$L=30-r$
$L=30-0$
$L=30$ open lockers

I This can also be done for any number.

87: $L=\sqrt{x}-r$
$L=\sqrt{87}-r$
$L\approx 9.3273791-r$
$L\approx 9.3273791-.3273791$
$L=9$ open lockers

1943: $L=\sqrt{x}-r$
$L=\sqrt{1943}-r$
$L\approx 44.079474-r$
$L\approx 44.079474-.079474$
$L=44$ open lockers

The equation again: $L=\sqrt{x}-r$

L P.S: I have a habit of repeating the equation in the end. Sorry.

Work Sample & Commentary: *Who Is the Best?*

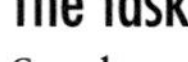

Number and Operation Concepts
Geometry & Measurement Concepts
Function & Algebra Concepts
Statistics & Probability Concepts M4
Problem Solving & Mathematical Reasoning
Mathematical Skills & Tools
Mathematical Communication
Putting Mathematics to Work

Mathematics performance descriptions in this commentary are excerpted. The complete performance descriptions are shown on pages 54-59.

The task

Students were presented with a scenario in which they had to determine which of three golfers is the "best" chipper. Each golfer chipped ten balls. The measured distances of the balls from the cup are given. The data for this problem were devised so that the average distance from the cup is the same for all three golfers. Thus, students had to use other appropriate statistical measures to analyze the situation. "Getting close and being consistent" are the criteria on which the students were to judge the golfers.

Circumstances of performance

This sample of student work was produced under the following conditions:

alone	√ in a group
√ in class	as homework
with teacher feedback	with peer feedback
timed	opportunity for revision

What the work shows

M4 a Statistics and Probability Concepts: The student…organizes data, and displays data with …graphs that are appropriate….

A The student rewrote Sarah's data in numerical order to illustrate median, quartiles, and extreme values of the range. It would have been good to see the same for Rick's and Mike's data.

B

This work sample illustrates a standard-setting performance for the following parts of the standards:

- **M4 a Statistics and Probability Concepts: Organize and display data.**
- **M4 b Statistics and Probability Concepts: Analyze data with respect to frequency and distribution.**
- **M4 c Statistics and Probability Concepts: Analyze central tendencies of data.**
- **M4 d Statistics and Probability Concepts: Make conclusions and recommendations based on data analysis.**

Name________________

Group________________

WHO IS THE BEST?

Rick, Mike and Sarah are all on their school's golf team. They have been practicing their chipping. Each player thinks s/he is the best chipper on the team. To decide who is right, they have a contest. Each player chips 10 balls onto the same green. The balls are different colors so they can tell them apart. When they finish they measure the distance from each ball to the cup in inches. Here are the results in no particular order:

Rick: 40, 60, 100, 120, 312, 320, 152, 105, 95, 46
Mike: 52, 76, 184, 288, 230, 120, 64, 60, 88, 188
Sarah: 84, 99, 130, 135, 200, 165, 120, 129, 136, 152

When the contest was over, the kids still couldn't decide who was the winner. The balls were all spread out. No one was close every time. They asked the coach for advice. He said, "In the game of golf, getting close and being consistent are important. So, you should consider who is closest and most consistent. Don't just consider who had the best shot. You're the math whizzes--I'm sure you can figure it out."

Help the kids decide who won. Analyze the results in as many different ways as you know. Present a **mathematical** argument to back up your decision about who the winner was and why s/he won.

Sarah: 84, 99, 120, 129, 130, 135, 136, 152, 165, 200

lower extreme — lower Quartile — 132.5 median — 152 upper Quartile — Upper extreme

A

Who's the Best January 21, 1996

Before I started this problem I thought that a plot would be the best way to represent this problem, but I had to think about which kind of plot would be the best to display and compare the data in the problem. There are three ranges of data, that I need to compare, Rick's chips, Mike's chips and Sarah's chips. I came to the conclusion that a box plot would be the most effective plot, because box plots can compare ranges of data to other ranges of data.

After I found the components necessary for a box plot (extremes, quartiles and the median) for each person I assembled a box plot (enclosed). From first glance you might say that Rick is the best chipper, because he has the over all closest shot. If you read the problem more closely you will see that the coach said to the young golfers "In the game of golf, getting close and being **C** consistent are important." Not only did Rick get the closest shot, he also got the farthest away shot. This means he is not very consistent.

D If you look at the plot closely you will see that Mike is not much better than Rick. Both of their inter-quartile ranges are quite large, which is another way to tell if a person is consistent. Rick's farthest away shot is an outlier **F** where Mike's is not. You can tell this by seeing if the upper extreme is, one and a half times the size of the inter-quartile range, above the upper quartile. This gives Rick an advantage, because it means his high shots were rare and flukes of a sort.

Who is the Best?

M4 b Statistics and Probability Concepts: The student analyzes data with respect to characteristics of frequency and distribution, including mode and range.

M4 c Statistics and Probability Concepts: The student analyzes appropriately central tendencies of data by considering mean and median.

C The student made meaningful comparisons of the data, keeping in mind the coach's criteria for good chipping.

D E The student was thinking mathematically of the coach's consistency criterion. He used the size of the inter-quartile range as a measure of consistency. Rick's and Mike's "quite large" ranges suggest some inconsistency, especially when compared with Sarah's smaller inter-quartile range. The inter-quartile range of the middle half of the data combines notions of distribution with those of central tendency.

B F Rick's farthest shot is recognized as an outlier. Indeed, his two chips that landed 312 and 320 inches away are both outliers. However, the student did not show them as such on the box-and-whiskers plot. He could have done so by plotting two isolated points at those two values instead of showing the range extending to 320 inches.

G The realization that "the total yardage…was the same" suggests an understanding of average as more than a computational procedure. The total yardages are the same, just like the averages, because the golfers made the same number of chips.

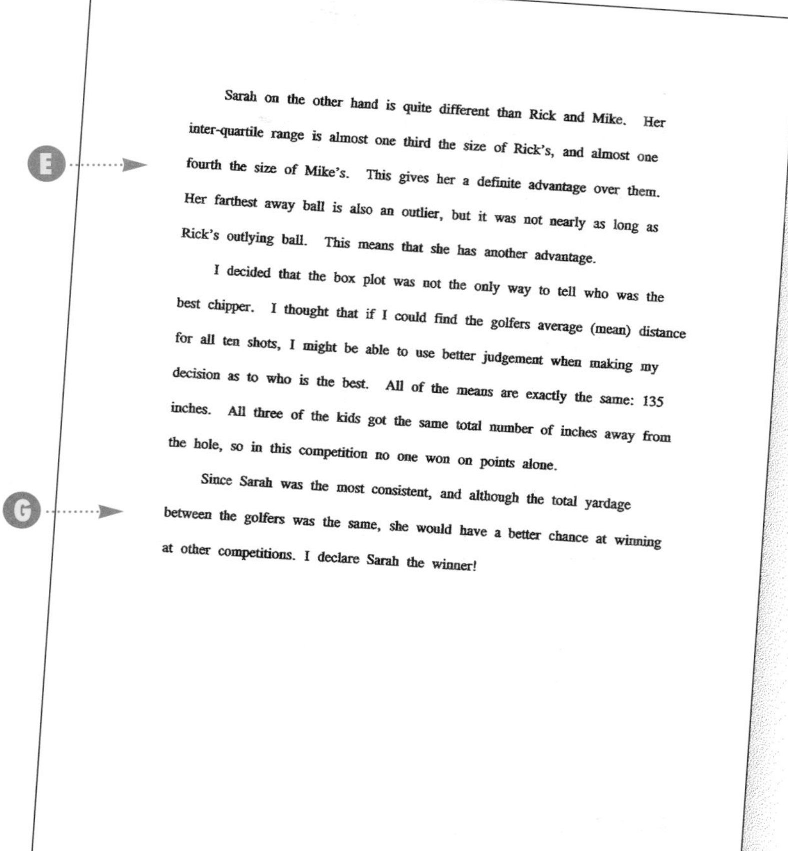

Sarah on the other hand is quite different than Rick and Mike. Her inter-quartile range is almost one third the size of Rick's, and almost one fourth the size of Mike's. This gives her a definite advantage over them. Her farthest away ball is also an outlier, but it was not nearly as long as Rick's outlying ball. This means that she has another advantage.

I decided that the box plot was not the only way to tell who was the best chipper. I thought that if I could find the golfers average (mean) distance for all ten shots, I might be able to use better judgement when making my decision as to who is the best. All of the means are exactly the same: 135 inches. All three of the kids got the same total number of inches away from the hole, so in this competition no one won on points alone.

Since Sarah was the most consistent, and although the total yardage between the golfers was the same, she would have a better chance at winning at other competitions. I declare Sarah the winner!

M4 d Statistics and Probability Concepts: The student makes conclusions…based on data analysis.

G The student justifiably declared Sarah the winner, particularly on grounds of consistency. A strong case could have been made for Rick, though. The median value of his chips is 30 inches less than that for Sarah. Furthermore, comparing their attempts in order from closest to farthest, each of Rick's best seven chips is closer than Sarah's corresponding chip. Their eighth best chips are equidistant, 152 inches away from the cup. Only Sarah's worst two chips are better than Rick's worst two.

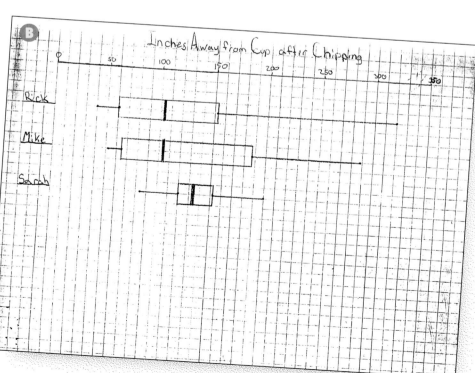

B

Inches Away from Cup after Chipping

0 50 100 150 200 250 300 350

Rick

Mike

Sarah

Work Sample & Commentary: *Probability Booth*

Mathematics performance descriptions in this commentary are excerpted. The complete performance descriptions are shown on pages 54-59.

The task

Students were given the following task:

The parent/teacher association is organizing the annual fundraising carnival. The eighth grade class will be allocated one booth in which to conduct a fundraising activity. About 500 people usually attend this event.

Your task is to design an activity that uses multiple probability events and that would attract lots of players. In your plan, please explain why you think your activity would be fun to play, how much you would charge to play, how much you would pay a winning contestant, and how much profit you would expect to make from your activity. A team of students and parents will select the proposal they think would be the most successful.

The task called for students to design an "unfair" game in which the organizers could be expected to make money. The game requires multiple probability events, which could be either independent or dependent events. The task includes a subjective criterion in requiring students to predict how many times the anticipated 500 attendees will play the game. Upon that assumption, students then needed to determine the expected pay-off of the proposed game of chance.

The task is clear in stating the information required if the student understands "multiple probability events," yet it also leaves much freedom for the student to develop the problem, both in concocting the game and in predicting how many players the game will draw.

This work sample illustrates a standard-setting performance for the following parts of the standards:

M4 h Statistics and Probability Concepts: Represent and determine probability, recognize equally likely outcomes, and construct sample spaces.

M4 i Statistics and Probability Concepts: Make predictions based on experimental or theoretical probabilities.

M4 j Statistics and Probability Concepts: Predict the result of a series of trials once the probability for one trial is known.

M5 a Problem Solving and Mathematical Reasoning: Formulation.

M7 b Mathematical Communication: Organize work, explain a solution orally and in writing, and use other techniques to make meaning clear to the audience.

M7 d Mathematical Communication: Exhibit developing reasoning abilities by justifying statements and defending work.

PROBABILITY BOOTH

My booth would have a coin and a pair of dice. To win you must correctly call "heads or tails" then roll an eleven or 12. I would charge $1 to play and give $10 to a winner. I feel this much of a payoff will attract many people. (C)

I think that about 200 people would play but they would play an average of two times making a total of 400 players.

The probability of winning is 1 in 24 because it's 1 in 2 (1/2) to win the coin toss and 1 in 12 (1/12) for the roll of the dice. The roll of the dice is 1 in 12 because out of the 36 possibilities in rolling the dice 3 of them will be 11 or 12. (A) This reduces

A good extension for this task would be to make conjectures about the numbers of game players when adjusting the values of either the prize money or the chances of winning. In this case, an optimization problem, based on the hypothesized numbers of players, manifests itself. The students' carnival choice could then be the one that would seem to yield maximum profit.

Circumstances of performance

This sample of student work was produced under the following conditions:

√ alone	in a group
√ in class	as homework
with teacher feedback	with peer feedback
√ timed	opportunity for revision

This is an unrevised draft of a timed assignment completed in 40 minutes.

Probability Booth

What the work shows

The work provides strong evidence for parts of M4. It provides evidence for determining probabilities of events, for example, the probabilities of coin tossing and dice throwing and of the multiple event created by combining the independent events into one game. The work shows the student computing the profit he can expect at the booth, based on his assumptions about how many people will play. The student works within the constraints of the task to formulate his game of chance and predict the profits to be made. Thus, his work provides evidence for part of M5. The solution is well-explained, providing evidence for M7.

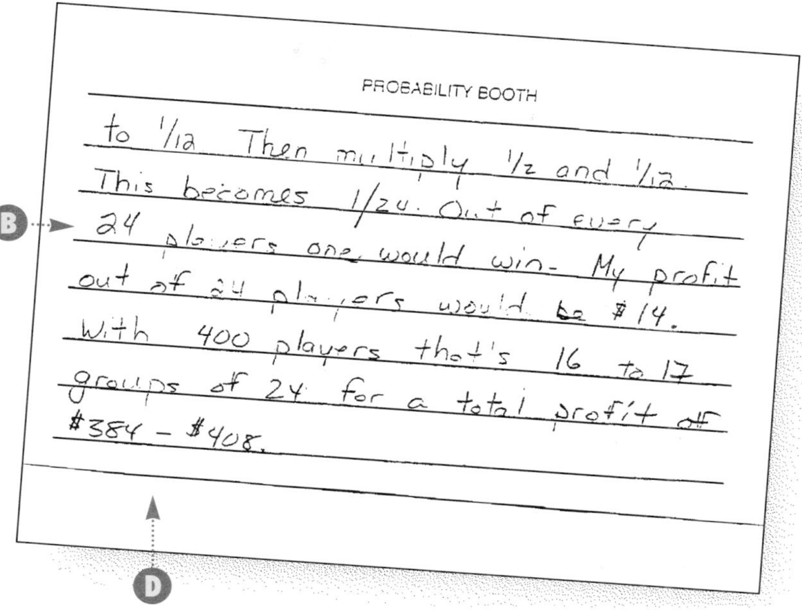

PROBABILITY BOOTH

to 1/12 Then multiply 1/2 and 1/12. This becomes 1/24. Out of every 24 players one would win. My profit out of 24 players would be $14. With 400 players that's 16 to 17 groups of 24 for a total profit of $384 – $408.

B

D

M4 h Statistics and Probability Concepts: The student represents and determines probability as a fraction of a set of equally likely outcomes; recognizes equally likely outcomes and constructs sample spaces....

A The student was careful to clarify and justify the claim that P[rolling 11 or 12] = 1/12, by alluding to the sample space of 36 equally likely outcomes when tossing two dice.

M4 i Statistics and Probability Concepts: The student makes predictions based on experimental or theoretical probabilities.

M4 j Statistics and Probability Concepts: The student predicts the result of a series of trials once the probability for one trial is known.

B The student displayed understanding of expected value, realizing that his 1/24 probability implied that he could expect one winner per 24 games played.

M5 a Problem Solving and Mathematical Reasoning: Formulation. The student formulates and solves a variety of meaningful problems....

C In the first two paragraphs, the student formulated the problem needing analysis by deciding on a game, a fee, and a prize, and by making a guess as to the number of people who will play. One could challenge the assumption of 400 game players. Would that many people really pay $1 for a chance to win $10 when the odds are so slim (1 in 24)?

D The student noted correctly that his expected profit is $14 for each group of 24 players. Since a total of 400 players contains between 16 and 17 groups of 24, his expected profit should be between 16 x $14 = $224 and 17 x $14 = $238, so the range $224 to $238 should replace the student's response of $384 to $408 (which are 16 x $24 and 17 x $24). This error does not detract from the evidence of understanding in the rest of the work.

M7 b Mathematical Communication: The student organizes work, explains facets of a solution orally and in writing, labels drawings, and uses other techniques to make meaning clear to the audience.

M7 d Mathematical Communication: The student exhibits developing reasoning abilities by justifying statements and defending work.

A The student was careful to clarify and justify the claim that P[rolling 11 or 12] = 1/12, by alluding to the sample space of 36 equally likely outcomes when tossing two dice.

Work Sample & Commentary: *Logic Puzzle*

Number and Operation Concepts M1
Geometry & Measurement Concepts
Function & Algebra Concepts
Statistics & Probability Concepts
Problem Solving & Mathematical Reasoning M5
Mathematical Skills & Tools
Mathematical Communication
Putting Mathematics to Work

Mathematics performance descriptions in this commentary are excerpted. The complete performance descriptions are shown on pages 54-59.

The task

Students were given the following assignment:

In the clues below, each variable represents a different digit 0-9. Determine the value of each variable.

g + g + g = d

j + e = j

$g^2 = d$

b + g = d

f - b = c

i / h = a (h > a)

a x c = a

Circumstances of performance

This sample of student work was produced under the following conditions:

√ alone	in a group
in class	√ as homework
with teacher feedback	with peer feedback
timed	opportunity for revision

What the work shows

The task is a logic puzzle. The work shows strength in mathematical reasoning. Strong knowledge of properties of numbers and operations is particularly evident.

April 22, 1996

Imagine for a minute that you're at the end of a good detective story. The crime has been solved, the criminals have been caught, and the detective whose incisive thinking solved the puzzle is being crowned as the hero of the day. Perhaps the detective is explaining how the mystery was solved. Most likely the sleuth used logic to solve the case. Logic is the process of using reason to solve a puzzle. From one clue, the detective deduces something, and from that deduction, deduces something more. Perhaps the sleuth induces as well. Anyway, without logic, the detective in the story would probably never have gone past step one.

Logic can be used to solve crimes and figure out the answers to other problems including math problems. One math problems easily solved by logic goes as follows:

In the clues below each variable represents a different digit 0-9. Determine the value of each variable.

g + g + g = d
j + e = j
$g^2 = d$
b + g = d
f - b = c
i / h = a (h > a)
a × c = a

Its solution is simple to reach if logical steps are followed.

(C) First, j + e = j. Since when e is added to j nothing happens, it can be deduced that e is 0. When 0 is added to another number, that number stays the same. Thus, e = 0.

(D) Second, a × c = a. The variable a does not change when it is multiplied by c. Here there are two possibilities. Either a = 0 as 0 times any number is still 0 or c = 1 as multiplying a number by 1 does not change the number. Because e is already 0 and each letter in the problem represents a different number, a cannot be 0. Therefore, c must be 1.

(A) Third, g^2 = d and g + g + g = d. By the transitive property of equality,

$g^2 = g + g + g$, or $g^2 = 3g$

divide each side by g

M1b Number and Operation Concepts: The student uses and understands the inverse relationships between addition and subtraction, multiplication and division...; uses the inverse operation to determine unknown quantities in equations.

(A) The student used transitivity and inverse operations to determine that g=3. A possible solution was inadvertently lost when the student decided to "divide each side by g," because division by zero is undefined. She should have been aware, though, that g=0 also satisfies g^2=3g. As in the second step, this possibility would have been dismissed because "e is already 0."

M1d Number and Operation Concepts: The student is familiar with characteristics of numbers...and with properties of operations....

(C) The student recognized the additive identity, 0.

(D) The student recognized the multiplicative identity, 1. She realized the effect of multiplication by zero. The latter was dismissed as a possibility because zero was used elsewhere.

This work sample illustrates a standard-setting performance for the following parts of the standards:

M1b Number and Operation Concepts: Use and understand the inverse relationships between multiplication and division, addition and subtraction.

M1d Number and Operation Concepts: Be familiar with characteristics of numbers and with properties of operations.

M5b Problem Solving and Mathematical Reasoning: Implementation.

M5c Problem Solving and Mathematical Reasoning: Conclusion.

M5d Problem Solving and Mathematical Reasoning: Mathematical reasoning.

Logic Puzzle

M5b Problem Solving and Mathematical Reasoning: Implementation. The student...
• invokes problem solving strategies...

E The student paused to review what she had done and what remained. Understanding and solving the remaining clues was easier after eliminating the digits already used once.
• solves for unknown or undecided quantities....

B F

M5c Problem Solving and Mathematical Reasoning: Conclusion. The student...verifies... results with respect to the original problem situation....

G

M5d Problem Solving and Mathematical Reasoning: Mathematical reasoning. The student...makes justified, logical statements.

D

H The "process of elimination" applies.

g = 3.

Then, by substitution,

3 + 3 + 3 = 9.

Thus, g = 3 and d = 9.

Fourth, b + g = d. If g is subtracted from both sides, the resulting equation is d - g = b. By substituting 9 for d and 3 for g, it becomes clear that b = 6.

Fifth, f - b = c. Add b to both sides, and one gets that c + b = f. Put 1 in for c and 6 in for b, and f is 7.

So far, the representations of six of the variables have been discovered. It is known that:

0 = e
1 = c
3 = g
6 = b
7 = f
9 = d

Only 2, 4, 5, and 8 and a, i, h, and j are left.

Sixth, i / h = a (h > a). One quick glance at the remaining numbers makes it clear that 2, 4, and 8 are going to be involved in this equation. They are powers of two. Since 5 is not a power of 2, it will not divide well with 2, 4, and 8.

Since h > a, h can't be 2 and a can't be 8. Neither 2 nor 4 yields a whole number when it is divided by 8. Thus, h must be 4. That i = 8 and a = 2 logically follows.

Seventh, the only remaining number is 5, and the only remaining variable is j. Thus, j = 5.

The list is now complete.

0 = e
1 = c
2 = a
3 = g
4 = h
5 = j
6 = b
7 = f
8 = i
9 = d

In order to be sure that all the variables are correct and no mistakes have been made, each number should be substituted for its variable in the original equations, and the math should be checked.

g + g + g = d
3 + 3 + 3 = 9 ✓

j + e = j
5 + 0 = 5 ✓

g^2 = d
3^2 = 9 ✓

b + g = d
6 + 3 = 9 ✓

f - b = c
7 - 6 = 1 ✓

i / h = a (h > a)
8 / 4 = 2 (4 > 2) ✓

a × c = a
2 × 1 = 2 ✓

Logic is a good skill to have. Good use of it can solve crimes, codes, other puzzles, and math problems such as the one presented above. Had trial and error been used to solve this problem instead of logic, finding the answer would have taken much longer than it did. Logic gets problems done well and quickly.

Work Sample & Commentary: *Scaling Project*

The quotations from the Mathematics performance descriptions in this commentary are excerpted. The complete performance descriptions are shown on pages 54-59.

The task

Students were given the following instructions:

Design and build a scale model enlarging or shrinking an everyday object using a ratio of 1:10 (or specify a different ratio) for each dimension. Describe the process you used to complete the model, the mathematics you used, the measurements of the original and the model including appropriate units, calculations of volume of the original and the scale model, and analyze the relationship between those calculations.

Circumstances of performance

This sample of student work was produced under the following conditions:

alone	√ in a group
in class	√ as homework
with teacher feedback	with peer feedback
timed	opportunity for revision

This work sample illustrates a standard-setting performance for the following parts of the standards:

M2 a Geometry and Measurement Concepts: Be familiar with two- and three-dimensional objects.

M2 d Geometry and Measurement Concepts: Determine and understand length, area, and volume.

M2 h Geometry and Measurement Concepts: Choose appropriate units of measure and convert with ease between like units.

M2 j Geometry and Measurement Concepts: Reason proportionally with measurements.

M6 d Mathematical Skills and Tools: Measure accurately.

M6 f Mathematical Skills and Tools: Use formulas appropriately.

M8 c Putting Mathematics to Work: Design a physical structure.

What the work shows

M2 a Geometry and Measurement Concepts: The student is familiar with assorted two- and three-dimensional objects....

M2 d Geometry and Measurement Concepts: The student determines and understands length, area, and volume (as well as the differences among these measurements)....

M2 h Geometry and Measurement Concepts: The student chooses appropriate units of measure and converts with ease between like units....

M2 j Geometry and Measurement Concepts: The student reasons proportionally with measurements...to make...larger scale drawings.

(A) The student appropriately used the 1:10 scale to increase each of the linear measurements. He converted to centimeters as appropriate, for instance, stating that two enlarged walls are 15 cm long instead of 150 mm long.

(B) (C) The student recognized that the half-centimeter thickness of the tagboard would be a factor in creating an accurate scale model, sixteen centimeters on each side. The two fifteen-centimeter walls each about two extra half centimeters where they touch the adjacent walls.

(D) The student recognized, correctly, that the volume of the enlargement is 10 x 10 x 10 = 1,000 times larger than the original. Some explanation is in order, though. Here, since the measurements of the original piece are stated, the smaller volume could have been computed and shown to be one-thousandth of the larger volume.

M6 d Mathematical Skills and Tools: The student measures length, area, [and] volume...accurately.

(D) (E)

M6 f Mathematical Skills and Tools: The student uses...formulas...appropriately.

(E) Standard formulas for volumes of rectangular prisms and of cylinders are applied accurately here. The student recognized that the volume of his creation is determined by adding the easily calculated volumes of the standard geometric shapes that are component parts.

There are two errors in the units of measure in the calculation of total volume. In the first line, "4 cm" should be "4 cm^2" since the 4 represents the square of the 2 cm radius. The student computed the volume of each of the four cylindrical "bumps" as V = [r^2 x π] x h. On the fifth line, "256 cc" should be "256 cm^2" since it is the area of the prism's square base computed from the previous line's "16 cm x 16 cm." The total volume determined is given with the correct units, cubic centimeters.

Scaling Project

M8 Putting Mathematics to Work: The student designs a physical structure, in which the student:

- generates a plan to build something....

C The paragraph describes the process of building the enlarged LEGO®. It also describes the design issues that arose in creating the components.

- uses mathematics from Standard 2 to make the design realistic or appropriate, e.g., areas and volumes in general and of specific geometric shapes.

E

- summarizes the important features of the structure....

C It would be helpful to the reader, and more appropriate mathematical communication, if the student had referred at least once to the "bumps" as "cylindrical bumps" or "cylinders." The student appears to have recognized them as such when using the formula for cylindrical volume in computing the total volume later in the piece. The student observed that these cylindrical bumps could be made from the same tagboard as the block by stacking four circular half-inch thick disks to make each two-inch tall cylinder.

- prepares a presentation or report that includes the question investigated, a detailed description of how the project was carried out, and an explanation of the findings.

C

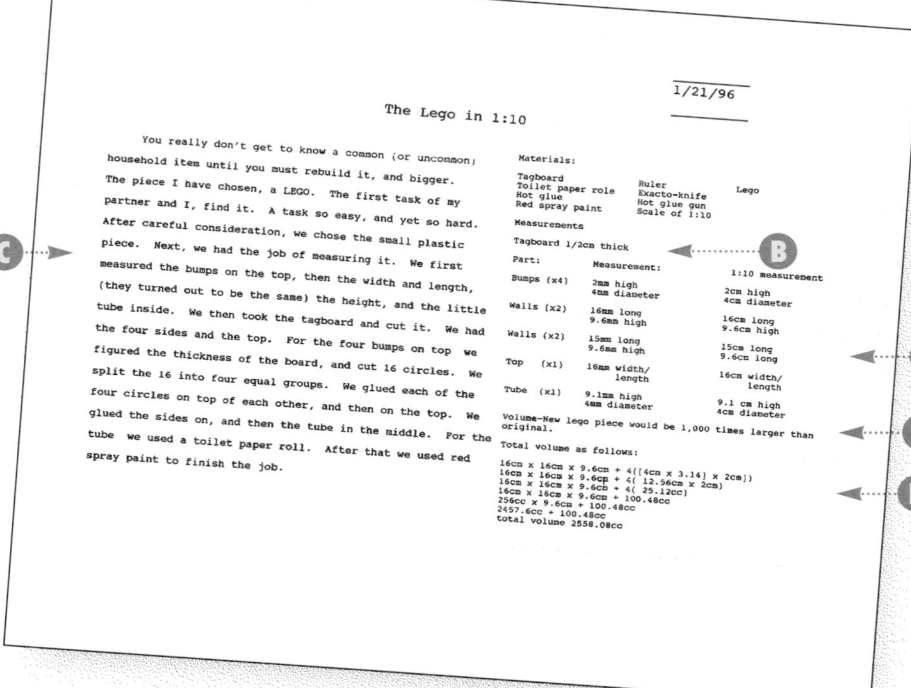

1/21/96

The Lego in 1:10

You really don't get to know a common (or uncommon) household item until you must rebuild it, and bigger. The piece I have chosen, a LEGO. The first task of my partner and I, find it. A task so easy, and yet so hard. After careful consideration, we chose the small plastic piece. Next, we had the job of measuring it. We first measured the bumps on the top, then the width and length, (they turned out to be the same) the height, and the little tube inside. We then took the tagboard and cut it. We had the four sides and the top. For the four bumps on top we figured the thickness of the board, and cut 16 circles. We split the 16 into four equal groups. We glued each of the four circles on top of each other, and then on the top. We glued the sides on, and then the tube in the middle. For the tube we used a toilet paper roll. After that we used red spray paint to finish the job.

Materials:

Tagboard
Toilet paper role
Hot glue
Red spray paint

Ruler
Exacto-knife
Hot glue gun
Scale of 1:10

Lego

Measurements

Tagboard 1/2cm thick

Part:	Measurement:	1:10 measurement
Bumps (x4)	2mm high 4mm diameter	2cm high 4cm diameter
Walls (x2)	16mm long 9.6mm high	16cm long 9.6cm high
Walls (x2)	15mm long 9.6mm high	15cm long 9.6cm long
Top (x1)	16mm width/ length	16cm width/ length
Tube (x1)	9.1mm high 4mm diameter	9.1 cm high 4cm diameter

Volume-New lego piece would be 1,000 times larger than original.

Total volume as follows:

16cm x 16cm x 9.6cm + 4([4cm x 3.14] x 2cm])
16cm x 16cm x 9.6cp + 4(12.56cm x 2cm)
16cm x 16cm x 9.6cb + 4(25.12cc)
16cm x 16cm x 9.6cm + 100.48cc
256cc x 9.6cm + 100.48cc
2457.6cc + 100.48cc
total volume 2558.08cc

Number and Operation Concepts
M2 Geometry & Measurement Concepts
Function & Algebra Concepts
Statistics & Probability Concepts
Problem Solving & Mathematical Reasoning
M6 Mathematical Skills & Tools
Mathematical Communication
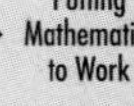
Putting Mathematics to Work

Work Sample & Commentary: *A New Look on a Budget*

The task

Students were given the following instructions:

Determine the cost of redecorating your room. You must carpet the room, paint two coats, and use wall-paper in some way. Draw to scale, on graph paper, each wall, including windows and doors.

This work sample illustrates a standard-setting performance for the following parts of the standards:

- **M1 a Number and Operation Concepts: Consistently and accurately multiply rational numbers.**
- **M1 c Number and Operation Concepts: Consistently and accurately apply and convert rational numbers.**
- **M1 e Number and Operation Concepts: Interpret percent as part of 100.**
- **M1 f Number and Operation Concepts: Reason proportionally to solve problems involving equivalent fractions.**
- **M2 d Geometry and Measurement Concepts: Determine and understand length and area.**
- **M2 h Geometry and Measurement Concepts: Choose appropriate units of measure and convert with ease between like units.**
- **M2 j Geometry and Measurement Concepts: Reason proportionally in situations with similar figures.**
- **M5 a Problem Solving and Mathematical Reasoning: Formulation.**
- **M5 b Problem Solving and Mathematical Reasoning: Implementation.**
- **M6 a Mathematical Skills and Tools: Compute accurately with arithmetic operations on rational numbers.**
- **M6 d Mathematical Skills and Tools: Measure accurately.**
- **M6 h Mathematical Skills and Tools: Use pencil and paper and measuring devices to achieve solutions.**
- **M7 a Mathematical Communication: Use mathematical language and representations with appropriate accuracy.**
- **M7 b Mathematical Communication: Organize work, explain a solution orally and in writing, and use other techniques to make meaning clear to the audience.**
- **M8 d Putting Mathematics to Work: Management and planning.**
- **E2 d Writing: Produce a narrative procedure.**
- **E4 a Conventions: Demonstrate an understanding of the rules of the English language.**

The quotations from the Mathematics performance descriptions in this commentary are excerpted. The complete performance descriptions are shown on pages 54-59.

A New Look On a Budget

Problem

Determine the cost of redecorating your room. You must carpet, paint 2 coats, and use wallpaper in some way. Draw to scale, on graph paper, each wall, including windows and doors.

Solution

After being in the same old, boring room for four years, it was time to redecorate. I had been annoying my mom about it for almost a year when she finally relented. She agreed to let me redecorate my room only under certain circumstances. She gave me a $700 budget, but I had to do all of the figuring (F) and calling. She also added that I could keep 50% of the remaining money, if there was any! After a few days of careful thought, I decided to take on this challenge.

I began my project by measuring each wall's dimensions carefully. I labeled the walls 1, 2, 3, and 4, so I could keep track of them. I measured the woodwork, doors, and windows separately because the woodwork and (H) doors would be a different color. I found the area of each wall by multiplying its length times height. I did the same for the woodwork, doors and windows. I kept all of this figuring in a notebook because my mind will not hold all of those numbers.

This planning project requires students to be skilled with one- and two-dimensional measurement and to compute quantities appropriately and accurately. Some formulation of the problem is necessary because students decide what information is needed when buying paint and when connecting that information to bedroom measurements. Students must also use proportional reasoning to make scale drawings of the redecorated space.

This project calls for skill with and understanding of two dimensional measurement as well as numbers and operations. It can also lend itself to consideration of volume or use of optimization, e.g., minimizing cost.

Work with three dimensional measurement could easily be included in or appended to this project. For example, because bedrooms normally include at least one bed, a dresser, and other items, volume and space considerations would arise.

Circumstances of performance

This sample of student work was produced under the following conditions:

√ alone	in a group
in class	√ as homework
with teacher feedback	with peer feedback
timed	opportunity for revision

A New Look on a Budget

This was an individual project completed primarily at home. Measuring instruments and calculators were allowed.

What the work shows

M1 a Number and Operation Concepts: The student consistently and accurately adds, subtracts, multiplies, and divides rational numbers using appropriate methods..., i.e., rationals written as decimals...or mixed fractions....

A The student realized that some computations would be redundant. That recognition spared her some calculation. The student also recognized that the opposite walls have equal sizes, thus avoiding some redundant computations. (This paragraph is an example of how work is often more wordy than it needs to be. A table would be a more effective means of communicating the areas of wall and of woodwork.)

B When rewriting areas as decimals instead of mixed fractions, some of the numbers (e.g., "241.86 square feet") are more precise than is necessary for this kind of project.

M1 c Number and Operation Concepts: The student consistently and accurately applies and converts the different kinds and forms of rational numbers.

B **C**

M1 e Number and Operation Concepts: The student interprets percent as part of 100 and as a means of comparing quantities of...changing sizes.

C

M1 f Number and Operation Concepts: The student...reasons proportionally to solve problems involving equivalent fractions [or] equal ratios....

D The computations are not shown. However, it is apparent that, even though each unit of the graph paper represents one half-foot, the student made conversions (e.g., 4 in. = ⅓ foot = ⅔ of one half-foot) so that she could mark off the inches (fractions of feet) with accuracy and according to scale.

M2 d Geometry and Measurement Concepts: The student determines and understands length, area...; uses units [and] square units...of measure correctly; computes areas of rectangles....

M2 h Geometry and Measurement Concepts: The student chooses appropriate units of measure and converts with ease between like units, e.g., inches and miles, within a customary or metric system.

E The conversions between square inches, square feet, and square yards are correct and significant. Many students would incorrectly use divisors of 12 and 3 instead of 12^2 and 3^2 when converting.

Here is the measuring method I used: Using a yardstick, I measured the walls in yards and inches. Then I converted the yards to inches and found the total inches. To convert yards to inches, I multiplied the number of yards times 36. Next I multiplied on my calculator the length and height in inches to find the square inches of each wall. I divided the area by 144 to find the **(E)** square feet. When necessary, I divided that by 9 to find the square yards. Because wall # 3 had a window, the area of the window was subtracted from the area of the wall. To find the area where I needed carpet, I multiplied the length of two walls that met at a 90 degree angle. I used the same process to find the area of the ceiling.

After doing what seemed like hours of figuring, I came up with my final figures. Wall #1 had 76 19/144 square feet of wall to be painted and 50 53/144 square feet of woodwork and doors to be painted. Wall #2 had 85 17/24 square feet of wall to be wallpapered and 5 1/24 square feet of woodwork to be painted. Wall #3 had 80 7/400 square feet of wall to be painted and 10 1/400 square feet of woodwork to be painted. Wall #4 had **(A)** the same amount of square feet as wall #2 because it is parallel to wall #2 and has no extra woodwork, doors, or windows. Wall #4's 85 17/24 square feet of wall would be painted instead of wallpapered.

(G) I went to ________________ to help me with the proper amount of paint and paper to purchase. They said that 1 gallon of paint for regular walls would cover 400 square feet and 1 quart would cover 100 square feet. They also quoted the price of $14.99 for 1 gallon of wall paint tinted to be Classic Aqua. For the ceiling, I decided to use a cheaper type of

---

M2 j Geometry and Number Concepts: The student reasons proportionally with measurements...to make...scale drawings.

D

M5 a Problem Solving and Mathematical Reasoning: Formulation. The student:

• formulates and solves...meaningful problems....

F The student planned to redecorate her room and created a realistic scenario with a constraint of $700 and the added "twist" of being able to keep 50% of the remainder, which impacts the decisions to be made in ways that the $700 upper limit could not. Formulating the problem of redecoration, imposing constraints not required by the task, and determining the information needed in order to proceed provide the evidence of **M5**.

• figures out what additional information is needed.

A New Look on a Budget

Reading
Writing E2
Speaking, Listening, and Viewing
Conventions, Grammar, and Usage of the English Language E4
Literature
Number and Operation Concepts M1
Geometry & Measurement Concepts M2
Function & Algebra Concepts
Statistics & Probability Concepts
Problem Solving & Mathematical Reasoning M5
Mathematical Skills & Tools M6
Mathematical Communication M7
Putting Mathematics to Work M8

M5 b Problem Solving and Mathematical Reasoning: Implementation. The student....

- invokes problem solving strategies, such as...organizing information....

H

- solves for unknown or undecided quantities using...sound reasoning....

I The decision to purchase one gallon and one quart of paint is conceived and explained well.

M6 a Mathematical Skills and Tools: The student computes accurately with arithmetic operations on rational numbers.

M6 d Mathematical Skills and Tools: The student measures length [and] area,...accurately.

M6 h Mathematical Skills and Tools: The student uses...pencil and paper, measuring devices,...[and] calculators,...to achieve solutions.

A B H

M7 a Mathematical Communication: The student uses mathematical language and representations with appropriate accuracy, including...diagrams.

M7 b Mathematical Communication: The student organizes work, explains facets of a solution orally and in writing,...[and] labels drawings...to make meaning clear to the audience.

D This diagram is very accurately drawn to scale and labeled well for clarity. (This is one of several scale drawings the student prepared.)

J This summary of costs in an organized array is clearer than additional prose would have been. Such a display would also have been appropriate at other points in this report. The summary explains the total cost of the renovation, and the subsequent diagrams show the configuration of the redecorated room.

M8 d Putting Mathematics to Work: The student conducts a management and planning project, in which the student:

- determines the needs of the event to be managed or planned, e.g., cost, supply, scheduling.

G

- notes any constraints that will affect the plan.

F

- determines a plan.

F

- uses concepts from any of Standards 1 to 4, depending on the nature of the project.

C E

- considers the possibility of a more efficient solution.

K

- prepares a presentation or report that includes the question investigated, a detailed description of how the project was carried out, and an explanation of the plan.

D J

E2 d Writing: The student produces a narrative procedure that:

- engages the reader by establishing a context, creating a persona, and otherwise developing reader interest;
- provides a guide to action for a relatively complicated procedure in order to anticipate a reader's needs; creates expectations through predictable structures, e.g., headings; and provides smooth transitions between steps;
- makes use of appropriate writing strategies such as creating a visual hierarchy and using white space and graphics as appropriate;
- includes relevant information;
- excludes extraneous information;
- anticipates problems, mistakes, and misunderstandings that might arise for the reader;
- provides a sense of closure to the writing.

The work engages the reader by establishing a context: redecorating a room on a budget.

F The established persona is maintained throughout the work.

The student anticipated the reader's needs and used predictable structures to fulfill those needs, such as headings ("Problem," "Solution"), a list of supplies needed, and a series of scale drawings of the room to be redecorated.

H The logical transitions for the procedure give the writing a narrative quality.

D J The proper use of several graphics helps to summarize the narrative.

The examples and explanations are clearly presented.

By writing clearly and concisely, the student ensured that the reader would be able to follow even the somewhat complicated explanations.

C The student closed the work appropriately, summarizing the narrative in a few brief sentences and filling in the last few pieces of information the reader might require.

A New Look on a Budget

white paint that only cost $8.99. I also selected a roll of Ocean Scene wallpaper for wall #2.

Before I could purchase the paint and wallpaper, I had to be sure how much to purchase. Under normal circumstances, the paint company would take the measurements and advise me how much to buy. My mom insisted

B that I do that figuring. The total amount of wall space to be painted was 241.86 square feet. The salesperson recommended two coats, which meant I actually had 483.72 square feet to paint. One gallon covers on an average 400 square feet and one quart covers 100 square feet. It was obvious that 1 gallon was not enough and 2 gallons was too much, so I purchased 1 gallon

I and 1 quart. This amount of paint should cover 500 square feet. The ceiling was 168.6 square feet and 1 gallon will be sufficient for two coats of paint. The wall to be papered was 85 17/24 square feet. One roll of wallpaper covers 56 square feet. Two rolls would be required, which is fine since the paper was only sold in double rolls. The wall paint cost was $14.99 for 1 gallon and $5.99 for 1 quart. The wallpaper cost $31.98

The next stop ______. I found this store advertised in the paper. The advertised price for paint tools was cheaper than 2 other hardware stores advertised in the same paper. These same items were much more expensive

K ______. The wood work and door surfaces to be painted were 70.45 square feet or 140.90 square feet allowing for the second coat of paint. I found I could not cover the surfaces with 1 quart and had to purchase 2 quarts. I bought 2 quarts of white woodwork paint for $11.98, a pan and paint roller kit for $5.49, and 2 paintbrushes for $4.90.

I ordered 19 square yards of Ivory Brilliant Saxony Carpet at ______ ______ for $16.99 a square yard. The salesperson reminded me about the closet that needed to be carpeted in the same color as the room. I had to go home, measure the closet, and then call him with the additional information. It was 1.46 square yards. Because the store sells in whole yards, not fractions, the final order was for 21 square yards of carpet, costing $356.79. This price included installation and padding

The total of all the purchases was $444.11. In Kentucky, tax is 6%. Six percent of $444.11 is $26.47. To calculate tax, I multiplied $444.11 times .06. When I added the tax, the grand total was $467.58. As stated earlier, my mom gave me a $700 budget. I was very pleased to find that I was $232.42

C below budget. I received 50% of that, or $116.21. I used that to go on a class trip.

J

Supplies	Cost
1 gallon of Classic Aqua Paint	14.99
1 quart of Classic Aqua Paint	5.99
2 qt of white woodwork paint	11.98
1 double roll of Ocean Scene wallpaper	31.98
1 gallon of regular white paint	8.99
Pan & paint roller kit	5.49
2 paintbrushes	4.90
21 yd. of Ivory Brilliant Saxony Carpet	356.79
TOTAL	$444.11
TAX	$26.47
GRAND TOTAL	$467.58

D

Wall #1

15ft, 4in.

3ft, 2in.

4ft, 8in.

8ft, 3in

6ft, 2in.

Door

6ft, 2in.

Doors

5½ in.

Woodwork

= 1 square foot

E4a Conventions, Grammar, and Usage of the English Language: The student demonstrates an understanding of the rules of the English language in written and oral work, and selects the structures and features of language appropriate to the purpose, audience, and context of the work. The student demonstrates control of:

- grammar;
- paragraph structure;
- punctuation;
- sentence construction;
- spelling;
- usage.

The student managed the conventions, grammar, and usage of English so that they aid rather than interfere with reading. In this case, management of conventions includes consistency in the use of numbers.

Work Sample & Commentary: *Candle Life*

The quotations from the Mathematics performance descriptions in this commentary are excerpted. The complete performance descriptions are shown on pages 54-59.

The task

Students were given worksheets from *Algebra Experiments, Book 1: Exploring Linear Functions*. The worksheets guide students through an experiment with analysis to determine the relationship between the volume of a container and the length of time a candle will burn when covered by it. Students must gather, record, and graph data in the coordinate plane, determine an equation and characteristics of a line, and use the equation of the line to determine one coordinate of a point on the line given the other coordinate. The questions, while they lead the student through the mathematics, are informative and instructional.

Circumstances of performance

This sample of student work was produced under the following conditions:

√ alone	in a group
in class	√ as homework
with teacher feedback	with peer feedback
timed	opportunity for revision

"Candle Life"

In my eighth grade algebra class, I performed an experiment to see if the time it took for a candle to extinguish was a function of how much air was in the glass container covering it. I gathered up twelve different containers of various sizes, a one-half inch food-warming candle, and a stopwatch. I lit the candle, placed the first container over it, and at the same time, started the stopwatch. At the moment the candle went out and I saw smoke, I stopped timing. I then repeated this procedure with the other eleven containers. Two more trials were done for each container. To measure the amount of air in each container, I filled them up with water and then poured it into a measuring cup marked in milliliters.

The data was graphed on a coordinate plane using the independent variable, x, as the size of the container used, and the dependent variable, y, as the time it took the candle to go out. The points I graphed formed a linear pattern. I drew a "line of best fit" and identified 2 points off of it. Using these points, I found the slope, y-intercept, and an equation for the line. The slope was 8/250, the y-intercept was 2, and the equation representing my data was y= 8/250x+2. This equation is a linear equation. The experiment showed that the time it took the candle to extinguish is a function of the volume of air surrounding it in an enclosed space.

D ▸ The slope of my line, 8/250, means that for every 250 milliliters, it will take 8 seconds for the candle to extinguish. The y-intercept, 2, means that 2 seconds will be added for each trial.

From my "line of best fit" and the equation I formed from 2 points on it, I can predict the time it would take the candle to extinguish for any amount of air in a container.

This work sample illustrates a standard-setting performance for the following parts of the standards:

- **M3 b Function and Algebra Concepts: Represent relationships.**
- **M3 d Function and Algebra Concepts: Find solutions for unknown quantities in linear equations.**
- **M4 a Statistics and Probability Concepts: Collect, organize, and display data.**
- **M6 a Mathematical Skills and Tools: Compute accurately with arithmetic operations on rational numbers.**
- **M6 c Mathematical Skills and Tools: Estimate numerically.**
- **M6 f Mathematical Skills and Tools: Use equations, formulas, and simple algebraic notation appropriately.**
- **M6 g Mathematical Skills and Tools: Read and organize data on charts and graphs.**

What the work shows

M3 b Function and Algebra Concepts: The student represents relationships with...verbal or symbolic rules.

A B The determination of slope and y-intercept provides strong evidence that the student can manipulate algebraic expressions and equations of lines.

M3 d Function and Algebra Concepts: The student finds solutions for unknown quantities in linear equations....

C

D This is a good interpretation of the slope of the line. The meaning ascribed to the y-intercept suffices only if detached from the scientific context of this task. The intercept is small (near zero), but it would be reasonable to expect the line to pass through the origin (0,0)—no volume, no time!

E The task's use of the phrase "best fit" is undefined here. Presumably, this phrase means "best fit to the naked eye," which is appropriate enough detail of this linear regression idea for middle school students. The student did not use two data points, as instructed, but the approach was sensible.

Candle Life

M4 a Statistics and Probability Concepts: The student collects data, organizes data, and displays data with tables…and graphs that are appropriate….

F G

M6 a Mathematical Skills and Tools: The student computes accurately with arithmetic operations on rational numbers.

A B C

M6 c Mathematical Skills and Tools: The student estimates numerically….

F After collecting data over three trials for each container, the student determined the "time to extinguish [the] candle" by choosing the intermediate value from each set of three trials. She did not compute an exact average, as encouraged by the task. Instead she opted to approximate the time needed to extinguish the candle by choosing an integer between, and often close to, two of the three trial values. She did this for each container, with one curious exception. This method of choosing intermediate values for this specific task is as appropriate as the ones offered in the instructions.

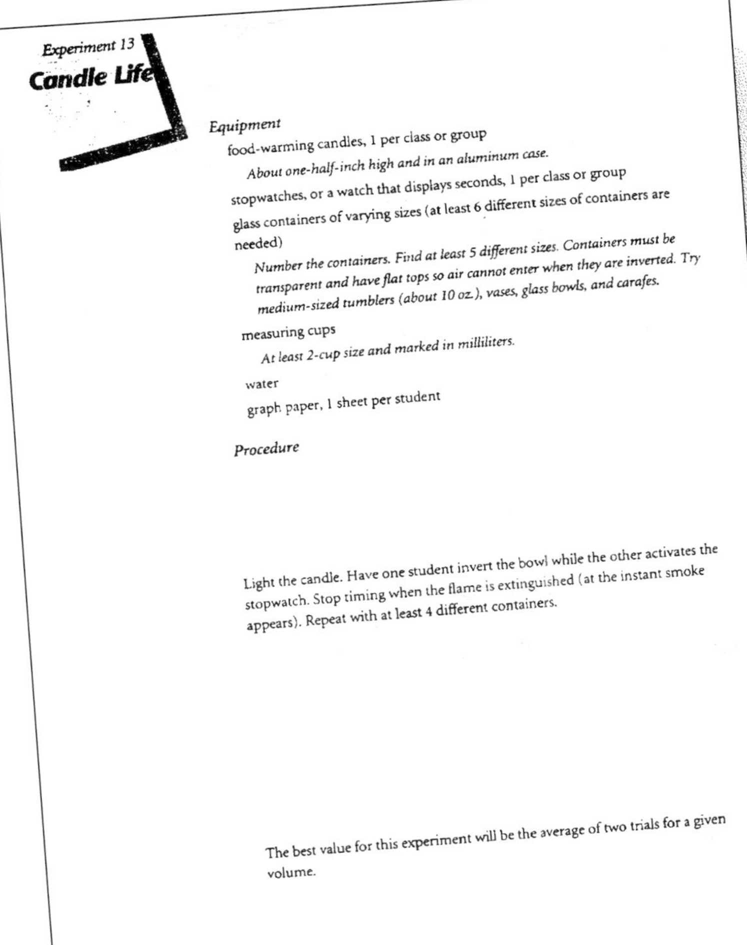

Experiment 13

Candle Life

Equipment

food-warming candles, 1 per class or group

About one-half-inch high and in an aluminum case.

stopwatches, or a watch that displays seconds, 1 per class or group

glass containers of varying sizes (at least 6 different sizes of containers are needed)

Number the containers. Find at least 5 different sizes. Containers must be transparent and have flat tops so air cannot enter when they are inverted. Try medium-sized tumblers (about 10 oz.), vases, glass bowls, and carafes.

measuring cups

At least 2-cup size and marked in milliliters.

water

graph paper, 1 sheet per student

Procedure

Light the candle. Have one student invert the bowl while the other activates the stopwatch. Stop timing when the flame is extinguished (at the instant smoke appears). Repeat with at least 4 different containers.

The best value for this experiment will be the average of two trials for a given volume.

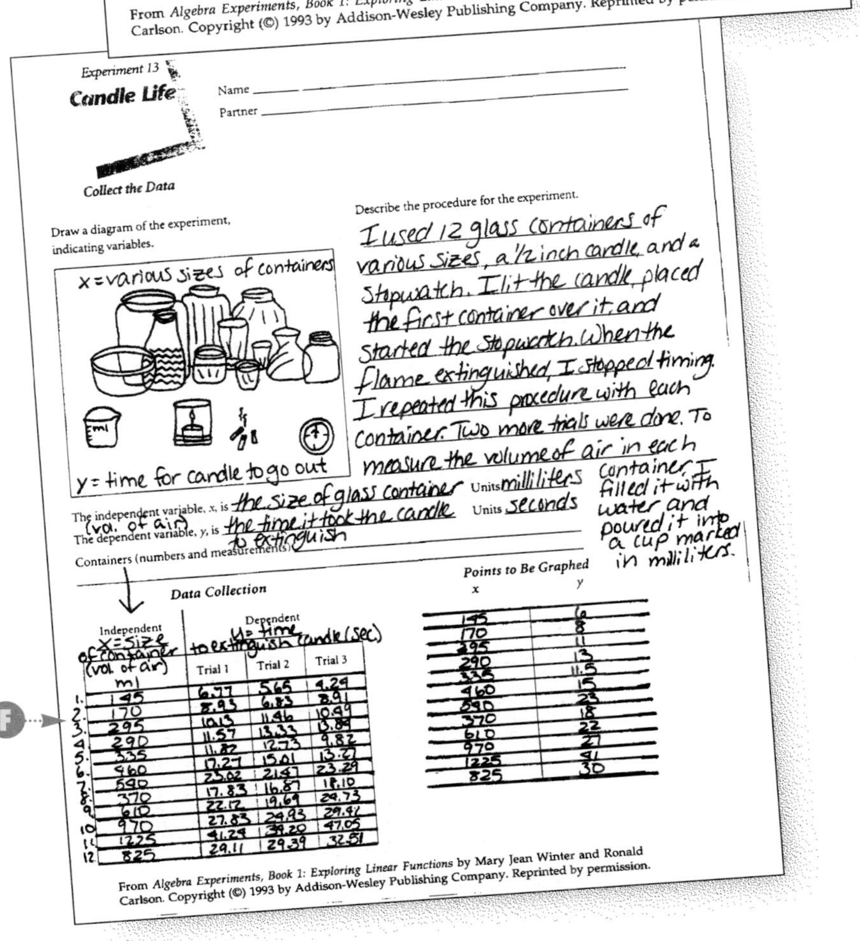

Experiment 13

Candle Life

Name ______

Partner ______

Collect the Data

Draw a diagram of the experiment, indicating variables.

Describe the procedure for the experiment.

I used 12 glass containers of various sizes, a ½ inch candle and a stopwatch. I lit the candle, placed the first container over it, and started the stopwatch. When the flame extinguished, I stopped timing. I repeated this procedure with each container. Two more trials were done. To measure the volume of air in each container, I filled it with water and poured it into a cup marked in milliliters.

The independent variable, *x*, is the size of glass container (vol. of air) Units milliliters

The dependent variable, *y*, is the time it took the candle to extinguish Units seconds

Containers (numbers and measurements)

Data Collection

	Independent x = size of container (vol. of air) ml	Dependent y = time to extinguish candle (sec) Trial 1	Trial 2	Trial 3
1.	145	6.77	5.65	4.29
2.	170	8.93	6.83	8.91
3.	295	10.13	11.46	10.99
4.	290	11.57	13.33	13.84
5.	335	11.82	12.73	9.82
6.	460	17.27	15.01	13.27
7.	590	25.02	21.47	23.29
8.	370	17.83	16.87	18.10
9.	610	22.12	19.69	24.73
10.	970	27.83	24.93	29.42
11.	1225	41.29	39.20	47.05
12.	825	29.11	29.39	32.51

Points to Be Graphed

x	y
145	6
170	8
295	11
290	13
335	11.5
460	15
590	23
370	18
610	22
970	27
1225	41
825	30

Candle Life

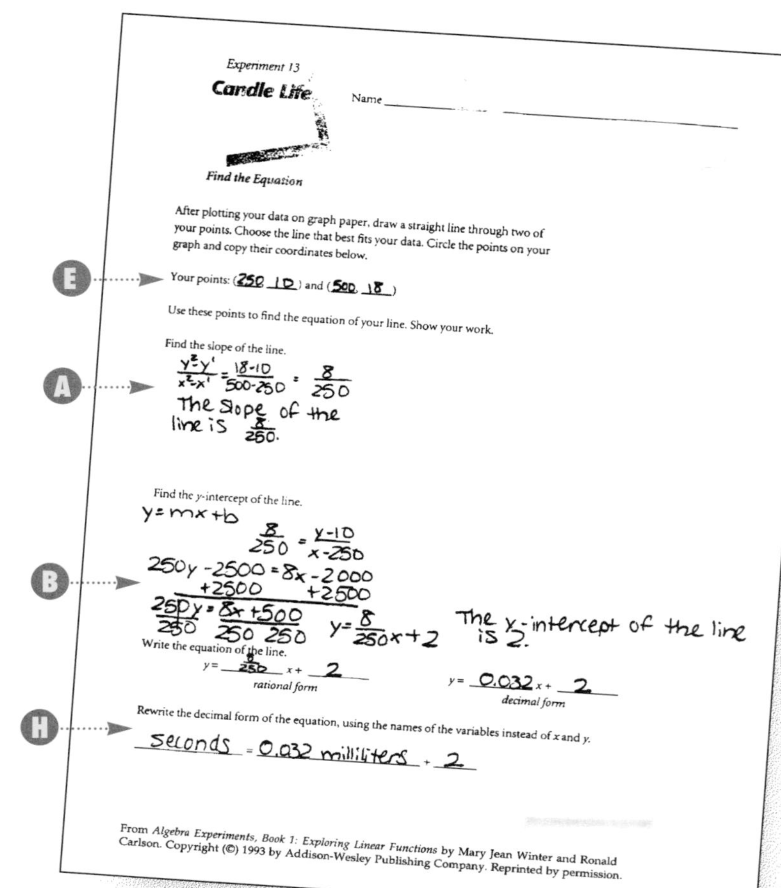

Experiment 13

Candle Life Name ________

Find the Equation

After plotting your data on graph paper, draw a straight line through two of your points. Choose the line that best fits your data. Circle the points on your graph and copy their coordinates below.

E ▸ Your points: (250, 10) and (500, 18)

Use these points to find the equation of your line. Show your work.

Find the slope of the line.

A ▸ $\frac{y^2 - y^1}{x^2 - x^1} = \frac{18-10}{500-250} = \frac{8}{250}$ The slope of the line is $\frac{8}{250}$.

Find the y-intercept of the line.

$y = mx + b$

$\frac{8}{250} = \frac{y-10}{x-250}$

B ▸ $250y - 2500 = 8x - 2000$

$+2500 \quad +2500$

$\frac{250y}{250} = \frac{8x + 500}{250 \quad 250}$ $y = \frac{8}{250}x + 2$ The y-intercept of the line is 2.

Write the equation of the line.

$y = \frac{8}{250}x + 2$ (rational form) $y = 0.032x + 2$ (decimal form)

Rewrite the decimal form of the equation, using the names of the variables instead of x and y.

H ▸ seconds = 0.032 milliliters + 2

From *Algebra Experiments, Book 1: Exploring Linear Functions* by Mary Jean Winter and Ronald Carlson. Copyright (©) 1993 by Addison-Wesley Publishing Company. Reprinted by permission.

Experiment 13

Candle Life Name ________

Interpret the Data

Write the decimal form of your equation here. $y = 0.032x + 2$

Use this equation to answer the questions. Show your work.

1. How long would the candle burn if you covered it with a 40-ml container? 3.28 sec.
   $y = 0.032(40) + 2$
   $y = 1.28 + 2$
   $y = 3.28$
2. Sandra's candle lasted 435 seconds. What size container had she used? 13531.25ml
   C ▸ $435 = 0.032x + 2$
   $-2 \quad -2$
   $\frac{433}{0.032} = \frac{0.032x}{0.032}$
3. Tom's candle lasted 213 seconds. What size container had he used? 6593.75ml
   $213 = 0.032x + 2$
   $-2 \quad -2$
   $\frac{211}{0.032} = \frac{0.032x}{0.032}$
4. Suppose a room measures 3 meters by 4 meters by 2.5 meters. What is the volume of the room in cubic centimeters? 30,000,000 cm³
   How long would a candle last in this room? 960002 sec.
   I ▸ $y = 0.032(30{,}000{,}000) + 2$
   $y = 960000 + 2$
   $y = 960002$
5. What conditions could produce a steeper line than yours?
   J ▸ A smaller volume resulting in a longer time

From *Algebra Experiments, Book 1: Exploring Linear Functions* by Mary Jean Winter and Ronald Carlson. Copyright (©) 1993 by Addison-Wesley Publishing Company. Reprinted by permission.

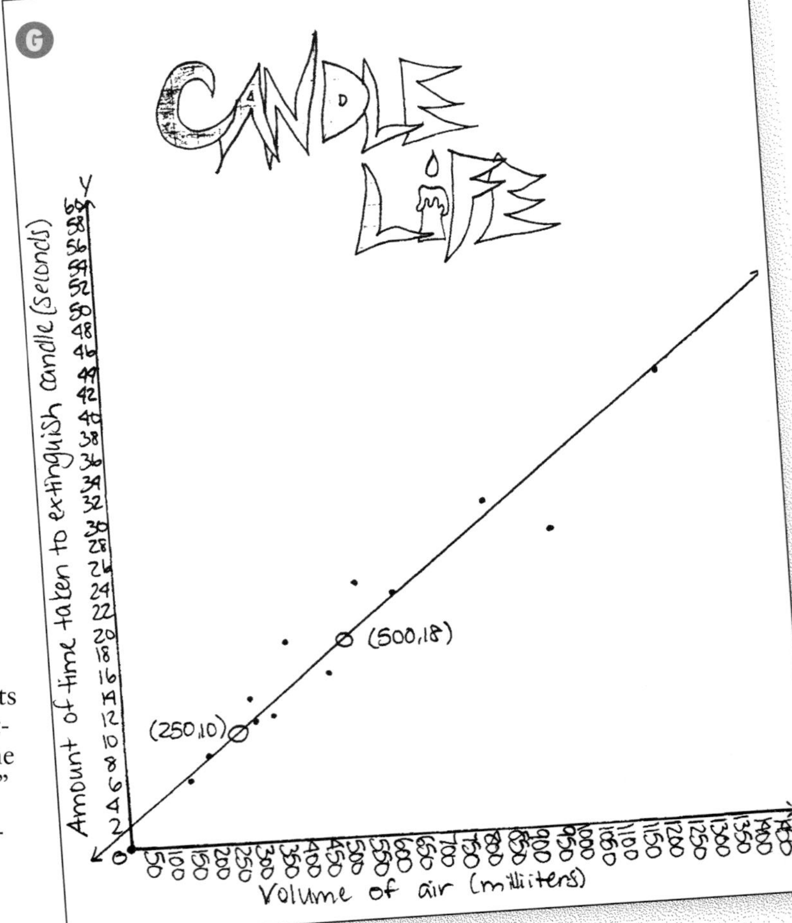

M6f Mathematical Skills and Tools: The student uses equations, formulas, and simple algebraic notation appropriately.

A B C

M6g Mathematical Skills and Tools: The student reads and organizes data on charts and graphs, including scatter plots,...[and] line... graphs....

G

H In the data collection table, the student correctly assigned names and units of measurement to her independent and dependent variables. Here, she incorrectly used only units of measurement. A corrected entry would read something like this:
"time (in sec.) = 0.032 · size (in ml) + 2."
Because the air is at room temperature and standard pressure, measuring the air in ml is equivalent to measuring in cm³.

I The 960,002 seconds are not appropriate units for this question. The student should have converted this length of time into units that would give the answer more meaning, e.g., "a little over 11 days."

J The trouble with this claim is that smaller volumes will not result in longer times. The data already suggest specific extinguishment times for candles in covered spaces of small and large volumes.

Number and Operation Concepts
Geometry & Measurement Concepts
Function & Algebra Concepts M3
Statistics & Probability Concepts M4
Problem Solving & Mathematical Reasoning
Mathematical Skills & Tools M6
Mathematical Communication
Putting Mathematics to Work

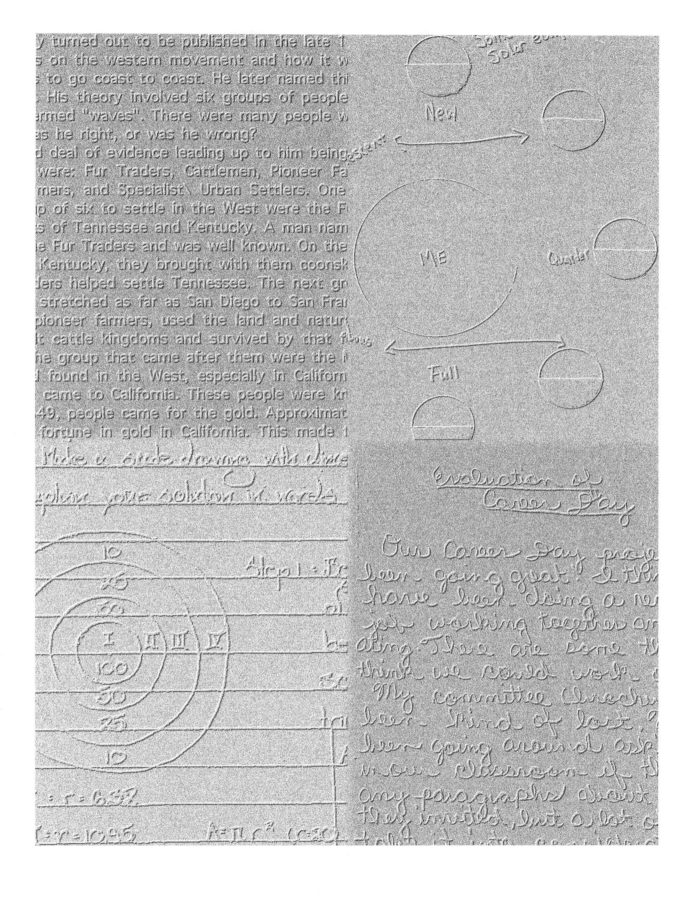

y turned out to be published in the late 1
s on the western movement and how it w
to go coast to coast. He later named thi
. His theory involved six groups of people
ermed "waves". There were many people w
as he right, or was he wrong?
d deal of evidence leading up to him being
were: Fur Traders, Cattlemen, Pioneer Fa
mers, and Specialist\ Urban Settlers. One
p of six to settle in the West were the F
s of Tennessee and Kentucky. A man nam
e Fur Traders and was well known. On the
Kentucky, they brought with them coonsk
ders helped settle Tennessee. The next gr
stretched as far as San Diego to San Fra
pioneer farmers, used the land and natur
lt cattle kingdoms and survived by that
ne group that came after them were the
d found in the West, especially in Californ
came to California. These people were kn
49, people came for the gold. Approximat
fortune in gold in California. This made t
New
ME
Quarter
Full
Evaluation of Career Day

Introduction to the performance standards for *Science*

There are two widely used and respected national documents in science which we have taken into account: the National Research Council (NRC) *National Science Education Standards* (1996) and the American Association for the Advancement of Science (AAAS) Project 2061 *Benchmarks for Science Literacy* (1993). We found the AAAS analysis of the Benchmarks and the NRC Draft to be helpful in seeing the substantial degree of agreement between the two documents. We also consulted New Standards partner statements about standards and international documents, including the work of the Third International Mathematics and Science Study and the Organisation for Economic Co-operation and Development. Many of these sources, like the *Benchmarks*, give greater emphasis to technology and the applications of science than does the NRC.

The framework for the Science performance standards reflects New Standards partner representatives' distillation of these several sources of guidance:

- **S1 Physical Sciences Concepts;**
- **S2 Life Sciences Concepts;**
- **S3 Earth and Space Sciences Concepts;**
- **S4 Scientific Connections and Applications;**
- **S5 Scientific Thinking;**
- **S6 Scientific Tools and Technologies;**
- **S7 Scientific Communication;**
- **S8 Scientific Investigation.**

As the amount of scientific knowledge explodes, the need for students to have deep understanding of fundamental concepts and ideas upon which to build increases; as technology makes information readily available, the need to memorize vocabulary and formulas decreases. There is general agreement among the science education community, in principle, that studying fewer things more deeply is the direction we would like to go. The choices about what to leave out and what to keep are hotly debated. There are 855 benchmarks and the content standards section of the NRC standards runs nearly 200 pages, so there are still choices to be made in crafting a reasonable set of performance standards.

When the goal is deep understanding, it is necessary to revisit concepts over time. Students show progressively deeper understanding as they use the concept in a range of familiar situations to explain observations and make predictions, then in unfamiliar situations; as they represent the concept in multiple ways (through words, diagrams, graphs, or charts), and explain the concept to another person. The conceptual understanding standards make explicit that students should be able to demonstrate understanding of a scientific concept "by using a concept accurately to explain observations and make predictions and by representing the concept in multiple ways (through words, diagrams, graphs, or charts, as appropriate)." Both aspects of understanding—explaining and representing—are required to meet these standards.

For most people and most concepts, there is a progression from phenomenological to empirical to theoretical, or from a qualitative to a quantitative understanding. We have chosen one important concept, density, to illustrate the progression. To do this we use "Flinkers" at the elementary school level (see Volume 1, page 136), "Discovering Density" at the middle school level (see page 101), and "The Density of Sand" at the high school level (see Volume 3, page 86). The expectation for any particular concept at any particular level can only be described with a satisfactory degree of precision and accuracy in the degree of detail adopted by AAAS and NRC; we strongly urge users of these performance standards to consult either or both of those documents for guidance on other concepts.

Complementing the conceptual understanding standards, S5-S8 focus on areas of the science curriculum that need particular attention and a new or renewed emphasis:

- **S5 Scientific Thinking;**
- **S6 Scientific Tools and Technologies;**
- **S7 Scientific Communication;**
- **S8 Scientific Investigation.**

Establishing separate standards for these areas is a mechanism for highlighting the importance of these areas, but does not imply that they are independent of conceptual understanding. The NRC standards, by declaring that inquiry is not only a teaching method but also an object of study, should put the time-worn "content versus process" debate to rest, and focus effort on combining traditionally defined content with process. As the work samples that follow illustrate, good work usually provides evidence of both.

Resources

Reviewers of drafts of these performance standards have pointed out that our expectations are more demanding, both in terms of student time and access to resources, than they consider reasonable for all students. We acknowledge the distance between our goals and the status quo, and the fact that there is a tremendous disparity in opportunities between the most and least advantaged students. We think that there are at least two strategies that must be pursued to achieve our goals—making better use of existing, out-of-school resources and making explicit the connection between particular resources and particular standards.

Best practice in science has always included extensive inquiry and investigation, but it is frequently given less emphasis in the face of competing demands for student time and teacher resources. An elementary teacher faced with the unfamiliar territory of project work in science or a secondary teacher faced with the prospect of guiding 180 projects and investigations can legitimately throw up his or her hands and cry, "Help!" Youth and community-based organizations, such as the Boy Scouts of America, Girl Scouts of the U.S.A., and 4-H, have science education on their agenda. Thus, we have incorporated examples of projects and investigations that are done outside of school to make clear that help is available.

We acknowledge that some of the performance descriptions and examples presuppose resources that are not currently available to all students, even those who take advantage of the out-of-school opportunities available to them. Yet, New Standards partners have adopted a Social Compact, which says, in part, "Specifically, we pledge to do everything in our power to ensure all students a fair shot at reaching the new performance standards...This means that they will be taught a curriculum that will prepare them for the assessments, that their teachers will have the preparation to enable them to teach it well, and there will be an equitable distribution of the resources the students and their teachers need to succeed."

All of the district, state, and national documents in science make explicit the need for students to have hands-on experience and to use information tools. Thus, for example, S6, Scientific Tools and Technologies, makes explicit reference to using telecommunications to acquire and share information. A recent National Center for Education Statistics survey recently reported that only 50% of schools and fewer than 9% of instructional rooms currently have access to the Internet. We know that this is an equity issue—that far more than 9% of the homes in the United States have access to the Internet and that schools must make sure that students' access to information and ideas does not depend on what they get at home—so we have crafted performance standards that would use the Internet so that people will make sure that all students have access to it. Since the New Standards partners have made a commitment to create the learning environments where students can develop the knowledge and skills that are delineated here, we hope that making these requirements explicit will help those who allocate resources to understand the consequences of their actions in terms of student performance.

Performance Descriptions *Science*

S1 Physical Sciences Concepts

The student demonstrates conceptual understanding by using a concept accurately to explain observations and make predictions and by representing the concept in multiple ways (through words, diagrams, graphs or charts, as appropriate). Both aspects of understanding—explaining and representing—are required to meet this standard.

The student produces evidence that demonstrates understanding of:

S1a Properties and changes of properties in matter, such as density and boiling point; chemical reactivity; and conservation of matter.

S1b Motions and forces, such as inertia and the net effects of balanced and unbalanced forces.

S1c Transfer of energy, such as transformation of energy as heat; light, mechanical motion, and sound; and the nature of a chemical reaction.

Examples of activities through which students might demonstrate conceptual understanding of physical sciences include:

- Use the concept of density to explain why some things float and others sink in water. **1a**
- Investigate the characteristics that are necessary to obtain an electric current from an electrochemical cell of metal(s) and a fluid medium. **1a**
- Explain the difference between recycling and reusing in terms of mass and energy conservation. **1a, 1c, 3a, 4b**
- Use the concept of force to explain the roles of front and rear brakes on a bicycle. **1b, 4d**
- Build a grandfather clock and explain how it works. **1b, 4d, 8c, A1a**
- Conduct an energy audit of the classroom and develop procedures for reducing waste. **1c, 4a, 4b, A1b**
- Evaluate the claims and potential benefits of sunglasses that are advertised to screen out ultraviolet light. **1c, 4a, 4b, 4c**

To see how these performance descriptions compare with the expectations for elementary school and high school, turn to pages 158-165.

The Science standards are founded upon both the National Research Council's *National Science Education Standards* and the American Association for the Advancement of Science's Project 2061 *Benchmarks for Science Literacy*. These documents, each of which runs to several hundred pages, contain detail that amplifies the meaning of the terms used in the performance descriptions.

S2 Life Sciences Concepts

The student demonstrates conceptual understanding by using a concept accurately to explain observations and make predictions and by representing the concept in multiple ways (through words, diagrams, graphs or charts, as appropriate). Both aspects of understanding—explaining and representing—are required to meet this standard.

The student produces evidence that demonstrates understanding of:

S2a Structure and function in living systems, such as the complementary nature of structure and function in cells, organs, tissues, organ systems, whole organisms, and ecosystems.

S2b Reproduction and heredity, such as sexual and asexual reproduction; and the role of genes and environment on trait expression.

S2c Regulation and behavior, such as senses and behavior; and response to environmental stimuli.

S2d Populations and ecosystems, such as the roles of producers, consumers, and decomposers in a food web; and the effects of resources and energy transfer on populations.

S2e Evolution, diversity, and adaptation of organisms, such as common ancestry, speciation, adaptation, variation, and extinction.

Examples of activities through which students might demonstrate conceptual understanding of life sciences include:

- Explain the effects of a particular disease (e.g., common cold) on an organism's internal structures and their related functions. **2a, 4a, 4c**
- Use drawings to demonstrate the structure and function relationships among a group of cells, tissues, or organs. **2a, 2c**
- Predict how long a plant will live planted in a closed glass jar located by a window; and explain what additional information regarding the plant and the surrounding environment would be needed to improve the prediction. **2a, 1a, 3a, 3b**
- Write a story about how a person learned to overcome an inherited physical limitation. **2b, 4b**
- Explain why offspring of organisms that reproduce sexually never look exactly like their parents. **2b, 2e**
- Earn the Bird Study Merit Badge (Boy Scouts of America) or complete the Plant Culture Project (Girl Scouts of the U.S.A.) and explain how it helped you to understand animal behavior, ecology, or regulation. **2c, 2d, 2e, 4a**
- Explain the physiology of sneezes, tears, or what happens when people laugh. **2c**
- Identify a pest in the immediate environment; and use an understanding of food webs to propose and test a way to eliminate the pest without introducing environmental poisons. **2d, 2e, 1c, 4b, 4c, 4d, 4e**
- Conduct an investigation to determine the kinds of seeds best suited to germination in a hydroponic system. **2a, 2d, 2e, 4b, 8a**
- Explain the lines of evidence showing that dogs and cats are related by common ancestors. **2b, 2c, 4a, 5c**
- Compare and contrast historical situations where species became extinct with situations where species survived due to differences in adaptive characteristics and the degree of environmental stress or change. **2b, 2c, 2d, 2e, 4a**

S3 Earth and Space Sciences Concepts

The student demonstrates conceptual understanding by using a concept accurately to explain observations and make predictions and by representing the concept in multiple ways (through words, diagrams, graphs or charts, as appropriate). Both aspects of understanding—explaining and representing—are required to meet this standard.

The student produces evidence that demonstrates understanding of:

S3a Structure of the Earth system, such as crustal plates and land forms; water and rock cycles; oceans, weather, and climate.

S3b Earth's history, such as Earth processes including erosion and movement of plates; change over time and fossil evidence.

S3c Earth in the Solar System, such as the predictable motion of planets, moons, and other objects in the Solar System including days, years, moon phases, and eclipses; and the role of the Sun as the major source of energy for phenomena on the Earth's surface.

S3d Natural resource management.

Examples of activities through which students might demonstrate conceptual understanding of Earth and space sciences include:

- Explain how earthquakes, volcanoes, and sea-floor spreading have a common cause. **3a, 3b, 4a, 4c**
- Write a story that describes what happens to a drop of water and the physical environment through which it flows as it travels from a lake to a river via the Earth's atmosphere. **3a, 3c, 1a, 4a**
- Complete the Geology Project (Girl Scouts of the U.S.A.) or earn the Astronomy Merit Badge (Boy Scouts of America) and explain what it helped you to understand about Earth processes and structures; fossil evidence; or aspects of the Solar System. **3a, 3b, 3c**
- Create a storybook to explain to a younger child how occasional catastrophes, such as the impact of an asteroid or comet, can influence the Earth's history. **3b, 3c, 2b, 2c, 2d, 2e**
- Predict what will happen to the reading of your weight on a bathroom scale while riding in an elevator, investigate your predication, and explain why the prediction was or was not accurate. **3c, 1b**
- Use the concept of gravity to explain why people can jump higher on the Moon than they can on Earth. **3c**
- Identify a place that is subject to periodic flooding, evaluate its positive and negative consequences, and study different ways of maintaining, reducing or eliminating the likelihood of flooding. **3d**

S4 Scientific Connections and Applications

The student demonstrates conceptual understanding by using a concept accurately to explain observations and make predictions and by representing the concept in multiple ways (through words, diagrams, graphs or charts, as appropriate). Both aspects of understanding—explaining and representing—are required to meet this standard.

The student produces evidence that demonstrates understanding of:

S4a Big ideas and unifying concepts, such as order and organization; models, form, and function; change and constancy; and cause and effect.

S4b The designed world, such as the reciprocal nature of science and technology; the development of agricultural techniques; and the viability of technological designs.

S4c Health, such as nutrition, exercise, and disease; effects of drugs and toxic substances; personal and environmental safety; and resources and environmental stress.

S4d Impact of technology, such as constraints and trade-offs; feedback; benefits and risks; and problems and solutions.

S4e Impact of science, such as historical and contemporary contributions; and interactions between science and society.

Examples of activities through which students might demonstrate conceptual understanding of scientific connections and applications include:

- Create a health pamphlet for a track team that travels around North America to help them adjust to altitudes different from the place where they usually train, and explain why these adjustments are necessary. **4a, 4d, 2c**
- Develop a plan to modify the school's fire warning system for students with disabilities. **4b, 4d**
- Analyze an automatic ice maker and explain how its design takes into account the differences in the properties of water in liquid and solid states. **4b, 4d, 1a**
- Identify a pest in a local agricultural setting; and compare and contrast the risks and benefits of chemical and biological pest control. **4b, 4c, 4d, 4e, 2d**
- Hypothesize why people tend to get more colds and flu in the winter and discuss ways to prevent the spread of illness. **4c, 2c**
- Investigate local water quality standards and make recommendations to school officials about water quality on and near the campus. **4c, 3a, A1b**

Samples of student work that illustrate standard-setting performances for these standards can be found on pages 96-111.

The examples that follow the performance descriptions for each standard are examples of the work students might do to demonstrate their achievement. The examples also indicate the nature and complexity of activities that are appropriate to expect of students at the middle school level.

The cross-references that follow the examples highlight examples for which the same activity, and possibly even the same piece of work, may enable students to demonstrate their achievement in relation to more than one standard. In some cases, the cross-references highlight examples of activities through which students might demonstrate their achievement in relation to standards for more than one subject matter.

S5 Scientific Thinking

The student demonstrates scientific inquiry and problem solving by using thoughtful questioning and reasoning strategies, common sense and conceptual understanding from Science Standards 1 to 4, and appropriate methods to investigate the natural world; that is, the student:

S5 a Frames questions to distinguish cause and effect; and identifies or controls variables in experimental and non-experimental research settings.

S5 b Uses concepts from Science Standards 1 to 4 to explain a variety of observations and phenomena.

S5 c Uses evidence from reliable sources to develop descriptions, explanations, and models.

S5 d Proposes, recognizes, analyzes, considers, and critiques alternative explanations; and distinguishes between fact and opinion.

S5 e Identifies problems; proposes and implements solutions; and evaluates the accuracy, design, and outcomes of investigations.

S5 f Works individually and in teams to collect and share information and ideas.

Examples of activities through which students might demonstrate skill in scientific thinking include:

- Investigate the results of two fellow students' plant growth experiments and recommend ways to enhance the information. **5a, 5b, 5c, 5d, 5e, 5f, 2a**
- Determine if the scientific evidence in the summary data chart in Consumer Reports substantiates recommendations about the "Best Buy" for a particular purchase. **5a, 5b, 5c, 5d, 5e**
- Work with another student to investigate the effects of several variables on oxygen production in an aquatic plant, e.g., nutrients, light, color of container. **5a, 5b, 5c, 5d, 5e, 5f, 2a, 2c**
- Evaluate the claims and potential risks and benefits of a newly advertised "diet pill." **5b, 5c, 5d, 5e, 2c, 4c**

To see how these performance descriptions compare with the expectations for elementary school and high school, turn to pages 158-165.

The Science standards are founded upon both the National Research Council's *National Science Education Standards* and the American Association for the Advancement of Science's Project 2061 *Benchmarks for Science Literacy.* These documents, each of which runs to several hundred pages, contain detail that amplifies the meaning of the terms used in the performance descriptions.

S6 Scientific Tools and Technologies

The student demonstrates competence with the tools and technologies of science by using them to collect data, make observations, analyze results, and accomplish tasks effectively; that is, the student:

S6 a Uses technology and tools (such as traditional laboratory equipment, video, and computer aids) to observe and measure objects, organisms, and phenomena, directly, indirectly, and remotely.

S6 b Records and stores data using a variety of formats, such as data bases, audiotapes, and videotapes.

S6 c Collects and analyzes data using concepts and techniques in Mathematics Standard 4, such as mean, median, and mode; outcome probability and reliability; and appropriate data displays.

S6 d Acquires information from multiple sources, such as print, the Internet, computer data bases, and experimentation.

S6 e Recognizes sources of bias in data, such as observer and sampling biases.

Examples of activities through which students might demonstrate competence with the tools and technologies of science include:

- Use a microcomputer-based investigation to compare the rates at which different carbonated beverages in a variety of containers lose their fizz. **6a, 1a, 4b, 5a**
- Complete the Animal Observation Project (Girl Scouts of the U.S.A.) and teach another student how to conduct field observations. **6a, 2d**
- Conduct a field research project to compare the distribution of birds near the school with a field guide for the region to see if local distributions are the same as regional. **6c, 6d, 2d**
- Compare the accuracy and timeliness of local weather information from a variety of sources. **6d, 3a**
- Exchange data on the acidity of rain with students from other states or countries. Figure out why the data differ, if they do. **6d, 1a, 3a**
- Use electronic data bases to get current information on the health effects of long-term space travel. **6d, 3c, 4c**

S7 Scientific Communication

The student demonstrates effective scientific communication by clearly describing aspects of the natural world using accurate data, graphs, or other appropriate media to convey depth of conceptual understanding in science; that is, the student:

S7 a Represents data and results in multiple ways, such as numbers, tables, and graphs; drawings, diagrams, and artwork; and technical and creative writing.

S7 b Argues from evidence, such as data produced through his or her own experimentation or by others.

S7 c Critiques published materials.

S7 d Explains a scientific concept or procedure to other students.

S7 e Communicates in a form suited to the purpose and the audience, such as by writing instructions that others can follow; critiquing written and oral explanations; and using data to resolve disagreements.

Examples of activities through which students might demonstrate competence in scientific communication include:

- Earn the Drafting Merit Badge. (Boy Scouts of America) **7a, 4b, 5c, 6a**
- Write an advertisement for a hair care product that explains the chemistry of how it works. **7b, 1a, 4b, 4c, 5d**
- Analyze and give a speech about a ballot initiative on toxic chemicals. **7c, 1a, 2c, 3a, 4b, 5d, 6d**
- Critique a *USA Today* article which reports that eating hot dogs in childhood causes adult leukemia. **7c, 2c, 4c, 5d**
- Write a review of an episode of *Beakman's World.* **7c, 5d, 6d**
- Make an animated video illustrating how white blood cells protect the body from infectious agents. **7d, 2a, 2c, 4c, 5c**

S8 Scientific Investigation

The student demonstrates scientific competence by completing projects drawn from the following kinds of investigations, including at least one full investigation each year and, over the course of middle school, investigations that integrate several aspects of Science Standards 1 to 7 and represent all four of the kinds of investigation:

S8 a Controlled experiment.

S8 b Fieldwork.

S8 c Design.

S8 d Secondary research, such as use of others' data.

A single project may draw on more than one type of investigation.

A full investigation includes:

- Questions that can be studied using the resources available.
- Procedures that are safe, humane, and ethical; and that respect privacy and property rights.
- Data that have been collected and recorded (see also Science Standard 6) in ways that others can verify, and analyzed using skills expected at this grade level (see also Mathematics Standard 4).
- Data and results that have been represented (see also Science Standard 7) in ways that fit the context.
- Recommendations, decisions, and conclusions based on evidence.
- Acknowledgment of references and contributions of others.
- Results that are communicated appropriately to audiences.
- Reflection and defense of conclusions and recommendations from other sources and peer review.

Examples of projects through which students might demonstrate competence in scientific investigation include:

- Analyze de-icers for relative effectiveness, cost, and environmental impact. **8a, 1a, 3d, 4d**
- Study different methods for cooking chicken considering health and aesthetics. **8a, 8c, 4c**
- Conduct a field study of monument degradation over time at a local cemetery. **8b, 1a, 3a**
- Adopt a stream and use that location to study habitat and water quality over time. **8b, 2d, 3a**
- Design a protective container for an uncooked egg using the concepts of force, motion, gravity, and acceleration and test the design by dropping the container (egg enclosed) from a one-story building. **8c, 1a, 1b**
- Research local climate changes over the last century. **8d, 3a**

Samples of student work that illustrate standard-setting performances for these standards can be found on pages 96-111.

The examples that follow the performance descriptions for each standard are examples of the work students might do to demonstrate their achievement. The examples also indicate the nature and complexity of activities that are appropriate to expect of students at the middle school level.

The cross-references that follow the examples highlight examples for which the same activity, and possibly even the same piece of work, may enable students to demonstrate their achievement in relation to more than one standard. In some cases, the cross-references highlight examples of activities through which students might demonstrate their achievement in relation to standards for more than one subject matter.

Work Sample & Commentary: *Light Reflection*

The task

The National Student Research Center encourages the establishment of student research centers in schools throughout the United States and around the world. The Center facilitates the exchange of information by publishing a journal of student investigations and by use of the Internet (nsrcmms@aol.com). It provides a standard format that students use to report their results. The format requires that students state a purpose and hypothesis; report their methods, data analysis, and conclusions; and suggest applications for their results.

Circumstances of performance

This sample of student work was produced under the following conditions:

	alone		in a group
√	in class		as homework
√	with teacher feedback	√	with peer feedback
	timed	√	opportunity for revision

Each student was allowed to select the topic for their study. This student chose to study the reflection of light on smooth surfaces. This investigation, therefore, adds to the components required for the format by providing evidence of an understanding of concepts in physical sciences.

The quotations from the Science performance descriptions in this commentary are excerpted. The complete performance descriptions are shown on pages 92-95.

S6 makes explicit reference to using telecommunications to acquire and share information. A recent National Center on Education Statistics survey recently reported that only 50% of schools and fewer than 9% of instructional rooms currently have access to the Internet. We know this is an equity issue—that far more than 9% of the homes in the United States have access to the Internet and that schools must make sure that students' access to information and ideas does not depend on what they get at home—so we have crafted performance standards that would use the Internet so that people will make sure that all students have access to it. New Standards partners have made a commitment to create the learning environments where students can develop the knowledge and skills delineated here.

TITLE: The Reflection of Light

(A) I. STATEMENT OF PURPOSE AND HYPOTHESIS:

I would like to do a scientific research project on the concept that light waves reflect
off smooth surfaces at the same angle they hit them. I want to see if this is true. My
hypothesis states that light waves do reflect off smooth surfaces at the same angle
they hit them.

(B) II. METHODOLOGY:

First, I wrote my statement of purpose. Then I wrote my review of literature. Next, I
developed my hypothesis. Then I wrote my methodology. Next, I wrote my list of
materials. Then I developed my observation and data collection form. Next, I began
my experimentation, observation, and data collection. I did my experimentation by
covering the lens of a flashlight with a black piece of paper. I then cut a hole at the
edge of the paper so that only one ray of light could escape. Then I put a white piece
of paper on the floor and put the mirror's edge on the paper so that a right angle
was made. I laid the flashlight down on the white paper with the hole on the black
paper covering the lens next to the floor. I set the flashlight at several angles to the
mirror on the floor. Then I shined the flashlight at the mirror. I drew a line on the
white paper following the ray hitting the mirror and the ray reflecting from the
mirror. I then drew a line running perpendicular to the mirror from the vertex of
the angle which the lines made and used a protractor to measure the two angles
created. I repeated this procedure for each angle. Then I wrote my analysis of data.
Next, I wrote my summary and conclusions where I accepted or rejected my
hypothesis. Then I applied my findings to the real world. Last, I sent my abstract to
the national journal of student research.

(C) III. ANALYSIS OF DATA:

I found that the in-going and out-going rays of light had the same angle. For the
first trial, I shined the flashlight at the mirror at a 29 degree angle and the light
reflected off at a 29 degree angle. For the second trial, I shined the flashlight at the
mirror at a ten degree angle and the light reflected off at a ten degree angle. For the
third trial, I shined the flashlight at the mirror at a 19 degree angle and the light
reflected off at a 19 degree angle.

IV. SUMMARY AND CONCLUSIONS:

My research indicates, that light reflects off smooth surfaces at the same angle it hits
them. Therefore, I accept my hypothesis which states that light waves do reflect off
smooth surfaces at the same angle they hit.

V. APPLICATION:

I will use my new knowledge to rearrange the mirrors in my room so that it will be
brighter inside.

The Student Researcher. Used by permission of the National Student Research Center, Dr. John I. Swang, Mandeville Middle School, 2525 Soult Street, Mandeville, Louisiana 70448. 504-626-5980 or nsrcmms@aol.com.

This work sample illustrates a standard-setting performance for the following parts of the standards:

- **S1 c Physical Sciences Concepts: Transfer of energy.**
- **S5 a Scientific Thinking: Frame questions and control variables.**
- **S5 c Scientific Thinking: Use evidence from reliable sources.**
- **S5 d Scientific Thinking: Distinguish between fact and opinion.**
- **S5 e Scientific Thinking: Evaluate accuracy, design, and outcomes.**
- **S5 f Scientific Thinking: Work in teams.**
- **S6 a Scientific Tools and Technologies: Use technology and tools to observe and measure.**

What the work shows

S1 c Physical Sciences Concepts: The student produces evidence that demonstrates understanding of transfer of energy, such as transformation of energy as...light....

This work is limited to a single but important concept. It provides evidence for understanding that light is reflected off smooth surfaces, that there is regularity to that process, and that there is a way to state the relationship between the "in-going" and "out-going" angles quantitatively.

S5 a Scientific Thinking: The student frames questions to distinguish cause and effect; and identifies or controls variables in experimental and non-experimental research settings.

(A) The question is direct and clear.

(B) The procedure is well detailed; its repetition shows evidence of controlling variables.

S5 c Scientific Thinking: The student uses evidence from reliable sources to develop descriptions, explanations, and models.

First hand experimentation is a reliable source, providing the procedures are clear and variables are controlled.

Light Reflection

S5d Scientific Thinking: The student proposes, recognizes, analyzes, considers, and critiques alternative explanations; and distinguishes between fact and opinion.

(A) There are many concepts in the physical sciences that students are expected to accept at face value. Many students find it necessary to experiment directly and to confirm for themselves things that are already "known." This experimentation is part of "distinguishes fact from opinion"; questioning "known facts" is an important part of Scientific Thinking at the middle school level.

S5e Scientific Thinking: The student identifies problems; proposes and implements solutions; and evaluates the accuracy, design, and outcomes of investigations.

S5f Scientific Thinking: The student works individually and in teams to collect and share information and ideas.

The format for work submitted to the National Student Research Center requires peer review to strengthen the work.

S6a Scientific Tools and Technologies: The student uses technology and tools (such as traditional laboratory equipment) to observe and measure objects... and phenomena, directly [and] indirectly....

(B) The somewhat complex method for gathering data is well designed to yield accurate measurements. The precise manipulation of a light source, a mirror, and a protractor to obtain accurate data is standard-setting work at the middle school level.

Work Sample & Commentary: *Cruise Boats*

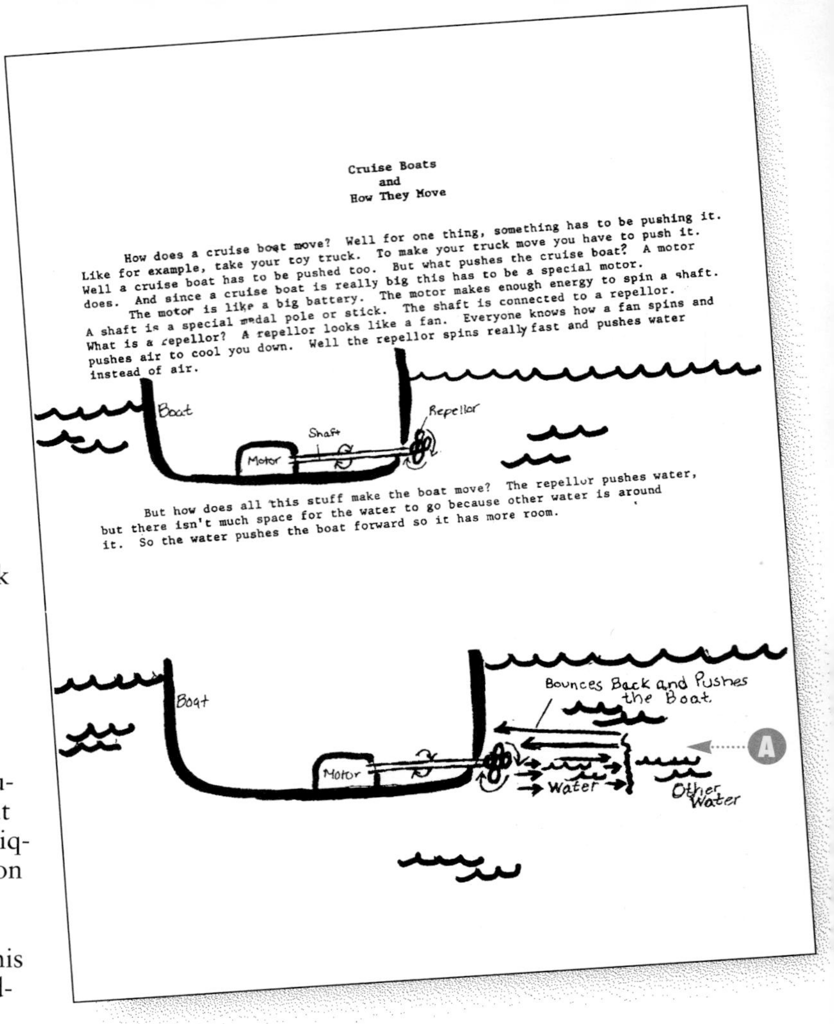

The task

After a unit of study on motions and forces, students were asked to explain how cruise boats worked. The explanation was supposed to be limited to two pages and written at a level that could be understood by a five to ten year-old child.

The quotations from the Science performance descriptions in this commentary are excerpted. The complete performance descriptions are shown on pages 92-95.

Circumstances of performance

This sample of student work was produced under the following conditions:

√ alone	in a group
√ in class	as homework
with teacher feedback	with peer feedback
timed	opportunity for revision

Science required by the task

The context of a liquid medium may have been confusing to the student. For a middle school student, it is somewhat advanced to understand that the same laws of motion apply to both gas and liquid environments (with forces modified by friction and resistance), when the student has probably learned about forces only in air. The student is asked only to tell what makes the boat move. This constraint makes the task manageable at the middle school level.

Cruise Boats
and
How They Move

How does a cruise boat move? Well for one thing, something has to be pushing it. Like for example, take your toy truck. To make your truck move you have to push it. Well a cruise boat has to be pushed too. But what pushes the cruise boat? A motor does. And since a cruise boat is really big this has to be a special motor.

The motor is like a big battery. The motor makes enough energy to spin a shaft. A shaft is a special medal pole or stick. The shaft is connected to a repellor. What is a repellor? A repellor looks like a fan. Everyone knows how a fan spins and pushes air to cool you down. Well the repellor spins really fast and pushes water instead of air.

Boat
Shaft
Repellor
Motor

But how does all this stuff make the boat move? The repellor pushes water, but there isn't much space for the water to go because other water is around it. So the water pushes the boat forward so it has more room.

Boat
Bounces Back and Pushes the Boat.
Motor
Water
Other Water
A

What the work shows

S1 b Physical Sciences Concepts: The student produces evidence that demonstrates understanding of motions and forces, such as inertia and the net effects of balanced and unbalanced forces.

The relationship between force and motion is easier to illustrate in a familiar environment. The student had to apply the concept in an unfamiliar setting in order to explain the forces in a liquid medium.

A This shows an accurate explanation of motions and forces by explaining that a force in one direction always results in a force in the opposite direction.

B Here is a correct explanation of the forces operating in this system. The student stated that the faster the movement of the water the faster the forward movement of the boat.

This work sample illustrates a standard-setting performance for the following parts of the standards:

- **S1 b Physical Sciences Concepts: Motions and forces.**
- **S4 a Scientific Connections and Applications: Big ideas and unifying concepts.**
- **S7 a Scientific Communication: Represent data in multiple ways.**
- **S7 e Scientific Communication: Communicate in a form suited to the purpose and the audience.**

Physical Sciences Concepts S1
Life Sciences Concepts
Earth and Space Sciences Concepts
Scientific Connections and Applications S4
Scientific Thinking
Scientific Tools and Technologies
Scientific Communication S7
Scientific Investigation

Cruise Boats

S4a Scientific Connections and Applications: The student produces evidence that demonstrates understanding of big ideas and unifying concepts, such as...cause and effect.

C The use of the fan to explain how ships might move faster is evidence for an understanding of the link between the shape of the fan and the behavior of a similar design in a different setting (water). The idea of cause and effect is illustrated in the explanation that, as the fans move faster, more water is pushed, causing greater forward motion.

S7a Scientific Communication: The student represents data and results in multiple ways, such as...drawings, diagrams, and artwork; and technical and creative writing.

The use of drawings to accompany the written explanation is an effective way to illustrate the forces operating in this system.

S7e Scientific Communication: The student communicates in a form suited to the purpose and the audience....

The task asked for an explanation to a specific audience (five- to ten-year-olds). This is an appropriate level of detail for a complete explanation to a younger student.

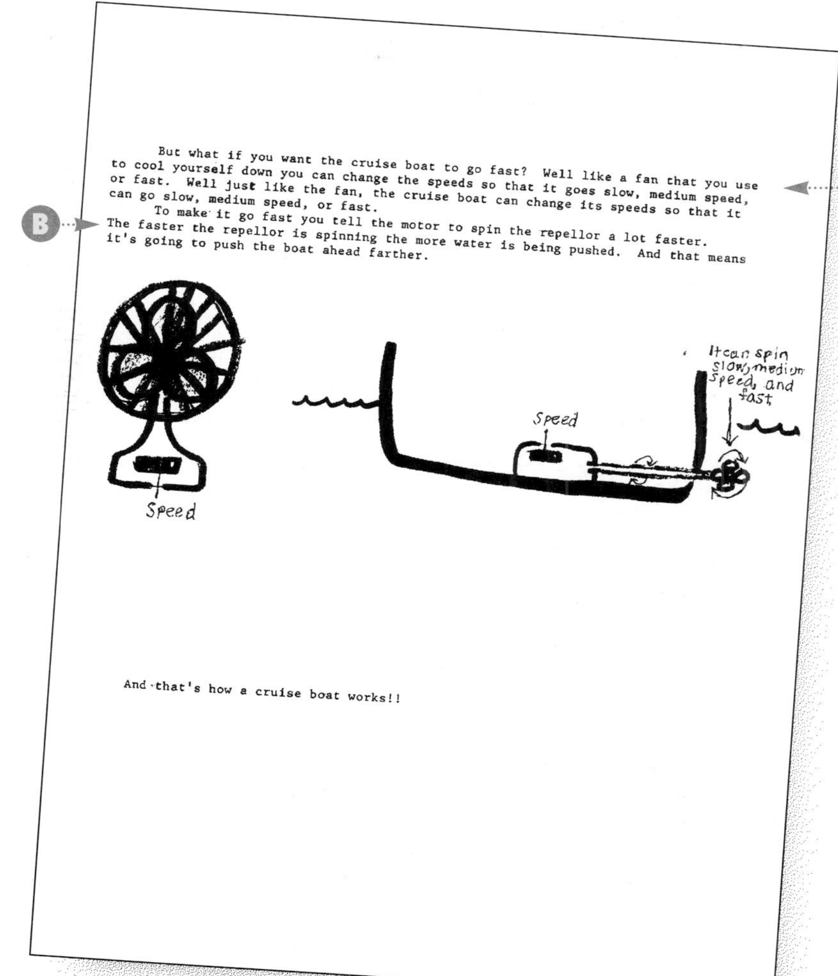

But what if you want the cruise boat to go fast? Well like a fan that you use to cool yourself down you can change the speeds so that it goes slow, medium speed, or fast. Well just like the fan, the cruise boat can change its speeds so that it can go slow, medium speed, or fast.

To make it go fast you tell the motor to spin the repellor a lot faster. The faster the repellor is spinning the more water is being pushed. And that means it's going to push the boat ahead farther.

Speed
Speed
It can spin slow, medium speed, and fast
B
C

And that's how a cruise boat works!!

Work Sample & Commentary: *Buoyancy*

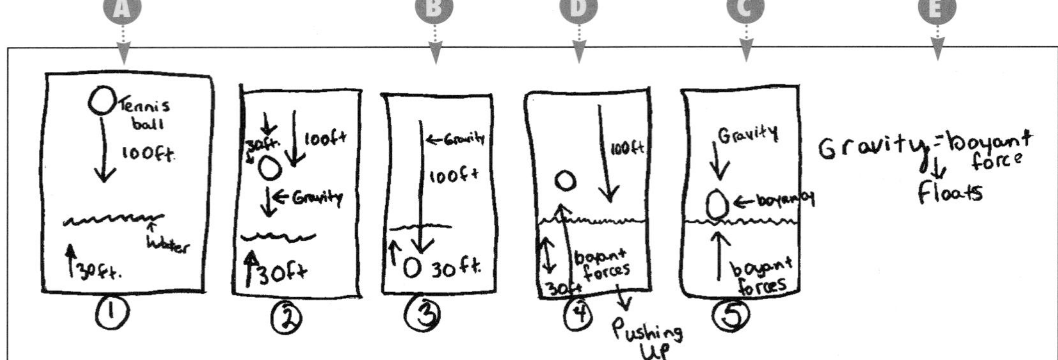

The quotations from the Science performance descriptions in this commentary are excerpted. The complete performance descriptions are shown on pages 92-95.

The task

Students who had been studying buoyant forces with vessels were asked to show what would happen to a tennis ball dropped from a height of 100 feet into 30 feet of water.

Circumstances of performance

This sample of student work was produced under the following conditions:

√ alone	in a group
√ in class	as homework
with teacher feedback	with peer feedback
timed	opportunity for revision

This task followed a unit of study on vessels in which forces and motions were studied in detail. Without this extended instruction, such a task would not ordinarily evoke a response such as this from a middle school student.

What the work shows

S1 b Physical Sciences Concepts: The student produces evidence that demonstrates understanding of motions and forces, such as...net effects of balanced and unbalanced forces.

The storyboard shows an analysis of the movement of the falling ball, seemingly a single action. The forces acting upon this moving object, however, are constantly changing, as represented by the changing lengths of the arrows.

A **B** The arrow lengths depict the forces acting upon the ball as unbalanced. The ball is either beneath the water or above the water.

C The arrows for gravity and buoyant forces are of equal length. The ball is depicted as floating, demonstrating that when the force of gravity is equal to the force of buoyancy, an object will float.

Note that the length of the arrows depicting the force of gravity should be constant across all frames, so there may be confusion between gravity and velocity.

D While the arrow depicting buoyancy appears to be acting outside the water in this frame, this misconception is not unusual for a middle school student.

E The evidence for conceptual understanding of balanced forces in the final frame is confirmed by the statement: "Gravity = buoyant force → floats."

This work sample illustrates a standard-setting performance for the following part of the standards:

S1 b Physical Sciences Concepts: Motions and forces.

Work Sample & Commentary: *Discovering Density*

The task

Following classroom discussion about the concept of density, students performed an extensive laboratory investigation. In the lab write up the students were asked to:

- discuss the definition of density;
- state a clear purpose for the investigation;
- give four clearly stated hypotheses;
- list all materials;
- clearly organize and label data;
- discuss any observed patterns;
- clearly explain laboratory procedures;
- summarize results;
- suggest ideas for future study.

Circumstances of performance

This sample of student work was produced under the following conditions:

	alone	√	in a group
√	in class		as homework
√	with teacher feedback	√	with peer feedback
	timed	√	opportunity for revision

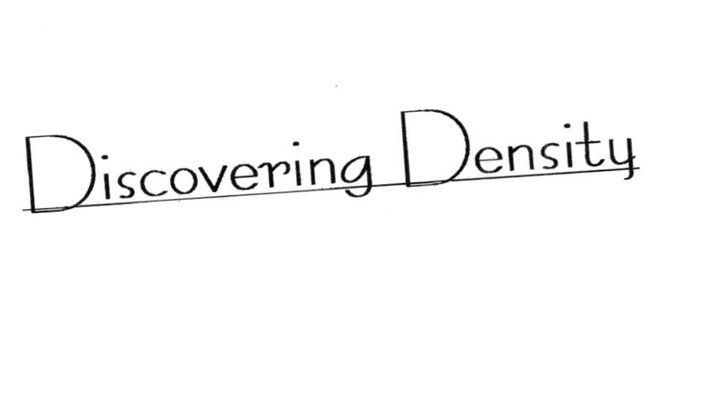
February 17, 1996

Discovering Density

This work sample illustrates a standard-setting performance for the following parts of the standards:

S1a Physical Sciences Concepts: Properties and changes of properties in matter.

S4a Scientific Connections and Applications: Big ideas and unifying concepts.

S5b Scientific Thinking: Use concepts from Science Standards 1 to 4 to explain observations and phenomena.

S5c Scientific Thinking: Use evidence from reliable sources.

S5e Scientific Thinking: Evaluate the accuracy, design, and outcomes of investigations.

S5f Scientific Thinking: Work individually and in teams.

S6a Scientific Tools and Technologies: Use technology and tools to observe and measure.

S7a Scientific Communication: Represent data and results in multiple ways.

S7e Scientific Communication: Communicate in a form suited to the purpose and the audience.

What the work shows

S1a Physical Sciences Concepts: The student produces evidence that demonstrates understanding of properties and changes of properties in matter, such as density....

(A) (B) There is clear evidence here and throughout the work that the student understands how volume and mass relate to density.

(C) There is a misconception stated here about air having zero mass.

S4a Scientific Connections and Applications: The student produces evidence that demonstrates understanding of big ideas and unifying concepts, such as order...; change and constancy; and cause and effect.

(D) (E) There are a number of places in this work where the student acknowledged that volume can remain constant and yet, if mass increases or decreases, the density is changed.

(F) The student provided evidence of understanding that if the density of an object is less than 1.0 g/ml the object will float in water.

The quotations from the Science performance descriptions in this commentary are excerpted. The complete performance descriptions are shown on pages 92-95.

Discovering Density

S5 b Scientific Thinking: The student uses concepts from Science Standards 1 to 4 to explain a variety of observations and phenomena.

E The conclusion ties together the concept of density and why objects in the experiment floated and why some sank. This shows that the student was able to use her conceptual understanding of density to predict whether an object would float or sink given information about the density of the medium into which the object is placed and the density of the object.

S5 c Scientific Thinking: The student uses evidence from reliable sources to develop descriptions, explanations, and models.

Throughout the work the student used information from reliable sources. One source was direct experimentation. However, the student took information, whether from the teacher or some other source, and explained some sophisticated concepts in her own voice.

Physical Sciences Concepts S1
Life Sciences Concepts
Earth and Space Sciences Concepts
Scientific Connections and Applications S4
Scientific Thinking S5
Scientific Tools and Technologies S6
Scientific Communication S7
Scientific Investigation

Past History

Density is a measurement of how close atoms and/or molecules are together, or in other words how concentrated they are. For instance, 1,000 lbs. of feathers are less dense than an ounce of gold, because gold molecules are all much closer together than the feather molecules are. We need to know how dense things are, to see if they float or sink, to see if we can break through them, to see how sturdy a substance is, and for many other reasons.

Purpose

The purpose of this laboratory experiment is to examine and determine the relationships between mass, volume, and density.

Hypothesis

A I believe that if the mass of an object goes up and the volume stays the same, the density will go up, because that means there are more molecules/atoms in the same amount of space. Accordingly, I think that if the volume of an object goes up and the mass stays the same, than then the density will go down, because there are the same amount of molecules/atoms in a larger amount of space. I think some objects float because there is space for air between molecules, and the molecules trap the are in the object so it floats. If the object is very dense, then there is no room for air in between the molecules, so it sinks. I think that a steel boat floats, because there are molecules that are not very dense, so air can go in the spaces between the molecules, and the sides of the boat add to that ability, because they constantly keep water from being on both the top and bottom of the molecules.

Materials

big block of wood
20 steal BB's
3 unknown liquids
little block of wood
balance
tape measure3
calculator
10 ml graduated cylinder
square piece of foil
rubber stoppers
50 ml graduated cylinder
50 ml beaker
1000 mlbeaker
balloon
1 cork stopper
100 ml beaker

K

Processes

Station 1 SMALL BLOCK/LARGE BLOCK

1. Mass the block of wood.
2. Measure the length, height, and width of the block in centimeters.
3. Calculate the volume using the formula for a rectangular solid.
4. Calculate the density of the block.
5. Fill one of the large beakers 2/3 of the way with water.
6. Gently place each block of wood into water to determine if it floats.
7. Remove the block from water.
8. Repeat for the other block.

Station 2 STEEL BB'S

1. Fill the graduated cylinder with 5.0 ml of water.
2. Mass the graduated cylinder and water.
3. Gently roll 20 beads into graduated cylinder.
4. Mass the graduates cylinder, water, and beads.
5. Calculate mass of the 20 beads.
6. Record the volume of water and 20 beads.
7. Calculate volume of the 20 beads.
8. Calculate density of the 20 beads.
9. Record whether or not the steel beads float.
10. Pour water back into the beaker and replace the beads into a petri dish.

Station 3 UNKNOWN LIQUIDS

1. Mass the graduated cylinder.
2. Pour approximately 30 ml of Liquid into the graduated cylinder.
3. Mass the graduated cylinder and the Liquid.
4. Record the exact volume of the Liquid that was poured into graduated cylinder.
5. Calculate the density of the Liquid.
6. Repeat for other Liquids.

L Station 4 BALLOON

1. Mass the balloon.
2. Use the tape measure to record the circumference if the balloon.
3. Calculate the radius of the balloon.
4. Using the following formula, calculate the volume of the balloon. v = 4 *pi* r^3/3 **H**
5. Calculate the density of the balloon.
6. Verify whether or not the balloon floats.

Station 5 RUBBER STOPPERS

1. Mass the rubber stopper.
2. Pour approximately 40 ml into the graduated cylinder.
3. Record exact volume of water in graduated cylinder.
4. Gently place rubber stopper into graduated cylinder.
5. Be sure rubber stopper is completely covered with water and measure the volume of water and stopper.
6. Calculate volume of stopper.
7. Calculate density of stopper.
8. Repeat for other stoppers.

Station 6 CORKS

1. Mass the cork.
2. Pour approximately 40 ml into graduated cylinder.
3. Record exact volume of water in graduated cylinder.
4. Gently place cork into graduated cylinder. **I**
5. Be sure cork is completely covered with water and measure volume of water and cork.
6. Calculate volume of cork.
7. Calculate density of cork.
8. Repeat for other corks.

Station 7 ALUMINUM FOIL BOAT/ALUMINUM BALL

1. Construct and aluminum boat following your instructor's instructions.
2. Mass the boat.
3. Measure the length, width, and height of the boat.
4. Calculate the volume of the boat.

Discovering Density

S5e Scientific Thinking: The student evaluates the accuracy, design, and outcomes of investigations.

G The student identified several reasonable sources of measurement error.

S5f Scientific Thinking: The student works individually and in teams to collect and share information and ideas.

S6a Scientific Tools and Technologies: The student uses technology and tools (such as traditional laboratory equipment…) to…measure objects…indirectly….

H The student determined the volume of the balloon by using the formula for a sphere.

I The student determined the volume of an irregularly shaped object by using water displacement.

S7a Scientific Communication: The student represents data and results in multiple ways, such as numbers, tables, and technical…writing.

J The student presented data in tabular form and analyzed the data in writing.

S7e Scientific Communication: The student communicates in a form suited to the purpose and the audience, such as by writing instructions that others can follow….

K **L** **M**

5. Calculate the density of the boat.
6. Determine whether the boat floats or sinks.
7. Squish the boat into a tight "cube" ball.
8. Record the mass of the ball.
9. Measure the length, width, and height of the aluminum ball to determine the volume of the ball.
10. Calculate the volume of the ball.
11. Calculate the density of the ball.
12. Determine if the boat floats or sinks.

Station 8 WATER

1. Mass the graduated cylinder.
2. Pour approximately 30 ml of water into the graduated cylinder.
3. Record the exact volume of the water in the graduated cylinder.
4. Mass the graduated cylinder and water.
5. Calculate the mass of the water in the graduated cylinder.
6. Calculate the density of the water.

Discussion **B**

The density of an object is most dependent on mass. This is because there are two factors concerning mass that contribute to the density of an object. At the atomic level each individual atom/molecule could weight a lot, thus effecting the mass which effects the density; or there could be a number of atoms/molecules squished up in a small area, which effects the mass and therefore effecting the volume. This is supported by all of the stations in this laboratory. In all of the stations, the mass and volume were taken, and in each case the individual weight of each atom/molecule and the weight of how ever many atoms/molecules there were affected the mass.

F Water's density is approximately 1.0 g/ml. You can see this in the Station 8 table of my data. With the data of all of the things that we testing whether they floated or sank it can be determined that things that float, have a density of less then 1.0 g/ml, and all of the things that sink have a density of greater than 1.0.

J

Floats	Density	Sinks	Density
Small Block	0.648 g/ml	Steel Beads	7 g/ml
Large Block	0.616 g/ml	Sm. Stopper	1.1 g/ml
Balloon	0.0052 g/ml	Med. Stopper	1.5 g/ml
Small Cork	0.15 g/ml	Lrg. Stopper	1.2 g/ml
Medium Cork	0.2 g/ml	Almn. Ball	1.2 g/ml
Large Cork	0.17 g/ml		
Almn. Boat	0.012 g/ml		

C The aluminum boat floated, because it's density was above 1.0 g/ml. Part of the reason, is because the empty space in the middle of the boat (which weighs nothing) is counted in the volume, then when you divide mass by volume the number drops greatly. With the ball you crammed alot of atoms/molecules into a small area, and the volume was so very small, when you divide the number stayed above 1.0 g/ml and it sinks.

D To find if what happens to the density of an object the mass of an object goes up, and the volume stays the same I looked in stations 5 and 6, and 3. If you look at the stoppers and corks that are the same volume, you will see that the mass of the stopper is larger. The density of the more massive object if higher in all three (small, medium, and large) cases. In the liquids station the volume always stayed the same, yet the more massive liquids always had a high density. So it can be concluded that if the mass of an object goes up and the volume stays the same, the density will go up.

To find what happens to the density of an object if the volume goes up and the mass stays the same I looked at station 7 backwards (if we had a aluminum ball first, then built it into a boat). When the aluminum was in a ball, the density was high, and when it was a boat the density was low. This is because the space in the object was counted as part of the object. In conclusion, if the volume of an object goes up and the mass stays the same, the density will go down.

To find out why things float I looked at all of the stations, and the table I made on the previous page, those things with a density lower than the density of the liquid they are in will float, and those things with a density higher than the liquid they are in will sink.

A steel boat floats, because it has sides on it. If it were simply a steel panel, in would sink like a rock. The space in the middle of the boat, counts as part of a boat, therefore making the boat much less dense than the water.

G Some things that might have affected my data, and made it wrong, could have been, water left on the objects, so they had the added mass of the water when they were weighed; how you measured the circumference of the balloon, because it was not a perfect sphere; the holes in the bottom of the stoppers could have filled up with air, and given a false volume reading; the scales might not have always been tared correctly; measurements of water in the graduated cylinders might not have been totally accurate; and when measuring the volume of objects that floated using water displacement, the objects might not have been in the water all of the way, giving and inaccurate reading on the graduated cylinder.

Conclusion

E This lab, has made it very easy to understand the relationships between mass, volume, and density. After completing this lab, it is easy to conclude, that if the mass of an object goes up and the volume stays the same the density will go up; that if the volume of an object goes up and the mass stays the same the density will go down; that objects float because they are less dense then the substance that they are in; and that a steel boat floats because it has side. With this new knowledge and understanding I personally know a little bit more about how this world works. I will also know how to find the density of things if I ever need to know if something floats, like if I ever need to construct a boat, or something like that. Now that I know how to find the density of an object, it would be interesting to go into some physics, and find how much force you would have to apply to break through things with different density's. Knowing how to calculate this, and being able to calculate this might be good for a job in making durable synthetic materials, or finding sturdy materials to make something which must be very strong.

Work Sample & Commentary: *Seeds*

The task

Students participated in a garden project as part of a community summer program. During the project they were given casual instruction on plants, seeds, and weeds. To identify weeds, the students walked through a vacant lot near the garden wearing socks over their shoes. They collected and analyzed the seeds from their socks. They then sorted the seeds according to their own classification scheme.

One student took the investigation a further step and compared the oil (fat) content of different dicots.

The quotations from the Science performance descriptions in this commentary are excerpted. The complete performance descriptions are shown on pages 92-95.

Best practice in science has always included intensive inquiry and investigation. There are many opportunities to learn science outside of school, including the Girl Scouts of the U.S.A., Boy Scouts of America, Boys and Girls Clubs of America, 4-H, and Future Farmers of America. The work done in these venues can and should be used to provide evidence of meeting these standards.

Circumstances of performance

This sample of student work was produced under the following conditions:

√ alone	in a group
in class	as homework
√ with teacher feedback	√ with peer feedback
timed	√ opportunity for revision

The fieldwork of gathering and classifying the seeds was done in a small group. The data analysis in both procedures was completed individually.

Project Seeds

Procedure I:

1. Went to big park across from Lydia House.
2. Put old socks over shoes.
3. Walked around the park for 10 minutes.
4. Came back and took off socks.
5. Took off all the seeds from socks.
6. Put seeds in envelopes.
7. Tried to find plants that seeds came from.
8. Went back to Lydia House.
9. Tape seeds that were the same on the same part of paper.
10. Put label on seeds that we knew what plant they came from.
11. Put label on monocots and dicots.

Data:

(A) Monocots are like grasses and corn and stuff like that. They have only one
part that is for food storage. Dicots are like peanuts that when you look at
them they have two parts and one part is for food storage and the other part
is too. So they have two parts for food storage. Some of the seeds were really
small and too small to see what they were with the magnifing lens. But if I
had a microscope I could find out what they were because I could see them
better.

Monocots:		Dicots:		Don't Know	
A:	11	A:	2	A:	13
B:	6	B.	2	B:	6
C:	26	C:	1	C:	12
D:	5			D:	8
E:	12				
F:	35				
G:	22				

Conclusions :

There were lots of more monocots than dicots. There were 117 monocots (B)
and 5 dicots. The ones I couldn't decide which they were probably
monocots. Thats because out of the ones I knew 96% of them were
monocots and only 4% were dicots. So the others were probably monocots
too. There was lots of grasses out in the park and weeds that looked like
grasses. So that was probably the reason there were lots more monocots (C)
because grasses are monocots. It must be that the dirt is better for
monocots. The dirt here was pretty dry . Or maybe the monocots are
(D) stronger and will push out the dicots from their space. There are some
weeds and grasses that grow in the garden and once they start growing they
get crowded and nothing else can grow there. When I pull up the grass
there is lots of roots that spread out and maybe dicots just go straight down
in the root.

What the work shows

S2 a Life Sciences Concepts: The student produces evidence that demonstrates understanding of structure and function in living systems, such as the complementary nature of structure and function....

(A) The classification based on a functional characteristic of seeds shows evidence of an understanding of structure and function.

S2 d Life Sciences Concepts: The student produces evidence that demonstrates understanding of populations and ecosystems, such as...the effects of resources and energy transfer on populations.

(B) The student identified the dominant group of plants in this particular population.

(C) The student identified a possible reason related to resources for the dominance of one species.

This work sample illustrates a standard-setting performance for the following parts of the standards:

- **S2 a Life Sciences Concepts: Structure and function.**
- **S2 d Life Sciences Concepts: Populations and ecosystems.**
- **S2 e Life Sciences Concepts: Adaptation of organisms.**
- **S5 a Scientific Thinking: Control variables.**
- **S5 b Scientific Thinking: Use concepts from Science Standards 1 to 4 to explain observations and phenomena.**
- **S5 d Scientific Thinking: Distinguish between fact and opinion.**
- **S5 e Scientific Thinking: Evaluate the accuracy, design, and outcomes of investigations.**

Seeds

S2e Life Sciences Concepts: The student produces evidence that demonstrates understanding of...adaptation of organisms....

(D) The student offered several possible adaptations to explain the population difference.

S5a Scientific Thinking: The student...controls variables in experimental and non-experimental research settings.

(E) The student critiqued his own procedure by identifying variables which might have been controlled.

S5b Scientific Thinking: The student uses concepts from Science Standards 1 to 4 to explain a variety of observations and phenomena.

(F) The student used the understanding necessary to identify dicots in order to control the variable of seed type.

S5d Scientific Thinking: The student...distinguishes between fact and opinion.

(G) The student based his conclusions on experimental data, not his opinion.

S5e Scientific Thinking: The student...evaluates the accuracy, design, and outcomes of investigations.

(H)

(F) Procedure II:

1. Get 5 kinds of dicots (walnuts, peanuts, limabean, pinto bean and soybean)
2. Get a hammer and some brown paper towels
3. Put one seed at a time in a paper towel in the middle
4. Hit the seed with the hammer real light because if you hit it hard you will tear the paper towel
5. Put the paper towels out where you can see them and let them sit for 10 minutes
6. Get a can of pop while you wait because you have time
7. Hold the paper towels up to the light and look at the oil spot.
8. Compare the oil spots and see which is largest.
9. Measure the oil spots at the widest part top to bottom and side to side.
10. The largest oil spot is the one with the most oil

Data:

It was hard to measure the way I thought because the oil spots were not round or square. So I held up two and picked the largest and then held it up to another one and then I found the largest and the next largest. The oil showed up best when I put it up in a window. The peanut had the biggest oil then the walnut then the soybean then the pinto bean and lima bean were the same.

(H) Conclusions:

(E) I should have let the paper towels dry more because I think some of the lima bean and the soybean may be water. But the peanut and the walnut had a lot of oil. (G) I was surprised by how the soybean was. I didn't think it would have any oil but it did. The oil is like fat and so it would be best if you ate the lima bean and the pinto beans. I would like to find other dicots and try them.

Work Sample & Commentary: *Passive Solar Homes*

The task

Students were asked to design and build a model that would illustrate a form of renewable energy and to make a presentation. They needed to complete background research in order to come up with an accurate design.

Circumstances of performance

This sample of student work was produced under the following conditions:

√ alone	in a group
√ in class	√ as homework
√ with teacher feedback	√ with peer feedback
timed	√ opportunity for revision

The quotations from the Science performance descriptions in this commentary are excerpted. The complete performance descriptions are shown on pages 92-95.

This student chose the topic of passive solar homes. Included here are the written report, a design drawing, and notes for the presentation. The model was built but is not included here.

What the work shows

S3d Earth and Space Sciences Concepts: The student produces evidence that demonstrates understanding of natural resource management.

Throughout the work, the student explained that solar energy is reliable and renewable, cost-efficient and less wasteful than conventional forms of home energy, and has minimum impact on the environment. For example solar energy is:

(A) reliable;

(B) renewable;

(C) cost-efficient and less wasteful than conventional forms of home energy; and has

(D) minimum impact on the environment.

This work sample illustrates a standard-setting performance for the following parts of the standards:

S3 d Earth and Space Sciences Concepts: Natural resource management.

S4 a Scientific Connections and Applications: Big ideas and unifying concepts.

S4 d Scientific Connections and Applications: Impact of technology.

Passive Solar Homes

Solar energy can be used in many ways. It can be used to heat water, cook food, and even heat and provide energy for homes. It is a (A) very reliable source.

Passive solar homes run on passive solar energy. The home is equipped with special devices to run on solar energy. It is equipped (E) with a black asphalt roof to collect, store, and distribute the heat. It also has full length windows on the south side for the sunlight to pass through and collect in the insulation inside the walls. There are also windows on a slanted roof for extra sunlight. The house has flagstone or adobe floors and walls for heat storage. To prevent overheating the house is equipped with ventilation, overhangs, shades, and landscaping.

The energy passes through the windows and heats the air. Then the walls and floors absorb and store excess heat. The stored heat is later released when the temperature falls. When the energy passes through the windows and is collected in the walls, then later released the energy conversion from this is light to heat. The sunlight is stored as heat and later released.

(B) Solar energy is a renewable source. It comes only from the sun. The sun can't run out of energy until it stops burning. The sun is always burning, therefore, solar energy is renewable. Solar energy will always be renewable until the sun stops burning.

(C) The cost efficiency for having a solar home is very inexpensive. The only thing needed for a solar home is large windows, insulation in the walls and floors, and adobe or flagstone. Solar energy does not need extra energy to run it, therefore, there are no extra costs. Solar energy is not wasteful and is a low-cost system.

A passive solar home provides day lighting and improves comfort with radiant heat. Solar energy is a renewable heating system that is quiet and reliable, has low maintenance, no moving parts, and lasts longer than other heating systems. The solar home also has a minimum (D) impact on the environment. It uses no gas, coal, petroleum, or any other polluting energy sources. It uses only the sun which does not pollute the environment or harm it in any way.

(F) Solar energy has very little impact on society. Positive impacts on society are that solar homes do not pollute, and are less costly for the government and homeowners. Negative impacts are that parts of society do not agree with the solar energy idea. Also, redesigning of houses and subdivisions would have to take place to fit the needs of solar energy.

Solar energy is a very easy and productive resource. It is environmentally safe and does not cost much at all. Solar energy is the ideal renewable energy source.

Passive Solar Homes

S4a Scientific Connections and Applications: The student produces evidence that demonstrates understanding of big ideas and unifying concepts, such as...form and function....

E The student carefully explained the purpose for each of the components in a passive solar home.

S4d Scientific Connections and Applications: The student produces evidence that demonstrates understanding of impact of technology, such as constraints and trade-offs....

F **G** The student analyzed the pros and cons of using solar energy. These concluding statements include consideration of some constraints and recognition of some trade-offs.

There are two constraints that are not mentioned: costs of technology and availability of sunshine. One could argue that the costs of technology would be underwritten and lowered if society as a whole had more enthusiasm for the concept. The availability of sunshine is less of a problem in the region where this student lives than in many other places in the United States.

Bibliography

Book
Keeter, Barbara. *Energy Alternatives.*
San Diego: Lucent Books, 1990.

Textbook
Christensen, John. *Global Science.*
Dabuque: Kendell Hunt, 1984.

Pamphlet
Passive Solar Retrofit.
Austin: Texas Energy Extension Service, 1994.

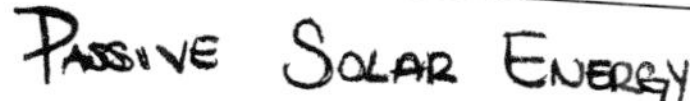

The sunlight passes through the window, then is collected and stored in the insulating barrier. Later when the temperature falls the heat is released.

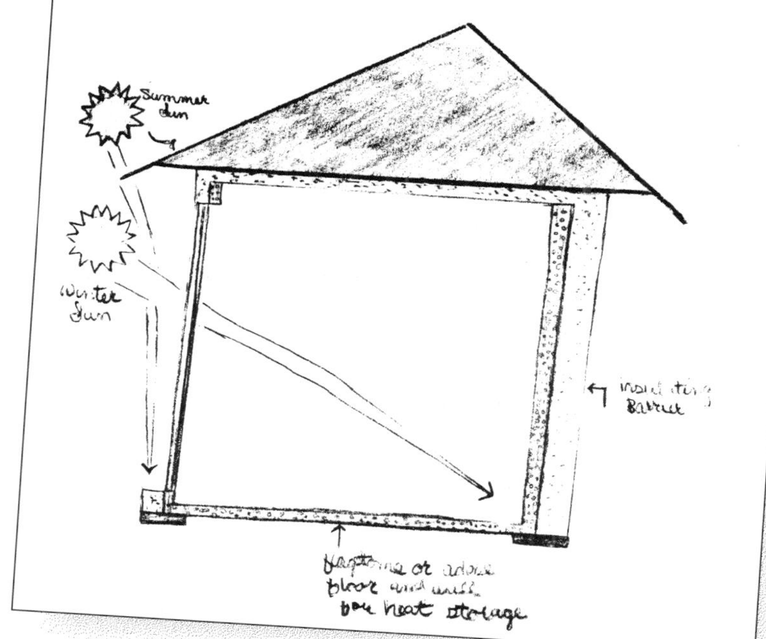

G

pros	cons
no polluting less costly environmentally safe not wasteful quiet	society dosen't agree w/solar energy idea redesign of houses to fit the solar plan sometimes not enough sunlight is collected

G Presentation

Solar Homes (Passive)

Demonstrate how home works.
- light goes through the windows
- is collected and stored in insulated walls
- black roof for storing heat
- skylights for extra solar energy.

Using the sun as a heat source. Read diagram. The energy conversions are: the light is collected and stored as heat.
Light - heat.

Physical Sciences Concepts
Life Sciences Concepts
S3 Earth and Space Sciences Concepts
S4 Scientific Connections and Applications
Scientific Thinking
Scientific Tools and Technologies
Scientific Communication
Scientific Investigation

Work Sample & Commentary: *Moon Study*

The task

Students who had been studying the Solar System were asked to pursue an individual project relating to the Solar System. This student chose to learn more about the phases of the Moon, a concept he had recently studied but did not understand.

Circumstances of performance

This sample of student work was produced under the following conditions:

√ alone	in a group
in class	√ as homework
√ with teacher feedback	with peer feedback
timed	√ opportunity for revision

The quotations from the Science performance descriptions in this commentary are excerpted. The complete performance descriptions are shown on pages 92-95.

What the work shows

S3 c Earth and Space Sciences Concepts: The student produces evidence that demonstrates understanding of earth in the Solar System, such as the predictable motion of planets, moons, and other objects in the Solar System including days, years, moon phases, and eclipses....

(A) The student demonstrated knowledge of the relative position of the Sun and Moon.

(A) (B) The student gave an accurate explanation of solar and lunar eclipses based on his observations.

S5 c Scientific Thinking: The student uses evidence from reliable sources to develop descriptions, explanations, and models.

(C) The student did not understand what had happened in class, so he used a book and observation to construct his understanding.

Moon Study

(C) My teacher tried to explain why there are phases of the moon. But, I really didn't understand even after the lab with the styrofoam ball. So, I went home and found a book that gave me some ideas about how to find out. This is what I did.

(D) Part 1: I made observations of the moon in the daytime from the full moon until the new moon (about a month). I counted the number of fists between the moon and the sun. I held my arm out as far as I could each time and I put my thumb fist side to the sun each time.

Day	Number of fists	moon
1	20	full
2	19	sort of full
3	cloudy	cloudy
4	cloudy	cloudy
5	15	gibbous
6	13	same
7	11	quarter (looks like half)
8	9	same
9	cloudy	cloudy
10	6	crescent (little sliver)
11	4	same
12	2	same
13	1	tiny crescent
14	1 (less than)	new moon (all shadow)
15	2	tiny crescent
16	3	same
17	5	crescent
18	7	same
19	9	crescent sort of
20	10	crescent
21	cloudy	
22	cloudy	
23	cloudy	
24	cloudy	
25	16	gibbous
26	18	same
27	19	almost full but not quite
28	cloudy	
29	cloudy	
30	cloudy	

(E)

(F) When the moon was full it was farther away from the sun than when it was crescent. I had to make some of my measures at different times of the day because of clouds. I guess that makes sense. Because when the moon is between the earth and the sun it would be super close to the sun and a new moon. Then when the moon moves it doesnt matter what way goes around the earth because it would be a crescent moon next. And the crescent moon was the next farthest by my fist measures. The full moon is when the moon is facing the sun so the earth is sort of between the moon and the sun. If (A) the sun was up over our back then it would still hit the moon and lite it up. If the sun was exactly behind the earth then we would have an eclipse of the moon because of the earth shadow. On the other side when the moon is in the new phase it could be a solar eclipse because the sun is blocked by the moon.

S6 a Scientific Tools and Technologies: The student uses technology and tools...to observe and measure objects...and phenomena,...remotely.

(D) The use of a fist as a measure is a traditional way to measure distance, but one that is an appropriate challenge to understand at the middle school level.

S7 a Scientific Communication: The student represents data and results in multiple ways, such as numbers, tables,...diagrams, and...writing.

(E) (F) (G)

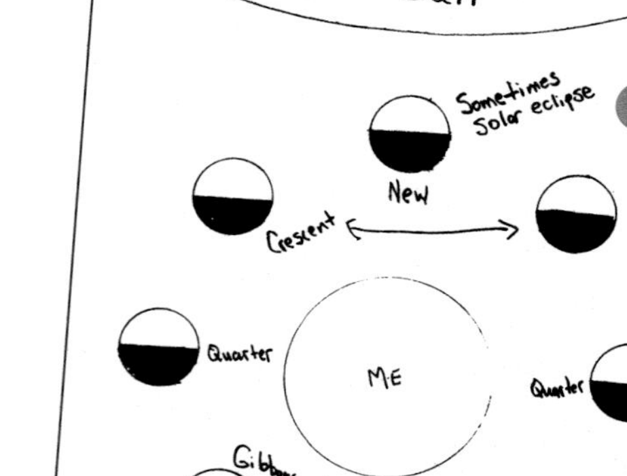

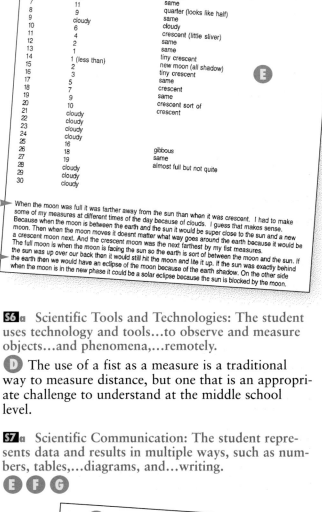

This work sample illustrates a standard-setting performance for the following parts of the standards:

S3 c Earth and Space Sciences Concepts: Earth in the Solar System.

S5 c Scientific Thinking: Use evidence from reliable sources.

S6 a Scientific Tools and Technologies: Use technology and tools to observe and measure.

S7 a Scientific Communication: Represent data and results in multiple ways.

Physical Sciences Concepts
Life Sciences Concepts
Earth and Space Sciences Concepts S3
Scientific Connections and Applications
Scientific Thinking S5
Scientific Tools and Technologies S6
Scientific Communication S7
Scientific Investigation

Work Sample & Commentary: *Spot Remover*

The task

In an on-demand task, students were asked to describe in detail an experiment that a person might perform to find out which of two spot removers is better for removing stains from fabrics.

Circumstances of performance

This sample of student work was produced under the following conditions:

√ alone	in a group
√ in class	as homework
with teacher feedback	with peer feedback
√ timed	opportunity for revision

This task was part of a state assessment and unrelated to the curriculum being studied.

What the work shows

S5a Scientific Thinking: The student frames questions to distinguish cause and effect; and identifies or controls variables in experimental and non-experimental research settings.

(A) In the first work sample, three variables are explicitly identified and controlled: "same material," "same amount on both shirts," and "same amount of time."

(B) In the second work sample, four variables are explicitly identified and controlled: "same material," "same amount of time [for staining]," and "same way," and "same amount of time [for washing]."

S7d Scientific Communication: The student explains a scientific concept or procedure to other students.

(A) (B) Both samples provide procedures that could be replicated by other students.

(B) Although not called for in the task, the second sample offers two explanations for the procedures, making the communication more effective.

(A)

A person wants to determine which of two spot removers is more effective. Describe in detail an experiment the person might perform in order to find out which spot remover is better for removing stains from fabrics.

Get some liquid that leaves spots, like spaghetti sauce or vegetable soup. Spot two shirts (of the same material) with it. Put the same amount on both shirts. Then soak one shirt in on spot remover and the other shirt in the other spot remover. leave the shirts in the liquid for the same amount of time. (leave the shirts in the spot remover for about 1 day.) Then take the shirts out, whichever spot remover got rid of the spots best is the best spot remover.

(B)

Instructions: Use this sheet to answer the question(s). Use the reverse side of this sheet if needed.

A person wants to determine which of two spot removers is more effective. Describe in detail an experiment the person might perform in order to find out which spot remover is better for removing stains from fabrics.

That person should find two old pieces of fabric made from the same material. The fabric should be old only because if the stain isn't removed, they won't be as disappointed. The fabric should be made from the same material just in case one kind of material stains worse. Next put a stain on each piece of fabric (grape juice, spaghetti sause). Let them sit for the same amount of time to make sure one doesn't stain worse because it sat longer. Then wash one with one spot remover and the other with the other spot remover. After they are washed the same way for the same amount of time, compare the stains. The person should buy the spot remover that removed the stain the best.

This works well plus it is a fun experiment to do!

These work samples illustrate standard-setting performances for the following parts of the standards:

S5a Scientific Thinking: Frame questions to distinguish cause and effect; identify or control variables in experimental and non-experimental research settings.

S7d Scientific Communication: Explain a scientific concept or procedure to other students.

The quotations from the Science performance descriptions in this commentary are excerpted. The complete performance descriptions are shown on pages 92-95.

Work Sample & Commentary: *Paper Towels*

Test #1

F **Problem:** Will the product, Brawny paper towels, be stronger than the other 3 brands of paper towels? Which brand is the strongest brand?

Research: Strength is a major part of this experiment. The word strong or strength doesn't necessarily have to deal with muscles. To be strong you must be powerful and able to resist attack. As well as being powerful, you must be well established, firm, solid, not easily broken, or steadfast. The word steadfast basically comes down to being firmly fixed, steady, and well built. The word strength has a similar meaning. To have strength it means to have the ability to endure, support, or force in numbers.

Paper is a material made by pressing pulp of rags, straw, or wood into thin sheets.

A towel can be cloth or paper. Based upon this experiment the towels being tested are made of paper. Drying is the major purpose for a paper towel, but sometimes they're used for scrubbing surfaces.

A **Hypothesis:** Based from the research, I think our product, the Brawny paper towel will be stronger. Being that the towel is made of thin sheets of paper, there is the likely reason that it will rip when wet. But unlike the other brands Brawny is thicker. When we compare the characteristics of strength Brawny fits all the characteristics. Brawny can resist attack. It is well established, firm, solid (thick, in other words), and well built. In our test we will actually find out if it can handle "force in numbers."

B **Set Up:** The paper towel will be laid over the rim of a plastic bowl, approximately 4 1/4 of an inch. The paper towel will be secured so that it is tight with a rubber band. The paper towel will be sprayed 20 times with a fine mist from a water bottle. Pennies (the weights) will be put on one at a time until the towel breaks. Then we'll count the pennies and record our data. The process will be repeated for the other brands as well.

The quotations from the Science performance descriptions in this commentary are excerpted. The complete performance descriptions are shown on pages 92-95.

The task

Students in a physical science class were asked to test the effectiveness of one of several different common products. The task required them to perform detailed and accurate testing and report results in a form for public presentation. Further, the students were asked to design and give a presentation promoting the most successful product.

Circumstances of performance

This sample of student work was produced under the following conditions:

	alone	√	in a group
√	in class		as homework
√	with teacher feedback	√	with peer feedback
	timed	√	opportunity for revision

Students had two weeks to complete the task which was part of a unit on scientific methodologies. While students videotaped a portion of their presentation, it is not included here.

Science required by the task

Paper towel testing is a common middle school activity, but many students select variables that are social in nature (e.g., cost, appearance) and are more easily measured than are strength or performance. This project tackled variables that required more imagination and effort to measure.

What the work shows

S4a Scientific Connections and Applications: The student produces evidence that demonstrates understanding of big ideas and unifying concepts, such as...form and function....

A The student related the thickness (form) of towels to the characteristic of strength (function).

This work sample illustrates a standard-setting performance for the following parts of the standards:

- **S4a Scientific Connections and Applications: Big ideas and unifying concepts.**
- **S4b Scientific Connections and Applications: The designed world.**
- **S5a Scientific Thinking: Frame questions to distinguish cause and effect; identify or control variables in experimental or non-experimental research settings.**
- **S7a Scientific Communication: Represent data and results in multiple ways.**
- **S8a Scientific Investigation: Controlled experiment.**

S4b Scientific Connections and Applications: The student produces evidence that demonstrates understanding of the designed world, such as...the viability of technological designs.

A The student provided evidence of thinking through the design of paper towels and how well they would serve the intended purpose.

S5a Scientific Thinking: The student frames questions to distinguish cause and effect; and identifies or controls variables in experimental and non-experimental research settings.

B C There is ample evidence of the student's recognition and control of variables.

S7a Scientific Communication: The student represents data and results in multiple ways, such as numbers, tables...drawings, diagrams, and artwork....

B C The experimental set-up is communicated in both words and drawings.

D E The results are communicated in tables, graphs, and words. The histogram is more effective than the pie chart. There is a reversal in the table for Test #2 (data for "Job Squad" and "Bounty"), but the multiple representations actually allow the reader to figure that out.

S8a Scientific Investigation: The student demonstrates scientific competence by completing a controlled experiment. A full investigation includes:

- Questions that can be studied using the resources available.

Paper Towels

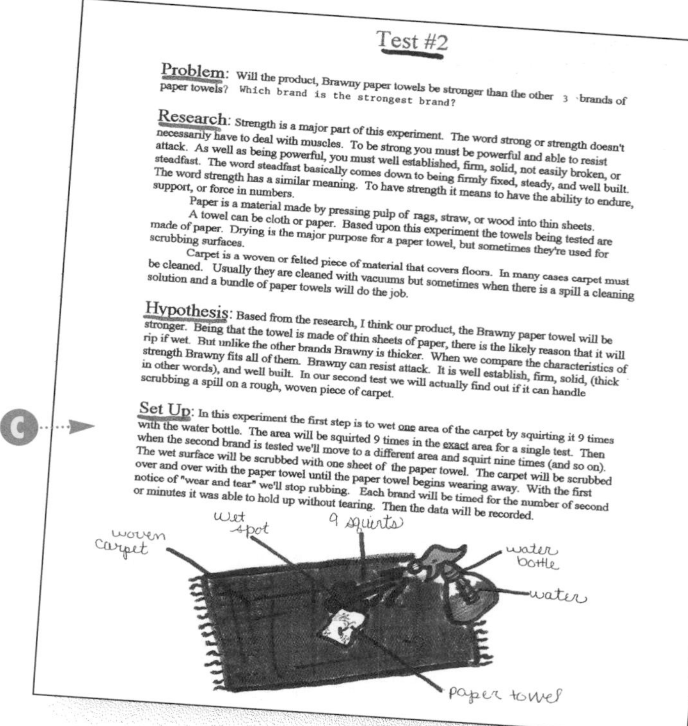

Test #2

Problem: Will the product, Brawny paper towels be stronger than the other 3 brands of paper towels? Which brand is the strongest brand?

Research: Strength is a major part of this experiment. The word strong or strength doesn't necessarily have to deal with muscles. To be strong you must be powerful and able to resist attack. As well as being powerful, you must well established, firm, solid, not easily broken, or steadfast. The word steadfast basically comes down to being firmly fixed, steady, and well built. The word strength has a similar meaning. To have strength it means to have the ability to endure, support, or force in numbers.

Paper is a material made by pressing pulp of rags, straw, or wood into thin sheets.

A towel can be cloth or paper. Based upon this experiment the towels being tested are made of paper. Drying is the major purpose for a paper towel, but sometimes they're used for scrubbing surfaces.

Carpet is a woven or felted piece of material that covers floors. In many cases carpet must be cleaned. Usually they are cleaned with vacuums but sometimes when there is a spill a cleaning solution and a bundle of paper towels will do the job.

Hypothesis: Based from the research, I think our product, the Brawny paper towel will be stronger. Being that the towel is made of thin sheets of paper, there is the likely reason that it will rip if wet. But unlike the other brands Brawny is thicker. When we compare the characteristics of strength Brawny fits all of them. Brawny can resist attack. It is well establish, firm, solid, (thick in other words), and well built. In our second test we will actually find out if it can handle scrubbing a spill on a rough, woven piece of carpet.

C → **Set Up**: In this experiment the first step is to wet one area of the carpet by squirting it 9 times with the water bottle. The area will be squirted 9 times in the exact area for a single test. Then when the second brand is tested we'll move to a different area and squirt nine times (and so on). The wet surface will be scrubbed with one sheet of the paper towel. The carpet will be scrubbed over and over with the paper towel until the paper towel begins wearing away. With the first notice of "wear and tear" we'll stop rubbing. Each brand will be timed for the number of second or minutes it was able to hold up without tearing. Then the data will be recorded.

- Procedures that are safe, humane, and ethical; and respect privacy and property rights.
- Data that have been collected and recorded (see also Science Standard 6) in ways that others can verify, and analyzed using skills expected at this grade level (see also Mathematics Standard 4).

B C D E

- Data and results that have been represented (see also Science Standard 7) in ways that fit the context.

D E

- Recommendations, decisions, and conclusions based on evidence.

G

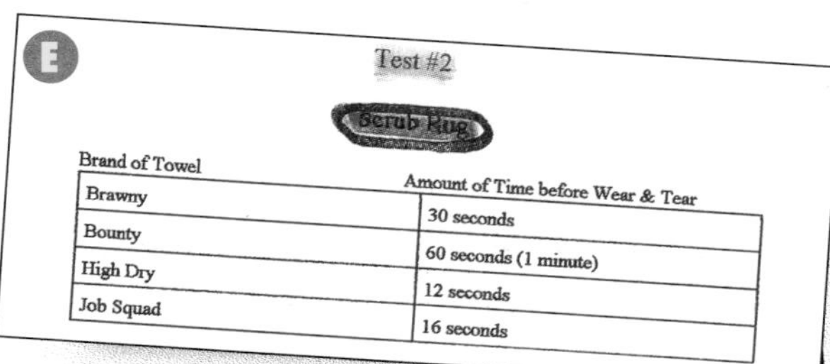

E

Test #2

Scrub Rug

Brand of Towel	Amount of Time before Wear & Tear
Brawny	30 seconds
Bounty	60 seconds (1 minute)
High Dry	12 seconds
Job Squad	16 seconds

Scrub & Rub

This bar graph shows which paper towel could stand up, and last the longest by rubbing it on a wet piece of carpet until it had a tear.

The x-axis names the brands of the 4 paper towels. The y-axis numbers by 5, with a range of 0 to 62 seconds. This axis is the time axis. By looking at the graph you can see that Job Squad lasted for 60 seconds until ripping. None of the other towels were close to Job Squad's time.

Brawny took 30 seconds until it wore away. Bounty took 16 seconds before wear and tear. High Dry came in last, with only 12 seconds.

SCRUB-&-RUB

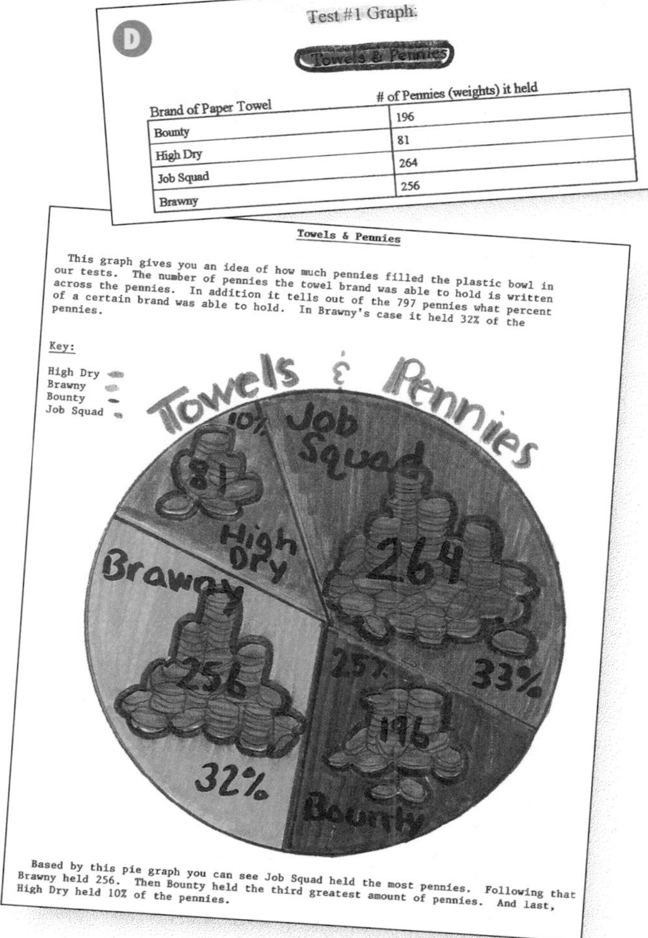

D

Test #1 Graph

Towels & Pennies

Brand of Paper Towel	# of Pennies (weights) it held
Bounty	196
High Dry	81
Job Squad	264
Brawny	256

Towels & Pennies

This graph gives you an idea of how much pennies filled the plastic bowl in our tests. The number of pennies the towel brand was able to hold is written across the pennies. In addition it tells out of the 797 pennies what percent of a certain brand was able to hold. In Brawny's case it held 32% of the pennies.

Key:

High Dry
Brawny
Bounty
Job Squad

Based by this pie graph you can see Job Squad held the most pennies. Following that Brawny held 256. Then Bounty held the third greatest amount of pennies. And last, High Dry held 10% of the pennies.

- Results that are communicated appropriately to audiences.

G

- Reflection and defense of conclusions and recommendations from other sources and peer review.

The student presented the work to others, though evidence of the presentation is not shown here.

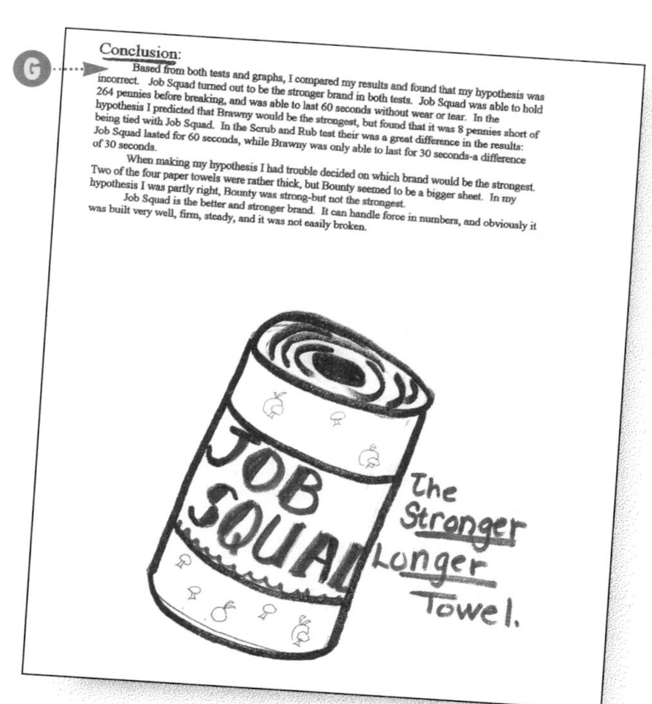

Conclusion:

G → Based from both tests and graphs, I compared my results and found that my hypothesis was incorrect. Job Squad turned out to be the stronger brand in both tests. Job Squad was able to hold 264 pennies before breaking, and was able to last 60 seconds without wear or tear. In the hypothesis I predicted that Brawny would be the strongest, but found that it was 8 pennies short of being tied with Job Squad. In the Scrub and Rub test their was a great difference in the results: Job Squad lasted for 60 seconds, while Brawny was only able to last for 30 seconds-a difference of 30 seconds.

When making my hypothesis I had trouble decided on which brand would be the strongest. Two of the four paper towels were rather thick, but Bounty seemed to be a bigger sheet. In my hypothesis I was partly right, Bounty was strong-but not the strongest.

Job Squad is the better and stronger brand. It can handle force in numbers, and obviously it was built very well, firm, steady, and it was not easily broken.

Introduction to the performance standards for *Applied Learning*

Applied Learning focuses on the capabilities people need to be productive members of society, as individuals who apply the knowledge gained in school and elsewhere to analyze problems and propose solutions, to communicate effectively and coordinate action with others, and to use the tools of the information age workplace. It connects the work students do in school with the demands of the twenty-first century workplace.

As a newer focus of study, Applied Learning does not have a distinct professional constituency producing content standards on which performance standards can be built. However, the Secretary's Commission on Achieving Necessary Skills (SCANS) laid a foundation for the field in its report, *Learning a Living: A Blueprint for High Performance* (1992) which defined the concept of "Workplace Know-how." We worked from this foundation and from comparable international work to produce our own "Framework for Applied Learning" (New Standards, 1994). That framework delineated nine areas of competence and spelled out their elements. The nine areas of competence were as follows:

- Collecting, analyzing, and organizing information;
- Communicating ideas and information;
- Planning and organizing resources;
- Working with others and in teams;
- Solving problems;
- Using mathematical ideas and techniques;
- Using technology;
- Teaching and learning on demand;
- Understanding and designing systems.

The Applied Learning performance standards have been built upon this framework. The standards have also been built on the experience of the Fort Worth Independent School District's applied learning initiative and the application projects developed by Mountlake Terrace High School in Washington.

We adopted the approach of developing distinct standards for Applied Learning rather than weaving them through the standards for the core subject areas. The advantage of establishing distinct standards for Applied Learning is that it focuses attention on the requirements of these standards and asserts an explicit role for Applied Learning as a domain for assessment and reporting of student achievement. "Cross-curricular" standards run the risk of being absorbed and lost within the expectations of the different subjects. However, the disadvantage of this approach is that it may be interpreted as advocating the development of Applied Learning as a subject in its own right to be studied in isolation from subject content. That is not the intention of these standards. We do not advocate development of Applied Learning as a separate subject. We expect that the work students do to meet the Applied Learning performance standards will take place generally within the context of a subject or will draw on content from more than one subject area. This expectation is stated in the performance description for A1, Problem Solving.

There are five performance standards for Applied Learning:

- **A1 Problem Solving;**
- **A2 Communication Tools and Techniques;**
- **A3 Information Tools and Techniques;**
- **A4 Learning and Self-management Tools and Techniques;**
- **A5 Tools and Techniques for Working With Others.**

A1, Problem Solving is the centerpiece of the standards. The performance description defines problem solving projects focused on productive activity and organized around three kinds of problem solving:

- Design a product, service or system in which the student identifies needs that could be met by new products, services, or systems and creates solutions for meeting them;
- Improve a System in which the student develops an understanding of the way systems of people, machines, and processes work; troubleshoots problems in their operation and devises strategies for improving their effectiveness;
- Plan and organize an event or an activity in which the student takes responsibility for all aspects of planning and organizing an event or an activity from concept to completion.

The performance description specifies the criteria for each kind of problem solving project. These criteria become progressively more demanding from elementary school to high school.

The four "tools and techniques" standards are designed to work in concert with the Problem Solving standard. Each of these standards describes tools and techniques that are needed for success in completing projects of the kinds outlined above.

The tools and techniques described in A2 - A5 (such as gathering information, conducting formal correspondence, learning from models, and taking responsibility for a component of a team project) are only meaningful when considered in the context of work that has a genuine purpose and audience. The key to effective use of these tools and techniques is the capacity to put them to use in an integrated way in the course of completing a real task. It is critical, therefore, that they be learned and used in such contexts rather than practiced in a piecemeal way as skills for their own sake. Students are expected to demonstrate their achievement of the tools and techniques standards in the context of problem solving projects. This is reflected in the examples listed under the performance descriptions. At the same time, it is unlikely that any one project will allow students to demonstrate their achievement in relation to all of the standards. This is evident from the work samples and commentaries. In fact, it is likely that a project that attempts to cover all of the parts of the standards will accomplish none of them well.

The Applied Learning performance standards reflect the nine areas of competence defined in the "Framework for Applied Learning." But the match is not complete. M6, M8, S6, and S8 embody many of the competencies that were defined by the "Framework for Applied Learning" in "Using mathematical tools and techniques" and "Using technology." These competencies have not been duplicated in Applied Learning. However, the Applied Learning standards do include an explicit requirement that students use information technology to assist in gathering, organizing, and presenting information. Given the importance of ensuring all students develop the capacity to make effective use of information technology, we resolved that the overlap among the standards in this area was warranted. (See "Introduction to the performance standards for Science," page 90, for discussion of the resource issues related to this requirement.)

Another area in which we decided that some overlap was warranted relates to A2. The first part of this standard, which requires an oral presentation, is similar to one of the requirements of E3. The difference is that A2a focuses explicitly on presenting project plans or results to an audience beyond the school, whereas the purpose and audience of the presentation are not specified in E3c. As the cross-referencing of examples under the performance descriptions indicates, oral presentations that meet the requirements of A2a may also satisfy the requirements of E3c; however, the reverse would not necessarily be the case.

The capacities defined by the tools and techniques standards (A2 - A5) are difficult to pin down. There is a tendency to describe them in terms of general dispositions that render them almost impossible to assess in any credible way. Each part of these standards is defined in terms of a work product or performance that students can use to provide concrete evidence of their achievement. The overall set of products and performances required to meet the standards is similar at each grade level, but the specific requirements differ and grow in demand from elementary to high school. (See "Appendix IV: The Grade Levels Compared: Applied Learning," page 166.)

The first year of developmental testing of Applied Learning portfolios in 1995-96 provided an opportunity to test these performance standards (as they were presented in the *Consultation Draft*) in practice. Students in about 50 classrooms conducted projects designed around the standards. Their experience and the experience of the teachers who supported them was a valuable source of information for refining the performance descriptions. Refinements were also made in response to reviews by representatives of business and industry groups and community youth organizations, such as 4-H, Girl Scouts of the U.S.A., Boy Scouts of America, Junior Achievement, and Girls and Boys Clubs of America. The refinements were largely confined to the detail of the performance descriptions, but there were two more significant changes, both related to A3. The first was the definition of more explicit requirements for using information technology, especially at the high school level, in response to comments from business and industry representatives. The second was the inclusion of a specific requirement for "research" as set out in A3a. Research was implicit in the draft performance standards. The decision to make it explicit arose in the process of review of student projects where it was clear that the successful projects were those in which students had invested energy in research and could demonstrate that research in the work they produced.

Experience in using the standards to shape student work raised several issues. It was notable that most projects focused on "design" and on "planning and organizing." There were fewer examples of "improving a system." This was not surprising, but indicates the need to focus attention on gathering examples of such projects.

The circumstances in which the projects were conducted varied markedly. Some projects were initiated by the teacher and some were initiated by students; some projects were conducted by whole classes, some by small groups of students, and some by individuals; some projects were conducted as part of classwork and some were conducted largely outside class. It was clear, however, that regardless of how a project was initiated, a critical part of its success was the development of a sense of responsibility among the students involved for figuring out the work that needed to be done to complete the project and for making sure that the work got done. What was less clear were the relative merits of different arrangements of whole class, small group, and individual projects. A further question was the appropriate level of scaffolding of projects by teachers and the degree of scaffolding that is appropriate at different grade levels. Our capacity to resolve this last issue was complicated by the fact that, for most of the teachers and students involved, these were the first projects of this sort they had ever undertaken. The work samples and commentaries should be read with this fact in mind. These are issues that can only be resolved through practice and experience.

A1 Problem Solving

Apply problem solving strategies in purposeful ways, both in situations where the problem and desirable solutions are clearly evident and in situations requiring a creative approach to achieve an outcome.

To see how these performance descriptions compare with the expectations for elementary school and high school, turn to pages 166-171.

The examples that follow the performance descriptions for each standard are examples of the work students might do to demonstrate their achievement. The examples also indicate the nature and complexity of activities that are appropriate to expect of students at the middle school level.

The cross-references that follow the examples highlight examples for which the same activity, and possibly even the same piece of work, may enable students to demonstrate their achievement in relation to more than one standard. In some cases, the cross-references highlight examples of activities through which students might demonstrate their achievement in relation to standards for more than one subject matter.

The student conducts projects involving at least two of the following kinds of problem solving each year and, over the course of middle school, conducts projects involving all three kinds of problem solving.

- Design a Product, Service, or System: Identify needs that could be met by new products, services, or systems and create solutions for meeting them.
- Improve a System: Develop an understanding of the way systems of people, machines, and processes work; troubleshoot problems in their operation and devise strategies for improving their effectiveness.
- Plan and Organize an Event or an Activity: Take responsibility for all aspects of planning and organizing an event or an activity from concept to completion, making good use of the resources of people, time, money, and materials and facilities.

Each project should involve subject matter related to the standards for English Language Arts, and/or Mathematics, and/or Science, and/or other appropriate subject content.

Design a Product, Service, or System

A1 a The student designs and creates a product, service, or system to meet an identified need; that is, the student:

- develops a range of ideas for design of the product, service, or system;
- selects one design option to pursue and justifies the choice with reference, for example, to functional, aesthetic, social, economic, or environmental considerations;
- establishes criteria for judging the success of the design;
- uses appropriate conventions to represent the design;
- plans and carries out the steps needed to create the product, service, or system;
- makes adjustments as needed to conform with specified standards or regulations regarding quality and safety;
- evaluates the quality of the design in terms of the criteria for success and by comparison with similar products, services, or systems.

Examples of designing a product, service, or system include:

- Design and produce a history periodical for students. **2b, 3b, 4a, 5a, E2c**
- Design and build a wheelchair access ramp. **2a, 3a, 5c, M2a, M2g, M2k, M8c, S8c**
- Design and implement an induction program for students new to the school, including a handbook and other informational materials. **2c, E2d**
- Design and conduct a community survey to inform local council decisions about the future use of a community owned building or resource area. **2a, 2c, 3b, 5a, M4a, M4b, M4c, M4d**
- Design and build a grandfather clock. **S1b, S4d, S8c**
- Design and stage a dramatic production. **2c, 4a, 5a, E5b**

Improve a System

A1 b The student troubleshoots problems in the operation of a system in need of repair or devises and tests ways of improving the effectiveness of a system in operation; that is, the student:

- describes the structure and management of the system in terms of its logic, sequences, and control;
- identifies the operating principles underlying the system, i.e., mathematical, scientific, organizational;
- evaluates the way the system operates;
- devises strategies for putting the system back in operation or improving its performance;
- evaluates the effectiveness of the strategies for improving the system and supports the evaluation with evidence.

Examples of troubleshooting problems in the operation of a system or improving the effectiveness of a system in operation include:

- Earn the Auto Mechanics Merit Badge (Boy Scouts of America) or complete the Auto Maintenance Project (Girl Scouts of the U.S.A.). **4a, S1c, S4b**
- Conduct an energy audit of the classroom and develop procedures for reducing waste. **S1c, S4b, S4d**
- Make recommendations to local officials about ways to improve water quality in the vicinity of the school. **3a, 3b, 5b, S3a, S3d, S4c**
- Design and equip a recreational area on one acre with a limited budget. **M1a, M2a, M2d, M2h, M2j, M8c**
- Propose ways of re-establishing a neighborhood crime prevention organization that has become defunct. **3a**

Plan and Organize an Event or an Activity

A1 c The student plans and organizes an event or activity; that is, the student:

- develops a plan that:
  - reflects research into relevant precedents and regulations;
  - includes all the factors and variables that need to be considered;
  - shows the order in which things need to be done;
  - takes into account the resources available to put the plan into action, including people and time;
- implements the plan in ways that:
  - reflect the priorities established in the plan;
  - respond effectively to unforeseen circumstances;
- evaluates the success of the event or activity;
- makes recommendations to others who might consider planning and organizing a similar event or activity.

Examples of planning and organizing an event or an activity include:

- Organize a science fair. **4a**
- Stage a dramatic production. **2c, 4a, 5a, E5b**
- Plan a field trip to study an ecosystem. **S2d**
- Organize a program for providing voluntary services in household help and maintenance to elderly people in the local area. **5c**
- Organize a school carnival. **2a, 2b, M4h, M4i, M8d**
- Organize a special event for a local organization, such as an awards night or end of season celebration. **2a, 2b, 5c**

A2 Communication Tools and Techniques

Communicate information and ideas in ways that are appropriate to the purpose and audience through spoken, written, and graphic means of expression.

A2 a The student makes an oral presentation of project plans or findings to an audience beyond the school; that is, the student:

- organizes the presentation in a logical way appropriate to its purpose;
- adjusts the style of presentation to suit its purpose and audience;
- speaks clearly and presents confidently;
- responds appropriately to questions from the audience;
- evaluates the effectiveness of the presentation.

Examples of oral presentations include:

- A presentation to the board of a local organization of a proposal for a special event to be organized on behalf of the organization. **1c, 2b, 5c, E3c**
- A presentation to the local council of results of a community survey designed to inform the council's decisions about future use of a community owned building or resource area. **1a, 2c, 3b, 5a, E3c**
- A presentation to a local business of plans for a school carnival and a request for assistance in running the event. **1c, 2b, E3c**
- A presentation to representatives of the school district's buildings and maintenance department of designs for a wheelchair access ramp. **1a, 3a, 5c, E3c**

A2 b The student conducts formal written correspondence with an organization beyond the school; that is, the student:

- expresses the information or request clearly for the purpose and audience;
- writes in a style appropriate to the purpose and audience of the correspondence.

Examples of formal written correspondence include:

- A letter to a museum seeking permission to reproduce artwork in a history periodical for students. **1a, 3b, 4a, 5a**
- A letter to a local business seeking financial support for a school carnival. **1c, 2a**
- Letters to the police and fire departments advising them of plans for a special event to be conducted on behalf of a local organization and seeking direction regarding safety regulations applicable to the event. **1c, 2a, 5c**

A2 c The student publishes information using several methods and formats, such as overhead transparencies, handouts, and computer generated graphs and charts; that is, the student:

- organizes the information into an appropriate form for use in the publication;
- checks the information for accuracy;
- formats the published material so that it achieves its purpose.

Examples of publishing information include:

- Publish a program for a dramatic production. **1a, 4a, 5a**
- Publish a brochure advertising the school for new students. **1a**
- Produce overhead transparencies and handouts to support a presentation to the local council on the results of a community survey designed to inform the council's decisions about future use of a community owned building or resource area. **1a, 2a, 3b, 5a**

A3 Information Tools and Techniques

Use information gathering techniques, analyze and evaluate information, and use information technology to assist in collecting, analyzing, organizing, and presenting information.

A3 a The student gathers information to assist in completing project work; that is, the student:

- identifies potential sources of information to assist in completing the project;
- uses appropriate techniques to collect the information, e.g., considers sampling issues in conducting a survey;
- interprets and analyzes the information;
- evaluates the information for completeness and relevance;
- shows evidence of research in the completed project.

Examples of gathering information to assist in completing project work include:

- Research regulations and building standards related to designing and building a wheelchair access ramp. **1a, 2a, 5c**
- Collect and test the quality of samples of water from nearby water sources. **1b, 3b, 5b, S6a**
- Survey other neighborhoods to gather information about neighborhood crime prevention organizations that work. **1b**

A3 b The student uses information technology to assist in gathering, analyzing, organizing, and presenting information; that is, the student:

- acquires information for specific purposes from on-line sources, such as the Internet, and other electronic data bases, such as a scientific data base on CD ROM;
- uses word-processing, graphics, data base, and spreadsheet programs to produce project reports and related materials.

Examples of using information technology to assist in gathering, analyzing, organizing, and presenting information include:

- Load, run, and use a data base program to manage data collected through a community survey. **1a, 2a, 2c, 5a**
- Use on-line sources to collect information about water quality in nearby areas to inform research into water quality in the local area. **1b, 3a, 5b, S6d**
- Use documentation and on-screen help to learn how to use a desktop publishing program for producing a history periodical for students. **1a, 2b, 4a, 5a**

Samples of student work that illustrate standard-setting performances for these standards can be found on pages 117-135.

The cross-references that follow the examples illustrate some of the ways by which a single Applied Learning project may provide a vehicle for demonstrating achievement of several parts of the standards. The cross-references are based on the examples that are linked to the Problem Solving standard. It is intended that students demonstrate their achievement of the four Tools and Techniques standards in conjunction with Problem Solving projects.

A4 Learning and Self-management Tools and Techniques

Manage and direct one's own learning.

A4 a The student learns from models; that is, the student:

- consults with or observes other students and adults at work, and identifies the main features of what they do and the way they go about their work;
- identifies models for the results of project work, such as professionally produced publications, and analyzes their qualities;
- uses what he or she learns from models to assist in planning and conducting project activities.

Examples of learning from models include:

- Examine professionally published journals to inform the design of a history journal for students. **1a, 2b, 3b, 5a**
- Visit a professionally organized exhibition to inform planning for a science fair. **1c**
- Make a field trip to study a dramatic production in rehearsal to inform design of the students' own production; interview people involved in the production, such as the director, stage manager, lighting director, publicity manager. **1a, 2c, 5a**
- Visit an auto repair shop and study how a mechanic diagnoses faults in motor vehicles. **1b**

To see how these performance descriptions compare with the expectations for elementary school and high school, turn to pages 166-171.

The examples that follow the performance descriptions for each standard are examples of the work students might do to demonstrate their achievement. The examples also indicate the nature and complexity of activities that are appropriate to expect of students at the middle school level.

The cross-references that follow the examples highlight examples for which the same activity, and possibly even the same piece of work, may enable students to demonstrate their achievement in relation to more than one standard. In some cases, the cross-references highlight examples of activities through which students might demonstrate their achievement in relation to standards for more than one subject matter.

A4 b The student develops and maintains a schedule of work activities; that is, the student:

- establishes a schedule of work activities that reflects priorities and deadlines;
- seeks advice on the management of conflicting priorities and deadlines;
- updates the schedule regularly.

Examples of tools and techniques for developing and maintaining a schedule of work activities include:

- Develop daily, weekly, or longer term work plans, as appropriate.
- Use timelines to identify conflicting priorities and deadlines, and seek advice on resolving conflicting priorities and deadlines from teachers, clients, or peers, as appropriate.
- Review and revise work plans at the end of each day, week, or other period of time, as appropriate.

A4 c The student sets goals for learning and reviews his or her progress; that is, the student:

- sets goals for learning;
- reviews his or her progress towards meeting the goals;
- seeks and responds to advice from others in setting goals and reviewing progress.

Examples of tools and techniques for setting and reviewing learning goals include:

- Establish learning goals in consultation with the teacher and use the goals to inform choices about project activities, e.g., choose activities that provide opportunities to work towards established goals.
- Review work on a completed project in light of established learning goals.
- Seek feedback from teachers, clients, and peers to help set goals and review progress towards meeting them.

A5 Tools and Techniques for Working With Others

Work with others to achieve a shared goal, help other people to learn on-the-job, and respond effectively to the needs of a client.

A5 a The student takes responsibility for a component of a team project; that is, the student:

- reaches agreement with team members on what work needs to be done to complete the task and how the work will be tackled;
- takes specific responsibility for a component of the project;
- takes all steps necessary to ensure appropriate completion of the specific component of the project within the agreed upon time frame.

Examples of taking responsibility for a component of a team project include:

- Take responsibility for preparing an article for publication in a history magazine for students. **1a, 2b, 3b, 4a**
- Take responsibility for the lighting aspects of a dramatic production. **1a, 2c, 4a**
- Take responsibility for coordinating the analysis of data collected in a community survey. **1a, 2a, 2c, 3b**

A5 b The student coaches or tutors; that is, the student:

- assists one or more others to learn on the job;
- analyzes coaching or tutoring experience to identify more and less effective ways of providing assistance to support on-the-job learning;
- uses the analysis to inform subsequent coaching or tutoring activities.

Examples of coaching or tutoring include:

- Coach another student in the use of a software program. **3b**
- Coach a group of younger students undertaking a project.
- Tutor other students in techniques for analyzing water quality. **1b, 3a, 3b, S7e**

A5 c The student responds to a request from a client; that is, the student:

- consults with a client to clarify the demands of a task;
- interprets the client's request and translates it into an initial plan for completing the task, taking account of available resources;
- negotiates with the client to arrive at an agreed upon plan.

Examples of responding to a request from a client include:

- Negotiate with disabled members of the school community to design a wheelchair access ramp appropriate to their needs. **1a, 2a, 3a**
- Negotiate with the board of a local organization to organize a special event on its behalf. **1c, 2a, 2b**
- Negotiate with a committee of elderly citizens to organize a program for providing voluntary services. **1a**

Work Sample & Commentary: *Video 2*

The task

Students in an English/reading class decided to produce news videos that could be used to inform students of events at the school, to recruit prospective students, and to orient students new to the school.

Circumstances of performance

Students in the class worked initially as a whole class group and then both individually and in groups. They received advice and feedback from the teacher and their peers. The students also obtained assistance from other school personnel. Much of the work was done at school; however, for the technical production of the video the students had access to the video editing equipment in the school district's instructional television department. They were trained in the use of the equipment by district personnel. The project lasted several months and the students produced two videos. The original plan was to produce one video in each reporting period, however, the time required to produce the videos and the limited availability of equipment reduced the number to two videos.

The written work included with this project contains some errors. For the main part the errors are confined to journal entries and other planning documents which were produced for personal use only and were not intended for publication. The two pieces of finished writing are the proposal and the letter to the business. These contain virtually error free writing.

What the work shows

A1 a Problem Solving: The student designs and creates a product, service, or system to meet an identified need; that is, the student:

- develops a range of ideas for design of the product, service, or system;
- selects one design option to pursue and justifies the choice with reference, for example, to functional, aesthetic, social, economic, or environmental considerations;
- establishes criteria for judging the success of the design;
- uses appropriate conventions to represent the design;
- plans and carries out the steps needed to create the product, service, or system;
- makes adjustments as needed to conform with specified standards or regulations regarding quality and safety;
- evaluates the quality of the design in terms of the criteria for success and by comparison with similar products, services, or systems.

This work sample illustrates a standard-setting performance for the following parts of the standards:

A1 a Problem Solving: Design a product, service, or system.

A2 b Communication: Conduct formal written correspondence.

A4 a Learning and Self-management: Learn from models.

A4 b Learning and Self-management: Develop and maintain a schedule of work activities.

A5 a Working With Others: Take responsibility for a component of a team project.

A

Title: Proposal letter for a video camera
To: Ms. ______
Ms. ______
From: Mrs. ______'s Applied Learning Class

SUMMARY:
We are going to make a news video for and about the entire
______ Middle School. This video would include special events going
on here at ______ plus different features that would be of interest
to all involved here at ______; students, teachers and parents. We
would make one video per six weeks period and make it available for
all the other grade levels and seventh grade classes to watch it.
It would also be available to either any of our feeder schools or
anyone else who is interested on knowing about ______.

PURPOSE:
The main purpose of our news video is to make ______ students
more aware or "educate" about what is going on here at our school
and in that process foster a higher level of "Cardinal Pride". Our
secondary purpose for making these videos, is their possible use as
"recruiting" videos or orientation material. One of these videos
could be formatted as an introduction\orientation to ______ for the
5th graders and their parents at our feeder elementary schools.
This video would "educate" these 5th graders about what a great
school ______ is and about all that it has to offer to its
students.
Because the videos will be made by kids, this "inside look" at the
school might have more credibility with other kids here and at our
feeder schools.

BUDGET:
We will need funding for one JVC GRAX34U video camera . The
best price we found, was $499.99 (not including tax). It comes with
two videos and a tripod. This offer is available from Best Buy
through Christmas. We would need 3 additional videos and a AC
adapter. If all this is purchased through the school we will not
have to pay taxes.

AUDIENCE:
The videos would be viewed by two different types of
audiences. The first audience for our news videos would be the
6th, 7th, and 8th grade Cardinals. The second type of audience
would be incoming fifth grade students, from our feeder schools,
and their parents. The videos will also be available to any
incoming or prospective seventh and eight grade students and
parents.

BENEFITS:
The benefits of a news video would be many and varied but
here are just a few that we think are pertinent. One benefit would
be that students who don't get the Clarion will know what is going
on at ______. This will encourage participation and will also
encourage school spirit. Another benefit of having a news video

encourage school spirit. Another benefit of having a news video
would be that after we are done using the video camera purchased or
the video, other teachers and students could use it. The news
video project," Dateline MMS", satisfies most seventh grade honors
English/reading objectives for speaking, listening, reading, and
writing for a real world purpose and audience other teachers could
also use the video camera for class projects, to record special
events, or anything else that a video camera might be used for.
One of the important benefits of having these videos is not
only educating ______ students, it is also to educate our local
community about what a great school ______ is. In recent years,
because of the perception that ______ was no longer a good
(academically) school, many of the feeder school parents of
children with academic choices have chosen either private or magnet
schools. The videos would be a way to communicate with these
parents and their children that they can get not only as good an
education at ______ but also the "extras". For all the incoming 5th
graders the video would be a big step towards adjusting to ______.
They could see that ______ is not really as scary as they might
think, that their middle school experience could be a memorable
experience, and that they all can be an important part of that.

The documentation presented from this project is not a comprehensive record of all work done as part of the project. It would be neither reasonable nor appropriate to ask students to keep detailed written records of every aspect of a project. This would defeat part of the purpose of applied learning which is for students to put their academic learning to work and to learn from projects that connect what they do at school to the demands of the twenty-first century workplace. Some of these standards lend themselves to assessment through observation and other less formal methods rather than through written work.

Video 2

The work shown here documents the process of designing and developing a product to solve a problem. The project, Video 2, was developed in direct response to several concerns of the English/reading class.

A The proposal contends that many of the students and their parents do not know "about what's going on at our school." Secondly, too many students at feeder schools are choosing to attend other middle schools. Thirdly, students new to the school have a "scary" time adjusting. The students proposed to address the problem by producing a video. The proposal includes evidence of background research and planning.

B This comparison chart records the findings of the students' research into video cameras as background for their proposal.

In many projects, the process of exploring a range of designs happens in class discussion. This was the case in this project and there is no surviving documentation of the initial planning process. Thus, the documents featured with this commentary trace the progression of the project after the students selected the design option, i.e., the news video. The documents demonstrate how the design plan was implemented.

C The extract from the draft script for Dateline MMS demonstrates use of one of the conventions appropriate for presenting the design for a video.

D One student's log entry records the process her group followed in planning and developing its story for the video.

E Another student's log explains how the video was taped and edited.

F Not only does the student work show the production process, it also links the initial criteria established for governing the quality of the product to the final evaluation of the video. In order to determine the features of a successful news program, the students viewed "Good Morning, America," a morning television program. After that, the students identified the factors they regarded as contributing to the success of the production and then grouped the factors by categories.

G The students used their list of effective features of a news production to produce a news video rubric for evaluating their work.

B

A	A	B	C	D	E	F
1	Manufacturer		RCA	Sony	Sony	JVC
2	Model		CC616	CCDFX33	CCDTR82	GRAX34U
3	Format		VHS-C	VHS-C	8mm	VHS-C
4	Zoom Range		12x	14x	12x	12x
5	Editing Features				X	X
6	Cost		$699.97	$599.97	$799.97	$499.99

COMPARISON OF VIDEO CAMERAS CHART

KEY: "X" INDICATES AVAILABLE FEATURES

C

Script for Dateline MMS

Introduction-

Phillip- Hello and welcome to Dateline MMS. I am Phillip _____ and Janel ____ will be telling you the highlights for this 6 weeks. Janel...

Janel- Thank you Phillip and this 6 weeks highlights are...
The M-Pact club with Janel _____
Who the top seller of the fund-raiser was with Lauren ______
The Door Decorating contest with Rachel _______
Intermurals with Phillip _______
The Faculty against the Lady Cardinals Volleyball Game with Jennifer ________ and Paxton ______
The ______ family's new arrival with Myranda ________
The Dubbing of the sixth grade Knight ceremony with Lauren ______
The McLean Cardinals Uncaged with Kimberley ________
and The Cafeteria Dont's with Lauren ______ and Jennifer ______

Rachel- I am Rachel ______ and those are this 6 weeks highlights and now back to Janel with the story of the M-Pact Club

Janel- M-Pact story

Phillip- Here is Lauren _____with the top seller of the fund-raiser.

Lauren- I am Lauren _____and the top seller of the fund-raiser was Michelle ____. She received a box of Gobstoppers Candy, Perpetual Motion Mobil, Box Camera, Yard of Gum, and the 3D Movie. Don't worry about not getting any of these wonderful prizes. There will be another fund-raiser next year. Back to you Phillip.

Phillip- And now here is Rachel with the Door Decorating Contest.

Rachel- Door Decorating Contest story

Janel- Thank you Rachel. And Philip will show us some footage on intermurals. Phillip...

Phillip- Intermural story

Rachel- Here are some details about the Volleyball game with Jennifer ______ and Paxton _____.

Problem Solving A1
Communication Tools and Techniques A2
Information Tools and Techniques
Learning and Self-management Tools and Techniques A4
Tools and Techniques for Working With Others A5

Video 2

C The rubric influenced the development of the project. An example is the Script for Dateline MMS that follows the format of professional news programs. For example, the video begins by announcing all the stories that will be featured; the anchors provide the linking information and hand off to reporters responsible for specific stories.

H Later the students used the criteria in their comparative evaluations of Video 1 and Video 2. This student considered the second video better than the first because of the stories, the topics' appeal to the targeted audience, fewer technical problems, and a more professional look. The evaluation's references to "improvement" imply that following the production of the first video, the process is adjusted to improve the quality of the second video. Suggestions to future video teams include the use of a body microphone in order to improve the sound quality.

A2b Communication Tools and Techniques: The student conducts formal written correspondence with an organization beyond the school; that is, the student:

- expresses the information or request clearly for the purpose and audience;
- writes in a style appropriate to the purpose and audience of the correspondence.

A The proposal for the purchase of a video camera was written to the principal rather than to an organization beyond the school. Nevertheless, it expresses the request clearly for the purpose and audience and is written in an appropriate style for a proposal of this sort. It opens with a summary of the proposal; makes good use of headings to organize the sections of the proposal; and restricts itself to information that is pertinent to the proposal.

I The letter to a business to request funding for a video camera is expressed clearly and is written in a style appropriate to its purpose and audience. The students attached their proposal to the brief letter rather than attempting to summarize it in the body of the letter. This strategy is typical of formal business correspondence.

J The business was unable to comply with the students' request but responded with an offer of an alternative solution.

D

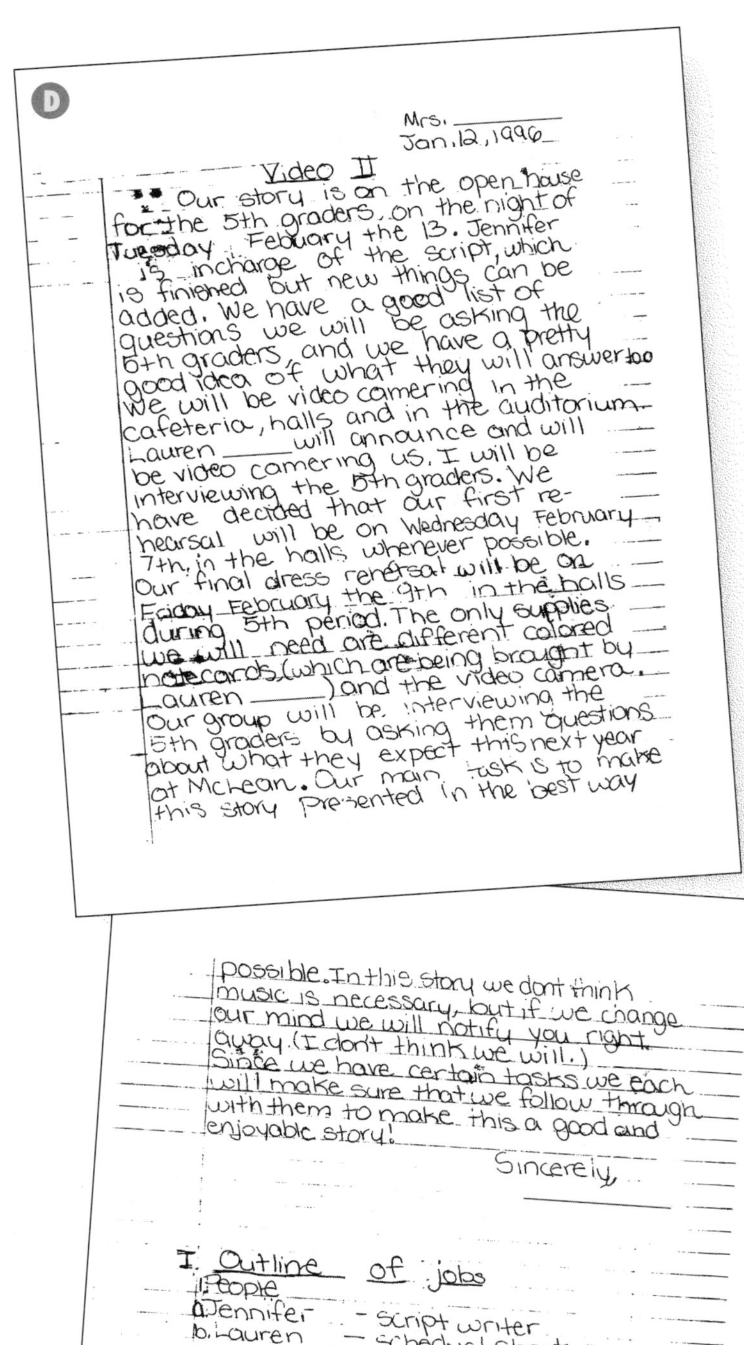

Mrs. ______
Jan. 12, 1996

Video II

Our story is on the open house for the 5th graders, on the night of Tuesday Febuary the 13. Jennifer is incharge of the script, which is finished but new things can be added. We have a good list of questions we will be asking the 5th graders, and we have a pretty good idea of what they will answer too. We will be video camering in the cafeteria, halls and in the auditorium. Lauren ______ will announce and will be video camering us. I will be interviewing the 5th graders. We have decided that our first rehearsal will be on Wednesday February 7th, in the halls whenever possible. Our final dress rehersal will be on Friday February the 9th in the halls during 5th period. The only supplies we will need are different colored notecards, (which are being brought by Lauren ______) and the video camera. Our group will be interviewing the 5th graders by asking them questions about what they expect this next year at McLean. Our main task is to make this story presented in the best way possible. In this story we dont think music is necessary, but if we change our mind we will notify you right away. (I dont think we will.) Since we have certain tasks we each will make sure that we follow through with them to make this a good and enjoyable story!

Sincerely,

I. Outline of jobs
1. People
a. Jennifer – script writer
b. Lauren – schedual shoot, announce.
c. Estela – Interviewer

Rehersal Dates

Sunday	Monday	Tuesday	Wednesday	Thursday	Friday	Saturday
				1	2	3
4	5	6	First	8	Dress	[illegible]
11	12	Open	14	15	16	17

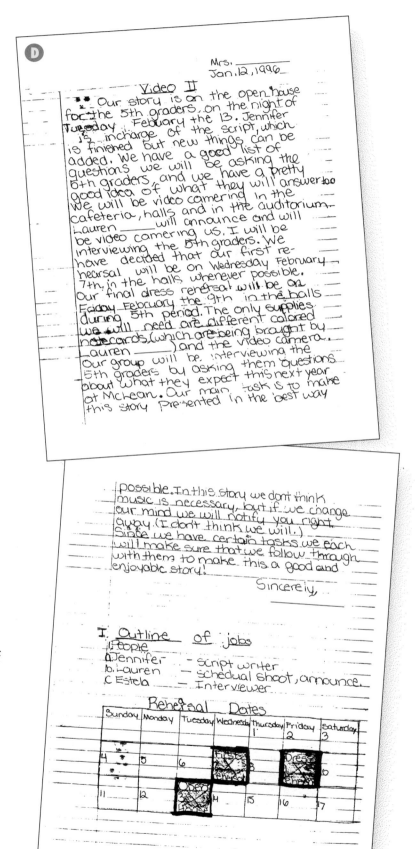

A1 Problem Solving
A2 Communication Tools and Techniques
Information Tools and Techniques
Learning and Self-management Tools and Techniques
A4
Tools and Techniques for Working With Others
A5

Video 2

12/8/95

ALP Log

In the process of learning how to edit I have had lots of fun and at the same time I have learned many new things. Some of the things we have done and learned are below.

In the editing process we, of course, have learned how to edit and use the editing machine. Robert ____ has explained in detail what buttons we will need to use in our editing process. He has also explained what we will need for each visit. Now I will explain what we have done each day through the past week at the ________ ITV building.

In the past week we have gone through some good and bad time. The first day we were at the ITV building we learned how to use the editing machine and constructed our own small video, which ownley lasted for about 15 seconds.

The second day we were there we learned of our first mistake. You see what happened was Parton accidentely recorded the tapes on SLP we were supposed to record them onto SP (Short Play). So we had to record the tape over at my house. That is the day that we came back early.

On Monday of this week we realized we needed more instruction on how to work the editing machine

#3

On Wednesday (yesterday) we actually began the real editing. We recorded footage of the V-ball game and that is all we got done. Editing is a slow process, but is fun also. Also, yesterday we recorded tape #2 onto a VCR tape. Philip and Paxton edited and Philip and I switched off in logging tape #2. That is all we have done the past week at the ITV building. If you have anymore questions you would like me to answer, feel free to ask.

A4a Learning and Self-management Tools and Techniques: The student learns from models; that is, the student:

- consults with or observes other students and adults at work, and identifies the main features of what they do and the way they go about their work;
- identifies models for the results of project work, such as professionally produced publications, and analyzes their qualities;
- uses what he or she learns from models to assist in planning and conducting project activities.

E The students learned video recording/editing skills from a professional media specialist. This log provides evidence that the students had a clear goal of learning how to use the equipment. After mistakes made early in the training, the students monitored their progress and "realized we needed more instruction." They negotiated additional training and reported beginning to do "real editing" later in the week. This is an example of students assuming responsibility for the direction of their learning.

Video 2

F G H The students used “Good Morning, America” as a model for the result of their work. The documents provide evidence of the students’ analysis of the qualities of the program, their use of the analysis to develop a rubric for evaluating their own production, and their evaluation of their work based on the elements of that rubric.

A4b Learning and Self-management Tools and Techniques: The student develops and maintains a schedule of work activities; that is, the student:

- establishes a schedule of work activities that reflects priorities and deadlines;
- seeks advice on the management of conflicting priorities and deadlines;
- updates the schedule regularly.

The students used a number of strategies for scheduling their work activities.

K This student used a calendar to schedule the work activities associated with the project as well as other commitments and events.

D This student used her log entry to establish a schedule of the work that needed to be done and incorporated a calendar into her plan.

L This student’s log offers suggestions for ways of improving the efficiency of the project’s operations to overcome clashes in the schedules of the various groups.

A5a Tools and Techniques for Working With Others: The student takes responsibility for a component of a team project; that is, the student:

- reaches agreement with team members on what work needs to be done to complete the task and how the work will be tackled;
- takes specific responsibility for a component of the project;
- takes all steps necessary to ensure appropriate completion of the specific component of the project within the agreed upon time frame.

Several documents show students working in teams and having a clear sense of the general task and also each individual member’s part of the task.

M The jobs list shows how the project was divided into components with a small group of students taking responsibility for each component.

N This student’s log makes explicit reference to the need for teamwork in order to get the work done.

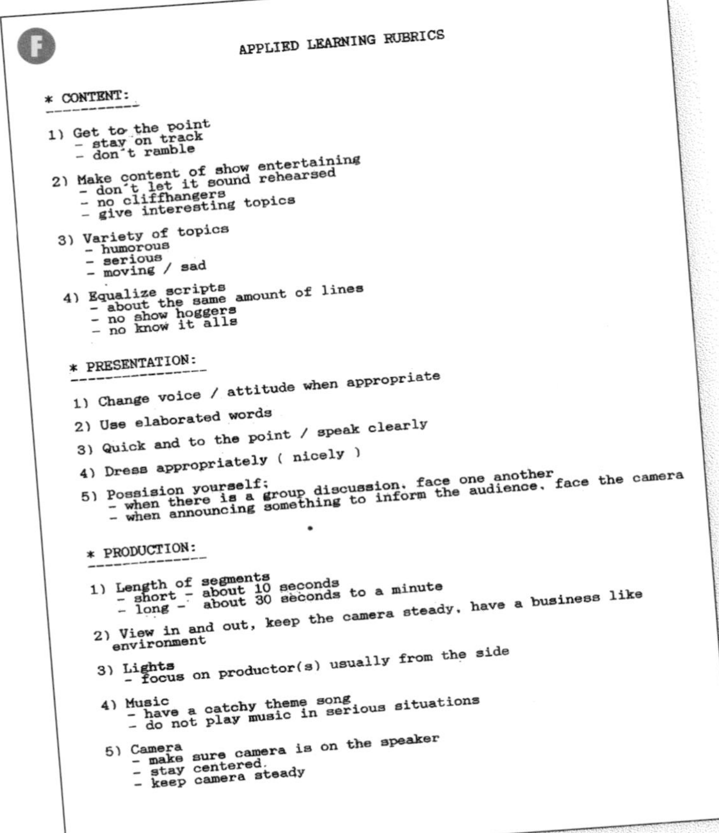

F

APPLIED LEARNING RUBRICS

* CONTENT:

1) Get to the point
   - stay on track
   - don't ramble
2) Make content of show entertaining
   - don't let it sound rehearsed
   - no cliffhangers
   - give interesting topics
3) Variety of topics
   - humorous
   - serious
   - moving / sad
4) Equalize scripts
   - about the same amount of lines
   - no show hoggers
   - no know it alls

* PRESENTATION:

1) Change voice / attitude when appropriate
2) Use elaborated words
3) Quick and to the point / speak clearly
4) Dress appropriately (nicely)
5) Possision yourself;
   - when there is a group discussion, face one another
   - when announcing something to inform the audience, face the camera

* PRODUCTION:

1) Length of segments
   - short - about 10 seconds
   - long - about 30 seconds to a minute
2) View in and out, keep the camera steady, have a business like environment
3) Lights
   - focus on productor(s) usually from the side
4) Music
   - have a catchy theme song
   - do not play music in serious situations
5) Camera
   - make sure camera is on the speaker
   - stay centered.
   - keep camera steady

G

News/Feature Video Rubric

4

Information presented in the video is informative, pertinent and accurate
Topics, features appeal to intended audiences' values/needs/knowledge
Presentation is clear, accurate, appealing, engaging
Technical elements are smooth, coherent, controlled, and non-intrusive

3

Information presented is accurate, but coverage is superficial
Topics, features may not target audience needs
Presentation is adequate, lacks sparkle
Technical elements merely adequate

2

Information is somewhat sketchy
Topic selection random
Presentation is self-conscious, not clear
Technical errors overpower message

1

Information may contain gaps or inaccuracies
Topic selection does not reflect needs of audience
Presentation detracts from message
Technical elements reflect no perceptible strategies

Video 2

H

April 19, 196

Video Comparison

Our class has worked very diligently producing our two news videos. Because our first video did not turn out the way we wanted it to, we decided it would be our practice video. However, I liked our second news video much more than I liked the first. In my opinion, what made the second better than the first, was that the content, organization, delivery, technical items were much better in our second video.

To begin with, the first video's and the second video's organization was totally different. In the first video we had two main anchors or hosts, (like in Good Morning America). We then had different people report on the stories. It was kind of choppy and did not seem to flow well. In our second video our organization was different and , in my opinion, much better. At the beginning of our second video, instead of the two anchors, we had an introduction involving the entire class that led into the first story. Each story was reported by one or two different people. Each new story was introduced with a printed title on the screen. This gave the second video more of a professional look.

Both videos were made with the intention that they could be used as an orientation tool for incoming fifth graders from our feeder schools. However, I feel that, our first video effort would not have been an effective orientation instrument. It didn't contain elements that the fifth graders could relate to. When we made the second video, we decided to make it from the perspective of "Bob," a fictional 5th grader. By doing this, I think, we made the video more "5th grader friendly".

One of our goals in both videos was to make them look as professional as possible. The first video was full of glitches, wobbly pictures and bad footage. By the second video, our "camera men" were more experienced and sure of themselves. Some of the wobbliness was eliminated, the frames were pretty much centered. The glitches were still there, (some worse) but this could not be avoided.

Another improvement of the second video over the first was the general mood of it. In the first, our presentation was very rigid, serious and we seemed nervous. This mood was reflected in the entire video. However by the time we did the second one, everyone was more relaxed and experienced. The second video has a casual laid back and creative feel to it.

The content of our videos also improved from one video to the other. For one thing, our creation of "fifth grade Bob," our narrator/eyes made it more interesting to the other fifth graders who would be viewing this. Also we made the stories in the second more interesting, funnier and more creative. Especially the ______ Industries project. (Ha, Ha, Ha.)

Being are first video production projects some things worked and some things didn't. One thing that didn't work was the interview with Mrs. ______. I thought it was quite to long. Another thing that didn't work was the story about the student and faculty volleyball game. I thought that it was too short. In the first video the color was a bit washed out, this didn't work either. One last thing that didn't work was that in the first video in the story about Mr. ______ new baby, I could hardly hear Maranda over the baby music.

If I was going to make another news video there is one revision I would make. The one revision I would make would be to wear a body mike at all times. Some stories were done outside and you could hardly hear over the wind. A body mike is a small microphone that you clip on to your clothes. With this tiny microphone, we would be able to hear all the stories much better.

I think that both videos one and two were great learning experiences for us. Just think, some of us might grow up to be broadcasters on Good Morning America or camera men (or women.) Our second video was better than the first, but I think they were both good tn their own way. Our first video was very good practice for us, and the second video was very good overall.

D The division of responsibility within teams and recognition of the importance of coordinating individual team members' efforts is evident in the student's comment, "Since we have certain tasks we each will make sure that we follow through with them to make this a good and enjoyable story!"

L Even though the work demonstrates recognition of individual responsibility and obvious agreement among group members, there is also the recognition that things could have been better. This log entry includes a suggestion for more efficient use of time through better communication among the several teams, possibly through the use of a bulletin board to share the schedules for all of the groups.

Problem Solving A1
Communication Tools and Techniques A2
Information Tools and Techniques
Learning and Self-management Tools and Techniques A4
Tools and Techniques for Working With Others A5

Video 2

I

FORT WORTH INDEPENDENT SCHOOL DISTRICT
McLean Middle School
3816 Stadium Drive
Fort Worth, Texas 76109
817 922-6830

December 12, 1995

Mr. Michael ________
________ Industries

Dear Sir:

Our seventh grade Applied Learning class is submitting the following proposal for a project that our class feels would be not only a great educational experience for us, but would also be of great benefit to McLean Middle School and the community it serves. We are hopeful that you will consider it worthy of helping us with the funding. Enclosed is information about our project and what we need to carry it out. Thank you for your consideration and time. We look forward to hearing from you.

Sincerely

Applied Learning Class

____
Approved

J

INTEROFFICE MEMO

Date: 01/10/96
To: Paulette ________
Sharon ________
From: Michael ________
Subject: Video Camera request

In response to your letter requesting funding for a video camera for use in your Applied Learning Class, we will regretfully be unable to fund the project at this time. However, we currently have a video camera that could be used for your project, provided the conditions in the following paragraph can be agreed to.

Per our phone conversation, it is our understanding that the camera will be used and operated only in the presence of a Teacher or other responsible party. Additionally, we understand that the camera will be secured at all times by a Teacher or other responsible party when not in use. In the event that Trinity should need the camera during your project, we will give reasonable notice and will expect to be able to use the camera for our purposes if the situation arises. We expect that the camera will be returned in the same condition as it was when you received it, and that you will be responsible for any damages to the camera and related equipment while in your possession.

Listed below are the following items to be loaned:

- Video Camera GE serial # 317610626
- Batteries 3 qty.
- Battery Charger
- Bag
- Tri-pod

Please sign below if the above terms are agreeable. We are excited about your project, and look forward to expanding our on-going partnership.

Sharon ________, Principal

Paulette ________, Teacher 1/11/96

Michael ________ Industries, Inc.

K

NOVEMBER 1995

SUNDAY	MONDAY	TUESDAY	WEDNESDAY	THURSDAY	FRIDAY	SATURDAY
			Persuasive Letter Due	Video News Project Task Analysis — sign up for a job	3	4
5	CMA video Analysis of Competent Adult Model Develop Rubric	Discussed important elements Plan to revise rubrics	8	9 Gather News *Revise Rubric	10 In-Service * No School!	11
12	13 Gather Plans for reporting (coverage) - Writing the script	14	(Filming	16	17 Titanic Project	18
19	20 Filming	21	22 Holiday	23 Thanks-giving	24 Yea!	25
26	27 Filming	28 [illegible] editing [illegible] Confirmed 12-2:20	29	30 Editing	Dec 1 Editing	Intramurals [illegible] Winners

Video 2

L

Mrs. ______
December 13, 1995

ALP Journal Entry
December 13, 1995

I planned what stories were to be done on what days. Actually I did not plan them the whole group did. We accomplished many diffrent tasks. We wrote and were at the scene of the stories. We learned that it takes many people to make a news video. Mainly everything wored very well. Digging up the news and writing the script worked very well. Some of the groups had problems and so did our group. One problem our group had was that we did not share with other people in other groups. I think that they should not have complained, because we were constantley around and about the school. We didn't have enough time to take a day out of our week to tell the whole class what we were doing. Maybe we could have a bulletin board where each group put up info. about what they were doing that week. I would make things more organized and a lot less goofing off. I extremely enjoyed doing this and hope to ~~do~~ experience this again.

M

VIDEOTAPE I JOBS LIST

ANNOUNCERS/ ANCHORS/ HOSTS
PHILLIP ______
RACHEL ______
JANEL ______

BROADCASTERS
KIMB ERLY ______
JENNIFER ______
LAUREN ______

CAMERA PERSON

PAXTON ______
COURTNEY ______
JOSEPH ______

DECORATORS
HEATHER ______
ERIN ______
CHRISTIAN ______
ANNE ______

DIRECTORS
JAMES ______
KEVIN ______
RYAN ______

EDITORS
MATT ______
CHRISTIAN ______
RACHEL ______

INTERVIEWERS
LAUREN ______
MYRANDA ______

MAKEUP/APPAREL

SARA ______
JESSICA ______

N

Mrs. ______
December 13, 1995

ALP Journal

I had a pretty big part in our news video. Although I was an anchor, I did most of my work behind the scenes. I was an editor. I never realized how much work it takes to edit a simple 10 min. video.

We had planned to have the video done and ready to show on December 4. Well, now it is December 13 and the video is not yet finished.

I learned a lot while working on this video. I learned how to edit, the quality of hard work, and most importantly, that if you want to get anything done, you have to work as a team.

I think that the anchors should have practiced some more. Then we would have been able to get the feel of each other and have been more relaxed.

Problem Solving
Communication Tools and Techniques A2
Information Tools and Techniques
Learning and Self-management Tools and Techniques A4
Tools and Techniques for Working With Others A5

Work Sample & Commentary: *Student Historical Magazines*

The task

Students on an English/history team designed and published a series of magazines organized around historical themes. The magazines provided entertaining, informative summer reading materials to middle school students who could not afford to buy magazines of this kind.

Circumstances of performance

On the basis of data gathered from a questionnaire that the class designed, distributed and collected, the students developed the magazines using historical themes that matched the interests of their audience. The students worked as individuals and as members of teams, with each team focusing on a specific theme. The history and English teachers served as consultants and monitors in order to ensure that students accomplished content objectives. The project lasted approximately three months and happened in conjunction with other class work.

What the work shows

A1 a Problem Solving: The student designs and creates a product, service, or system to meet an identified need; that is, the student:

- develops a range of ideas for design of the product, service, or system;
- selects one design option to pursue and justifies the choice with reference, for example, to functional, aesthetic, social, economic, or environmental considerations;
- establishes criteria for judging the success of the design;
- uses appropriate conventions to represent the design;
- plans and carries out the steps needed to create the product, service, or system;
- makes adjustments as needed to conform with specified standards or regulations regarding quality and safety;
- evaluates the quality of the design in terms of the criteria for success and by comparison with similar products, services, or systems.

A

Dear Ms. _____ and Ms. _____

Our Applied Learning group is planning on doing a magazine. It will focus on the subject of modern art in the late nineteenth century to the early twentieth century. We feel that this magazine is a worthwhile project for many reasons. First, this magazine will provide a source of education for our group as well as the readers. We will learn a lot more from our research because our main goal is to inform the reader. The reader will benefit because they will learn throughout this interactive magazine. Second, the magazine will entertain the reader.

This whole project will be a worthwhile experience. We hope that you will consider the ideas that we have setforth throughout this proposal. Thank you for your time.

Sincerely,

Melissa _____ Melissa
Natalie _____ Natalie
Dusty _____ Dusty
Kimberly _____ Kimberly
Jamie _____ Jamie

B

Dear Ms. ____ and Ms. _____:

I had no idea of the magnitude of hard work and effort it takes to do research and endless drafts, artwork, text and layouts, and how difficult it is sometimes to work in a group. Though we encountered some minor, and major snags along the way, I was very pleased with the final product and feel that I have learned a lot of valuable lessons and skills as a result of his project.

The first step we had to take in developing our magazine before we even thought of writing articles, was to design it. I first came up with the idea of using entertainment for our theme because on our list of our audience's needs and values, we had entertainment listed as one of the main items. We later developed it to include music, games, and television, because these are things that we ourselves find interesting. As far as deciding what to include in our magazine goes, we started out by identifying the needs, values, and knowledge of our audience. Each member of our group made their own list and then we combined them during class After we had a better feeling for who we were writing for, we brought in several magazines, like Seventeen, as competent adult models (See Daily Log, 2\22). Then we each made lists of content and visual items that we liked and wanted to try and include in our own magazine. We noted things like bright headlines, different types of layouts, lots of artwork, varying colors, and easy to follow articles about interesting topics. Our group worked really well together on this aspect and we each contributed about equally to discussions and ideas. After we had the basic theme, we had to develop it in all of the given categories I came up with the idea to do an extra section about interesting and strange facts about the history of television and where it is today, and ended up actually doing it in the end. For my other sections I found it pretty easy to decide what to write about. For example, in the creative writing section I decided to write about a roller coaster because the average teenager loves amusement parks and rides, and for the time capsule I just researched fun and interesting events about the history of television, music, and games Once we finished developing our project, we test ran it and evaluated the results by having two groups of people look at it and make comments. Because we got semi-low marks on original artwork and the creative writing section, I tried to improve the quality of these sections as well as include lots more artwork in my time capsule (See Daily Log, 4\19 and 4\23).

This work sample illustrates a standard-setting performance for the following parts of the standards:

A1 a Problem Solving: Design a product, service, or system.

A2 c Communication: Publish information using several methods and formats.

A3 a Information: Gather information.

A3 b Information: Use information technology.

A4 b Learning and Self-management: Develop and maintain a schedule of work activities.

A5 a Working With Others: Take responsibility for a component of a team project.

The documentation presented from this project is not a comprehensive record of all work done as part of the project. It would be neither reasonable nor appropriate to ask students to keep detailed written records of every aspect of a project. This would defeat part of the purpose of applied learning which is for students to put their academic learning to work and to learn from projects that connect what they do at school to the demands of the twenty-first century workplace. Some of these standards lend themselves to assessment through observation and other less formal methods rather than through written work.

Student Historical Magazines

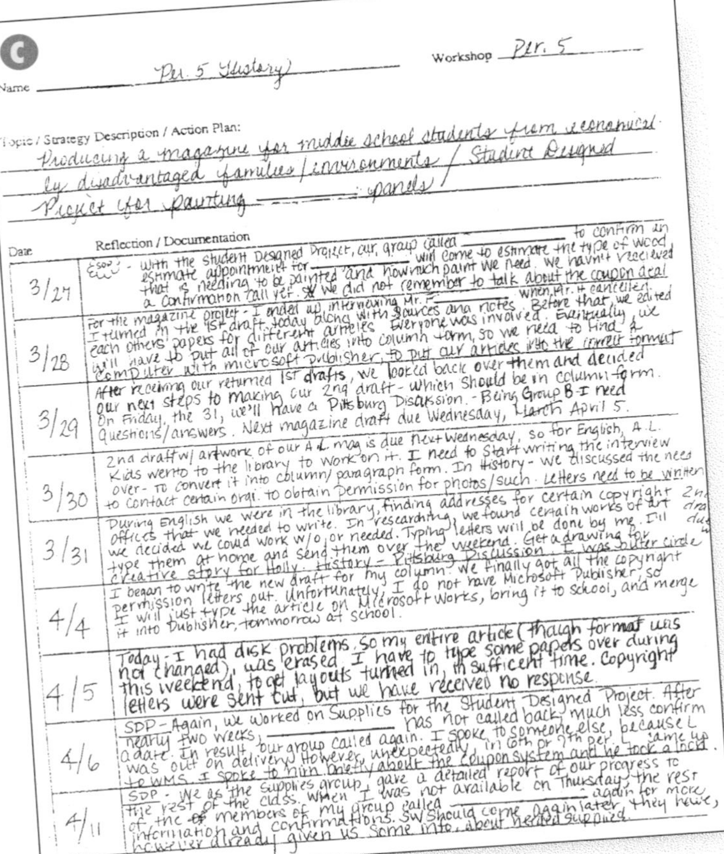

C

Name: Per. 5 History) Workshop: Per. 5

Topic / Strategy Description / Action Plan: Producing a magazine for middle school students from economical by disadvantaged families / environments / Student Designed Project for painting ______ panels /

Date	Reflection / Documentation
3/27	SDP - With the student Designed Project, our group called ______ to confirm an estimate appointment for ______ will come to estimate the type of wood that is needing to be painted and how much paint we need. We haven't received a confirmation call yet. We did not remember to talk about the coupon deal when Mr. H cancelled.
3/28	For the magazine project - I ended up interviewing Mr. F______. Before that, we edited each others' papers for different articles. Everyone was involved. Eventually, we I turned in the 1st draft today along with sources and notes. will have to put all of our articles into column form, so we need to find a computer with microsoft publisher, to put our articles into the correct format
3/29	After receiving our returned 1st drafts, we looked back over them and decided our next steps to making our 2nd draft - which should be in column form. On Friday, the 31, we'll have a Pittsburg Discussion. - Being Group B I need Questions/answers. Next magazine draft due Wednesday, ~~March~~ April 5.
3/30	2nd draft w/ artwork of our A.L. mag is due next Wednesday, so for English, A.L. Kids went to the library to work on it. I need to start writing the interview over - to convert it into column/paragraph form. In History - we discussed the need to contact certain orgs. to obtain permission for photos/such. Letters need to be written
3/31	During English we were in the library, finding addresses for certain copyright offices that we needed to write. In researching, we found certain works of art we decided we could work w/o, or needed. Typing letters will be done by me. I'll type them at home and send them over the weekend. Get a drawing for creative story for Holly. History - Pittsburg Discussion. I was outer circle
4/4	I began to write the new draft for my column. We finally got all the copyright permission letters out. Unfortunately, I do not have Microsoft Publisher, so I will just type the article on Microsoft Works, bring it to school, and merge it into Publisher, tommorrow at school.
4/5	Today - I had disk problems, so my entire article (though format was not changed), was erased. I have to type some papers over during this weekend, to get layouts turned in, in sufficent time. Copyright letters were sent out, but we have received no response.
4/6	SDP - Again, we worked on Supplies for the Student Designed Project. After nearly two weeks, ______ has not called back, much less confirm a date. In result, our group called again. I spoke to someone else, because L was out on delivery. However, unexpectedly, in 6th or 7th per. L came up to WMS. I spoke to him briefly about the coupon system and he took a look.
4/11	SDP - We as the supplies group, gave a detailed report of our progress to the rest of the class. When I was not available on Thursday, the rest of the ~~of~~ members of my group called ______ again for more information and confirmations. SW should come again later, they have, however already given us some info. about needed supplies.

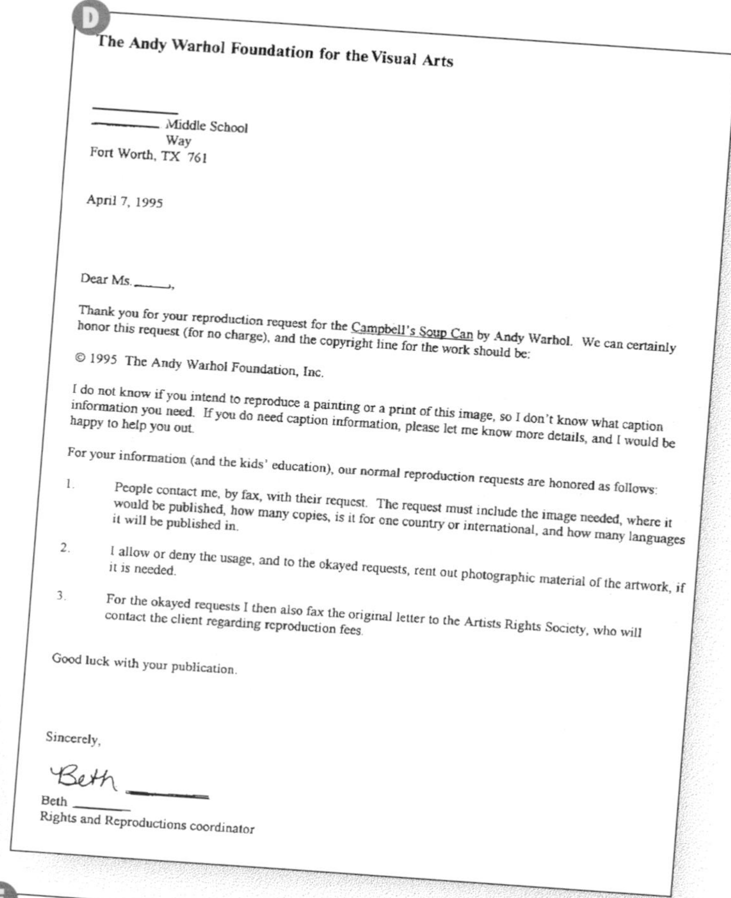

D

The Andy Warhol Foundation for the Visual Arts

______
______ Middle School
Way
Fort Worth, TX 761

April 7, 1995

Dear Ms. ______,

Thank you for your reproduction request for the Campbell's Soup Can by Andy Warhol. We can certainly honor this request (for no charge), and the copyright line for the work should be:

© 1995 The Andy Warhol Foundation, Inc.

I do not know if you intend to reproduce a painting or a print of this image, so I don't know what caption information you need. If you do need caption information, please let me know more details, and I would be happy to help you out.

For your information (and the kids' education), our normal reproduction requests are honored as follows:

1. People contact me, by fax, with their request. The request must include the image needed, where it would be published, how many copies, is it for one country or international, and how many languages it will be published in.
2. I allow or deny the usage, and to the okayed requests, rent out photographic material of the artwork, if it is needed.
3. For the okayed requests I then also fax the original letter to the Artists Rights Society, who will contact the client regarding reproduction fees.

Good luck with your publication.

Sincerely,

Beth ______

Beth ______
Rights and Reproductions coordinator

A The brief proposal explains that the magazines "will provide a source of [historical] education for our group as well as the readers."

B The students reviewed the design of a number of professionally produced magazines before settling on their own. These professional magazines also provided the criteria that the students used to determine the qualities that characterize successful magazines. Students tested the product before launching into final production and made adjustments to improve the quality of several aspects of the magazine: "Once we finished developing our project, we test ran it and evaluated the results by having two groups of people look at it and make comments."

C In carrying out the steps in the production process, e.g., the planning described in this student's log, there is also evidence that the students learned about and followed some of the regulations that apply to magazine publication. See the entries for 3/30 and 3/31.

D **E** This letter gives permission to reproduce artwork. The cover of one issue of the magazine incorporates that reproduced work.

The documentation provides evidence of the students assuming responsibility for the design and implementation of the product.

Problem Solving A1
Communication Tools and Techniques A2
Information Tools and Techniques A3
Learning and Self-management Tools and Techniques A4
Tools and Techniques for Working With Others A5

Student Historical Magazines

F

The Peanut Man

George Washington Carver

Captain George Washington Carver of the National Guard at Iowa State University.

A peanut can't be worth much... or so some people think. After all, what can you do with a one-inch long nut other than eat it or feed it to an elephant? George Washington Carver asked himself this and developed 145 ways to use the peanut, such as flour, breakfast foods, imitation coffee, and cosmetics. How could one person think of something as crazy as that?

George Washington Carver was born near Diamond, Missouri in 1864. His parents were slaves, but he found a way out of it and worked his way through high school in Minneapolis, Kansas.

In 1894, Carver graduated from Iowa State University and then joined the faculty as a lab scientist in botany, the study of plant life.

By 1896, he was director of Tuskegee Institute, where he began his studies on sweet potatoes and soy beans. However, because he did not write down any formulas for his products before he died, his products were never manufactured. However, his discoveries and developments influenced southern farmers to raise other crops besides cotton and tobacco, helping the South have an agricultural diversity.

Carver won the Spingarn Medal in 1923, which was given to him by the National Association for the Advancement of Colored People (NAACP). He was also given a high position in the U.S. Department of Agriculture in 1935. Carver gave all his savings to the establishment of the George Washington Carver Foundation of Tuskegee for research on natural science.

On January 5, 1943, he died at Tuskegee. His birthplace is now a national monument.

From now on you can think of George Washington Carver when you pick up a peanut to munch on.

Dr. James Naismith

What would you do if someone told you to invent a new game? James Naismith was told, and he ended up creating one of America's most popular sports....

Basketball, Anyone?

By

It's most likely that when you're shootin' hoops after school, you don't think about where the game of basketball came from. It was invented more than a hundred years ago by Dr. James Naismith, an instructor at the International YMCA Training School in Springfeld, Massachusetts.

It all started when the college's athletic head, Dr. Luther Gulick figured that the students needed something to do in the winter between the football and baseball seasons. It was too cold outside, and there was nothing to do inside. So he asked Naismith to invent a new indoor game.

When Naismith started out, he didn't know what he was going to do. He tried different variations of outdoor sports, but it didn't work. He wanted a game which was not full contact so the players wouldn't get hurt as easily.

He finally got the idea of what we know as basketball. To make it harder, Naismith put the goal above head level.

It was only a matter of teaching the players the game, and he had himself a basketball team. The first demonstration game was played with two peach baskets nailed to opposite ends of the gym wall. The players used a soccer ball, and had thirteen rules to follow. Most of these rules are still used today.

Basketball was an instant success. Everyone started playing-- colleges, YMCA's, high schools, even regular kids just like you. So next time you pick up your basketball, tip your cap to Naismith. You wouldn't be playing if it wasn't for him.

H

Getting Around From Then To Now

YEAR	TYPE	ADVANTAGES	DISADVANTAGES	HOW IT CHANGED
Prehistoric	Sledge- like a sled of today	carried food and freshly killed prey	heavy and hard to pull	one of first modes of transportation known today
Prehistoric	Travois- like sledge but larger	moved supplies over short distances	awkward to carry- had to be drug along ground	larger and more efficient for carrying food
Ancient	Etrusion Chariot	made good racing vehicle	off balance- only two wheels	developed the first wheels used in Olympics
Ancient	Scythian Oxcart	pulled heavy items	had to have an ox to pull it	had an ox pull it\ more on balance
1400's	Ocean liners	went across large areas of water	took a long time- months	could float on water
1600-1700's	Wagons	went long distances	not very sturdy- no motors	had four wheels\ could carry a lot
1800's	Horse- drawn car	traveled short distances fast	cost a lot of money to own- had to have a horse	developed many streets in cities and towns
1800's	Locomotive	used steam	had to follow tracks	used steam to operate
Early 1900's	Electric car	no animals	very expensive	no animals\ engines
1900's	Zeppelin Airship	flew distances over land	crashed down- killed many people	able to travel through the air
1930's	Ferry	lots of people	short distances	some could carry vehicles
1990's	Planes\jets	fast for long flights	costly- airfare sometimes over $150	uses fuel\ travels very fast
1900's	Motor cars	very common	many accidents	many styles

-Jennifer

A2 Communication Tools and Techniques: The student publishes information using several methods and formats, such as overhead transparencies, handouts, and computer generated graphs and charts; that is, the student:

- organizes the information into an appropriate form for use in the publication;
- checks the information for accuracy;
- formats the published material so that it achieves its purpose.

E F G H I The work includes several examples of organizing and communicating information for publication using different methods and formats, e.g., the cover of one of the magazines which incorporates headlines to attract the reader to look inside; articles for the magazine; and a chart prepared to show changes in transportation over time.

I See page 32 for commentary on this article as a report within the requirements of the English Language Arts standards.

Student Historical Magazines

I

Interview With the Vet

It was a silent night in 1968. The day was rather hot, with some steamy wetness in the tropical Vietnamese climate. The night was a pretty normal one for twenty-one year old Corporal. Fransisco "Frank"________. Patrolling had been rather uneventful, and the quiet night air was relaxing for the members of ________'s group. Men silently prowled the grounds amidst the looming compound in Da Nang, Vietnam, watching intently for any signs of disturbance. Cpl. ________ stood still, relaxed, taking it easy after a lonely, difficult day at work. But, how could you ever say that war was easy? The seemingly unnecessary and costly Vietnam War had been going on for several years, and Frank was there to do his job for right now. However, right then, Frank began to get some of his soldiers instinct for danger. He saw that the other soldiers on the patrol had also begun to look up with alertness. The night had grown deathly quiet in a normally noisy part of the land.

Just as Frank decided that it had definitely grown too quiet, whistling mortar shells and booming gunfire shattered the peaceful calm of the compound with shrieking and deafening noises. Everything seemed to be raining down from the pitch black sky, sending with it shards of powder, metal and debris. In the few seconds that all this occurred, Frank suddenly felt a searing, intense pain in his gut, near his stomach. He leaped to the ground for safety as emergency teams got him to the hospital. As he was rushed there, he got scared at the thought of a bullet hitting him. When he entered the

Frank________ as a young soldier in Vietnam in 1968.

emergency room, the medics immediately began looking for the bullet hole, except it was never found. The sudden event had scared Frank so immensely that he had formed a huge ulcer in the pit of his stomach fear gripping him from the real world.

Mr. ________, now age forty-nine, looks back on that incident with a chuckle because he remembers how one of his first encounters scared him thoroughly. Although many followed after that one in that foreign land, he looks back saying, "It scared the heck outta me...I'll never forget that night." That night was one of a lifetime for Frank while he served in the U.S. Marine Corps during the Vietnam War.

Although there were a few good times and a duty to finish out, Mr. ________ never quite got over the fact that this political war was fought for the wrong reasons. In his opinion and other's view on this war, "Everyone was out to profit or gain from this war. Generals got promoted, business boomed for the defense industry, new jobs were made in Vietnam and America alike. I really think that the basic effort of this whole operation was a wasted one." Vietnam was remembered to many as an unnecessary, cruel war that ruined two countries.

But how did this affair start? Well, you could say that it began with the end of World War II. During the reconstruction period after World War II, President Truman and other leaders of America, one of the most powerful nations during that time, wanted to have capitalism, which is when most property is owned privately by people or corporations. Communism was

corporations. **Communism,** a system where all businesses and properties are owned by the government. was also and idea spreading quickly. In an effort to prevent communism from taking over the foreign policies of that era, Truman and his colleagues promised to help any country trying to resist communism. In short, throughout the years of Eisenhower, Kennedy, Johnson, and Nixon, many efforts were made for the prevention it spreading through Vietnam.

Born in Big Spring, Texas, 250 miles west of Fort Worth, Fransisco ________ was born to a Hispanic family, who also had roots in the border city of Presidio, where his father worked for the Air Force. Frank went through high school in Big Spring and graduated there. After graduation, he joined the Marine Corps and fought in Vietnam. His jobs there consisted of being an administrative clerk, and translator, the only one in his unit. Returning from Vietnam, he began attending ________ County Junior College and earned an associate degree in general business. Soon after, he met and married his wife, Elizabeth. They have two daughters, who are adults now. Their eldest had a son, Frank's first grandson.

I had wondered, however, if he had ever had any trouble with his race, a rather controversial issue in the world, then and now. He explained, "In getting my education in the schools, I had little problem getting to where I eventually got. If I did, I probably ignored it. I mean, that's what you have to do. When I was in the boot and infantry camps, and even on the battleground, there were mainly blacks, whites, and I was the only Hispanic there. The people there in my unit didn't

Frank with the kids in the orphanage

bother me much; we were too busy working on a job that we had to do. I had a goal to accomplish, and I really didn't let any racism get in my way."

Basically, Frank was not quite satisfied with his one degree and started pursuing another one recently. He is currently attending ________ University to earn a Bachelor's degree in business. He is, however, already a successful man, working for ________ at its Fort Worth plant. Although he only had one degree, he worked himself up from the bottom several steps to become steps to become an English supervisor in the plant. With even more education, he will work his way up in the business world. It just goes to show what one can accomplish with a sufficient education. In addition to his hard work at ________, he is in the Army Reserve with the rank of Sergeant Major and is a member of the Vietnam Veterans Association.

Mr. ________ turned out to be a very successful and well-grounded individual despite the effect the war had on him. He did have a suggestion for minorities or anyone else willing to join efforts in the military, though. He pointedly stated, "Get the best education you can while you are at it. Goofing off is never going to get you anywhere. If you do your best, never hesitate on being the leader. Lead you own crowd if you have to. The leaders of this day and age always get the best jobs in the military. Only the smart, intelligent and hardest workers get promoted to the senior stage. Always keep a positive outlook on the world, because war in one of the most negative things you'll mess with. It can really test you because it is never what you think it is. Just keep that positive outlook on life."

English/History

March 28, 1995

Bibliography for Interview

1. Collier's Encyclopedia Copyright 1972 Crowell-Collier Educational Corporation Volume USA to ZWINGLI Topic: Vietnam War

Summary: A political and military war fought in the country of Vietnam. War plans, conflicts, and tensions that arose during this war. I just got some information on the war so that the interview with Mr. Fransisco________ would be smoother.

2. Tell me About Yourself - How to Interview by D.L. Maybery Copyright © 1985 by Lerner Publications Company

Summary: This book guided me in presenting and doing interviews, (Fact Finding / Informational) and doing useful and proper research, preparing questions, and all the arrangements needed to conduct the interview.

3. Interview Questions (Written by me)

I researched some Vietnam War facts / and questions to ask and this is what I came up with. →

F.P. - I did attend a Marine Corps Infantry Camp, that educated me in academics and the steps
to taking measures on the combat field. I also, to become an interpreter, had to go to a
language school in Vietnam. In the physical training, I had to go to some field training that was
tough, but essential.
M.L. - How do you feel about the efforts spent on this war? Were they worth it?
F.P. - Definitely not. The whole deal was based on the fact that certain companies wanted
money for their planes or jets, the government wanted to gain something. All the business
enterprise all wanted to earn profits from this ridiculous political war. Generals got promoted,
new jobs were established in Vietnam and America alike. I believe that the whole effort was a
wasted one, but I still fought in it, because I had a duty and a promise to the United States.
M.L. - In the end, how did this war affect your life or any of your loved ones? Did any new
relationships form?
F.P. - Yes, definitely. This war affected me for a long, long time. I was all bent out of shape with
anger towards the government. I had an immense anger in me that was kept inside for the
longest time. I couldn't talk to anybody. To me, there was no one there that understood how I
felt. I felt as if the government had treated me like dirt. They didn't seem to give me a chance
to decide for my own. Fortunately, I found new friends in special programs for Vietnam
veterans. I had the opportunity to talk to lots of people that could relate with the way I felt. In the
compound that I was in, most everyone had bad attitudes, because nobody thought that this was
a necessary war. The worst thing I saw was how traumatized some people were after they
fought in Vietnam. Many had drug or marital problems later.
M.L. - Did your race ever get in your way? Did it receive mixed reactions or ever stand as an
obstacle?
F.P. - In getting my education in the schools, I had little problem getting to where I eventually
got. If I did, I probably ignored it. I mean, that's what you have to do. When I was in Vietnam,
there were mainly blacks, whites, and I was the only Hispanic or Mexican. The people there in
the infantry never really bothered me, we were too busy working on a job that we had to do.
M.L. - What would you suggest to a minority or anyone else who wants to join the armed forces?
F.P. - I would just tell them to get the best education that they could get while they are at it.
Goofing off is never going to get you anywhere. If you do your best, never hesitate on being the
leader. Lead your own crowd if you have to. The leaders of this day and age always get the
best jobs in the military. Only the smart, intelligent and hardest working get promoted to the
officers' stage. Always keep a positive outlook on the world, because war is one of the most
negative things you'll mess with. It can really test you because it is never what you think it is.
Just keep that positive outlook on life.

Problem Solving A1
Communication Tools and Techniques A2
Information Tools and Techniques A3
Learning and Self-management Tools and Techniques A4
Tools and Techniques for Working With Others A5

Student Historical Magazines

A3a Information Tools and Techniques: The student gathers information to assist in completing project work; that is, the student:

- identifies potential sources of information to assist in completing the project;
- uses appropriate techniques to collect the information, e.g., considers sampling issues in conducting a survey;
- interprets and analyzes the information;
- evaluates the information for completeness and relevance;
- shows evidence of research in the completed project.

I J K These documents trace the development of a single article from research, both into the topic for the article and into the use of interviews to obtain information, to a transcript of the interview and, finally, to the completed article for publication. These documents provide evidence for collection of information from several sources and organization of the information into a form appropriate for a journalistic article. The article reports the interviewee's words faithfully.

A3b Information Tools and Techniques: The student uses information technology to assist in gathering, analyzing, organizing, and presenting information; that is, the student:

- acquires information for specific purposes from on-line sources, such as the Internet, and other electronic data bases, such as a scientific data base on CD ROM;
- uses word-processing, graphics, data base, and spreadsheet programs to produce project reports and related materials.

F G H K The magazines are desktop publications that were word-processed. The articles and chart were produced on desktop publishing software.

C This student's log provides evidence of a familiarity with the use of information tools and techniques, e.g., the entry dated 4/4 includes, "I do not have Microsoft Publisher, so I will just type the article on Microsoft Works, bring it to school, and merge it into Publisher, tomorrow at school," and the log entry dated 4/5 includes, "Today I had disk problems, so my entire article (though format was not changed), was erased. I have to type some papers over during this weekend, to get layouts turned in, in sufficient time."

A4b Learning and Self-management Tools and Techniques: The student develops and maintains a schedule of work activities; that is, the student:

- establishes a schedule of work activities that reflects priorities and deadlines;
- seeks advice on the management of conflicting priorities and deadlines;
- updates the schedule regularly.

L

Division of Responsibilities/Value of project

In our group, we have divided the responsibilities up equally, according to each person's interests. Heather is the Art Director, Jennifer is the Production Manager, Maureen is the Editor, and Alex the Financial Manager.

In the actual magazine, Jennifer and Maureen are working on the time capsule, Alex is doing the craft kit, Heather the interview, Maureen the classical focus, and everyone is contributing to creative writing.

The kids who read this magazine will value it because it will be fun to read and interesting. The articles will be written in a sort of entertaining style so they won't get bored. Both our audience and us will appreciate our magazine because inventions and discoveries are an important part of our ever-growing nation.

C This is an example of a work schedule, in this case in the form of a log produced on a daily basis in which each day's record grows out of the previous day's work and closes with tasks established for the next day. The log records work activities associated with two concurrent projects. It would provide a valuable memory aid to assist the process of reviewing progress towards achieving learning goals.

A5a Tools and Techniques for Working With Others: The student takes responsibility for a component of a team project; that is, the student:

- reaches agreement with team members on what work needs to be done to complete the task and how the work will be tackled;
- takes specific responsibility for a component of the project;
- takes all steps necessary to ensure appropriate completion of the specific component of the project within the agreed upon time frame.

L This student's record provides evidence for students' reaching agreement among team members on the work to be done and how it would be tackled, and for students' taking responsibility for specific components of the project.

Work Sample & Commentary: *Career Day*

The task

An English class was asked by the principal to plan a career day event for the entire school.

Circumstances of performance

The students had approximately six weeks to plan, organize, and stage the career day. The students were responsible for contacting people, organizing the schedule, and keeping the students and teachers in the school informed. The students had the benefit of examining the previous year's career day which had also been a student-directed event. During the fall semester, the students performed writing tasks and a one day work internship at a place of business that helped prepare them for the project. Most of the work was completed in class with feedback from peers and the teacher. Other adults in the building, including secretaries and administrators, assisted students with tasks such as phone calls, permission forms, and advertisements. The students worked on the project while completing other assigned tasks in the class.

The written work included with this project contains some errors. For the main part the errors are confined to journal entries and other planning documents which were produced for personal use only and were not intended for publication. The pieces of finished writing are the proposal to the principal, the document titles, "Career Day," the note to parents, the handout for teachers, the brochure, the map, and the evaluation forms. These contain virtually error free writing.

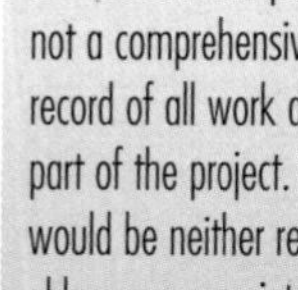

The documentation presented from this project is not a comprehensive record of all work done as part of the project. It would be neither reasonable nor appropriate to ask students to keep detailed written records of every aspect of a project. This would defeat part of the purpose of applied learning which is for students to put their academic learning to work and to learn from projects that connect what they do at school to the demands of the twenty-first century workplace. Some of these standards lend themselves to assessment through observation and other less formal methods rather than through written work.

What the work shows

A1c Problem Solving: The student plans and organizes an event or activity; that is, the student:

- develops a plan that:
  - reflects research into relevant precedents and regulations;
  - includes all the factors and variables that need to be considered;
  - shows the order in which things need to be done;
  - takes into account the resources available to put the plan into action, including people and time;

This work sample illustrates a standard-setting performance for the following parts of the standards:

A1c Problem Solving: Plan and organize an event or an activity.

A2c Communication: Publish information.

A3b Information: Use information technology.

A4c Learning and Self-management: Set learning goals and review progress.

Mrs. ______ Class
Wedgwood Middle School
Fort Worth , Texas 76133
September 28, 1995

Mrs. ______ Principal,
Wedgwood Middle School

Fort Worth, TX 76133

Dear Mrs. ______,

Mrs. ______'s class of honors English would savor the opportunity to be a part of Vital Link in our class. I will attempt to convince you that we should participate in this event. We are requesting your permission to follow through with this project. The following reasons I hope will do just that.

Our first reason is that it would be a good experience for all of the students. They could see what a real business is like. We will learn about the skills you need and the type of person you need to be in the field you choose. It will teach us that at work you have to work in cooperative groups and other skills.

The second reason that I had in mind is that this project would help us learn about a business, and it would help us know what we have to work for. If you wanted a certain job when you grow up, and you picked it for Vital Link, you would know what type of skills you would need for the job. That might lead us to stay in school and continue until college and get a degree.

Our third and final reason is it would help lead us toward a Career Day at our school. If we were involved in Vital Link we would know the people that worked at the business. We could invite them to come talk to students, now, not only to teach us but to teach other students that,that job would be an interesting career to set for their goal in life.

In conclusion I ask you again to grant Mrs. ______'s first period honors English class permission to take part in Vital Link.

Sincerely,
Mrs. ______'s
(first period)

B

CAREER DAY

______
______'S 1st PERIOD
By: ______

On March 7,1996, our 1st period Applied Learning in English class presented a Career Day for the entire school. The students wrote Mrs.______, our principal, for permission to have a school-wide Career Day.

Our class was assigned a committee that they were going to strive to finish before the day Career Day arrived. The committees were as follows: Scheduling Committee, Welcoming Committee, Telephone Committee, Evaluation Committee, and Coordinating the Host/Hostesses.

The Scheduling Committee made the schedule and made sure that every homeroom has three speakers. The scheduling committee made spread sheets on the computer to assure that all homerooms were covered for each session and that there were a variety of occupation for each homeroom. They also planned how long Career Day was going to be.

The Welcoming Committee planned and scheduled the brunch for the participants in the Career Day. The brunch lasted for about 30 minutes in the morning. The students planned the refreshments and the decorations.

The Telephone Committee called all the participants in Career Day to ask them to speak, and to schedule them. They also wrote the letter to confirm when they were coming.

The Evaluation Committee made all the evaluations for the students, teachers, and speakers. They were also responsible for collecting and evaluating them.

The Host/Hostesses were assigned to speakers and homerooms. They were given maps of the school and a master schedule list. Each host/hostess introduced the speakers.

A brochure was prepared by the class including all of the speakers and a brief description of their occupation for each student in the school. Each student completed a short profile of the guest who they invited. The committee typed and formatted the brochure. An expert on computer programing came to show us how to format the brochure so that it would look professional. We bought brochure paper and ran enough copies for every student in the school to have a brochure with all of the participants included.

The Career Day was very well received. The students learned a great deal from their experiences.

- implements the plan in ways that:
  - reflect the priorities established in the plan;
  - respond effectively to unforeseen circumstances;
- evaluates the success of the event or activity;
- makes recommendations to others who might consider planning and organizing a similar event or activity.

Problem Solving A1
Communication Tools and Techniques A2
Information Tools and Techniques A3
Learning and Self-management Tools and Techniques A4
Tools and Techniques for Working With Others

Career Day

C

Jan. 29, 1996

Evaluation of
Career Day

Our Career Day project has
been going great! I think we
have been doing a really good
job working together and cooper-
ating. There are some things I
think we could work on though.
My committee (brochure) has
been kind of lost. We have
been going around asking people
in our classroom if they've written
any paragraphs about the person
they invited, but a lot of them don't
take it into consideration and
haven't written a word yet. On the
computer, we're not really sure
what to do either. Once we get
paragraphs put together, what do
we do with them?
I know Chanel and I haven't
gone to vital link yet, but at least
we have gotten in contact with Sharon
and have tried to make things
work.
I appreciate all your help with
Career Day and I think we're
doing wonderful!

D

3-8-96

Evaluation 4
Career Day!

On March 7, my Applied Learning
English class organized a career day.
It was hard work but in the end
everything turned out kind of according
to plans

I learned many things, like
scheduale is everything! I learned
that when you have things to do and
time is running out, you get nervouse!
I learned by some friends that you
can never trust a big shot!

A lot of things worked, my
guy came on time, the brunch went
great, most of the kids enjoyed it,
and everyone had something to do!
But there were some things that
didn't go right, like somebody's man
didn't show up, the balloons said "Happy
Birthday!" (but that was okay!) I don't
know why it didn't work, maybe because
some people weren't sure of what
was going on, or some people forgot.

I wouldn't do anything differently
if we did it over, except let the
homerooms decide which person they
wanted to talk to. I would do everything
the same. I thought it went really well.

I hope that maybe next year
my honors English class will do a
career day next year!

THEND

A This proposal to the principal seeks permission for the students to take part in Vital Link, a program of one-day internships in businesses. The last paragraph points to the development of the career day as an outgrowth of the students' participation in Vital Link. The proposal also states the connection to goals and other learning that would be important to the principal.

B This document relates to the overall organization, purpose, and evaluation of the event. All variables that need to be considered are included such as the committees and the duties of each. The document makes sense in terms of the order of assignments to be accomplished. This document is clear enough for someone else to use when developing a similar project.

C **D** **E** These student records evaluate the plan both in progress and in retrospect. The records include statements concerning adjustments and recommendations to correct problems if the event were to be staged again. The evaluations make reference to unforeseen circumstances that arose and other published documents confirm that the students overcame the problems.

A1 Problem Solving
A2 Communication Tools and Techniques
A3 Information Tools and Techniques
A4 Learning and Self-management Tools and Techniques
Tools and Techniques for Working With Others

Career Day

E

3/8/96

Career Day Evaluation

I learned about my guests that I introduced, I also learned how to apply my listening and speaking skills. Everything worked smoothly. The schedule went really good, everyone got to the correct place at the right time. I think everything went good, I only had one problem, and that was one of the speakers went over the session time, and made my speaker have less time to talk. If we had another Career Day I would think we would need to have more connections with the speakers that are coming like call our speaker several days before and make sure their coming and ask them if their bringing any other guests with them. I would still have a brunch and have special committee's and have it set up as it was. I think we did a good job, and everyone had a part in being a speaker so no one got left out. I would definetly do it again any time and I know others will agree. Thanks Mrs. ______ for your hard work in this, it was lots of fun.

A2 c Communication Tools and Techniques: The student publishes information using several methods and formats, such as overhead transparencies, handouts, and computer generated graphs and charts; that is, the student:

- organizes the information into an appropriate form for use in the publication;
- checks the information for accuracy;
- formats the published material so that it achieves its purpose.

F This is a note written to parents and guardians seeking help in identifying businesses to participate in the Vital Link component of the project. The students adopted a style common for such notes from school to home.

F

October 18, 1995

Dear Parents or Guardian,

Mrs. ______'s 1st period English class has chosen Vital Link for our applied learning project for this year. Vital Link is where students go to places of work for a day.

This will help your child and other children in the future by giving them leadership skills and know of skills needed in the real world. We can also find out why parents come home so stressed out.

We need some help from *you* parents so we can succeed in this project. If you are interested in having a student from our class visit your business, or if you can provide transportation for your child, please complete and detach the permission slip below. This project will take place Nov. 1- Nov. 10.

Approved

Thank you,
Dusty ______
Adam ______
Robert ______
Kevin ______
Mallory ______
Lacie ______
Chanel ______

______I will allow my child to go to an adults office for a day.

______I can provide transportation to the offices. My daytime phone number is ______-______

______I would be willing to have a child to come and work with me.

My job is ____________________ My work number is ______-______

______I will not allow my child to participate in this activity

Child's Name ____________________ Parents Name ______________

Parent's Signature ____________________

Career Day

G

Schedule For Career Day

Remain in advisory from 9:00-11:15
9:05-9:20- Advisory
9:20-9:50-1st Speaker
9:50-10:20-2nd Speaker
10:20-10:30-Break
10:30-11:00-3rd speaker
11:00-11:15-Evaluations by students,teachers and participants

Career Day Notice

Thank you for your cooperation concerning Career Day. The students will remain in their homeroom, and a Career Day host and a guest speaker will come to your room. Each student in the their first session will receive a brochure. The guest will speak about their occupation. The host will also be passing out student evaluations after the 3rd session. Thank you.

Mrs. ______'s Applied Learning Class

H

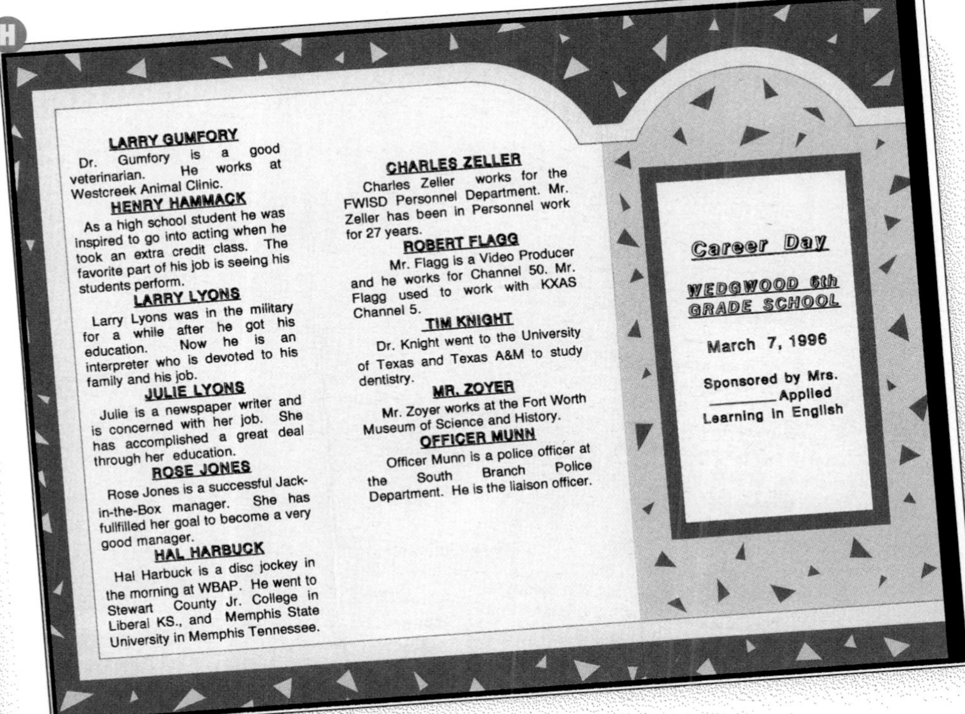

LARRY GUMFORY
Dr. Gumfory is a good veterinarian. He works at Westcreek Animal Clinic.

HENRY HAMMACK
As a high school student he was inspired to go into acting when he took an extra credit class. The favorite part of his job is seeing his students perform.

LARRY LYONS
Larry Lyons was in the military for a while after he got his education. Now he is an interpreter who is devoted to his family and his job.

JULIE LYONS
Julie is a newspaper writer and is concerned with her job. She has accomplished a great deal through her education.

ROSE JONES
Rose Jones is a successful Jack-in-the-Box manager. She has fullfilled her goal to become a very good manager.

HAL HARBUCK
Hal Harbuck is a disc jockey in the morning at WBAP. He went to Stewart County Jr. College in Liberal KS., and Memphis State University in Memphis Tennessee.

CHARLES ZELLER
Charles Zeller works for the FWISD Personnel Department. Mr. Zeller has been in Personnel work for 27 years.

ROBERT FLAGG
Mr. Flagg is a Video Producer and he works for Channel 50. Mr. Flagg used to work with KXAS Channel 5.

TIM KNIGHT
Dr. Knight went to the University of Texas and Texas A&M to study dentistry.

MR. ZOYER
Mr. Zoyer works at the Fort Worth Museum of Science and History.

OFFICER MUNN
Officer Munn is a police officer at the South Branch Police Department. He is the liaison officer.

Career Day
WEDGWOOD 6th GRADE SCHOOL
March 7, 1996
Sponsored by Mrs. ________ Applied Learning in English

I

MARY PRINE
Mary is an excellent counselor for Bruce Shulkey Elementary. She takes her day and uses it to help kids with their problems.

DARREN TURNER
Darren Turner is the director of student affairs at TCU. He used to play in the NFL with the Chicago Bears.

TOM WAINEWRIGHT
Mr. Tom Wainewright is a comptroller of currency. He makes sure the banks are running smoothly.

JEAN DENTON
Mrs. Denton is a very good cartoonist. She has written for the newspaper. She was a sports writer for The Star Telegram. Her cartoons appear in the newspaper and magazines.

BARBARA BIRDWELL
Dr. Barbara Birdwell is a family doctor who attended TCU. After that, she went to U. T. Medical School in San Antonio.

HOLLYWOOD HENDERSON
Hollywood joins 106.1 KISS-FM for the afternoon. He lives in Dallas with his wife, Cara and his son, Samuel.

SHARON COX
Sharon Cox is an editor for Class Acts. She got her master's degree in journalism and education .

MARILYN BURT
Mrs. Burt worked with All Saints Home Care as Manager for the Private Duty and Nursing Agency and Marketing . She retired in April of 1995.

JEFF BUELL
Jeff works at McKinney Bible Church as a Youth Minister. He teaches kids about the Bible. Jeff also helps with events at his church.

RANDY SMITH
Mr. Smith is a videographer. He went to Video Technical Institute and got an Associate Degree of Applied Science in video technology.

SUSAN GEURTZ
Susan Guertz is an interpreter for the deaf. She taught at Goodman Elementary in Arlington. Now she interprets for deaf children at Trimble Tech High School.

FRANCES LEA
Frances Lea is a dance instructor at her own studio. The classes she teaches are tap, jazz, clogging and aerobics.

PAT WILLBURN
Pat Willburn is a devoted plumber for Dyna Ten. He supervises and instructs other plumbers.

MANUEL GONZALEZ
For two years, Mr. Manuel Gonzalez was the superintendent of training devices at Carswell AFB.

RICHARD WISEMAN
Richard Wiseman is a successful lawyer. He is devoted to his career at Herman, Scott, Dean and Miles.

STEVE THORNTON
Steve Thorton is a firefighter. As part of Mr. Thornton's job, he trains recruits.

BOB RAY SANDERS
Bob Ray Sanders is a commentary journalist at the *Fort Worth Star Telegram*. Mr. Sanders also works for Channel 13. He has won several awards.

GERALD MARCELL
Mr. Marcell is a Computer Programmer/Analyst for Union Pacific Resources Company. He has worked there for 11 years.

G This handout was prepared to inform teachers about the schedule and other arrangements for the career day. It is presented in a format appropriate to its purpose and anticipates the readers' needs by providing information in addition to the schedule.

H I These pages are the front and back of an informational brochure that was given to each student in the school on the career day.

J This document demonstrates one student's translation of background information collected prior to the career day into a format written for an oral presentation. This same information in a briefer form appears in the brochure.

K The students prepared this map of the school to help direct the speakers visiting the school on the career day.

Career Day

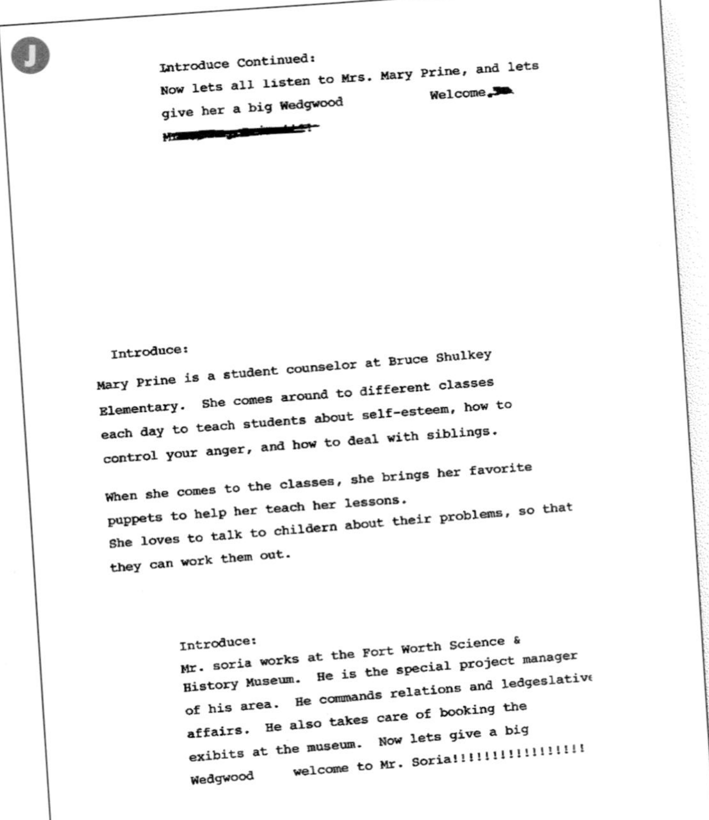

J

Introduce Continued:
Now lets all listen to Mrs. Mary Prine, and lets give her a big Wedgwood   Welcome.

Introduce:
Mary Prine is a student counselor at Bruce Shulkey Elementary. She comes around to different classes each day to teach students about self-esteem, how to control your anger, and how to deal with siblings.

When she comes to the classes, she brings her favorite puppets to help her teach her lessons. She loves to talk to childern about their problems, so that they can work them out.

Introduce:
Mr. soria works at the Fort Worth Science & History Museum. He is the special project manager of his area. He commands relations and ledgeslative affairs. He also takes care of booking the exibits at the museum. Now lets give a big Wedgwood   welcome to Mr. Soria!!!!!!!!!!!!!!!!!

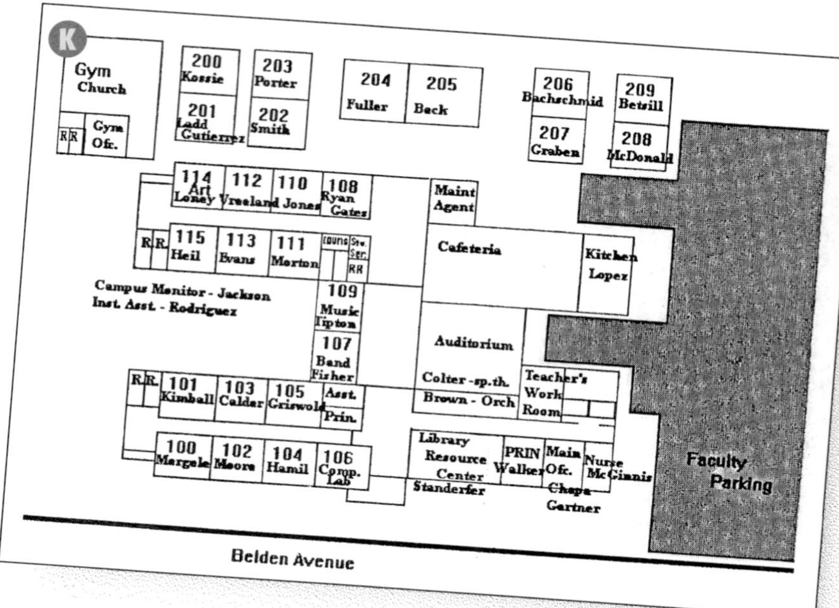

L

	A	B	C	D	E
1	Speakers	Occupation	Sessions	HOST/HOSTESS	Classroom
2	Officer Munn	police	1,2,&3	Erick ______	A.100 B.107 C.115
3	Bob Ray Sanders	newspaper	1,2,&3	Kevin ______	A.102 B.100 C.101
4	Jean Denton	cartoonist	1,2,&3	Katherine ______	A.104 B.110 C.100
5	Mary Prine	counselor	1	Beth ______	A.101
6	Frances Lea	dance inst	1&2	Dee Dee ______	A.111 B.101
7	Dr. Gumfory	vet	1&2	Greg ______	A.206 B.102
8	Jeff Buell	minister	1,2,&3	Dusty ______	A.110 B.202 C.102
9	Rose Jones	Jack in Box	1,2,&3	Brian ______	A.103 B.105 C.104
10	Mr. Gonzalez	military	1&3	Lacie ______	A.203 C.105
11	Gerald Marcell	computer	3	Greg ______	C.103
12	Pat Willburn	plumber	3	Charkesia ______	C.110
13	Tim Knight	dentist	1,2,&3	DeAndre ______	A.105 B.104 C.204
14	Tom Wainewright	OCC	1,2,&3	Lindsey ______	A.107 B.111 C.112
15	Charles Zeller	FWISD personnel	2&3	April ______	B.112 C.107
16	Marilyn Burt	health care	1	Charlie ______	A.113
17	Susan Geurtz	deaf	3	Davin ______	C.111
18	Randy Smith	video	1,2,&3	Sidnie ______	A.112 B.113 C.202
19	Larry Lyons	military	1,2,&3	Jamaal ______	A.115 B.205 C.113
20	Julie Lyons	newspaper	1&2	Charkesia ______	A.202 B.115
21	Steve Thronton	fireman	1&2	Andy ______	A.209 B.203
22	Dr. Barbara Birdwell	doctor	3	Jennifer ______	C.203
23	Richard Wiseman	lawyer	1	Mallory ______	A.204
24	Sharon Cox	Class Acts	1&2	Chanel ______	A.205 B.206
25	Robert Flagg	FWISD TV	1,2,&3	Taylor ______	A.208 B.103 C.205
26	Hal Harbrook	DJ WBAP	3	Brett ______	C.206
27	Henry Hammock	theatre	2	Lacie ______	B.208
28	Mr. Soria	museum	3	Beth ______	C.208
29	Darren Turner	TCU	2	Adam ______	B.209
30	Hollywood Henderson	DJ KISS F.M.	2&3	Jennifer ______ & Dee Dee ______	B.204 C.209

Official 3/5/96

A3b Information Tools and Techniques: The student uses information technology to assist in gathering, analyzing, organizing, and presenting information; that is, the student:

- acquires information for specific purposes from on-line sources, such as the Internet, and other electronic data bases, such as a scientific data base on CD ROM;
- uses word-processing, graphics, data base, and spreadsheet programs to produce project reports and related materials.

The students used word-processing programs to produce a range of materials.

K L M Students used a graphics package to produce the school map and a spreadsheet package to produce the charts scheduling the speakers.

A4c Learning and Self-management Tools and Techniques: The student sets goals for learning and reviews his or her progress; that is, the student:

- sets goals for learning;
- reviews his or her progress towards meeting the goals;
- seeks and responds to advice from others in setting goals and reviewing progress.

A B D E F These documents demonstrate that goals and a system of self-management were in place. The student evaluations indicate the things that went well. Areas for improvement such as the student's frustration with other students meeting their responsibilities by writing descriptive paragraphs, and the need to make phone calls to adults prior to the adults showing up on the assigned day, demonstrate a capacity to review progress toward goals as well as the management of conflicting priorities. Students commented about both the features of the career day that went well, such as the brunch, and the things that went less well, such as the balloons that said happy birthday.

N O P Through the formal evaluation forms, the students collected information to check their understanding of how well the event was planned and staged against the perceptions of the adults and students who participated in the event.

Career Day

M

	A	B	C
1	**Classroom**		**Speakers**
2	100		A. Officer Munn, B. Bob Ray Sanders, C. Jean Denton
3	101		A. mary Prine, B. Frances Lea, C. Bob Ray Sanders
4	102		A. Bob Ray Sanders, B. Dr. Gumfory, C. Jeff Buell
5	103		A. Rose Jones, B. Robert Flagg, C. Gerald Marcell
6	104		A. Jean Denton, B. Tim Knight, C. Rose Jones
7	105		A. Tim Knight B. Rose Jones, C. Mr. Gonzalez
8	107		A. Tom Wainewright, B. Officer Munn, C. Charles Zeller
9	110		A. Jeff Buell, B. Jean Denton, C. Pat Willburn
10	111		A. Frances Lea, B. Tom Wainewright, C. Susan Geurtz
11	112		A. Randy Smith, B. Charles Zeller, C. Tom Wainewright
12	113		A. Marilyn Burt, B. Randy Smith, C. Larry Lyons
13	115		A. Larry Lyons, B. Julie Lyons, C. Officer Munn
14	202		A. Julie lyons, B. Jeff Buell, C. Randy Smith
15	203		A. Mr. Gonzalez, B. Steve Thornton, C. Dr. Barbara Birdwell
16	204		A. Richard Wiseman, B. Hollywood Henderson, C. Tim Knight
17	205		A. Sharon Cox, B. Larry Lyons, C. Robert Flagg
18	206		A. Dr. Gumfory, B. Sharon Cox, C. Hal Harbuck
19	208		A. Robert Flagg, B. Henry Hammock, C. Mr. Soria
20	209		A. Steve Thornton, B. Darren Turner, C. Hollywood Henderson

N

TEACHER EVALUATION

1.) In what ways do you think your students enjoyed Career Day?

2.) Did you enjoy Career Day? Explain why or why not.

3.) How do you think this event helped your students decide what they want to be as an adult?

4.) Did your students behave and treat the guest(s) with respect?

5.) What suggestions do you have for Career Day for next year?

O

Guest Evaluation

1.What is your name and occupation?________

2.Did you enjoy our March 7, 1996 Career Day?____

3. Do you think the students enjoyed your speaking? Why?

4. Were the Welcoming committee, and Host/Hostess polite?

5.If you were invited again would you come? Why?

6.On a scale of 1-10, how would you rate our Career Day? Why?

7.What suggestions do you have about Career Day?

P

Name____________

Student Evaluation

1.) Who came to your classroom? List their occupation, please.

A.)

B.)

C.)

2.)What interested you the most about the presentation of speakers?

3.)Did the speaker's information have an effect on what you want be when you become an adult?

4.)What rating would you give Career day on a scale to 1-10, 10 being the greatest?

5.)How do you think we could improve Career Day?

E1 Reading / E6 Public Documents / E7 Functional Documents

APPENDIX I

The elementary school standards are set at a level of performance approximately equivalent to the end of fourth grade. The middle school standards are set at a level of performance approximately equivalent to the end of eighth grade. The high school standards are set at a level of performance approximately equivalent to the end of tenth grade. It is expected that some students might achieve these levels earlier and others later than these grades.

An array of work is required to achieve any single standard. The work becomes increasing refined and sophisticated as students get older. The complexity of the tasks used to generate the work also increases. This notion of requiring students to hone the sophistication of their performances while simultaneously working with increasingly complex assignments cuts across all the English Language Arts standards.

These standards allow for oral performances of student work whenever appropriate.

Elementary School

E1 a The student reads at least twenty-five books or book equivalents each year. The quality and complexity of the materials to be read are illustrated in the sample reading list. The materials should include traditional and contemporary literature (both fiction and non-fiction) as well as magazines, newspapers, textbooks, and on-line materials. Such reading should represent a diverse collection of material from at least three different literary forms and from at least five different writers.

E1 b The student reads and comprehends at least four books (or book equivalents) about one issue or subject, or four books by a single writer, or four books in one genre, and produces evidence of reading that:

- makes and supports warranted and responsible assertions about the texts;
- supports assertions with elaborated and convincing evidence;
- draws the texts together to compare and contrast themes, characters, and ideas;
- makes perceptive and well developed connections;
- evaluates writing strategies and elements of the author's craft.

E1 c The student reads and comprehends informational materials to develop understanding and expertise and produces written or oral work that:

- restates or summarizes information;
- relates new information to prior knowledge and experience;
- extends ideas;
- makes connections to related topics or information.

E1 d The student reads aloud, accurately (in the range of 85-90%), familiar material of the quality and complexity illustrated in the sample reading list, and in a way that makes meaning clear to listeners by:

- self correcting when subsequent reading indicates an earlier miscue;
- using a range of cueing systems, e.g., phonics and context clues, to determine pronunciation and meanings;
- reading with a rhythm, flow, and meter that sounds like everyday speech.

Middle School

E1 a The student reads at least twenty-five books or book equivalents each year. The quality and complexity of the materials to be read are illustrated in the sample reading list. The materials should include traditional and contemporary literature (both fiction and non-fiction) as well as magazines, newspapers, textbooks, and on-line materials. Such reading should represent a diverse collection of material from at least three different literary forms and from at least five different writers.

E1 b The student reads and comprehends at least four books (or book equivalents) about one issue or subject, or four books by a single writer, or four books in one genre, and produces evidence of reading that:

- makes and supports warranted and responsible assertions about the texts;
- supports assertions with elaborated and convincing evidence;
- draws the texts together to compare and contrast themes, characters, and ideas;
- makes perceptive and well developed connections;
- evaluates writing strategies and elements of the author's craft.

E1 c The student reads and comprehends informational materials to develop understanding and expertise and produces written or oral work that:

- restates or summarizes information;
- relates new information to prior knowledge and experience;
- extends ideas;
- makes connections to related topics or information.

E1 d The student demonstrates familiarity with a variety of public documents (i.e., documents that focus on civic issues or matters of public policy at the community level and beyond) and produces written or oral work that does one or more of the following:

- identifies the social context of the document;
- identifies the author's purpose and stance;
- analyzes the arguments and positions advanced and the evidence offered in support of them, or formulates an argument and offers evidence to support it;

High School

E1 a The student reads at least twenty-five books or book equivalents each year. The quality and complexity of the materials to be read are illustrated in the sample reading list. The materials should include traditional and contemporary literature (both fiction and non-fiction) as well as magazines, newspapers, textbooks, and on-line materials. Such reading should represent a diverse collection of material from at least three different literary forms and from at least five different writers.

E1 b The student reads and comprehends at least four books (or book equivalents) about one issue or subject, or four books by a single writer, or four books in one genre, and produces evidence of reading that:

- makes and supports warranted and responsible assertions about the texts;
- supports assertions with elaborated and convincing evidence;
- draws the texts together to compare and contrast themes, characters, and ideas;
- makes perceptive and well developed connections;
- evaluates writing strategies and elements of the author's craft.

E1 c The student reads and comprehends informational materials to develop understanding and expertise and produces written or oral work that:

- restates or summarizes information;
- relates new information to prior knowledge and experience;
- extends ideas;
- makes connections to related topics or information.

E6 Public Documents

E6 a The student critiques public documents with an eye to strategies common in public discourse, including:

- effective use of argument;
- use of the power of anecdote;
- anticipation of counter-claims;
- appeal to audiences both friendly and hostile to the position presented;
- use of emotionally laden words and imagery;
- citing of appropriate references or authorities.

Much writing can be classified as belonging to the public arena. New Standards, however, defines public documents to mean those pieces of text that are concerned with public policy, that address controversial issues confronting the public, or that arise in response to controversial issues or public policy. Public documents are included in the Reading standard at middle school level (E1 d) and constitute a separate standard at high school level (E6). At the middle school level, the issues students write about come primarily from the school or local community. At high school, students should address issues which are of national importance.

Functional writing is writing that exists in order to get things done. Functional writing is ordinarily considered technical writing and, as such, is often not part of the typical English curriculum. New Standards requires students to demonstrate proficiency with functional writing because such writing is of increasing importance to the complex literacy of our culture. Functional documents are included in the Reading standard at middle school level (E1 e) and constitute a separate standard at high school level (E7).

- examines or makes use of the appeal of a document to audiences both friendly and hostile to the position presented;
- identifies or uses commonly used persuasive techniques.

E1 e The student demonstrates familiarity with a variety of functional documents (i.e., documents that exist in order to get things done) and produces written or oral work that does one or more of the following:

- identifies the institutional context of the document;
- identifies the sequence of activities needed to carry out a procedure;
- analyzes or uses the formatting techniques used to make a document user-friendly;
- identifies any information that is either extraneous or missing in terms of audience and purpose or makes effective use of relevant information.

E6 b The student produces public documents, in which the student:

- exhibits an awareness of the importance of precise word choice and the power of imagery and/or anecdote;
- utilizes and recognizes the power of logical arguments, arguments based on appealing to a reader's emotions, and arguments dependent upon the writer's persona;
- uses arguments that are appropriate in terms of the knowledge, values, and degree of understanding of the intended audience;
- uses a range of strategies to appeal to readers.

E7 Functional Documents

E7 a The student critiques functional documents with an eye to strategies common to effective functional documents, including:

- visual appeal, e.g., format, graphics, white space, headers;
- logic of the sequence in which the directions are given;
- awareness of possible reader misunderstandings.

E7 b The student produces functional documents appropriate to audience and purpose, in which the student:

- reports, organizes, and conveys information and ideas accurately;
- includes relevant narrative details, such as scenarios, definitions, and examples;
- anticipates readers' problems, mistakes, and misunderstandings;
- uses a variety of formatting techniques, such as headings, subordinate terms, foregrounding of main ideas, hierarchical structures, graphics, and color;
- establishes a persona that is consistent with the document's purpose;
- employs word choices that are consistent with the persona and appropriate for the intended audience.

E1 Reading *continued*

APPENDIX I

The number of books required for E1a does not increase as students get older, but the length and complexity of what is read does increase (as indicated by the sample reading lists), so, this standard becomes increasingly formidable.

E1a assumes an adequate library of appropriate reading material. In some places, library resources are too meager to support the amount of reading required for every student to achieve this standard. Where a shortage of books exists, better use of out-of-school resources must be made; for example, students may have to be assured access to local or county libraries.

Reading twenty-five books a year entails a substantial amount of time. Students may use materials read in conjunction with their regular class work, including courses other than English, to satisfy this requirement.

Elementary School

Fiction

Brink, *Caddie Woodlawn;*
Cleary, *Ramona and Her Father;*
Coerr, *The Josefina Story Quilt;*
Cohen, *Fat Jack;*
De Saint-Exupery, *The Little Prince;*
Hamilton, *Zeely;*
Hansen, *The Gift-Giver;*
Lord, *In the Year of the Boar and Jackie Robinson;*
Mendez and Byard, *The Black Snowman;*
Naidoo, *Journey to Jo'Burg;*
O'Dell, *Zia;*
Ringgold, *Tar Beach;*
Speare, *The Sign of the Beaver;*
Yep, *Child of the Owl.*

Non-Fiction

Aliki, *Corn Is Maize: The Gift of the Indians;*
Baylor, *The Way to Start a Day;*
Cherry, *The Great Kapok Tree;*
Epstein, *History of Women in Science for Young People;*
Fritz, *And Then What Happened, Paul Revere?;*
Godkin, *Wolf Island;*
Greenfield, *Childtimes: A Three-Generation Memoir;*
Hamilton, *Anthony Burns: The Defeat and Triumph of a Fugitive Slave;*
McGovern, *The Secret Soldier: The Story of Deborah Sampson;*
McKissack, *Frederick* Douglass: *The Black Lion;*
Politi, *Song of the Swallows;*
Sattler, *Dinosaurs of North America.*

Poetry

Ahlberg, *Heard It in the Playground;*
Blishen and Wildsmith, *Oxford Book of Poetry for Children;*
De Regniers, Moore, White, and Carr, eds., *Sing a Song of Popcorn;*
Giovanni, *Ego-Tripping and Other Poems for Young People;*
Greenfield, *Honey, I Love and Other Love Poems;*
Heard, *For the Good of the Earth and Sun;*
Janeczko, *Strings: A Gathering of Family Poems;*
Koch and Farrell, eds., *Talking to the Sun;*
Lobel, ed., *The Random House Book of Mother Goose;*
Manguel, ed., *Seasons;*
Mathis, *Red Dog, Blue Fly: Football Poems;*
Silverstein, *Where the Sidewalk Ends.*

Folklore

French, *Snow White in New York;*
Goble, *Buffalo Woman;*
Griego y Maestas, *Cuentos: Tales From the Hispanic Southwest;*
Huck and Lobel, *Princess Furball;*
Kipling, *The Elephant's Child;*

Middle School

Fiction

Anaya, *Bless Me, Ultima;*
Armstrong, *Sounder;*
Bonham, *Durango Street;*
Cohen, *Tell Us Your Secret;*
Collier, *My Brother Sam Is Dead;*
Cormier, *I Am the Cheese;*
Danziger, *The Cat Ate My Gymsuit;*
Fast, *April Morning;*
Gaines, *A Gathering of Old Men;*
Goldman, *The Princess Bride;*
Greene, *Summer of My German Soldier;*
Hansen, *Which Way Freedom;*
Hinton, *The Outsiders;*
Holman, *Slake's Limbo;*
London, *The Call of the Wild;*
Mathis, *Listen for the Fig Tree;*
Mohr, *Nilda;*
Neufeld, *Lisa, Bright and Dark;*
O'Brien, *Z for Zachariah;*
Schaefer, *Shane;*
Stevenson, *Treasure Island;*
Voigt, *Dicey's Song;*
Walker, *To Hell With Dying;*
Walter, *Because We Are;*
Zindel, *The Pigman.*

Non-Fiction

Amory, *The Cat Who Came for Christmas;*
Berck, *No Place to Be: Voices of Homeless Children;*
Frank, *The Diary of a Young Girl;*
George, *The Talking Earth;*
Gilbreth, *Cheaper by the Dozen;*
Haskins, *Outward Dreams;*
Hautzig, *Endless Steppe: A Girl in Exile;*
Herriott, *All Creatures Great and Small;*
Lester, *To Be a Slave;*
Meyers, *Pearson, a Harbor Seal Pup;*
Reiss, *The Upstairs Room;*
Soto, *Living Up the Street;*
White, *Ryan White: My Own Story;*
Yates, *Amos Fortune, Free Man.*

Poetry

Adams, *Poetry of Earth and Sky;*
Eliot, *Old Possum's Book of Practical Cats;*
Frost, *You Come Too;*
Greenfield, *Night on Neighborhood Street;*
Livingston, *Cat Poems.*

Drama

Blinn, *Brian's Song;*
Davis, *Escape to Freedom;*
Gibson, *The Miracle Worker;*
Lawrence and Lee, *Inherit the Wind;*
Osborn, *On Borrowed Time;*

High School

Fiction

Carroll, *Alice in Wonderland;*
Cisneros, *The House on Mango Street;*
Clark, *The Ox-Bow Incident;*
Golding, *Lord of the Flies;*
Hawthorne, *The Scarlet Letter;*
Hemingway, *For Whom the Bell Tolls;*
Hentoff, *The Day They Came to Arrest the Book;*
Hilton, *Goodbye, Mr. Chips;*
Kinsella, *Shoeless Joe;*
Knowles, *A Separate Peace;*
Lee, *To Kill a Mockingbird;*
McCullers, *The Heart Is a Lonely Hunter;*
Orwell, *1984;*
Paulsen, *Canyons;*
Portis, *True Grit;*
Potok, *Davita's Harp;*
Stoker, *Dracula;*
Wartski, *A Boat to Nowhere;*
Welty, *The Golden Apples.*

Non-Fiction

Angell, *Late Innings;*
Angelou, *I Know Why the Caged Bird Sings;*
Ashe, *Days of Grace;*
Beal, *"I Will Fight No More Forever": Chief Joseph and the Nez Perce War;*
Bishop, *The Day Lincoln Was Shot;*
Bloom, *The Closing of the American Mind;*
Campbell, *The Power of Myth;*
Covey, *Seven Habits of Highly Effective People;*
Galarza, *Barrio Boy;*
Hawking, *A Brief History of Time;*
Houston, *Farewell to Manzanar;*
Kennedy, *Profiles in Courage;*
Kingsley and Levitz, *Count Us In: Growing Up With Down Syndrome;*
Kingston, *Woman Warrior;*
Mazer, ed., *Going Where I'm Coming From;*
Momaday, *The Way to Rainy Mountain;*
Rodriguez, *Hunger of Memory;*
Sternberg, *User's Guide to the Internet;*
Wright, *Black Boy.*

Poetry

Angelou, *I Shall Not be Moved;*
Bly, ed., *News of the Universe;*
Carruth, ed., *The Voice That Is Great Within Us;*
Cummings, *Collected Poems;*
Dickinson, *Complete Poems;*
Hughes, *Selected Poems;*
Knudson and Swenson, eds., *American Sports Poems;*
Longfellow, *Evangeline;*
Randall, ed., *The Black Poets;*
Wilbur, *Things of This World.*

Luenn, *The Dragon Kite;*
Steptoe, *Mufaro's Beautiful Daughters;*
Steptoe, *The Story of Jumping Mouse.*

Modern Fantasy and Science Fiction

Andersen, *The Ugly Duckling;*
Bond, *A Bear Called Paddington;*
Dahl, *James and the Giant Peach;*
Grahame, *The Wind in the Willows;*
Lewis, *The Lion, the Witch and the Wardrobe;*
Norton, *The Borrowers;*
Van Allsburg, *Jumanji;*
White, *Charlotte's Web.*

Children's magazines

Action (Scholastic);
Creative Classroom;
News (Scholastic);
Social Studies for the Young Learner;
TIME FOR KIDS;
Weekly Reader;
World (National Geographic).

Other

Newspapers, manuals appropriate for elementary school children, e.g., video game instructions, computer manuals.

Shakespeare, *A Midsummer Night's Dream;*
Stone, *Metamora, or, the Last of the Wampanoags.*

Folklore/Mythology

Blair, *Tall Tale America;*
Bruchac, *The First Strawberries: A Cherokee Story;*
Bryan, *Beat the Story-Drum, Pum-Pum;*
D'Aulaire, *Norse Gods and Giants;*
Gallico, *The Snow Goose;*
Lee, *Toad Is the Uncle of Heaven: A Vietnamese Folk Tale;*
Pyle, *Merry Adventures of Robin Hood.*

Modern Fantasy and Science Fiction

Babbitt, *Tuck Everlasting;*
Bradbury, *Dandelion Wine;*
Cooper, *The Grey King;*
Hamilton, *The Magical Adventures of Pretty Pearl;*
L'Engle, *A Wrinkle in Time;*
Tolkien, *The Hobbit;*
Yep, *Dragon of the Lost Sea.*

Magazines/Periodicals

Calliope (world history);
Cobblestone (American history);
Faces (anthropology);
Junior Scholastic (Scholastic);
Odyssey (science);
Science World (Scholastic);
Scope (Scholastic);
World (National Geographic);.

Other

Computer manuals; instructions; contracts. See also the reading lists included in award books corresponding to reading provided by the Girl Scouts of the U.S.A. and the Boy Scouts of America.

Drama

Christie, *And Then There Were None;*
Hansberry, *A Raisin in the Sun;*
McCullers, *The Member of the Wedding;*
Pomerance, *The Elephant Man;*
Rose, *Twelve Angry Men;*
Rostand, *Cyrano de Bergerac;*
Shakespeare, *Romeo and Juliet; Julius Caesar;*
Van Druten, *I Remember Mama;*
Wilder, *The Skin of Our Teeth;*
Wilson, *The Piano Lesson.*

Folklore/Mythology

Burland, *North American Indian Mythology;*
Evslin, *Adventures of Ulysses;*
Pinsent, *Greek Mythology;*
Stewart, *The Crystal Cave;*
White, *The Once and Future King.*

Modern Fantasy and Science Fiction

Adams, *Watership Down;*
Asimov, *Foundation;*
Bradbury, *The Martian Chronicles;*
Clarke, *2001: A Space Odyssey;*
Clarke, *Childhood's End;*
Frank, *Alas, Babylon;*
Herbert, *Dune;*
Lewis, *Out of the Silent Planet;*
McCaffrey, *Dragonflight;*
Twain, *A Connecticut Yankee in King Arthur's Court;*
Verne, *20,000 Leagues Under the Sea.*

Magazines and Newspapers

Literary Cavalcade (Scholastic);
National Geographic;
Newsweek;
Omni;
Smithsonian;
Sports Illustrated;
Time.

Other

Computer manuals; instructions; contracts; technical materials.

E2 Writing

APPENDIX I

E2b is meant to replace the repertoire of responses that students traditionally write when they respond to literature. This type of response requires an understanding of writing strategies.

The work students produce to meet the English Language Arts standards does not all have to come from an English class. Students should be encouraged to use work from subjects in addition to English to demonstrate their accomplishments. The work samples include some examples of work produced in other classes that meet requirements of these standards.

Elementary School

E2a The student produces a report that:

- engages the reader by establishing a context, creating a persona, and otherwise developing reader interest;
- develops a controlling idea that conveys a perspective on the subject;
- creates an organizing structure appropriate to a specific purpose, audience, and context;
- includes appropriate facts and details;
- excludes extraneous and inappropriate information;
- uses a range of appropriate strategies, such as providing facts and details, describing or analyzing the subject, and narrating a relevant anecdote;
- provides a sense of closure to the writing.

E2b The student produces a response to literature that:

- engages the reader by establishing a context, creating a persona, and otherwise developing reader interest;
- advances a judgment that is interpretive, analytic, evaluative, or reflective;
- supports judgment through references to the text, references to other works, authors, or non-print media, or references to personal knowledge;
- demonstrates an understanding of the literary work;
- provides a sense of closure to the writing.

E2c The student produces a narrative account (fictional or autobiographical) that:

- engages the reader by establishing a context, creating a point of view, and otherwise developing reader interest;
- establishes a situation, plot, point of view, setting, and conflict (and for autobiography, the significance of events);
- creates an organizing structure;
- includes sensory details and concrete language to develop plot and character;
- excludes extraneous details and inconsistencies;
- develops complex characters;
- uses a range of appropriate strategies, such as dialogue and tension or suspense;
- provides a sense of closure to the writing.

Middle School

E2a The student produces a report that:

- engages the reader by establishing a context, creating a persona, and otherwise developing reader interest;
- develops a controlling idea that conveys a perspective on the subject;
- creates an organizing structure appropriate to purpose, audience, and context;
- includes appropriate facts and details;
- excludes extraneous and inappropriate information;
- uses a range of appropriate strategies, such as providing facts and details, describing or analyzing the subject, narrating a relevant anecdote, comparing and contrasting, naming, and explaining benefits or limitations;
- provides a sense of closure to the writing.

E2b The student produces a response to literature that:

- engages the reader through establishing a context, creating a persona, and otherwise developing reader interest;
- advances a judgment that is interpretive, analytic, evaluative, or reflective;
- supports a judgment through references to the text, references to other works, authors, or non-print media, or references to personal knowledge;
- demonstrates an understanding of the literary work;
- anticipates and answers a reader's questions;
- provides a sense of closure to the writing.

E2c The student produces a narrative account (fictional or autobiographical) that:

- engages the reader by establishing a context, creating a point of view, and otherwise developing reader interest;
- establishes a situation, plot, point of view, setting, and conflict (and for autobiography, the significance of events and of conclusions that can be drawn from those events);
- creates an organizing structure;
- includes sensory details and concrete language to develop plot and character;
- excludes extraneous details and inconsistencies;

High School

E2a The student produces a report that:

- engages the reader by establishing a context, creating a persona, and otherwise developing reader interest;
- develops a controlling idea that conveys a perspective on the subject;
- creates an organizing structure appropriate to purpose, audience, and context;
- includes appropriate facts and details;
- excludes extraneous and inappropriate information;
- uses a range of appropriate strategies, such as providing facts and details, describing or analyzing the subject, narrating a relevant anecdote, comparing and contrasting, naming, explaining benefits or limitations, demonstrating claims or assertions, and providing a scenario to illustrate;
- provides a sense of closure to the writing.

E2b The student produces a response to literature that:

- engages the reader through establishing a context, creating a persona, and otherwise developing reader interest;
- advances a judgment that is interpretive, analytic, evaluative, or reflective;
- supports a judgment through references to the text, references to other works, authors, or non-print media, or references to personal knowledge;
- demonstrates understanding of the literary work through suggesting an interpretation;
- anticipates and answers a reader's questions;
- recognizes possible ambiguities, nuances, and complexities;
- provides a sense of closure to the writing.

E2c The student produces a narrative account (fictional or autobiographical) that:

- engages the reader by establishing a context, creating a point of view, and otherwise developing reader interest;
- establishes a situation, plot, point of view, setting, and conflict (and for autobiography, the significance of events and of conclusions that can be drawn from those events);
- creates an organizing structure;
- includes sensory details and concrete language to develop plot and character;
- excludes extraneous details and inconsistencies;
- develops complex characters;
- uses a range of appropriate strategies, such as dialogue, tension or suspense, naming, pacing,

E2 d The student produces a narrative procedure that:

- engages the reader by establishing a context, creating a persona, and otherwise developing reader interest;
- provides a guide to action that anticipates a reader's needs; creates expectations through predictable structures, e.g., headings; and provides transitions between steps;
- makes use of appropriate writing strategies such as creating a visual hierarchy and using white space and graphics as appropriate;
- includes relevant information;
- excludes extraneous information;
- anticipates problems, mistakes, and misunderstandings that might arise for the reader;
- provides a sense of closure to the writing.

- develops complex characters;
- uses a range of appropriate strategies, such as dialogue, tension or suspense, naming, and specific narrative action, e.g., movement, gestures, expressions;
- provides a sense of closure to the writing.

E2 d The student produces a narrative procedure that:

- engages the reader by establishing a context, creating a persona, and otherwise developing reader interest;
- provides a guide to action for a relatively complicated procedure in order to anticipate a reader's needs; creates expectations through predictable structures, e.g., headings; and provides transitions between steps;
- makes use of appropriate writing strategies such as creating a visual hierarchy and using white space and graphics as appropriate;
- includes relevant information;
- excludes extraneous information;
- anticipates problems, mistakes, and misunderstandings that might arise for the reader;
- provides a sense of closure to the writing.

E2 e The student produces a persuasive essay that:

- engages the reader by establishing a context, creating a persona, and otherwise developing reader interest;
- develops a controlling idea that makes a clear and knowledgeable judgment;
- creates and organizes a structure that is appropriate to the needs, values, and interests of a specified audience, and arranges details, reasons, examples, and anecdotes effectively and persuasively;
- includes appropriate information and arguments;
- excludes information and arguments that are irrelevant;
- anticipates and addresses reader concerns and counter-arguments;
- supports arguments with detailed evidence, citing sources of information as appropriate;
- provides a sense of closure to the writing.

and specific narrative action, e.g., movement, gestures, expressions;

- provides a sense of closure to the writing.

E2 d The student produces a narrative procedure that:

- engages the reader by establishing a context, creating a persona, and otherwise developing reader interest;
- provides a guide to action for a complicated procedure in order to anticipate a reader's needs; creates expectations through predictable structures, e.g., headings; and provides smooth transitions between steps;
- makes use of appropriate writing strategies, such as creating a visual hierarchy and using white space and graphics as appropriate;
- includes relevant information;
- excludes extraneous information;
- anticipates problems, mistakes, and misunderstandings that might arise for the reader;
- provides a sense of closure to the writing.

E2 e The student produces a persuasive essay that:

- engages the reader by establishing a context, creating a persona, and otherwise developing reader interest;
- develops a controlling idea that makes a clear and knowledgeable judgment;
- creates an organizing structure that is appropriate to the needs, values, and interests of a specified audience, and arranges details, reasons, examples, and anecdotes effectively and persuasively;
- includes appropriate information and arguments;
- excludes information and arguments that are irrelevant;
- anticipates and addresses reader concerns and counter-arguments;
- supports arguments with detailed evidence, citing sources of information as appropriate;
- uses a range of strategies to elaborate and persuade, such as definitions, descriptions, illustrations, examples from evidence, and anecdotes;
- provides a sense of closure to the writing.

E2 f The student produces a reflective essay that:

- engages the reader by establishing a context, creating a persona, and otherwise developing reader interest;
- analyzes a condition or situation of significance;
- develops a commonplace, concrete occasion as the basis for the reflection, e.g., personal observation or experience;
- creates an organizing structure appropriate to purpose and audience;
- uses a variety of writing strategies, such as concrete details, comparing and contrasting, naming, describing, creating a scenario;
- provides a sense of closure to the writing.

E3 Speaking, Listening, and Viewing

Elementary School

E3a The student participates in one-to-one conferences with a teacher, paraprofessional, or adult volunteer, in which the student:

- initiates new topics in addition to responding to adult-initiated topics;
- asks relevant questions;
- responds to questions with appropriate elaboration;
- uses language cues to indicate different levels of certainty or hypothesizing, e.g., "what if...," "very likely...," "I'm unsure whether...";
- confirms understanding by paraphrasing the adult's directions or suggestions.

E3b The student participates in group meetings, in which the student:

- displays appropriate turn-taking behaviors;
- actively solicits another person's comment or opinion;
- offers own opinion forcefully without dominating;
- responds appropriately to comments and questions;
- volunteers contributions and responds when directly solicited by teacher or discussion leader;
- gives reasons in support of opinions expressed;
- clarifies, illustrates, or expands on a response when asked to do so; asks classmates for similar expansions.

E3c The student prepares and delivers an individual presentation, in which the student:

- shapes information to achieve a particular purpose and to appeal to the interests and background knowledge of audience members;
- shapes content and organization according to criteria for importance and impact rather than according to availability of information in resource materials;
- uses notes or other memory aids to structure the presentation;
- engages the audience with appropriate verbal cues and eye contact;
- projects a sense of individuality and personality in selecting and organizing content, and in delivery.

Middle School

E3a The student participates in one-to-one conferences with a teacher, paraprofessional, or adult volunteer, in which the student:

- initiates new topics in addition to responding to adult-initiated topics;
- asks relevant questions;
- responds to questions with appropriate elaboration;
- uses language cues to indicate different levels of certainty or hypothesizing, e.g., "what if...," "very likely...," "I'm unsure whether...";
- confirms understanding by paraphrasing the adult's directions or suggestions.

E3b The student participates in group meetings, in which the student:

- displays appropriate turn-taking behaviors;
- actively solicits another person's comment or opinion;
- offers own opinion forcefully without dominating;
- responds appropriately to comments and questions;
- volunteers contributions and responds when directly solicited by teacher or discussion leader;
- gives reasons in support of opinions expressed;
- clarifies, illustrates, or expands on a response when asked to do so; asks classmates for similar expansions;
- employs a group decision-making technique such as brainstorming or a problem-solving sequence (e.g., recognize problem, define problem, identify possible solutions, select optimal solution, implement solution, evaluate solution).

E3c The student prepares and delivers an individual presentation in which the student:

- shapes information to achieve a particular purpose and to appeal to the interests and background knowledge of audience members;
- shapes content and organization according to criteria for importance and impact rather than according to availability of information in resource materials;
- uses notes or other memory aids to structure the presentation;

High School

E3a The student participates in one-to-one conferences with a teacher, paraprofessional, or adult volunteer, in which the student:

- initiates new topics in addition to responding to adult-initiated topics;
- asks relevant questions;
- responds to questions with appropriate elaboration;
- uses language cues to indicate different levels of certainty or hypothesizing, e.g., "what if...," "very likely...," "I'm unsure whether...";
- confirms understanding by paraphrasing the adult's directions or suggestions.

E3b The student participates in group meetings, in which the student:

- displays appropriate turn-taking behaviors;
- actively solicits another person's comment or opinion;
- offers own opinion forcefully without dominating;
- responds appropriately to comments and questions;
- volunteers contributions and responds when directly solicited by teacher or discussion leader;
- gives reasons in support of opinions expressed;
- clarifies, illustrates, or expands on a response when asked to do so; asks classmates for similar expansions;
- employs a group decision-making technique such as brainstorming or a problem-solving sequence (e.g., recognize problem, define problem, identify possible solutions, select optimal solution, implement solution, evaluate solution);
- divides labor so as to achieve the overall group goal efficiently.

E3c The student prepares and delivers an individual presentation, in which the student:

- shapes information to achieve a particular purpose and to appeal to the interests and background knowledge of audience members;
- shapes content and organization according to criteria for importance and impact rather than according to availability of information in resource materials;

E3d The student makes informed judgments about television, radio, and film productions; that is, the student:

- demonstrates an awareness of the presence of the media in the daily lives of most people;
- evaluates the role of the media in focusing attention and in forming an opinion;
- judges the extent to which the media provide a source of entertainment as well as a source of information;
- defines the role of advertising as part of media presentation.

- develops several main points relating to a single thesis;
- engages the audience with appropriate verbal cues and eye contact;
- projects a sense of individuality and personality in selecting and organizing content, and in delivery.

E3d The student makes informed judgments about television, radio, and film productions; that is, the student:

- demonstrates an awareness of the presence of the media in the daily lives of most people;
- evaluates the role of the media in focusing attention and in forming opinion;
- judges the extent to which the media are a source of entertainment as well as a source of information;
- defines the role of advertising as part of media presentation.

- uses notes or other memory aids to structure the presentation;
- develops several main points relating to a single thesis;
- engages the audience with appropriate verbal cues and eye contact;
- projects a sense of individuality and personality in selecting and organizing content, and in delivery.

E3d The student makes informed judgments about television, radio, and film productions; that is, the student:

- demonstrates an awareness of the presence of the media in the daily lives of most people;
- evaluates the role of the media in focusing attention and in forming opinion;
- judges the extent to which the media are a source of entertainment as well as a source of information;
- defines the role of advertising as part of media presentation.

E3e The student listens to and analyzes a public speaking performance; that is, the student:

- takes notes on salient information;
- identifies types of arguments (e.g., causation, authority, analogy) and identifies types of logical fallacies (e.g., ad hominem, inferring causation from correlation, over-generalization);
- accurately summarizes the essence of each speaker's remarks;
- formulates a judgment about the issues under discussion.

E4 Conventions, Grammar, and Usage of the English Language

Elementary School

E4 a The student demonstrates a basic understanding of the rules of the English language in written and oral work, and selects the structures and features of language appropriate to the purpose, audience, and context of the work. The student demonstrates control of:

- grammar;
- paragraph structure;
- punctuation;
- sentence construction;
- spelling;
- usage.

E4 b The student analyzes and subsequently revises work to clarify it or make it more effective in communicating the intended message or thought. The student's revisions should be made in light of the purposes, audiences, and contexts that apply to the work. Strategies for revising include:

- adding or deleting details;
- adding or deleting explanations;
- clarifying difficult passages;
- rearranging words, sentences, and paragraphs to improve or clarify meaning;
- sharpening the focus;
- reconsidering the organizational structure.

Middle School

E4 a The student demonstrates an understanding of the rules of the English language in written and oral work, and selects the structures and features of language appropriate to the purpose, audience, and context of the work. The student demonstrates control of:

- grammar;
- paragraph structure;
- punctuation;
- sentence construction;
- spelling;
- usage.

E4 b The student analyzes and subsequently revises work to clarify it or make it more effective in communicating the intended message or thought. The student's revisions should be made in light of the purposes, audiences, and contexts that apply to the work. Strategies for revising include:

- adding or deleting details;
- adding or deleting explanations;
- clarifying difficult passages;
- rearranging words, sentences, and paragraphs to improve or clarify meaning;
- sharpening the focus;
- reconsidering the organizational structure.

High School

E4 a The student independently and habitually demonstrates an understanding of the rules of the English language in written and oral work, and selects the structures and features of language appropriate to the purpose, audience, and context of the work. The student demonstrates control of:

- grammar;
- paragraph structure;
- punctuation;
- sentence construction;
- spelling;
- usage.

E4 b The student analyzes and subsequently revises work to clarify it or make it more effective in communicating the intended message or thought. The student's revisions should be made in light of the purposes, audiences, and contexts that apply to the work. Strategies for revising include:

- adding or deleting details;
- adding or deleting explanations;
- clarifying difficult passages;
- rearranging words, sentences, and paragraphs to improve or clarify meaning;
- sharpening the focus;
- reconsidering the organizational structure;
- rethinking and/or rewriting the piece in light of different audiences and purposes.

E5 Literature

Elementary School

E5a The student responds to non-fiction, fiction, poetry, and drama using interpretive, critical, and evaluative processes; that is, the student:

- identifies recurring themes across works;
- analyzes the impact of authors' decisions regarding word choice and content;
- considers the differences among genres;
- evaluates literary merit;
- considers the function of point of view or persona;
- examines the reasons for a character's actions, taking into account the situation and basic motivation of the character;
- identifies stereotypical characters as opposed to fully developed characters;
- critiques the degree to which a plot is contrived or realistic;
- makes inferences and draws conclusions about contexts, events, characters, and settings.

E5b The student produces work in at least one literary genre that follows the conventions of the genre.

Middle School

E5a The student responds to non-fiction, fiction, poetry, and drama using interpretive, critical, and evaluative processes; that is, the student:

- identifies recurring themes across works;
- interprets the impact of authors' decisions regarding word choice, content, and literary elements;
- identifies the characteristics of literary forms and genres;
- evaluates literary merit;
- identifies the effect of point of view;
- analyzes the reasons for a character's actions, taking into account the situation and basic motivation of the character;
- makes inferences and draws conclusions about fictional and non-fictional contexts, events, characters, settings, and themes;
- identifies stereotypical characters as opposed to fully developed characters;
- identifies the effect of literary devices such as figurative language, allusion, diction, dialogue, and description.

E5b The student produces work in at least one literary genre that follows the conventions of the genre.

High School

E5a The student responds to non-fiction, fiction, poetry, and drama using interpretive, critical, and evaluative processes; that is, the student:

- makes thematic connections among literary texts, public discourse, and media;
- evaluates the impact of authors' decisions regarding word choice, style, content, and literary elements;
- analyzes the characteristics of literary forms and genres;
- evaluates literary merit;
- explains the effect of point of view;
- makes inferences and draws conclusions about fictional and non-fictional contexts, events, characters, settings, themes, and styles;
- interprets the effect of literary devices, such as figurative language, allusion, diction, dialogue, description, symbolism;
- evaluates the stance of a writer in shaping the presentation of a subject;
- interprets ambiguities, subtleties, contradictions, ironies, and nuances;
- understands the role of tone in presenting literature (both fictional and non-fictional);
- demonstrates how literary works (both fictional and non-fictional) reflect the culture that shaped them.

E5b The student produces work in at least one literary genre that follows the conventions of the genre.

M1 Arithmetic and Number Concepts/Number and Operation Concepts

APPENDIX II

The elementary school standards are set at a level of performance approximately equivalent to the end of fourth grade. The middle school standards are set at a level of performance approximately equivalent to the end of eighth grade. The high school standards are set at a level of performance approximately equivalent to the end of tenth grade or the end of the common core. It is expected that some students might achieve these levels earlier and others later than these grades.

Elementary School

The student produces evidence that demonstrates understanding of arithmetic and number concepts; that is, the student:

M1 a Adds, subtracts, multiplies, and divides whole numbers, with and without calculators; that is:

- adds, i.e., joins things together, increases;
- subtracts, i.e., takes away, compares, finds the difference;
- multiplies, i.e., uses repeated addition, counts by multiples, combines things that come in groups, makes arrays, uses area models, computes simple scales, uses simple rates;
- divides, i.e., puts things into groups, shares equally; calculates simple rates;
- analyzes problem situations and contexts in order to figure out when to add, subtract, multiply, or divide;
- solves arithmetic problems by relating addition, subtraction, multiplication, and division to one another;
- computes answers mentally, e.g., 27 + 45, 30 x 4;
- uses simple concepts of negative numbers, e.g., on a number line, in counting, in temperature, "owing."

M1 b Demonstrates understanding of the base ten place value system and uses this knowledge to solve arithmetic tasks; that is:

- counts 1, 10, 100, or 1,000 more than or less than, e.g., 1 less than 10,000, 10 more than 380, 1,000 more than 23,000, 100 less than 9,000;
- uses knowledge about ones, tens, hundreds, and thousands to figure out answers to multiplication and division tasks, e.g., 36 x 10, 18 x 100, 7 x 1,000, 4,000 ÷ 4.

M1 c Estimates, approximates, rounds off, uses landmark numbers, or uses exact numbers, as appropriate, in calculations.

M1 d Describes and compares quantities by using concrete and real world models of simple fractions; that is:

- finds simple parts of wholes;
- recognizes simple fractions as instructions to divide, e.g., $\frac{1}{4}$ of something is the same as dividing something by 4;
- recognizes the place of fractions on number lines, e.g., in measurement;

Middle School

The student produces evidence that demonstrates understanding of number and operation concepts; that is, the student:

M1 a Consistently and accurately adds, subtracts, multiplies, and divides rational numbers using appropriate methods (e.g., the student can add $\frac{1}{2} + \frac{5}{6}$ mentally or on paper but may opt to add $\frac{13}{24} + \frac{57}{68}$ on a calculator) and raises rational numbers to whole number powers. (Students should have facility with the different kinds and forms of rational numbers, i.e., integers, both whole numbers and negative integers; and other positive and negative rationals, written as decimals, as percents, or as proper, improper, or mixed fractions. Irrational numbers, i.e., those that cannot be written as a ratio of two integers, are not required content but are suitable for introduction, especially since the student should be familiar with the irrational number π.)

M1 b Uses and understands the inverse relationships between addition and subtraction, multiplication and division, and exponentiation and root-extraction (e.g., squares and square roots, cubes and cube roots); uses the inverse operation to determine unknown quantities in equations.

M1 c Consistently and accurately applies and converts the different kinds and forms of rational numbers.

M1 d Is familiar with characteristics of numbers (e.g., divisibility, prime factorization) and with properties of operations (e.g., commutativity and associativity), short of formal statements.

M1 e Interprets percent as part of 100 and as a means of comparing quantities of different sizes or changing sizes.

M1 f Uses ratios and rates to express "part-to-part" and "whole-to-whole" relationships, and reasons proportionally to solve problems involving equivalent fractions, equal ratios, or constant rates, recognizing the multiplicative nature of these problems in the constant factor of change.

M1 g Orders numbers with the > and < relationships and by location on a number line; estimates and compares rational numbers using sense of the magnitudes and relative magnitudes of numbers and of base-ten place values (e.g., recognizes relationships to "benchmark" numbers $\frac{1}{2}$ and 1 to conclude that the sum $\frac{1}{2} + \frac{5}{6}$ must be between 1 and $1\frac{1}{2}$ (likewise, $\frac{13}{24} + \frac{57}{68}$)).

High School

The student produces evidence that demonstrates understanding of number and operation concepts; that is, the student:

M1 a Uses addition, subtraction, multiplication, division, exponentiation, and root-extraction in forming and working with numerical and algebraic expressions.

M1 b Understands and uses operations such as opposite, reciprocal, raising to a power, taking a root, and taking a logarithm.

M1 c Has facility with the mechanics of operations as well as understanding of their typical meaning and uses in applications.

M1 d Understands and uses number systems: natural, integer, rational, and real.

M1 e Represents numbers in decimal or fraction form and in scientific notation, and graphs numbers on the number line and number pairs in the coordinate plane.

M1 f Compares numbers using order relations, differences, ratios, proportions, percents, and proportional change.

M1 g Carries out proportional reasoning in cases involving part-whole relationships and in cases involving expansions and contractions.

M1 h Understands dimensionless numbers, such as proportions, percents, and multiplicative factors, as well as numbers with specific units of measure, such as numbers with length, time, and rate units.

M1 i Carries out counting procedures such as those involving sets (unions and intersections) and arrangements (permutations and combinations).

M1 j Uses concepts such as prime, relatively prime, factor, divisor, multiple, and divisibility in solving problems involving integers.

M1 k Uses a scientific calculator effectively and efficiently in carrying out complex calculations.

M1 l Recognizes and represents basic number patterns, such as patterns involving multiples, squares, or cubes.

- uses drawings, diagrams, or models to show what the numerator and denominator mean, including when adding like fractions, e.g., $\frac{1}{8}$ + $\frac{5}{8}$, or when showing that $\frac{3}{4}$ is more than $\frac{3}{8}$;
- uses beginning proportional reasoning and simple ratios, e.g., "about half of the people."

M1 e Describes and compares quantities by using simple decimals; that is:

- adds, subtracts, multiplies, and divides money amounts;
- recognizes relationships among simple fractions, decimals, and percents, i.e., that $\frac{1}{2}$ is the same as 0.5, and $\frac{1}{2}$ is the same as 50%, with concrete materials, diagrams, and in real world situations, e.g., when discovering the chance of a coin landing on heads or tails.

M1 f Describes and compares quantities by using whole numbers up to 10,000; that is:

- connects ideas of quantities to the real world, e.g., how many people fit in the school's cafeteria; how far away is a kilometer;
- finds, identifies, and sorts numbers by their properties, e.g., odd, even, multiple, square.

M2 Geometry and Measurement Concepts

APPENDIX II

Elementary School

The student produces evidence that demonstrates understanding of geometry and measurement concepts; that is, the student:

M2a Gives and responds to directions about location, e.g., by using words such as "in front of," "right," and "above."

M2b Visualizes and represents two dimensional views of simple rectangular three dimensional shapes, e.g., by showing the front view and side view of a building made of cubes.

M2c Uses simple two dimensional coordinate systems to find locations on a map and to represent points and simple figures.

M2d Uses many types of figures (angles, triangles, squares, rectangles, rhombi, parallelograms, quadrilaterals, polygons, prisms, pyramids, cubes, circles, and spheres) and identifies the figures by their properties, e.g., symmetry, number of faces, two- or three-dimensionality, no right angles.

M2e Solves problems by showing relationships between and among figures, e.g., using congruence and similarity, and using transformations including flips, slides, and rotations.

M2f Extends and creates geometric patterns using concrete and pictorial models.

M2g Uses basic ways of estimating and measuring the size of figures and objects in the real world, including length, width, perimeter, and area.

M2h Uses models to reason about the relationship between the perimeter and area of rectangles in simple situations.

M2i Selects and uses units, both formal and informal as appropriate, for estimating and measuring quantities such as weight, length, area, volume, and time.

M2j Carries out simple unit conversions, such as between cm and m, and between hours and minutes.

M2k Uses scales in maps, and uses, measures, and creates scales for rectangular scale drawings based on work with concrete models and graph paper.

Middle School

The student produces evidence that demonstrates understanding of geometry and measurement concepts in the following areas; that is, the student:

M2a Is familiar with assorted two- and three-dimensional objects, including squares, triangles, other polygons, circles, cubes, rectangular prisms, pyramids, spheres, and cylinders.

M2b Identifies similar and congruent shapes and uses transformations in the coordinate plane, i.e., translations, rotations, and reflections.

M2c Identifies three dimensional shapes from two dimensional perspectives; draws two dimensional sketches of three dimensional objects that preserve significant features.

M2d Determines and understands length, area, and volume (as well as the differences among these measurements), including perimeter and surface area; uses units, square units, and cubic units of measure correctly; computes areas of rectangles, triangles, and circles; computes volumes of prisms.

M2e Recognizes similarity and rotational and bilateral symmetry in two- and three-dimensional figures.

M2f Analyzes and generalizes geometric patterns, such as tessellations and sequences of shapes.

M2g Measures angles, weights, capacities, times, and temperatures using appropriate units.

M2h Chooses appropriate units of measure and converts with ease between like units, e.g., inches and miles, within a customary or metric system. (Conversions between customary and metric are not required.)

M2i Reasons proportionally in situations with similar figures.

M2j Reasons proportionally with measurements to interpret maps and to make smaller and larger scale drawings.

M2k Models situations geometrically to formulate and solve problems.

High School

The student produces evidence that demonstrates understanding of geometry and measurement concepts; that is, the student:

M2a Models situations geometrically to formulate and solve problems.

M2b Works with two- and three-dimensional figures and their properties, including polygons and circles, cubes and pyramids, and cylinders, cones, and spheres.

M2c Uses congruence and similarity in describing relationships between figures.

M2d Visualizes objects, paths, and regions in space, including intersections and cross sections of three dimensional figures, and describes these using geometric language.

M2e Knows, uses, and derives formulas for perimeter, circumference, area, surface area, and volume of many types of figures.

M2f Uses the Pythagorean Theorem in many types of situations, and works through more than one proof of this theorem.

M2g Works with similar triangles, and extends the ideas to include simple uses of the three basic trigonometric functions.

M2h Analyzes figures in terms of their symmetries using, for example, concepts of reflection, rotation, and translation.

M2i Compares slope (rise over run) and angle of elevation as measures of steepness.

M2j Investigates geometric patterns, including sequences of growing shapes.

M2k Works with geometric measures of length, area, volume, and angle; and non-geometric measures such as weight and time.

M2l Uses quotient measures, such as speed and density, that give "per unit" amounts; and uses product measures, such as person-hours.

M2m Understands the structure of standard measurement systems, both SI and customary, including unit conversions and dimensional analysis.

M2n Solves problems involving scale, such as in maps and diagrams.

M2o Represents geometric curves and graphs of functions in standard coordinate systems.

M2p Analyzes geometric figures and proves simple things about them using deductive methods.

M2q Explores geometry using computer programs such as CAD software, Sketchpad programs, or LOGO.

M3 Function and Algebra Concepts

Elementary School

The student produces evidence that demonstrates understanding of function and algebra concepts; that is, the student:

M3 a Uses linear patterns to solve problems; that is:

- shows how one quantity determines another in a linear ("repeating") pattern, i.e., describes, extends, and recognizes the linear pattern by its rule, such as, the total number of legs on a given number of horses can be calculated by counting by fours;
- shows how one quantity determines another quantity in a functional relationship based on a linear pattern, e.g., for the "number of people and total number of eyes," figure out how many eyes 100 people have all together.

M3 b Builds iterations of simple non-linear patterns, including multiplicative and squaring patterns (e.g., "growing" patterns) with concrete materials, and recognizes that these patterns are not linear.

M3 c Uses the understanding that an equality relationship between two quantities remains the same as long as the same change is made to both quantities.

M3 d Uses letters, boxes, or other symbols to stand for any number, measured quantity, or object in simple situations with concrete materials, i.e., demonstrates understanding and use of a beginning concept of a variable.

Middle School

The student produces evidence that demonstrates understanding of function and algebra concepts; that is, the student:

M3 a Discovers, describes, and generalizes patterns, including linear, exponential, and simple quadratic relationships, i.e., those of the form $f(n)=n^2$ or $f(n)=cn^2$, for constant c, including $A=\pi r^2$, and represents them with variables and expressions.

M3 b Represents relationships with tables, graphs in the coordinate plane, and verbal or symbolic rules.

M3 c Analyzes tables, graphs, and rules to determine functional relationships.

M3 d Finds solutions for unknown quantities in linear equations and in simple equations and inequalities.

High School

The student produces evidence that demonstrates understanding of function and algebra concepts; that is, the student:

M3 a Models given situations with formulas and functions, and interprets given formulas and functions in terms of situations.

M3 b Describes, generalizes, and uses basic types of functions: linear, exponential, power, rational, square and square root, and cube and cube root.

M3 c Utilizes the concepts of slope, evaluation, and inverse in working with functions.

M3 d Works with rates of many kinds, expressed numerically, symbolically, and graphically.

M3 e Represents constant rates as the slope of a straight line graph, and interprets slope as the amount of one quantity (y) per unit amount of another (x).

M3 f Understands and uses linear functions as a mathematical representation of proportional relationships.

M3 g Uses arithmetic sequences and geometric sequences and their sums, and sees these as the discrete forms of linear and exponential functions, respectively.

M3 h Defines, uses, and manipulates expressions involving variables, parameters, constants, and unknowns in work with formulas, functions, equations, and inequalities.

M3 i Represents functional relationships in formulas, tables, and graphs, and translates between pairs of these.

M3 j Solves equations symbolically, graphically, and numerically, especially linear, quadratic, and exponential equations; and knows how to use the quadratic formula for solving quadratic equations.

M3 k Makes predictions by interpolating or extrapolating from given data or a given graph.

M3 l Understands the basic algebraic structure of number systems.

M3 m Uses equations to represent curves such as lines, circles, and parabolas.

M3 n Uses technology such as graphics calculators to represent and analyze functions and their graphs.

M3 o Uses functions to analyze patterns and represent their structure.

M4 Statistics and Probability Concepts

Elementary School

The student produces evidence that demonstrates understanding of statistics and probability concepts in the following areas; that is, the student:

M4a Collects and organizes data to answer a question or test a hypothesis by comparing sets of data.

M4b Displays data in line plots, graphs, tables, and charts.

M4c Makes statements and draws simple conclusions based on data; that is:

- reads data in line plots, graphs, tables, and charts;
- compares data in order to make true statements, e.g., "seven plants grew at least 5 cm";
- identifies and uses the mode necessary for making true statements, e.g., "more people chose red";
- makes true statements based on a simple concept of average (median and mean), for a small sample size and where the situation is made evident with concrete materials or clear representations;
- interprets data to determine the reasonableness of statements about the data, e.g., "twice as often," "three times faster";
- uses data, including statements about the data, to make a simple concluding statement about a situation, e.g., "This kind of plant grows better near sunlight because the seven plants that were near the window grew at least 5 cm."

M4d Gathers data about an entire group or by sampling group members to understand the concept of sample, i.e., that a large sample leads to more reliable information, e.g., when flipping coins.

M4e Predicts results, analyzes data, and finds out why some results are more likely, less likely, or equally likely.

M4f Finds all possible combinations and arrangements within certain constraints involving a limited number of variables.

Middle School

The student produces evidence that demonstrates understanding of statistics and probability concepts; that is, the student:

M4a Collects data, organizes data, and displays data with tables, charts, and graphs that are appropriate, i.e., consistent with the nature of the data.

M4b Analyzes data with respect to characteristics of frequency and distribution, including mode and range.

M4c Analyzes appropriately central tendencies of data by considering mean and median.

M4d Makes conclusions and recommendations based on data analysis.

M4e Critiques the conclusions and recommendations of others' statistics.

M4f Considers the effects of missing or incorrect information.

M4g Formulates hypotheses to answer a question and uses data to test hypotheses.

M4h Represents and determines probability as a fraction of a set of equally likely outcomes; recognizes equally likely outcomes, and constructs sample spaces (including those described by numerical combinations and permutations).

M4i Makes predictions based on experimental or theoretical probabilities.

M4j Predicts the result of a series of trials once the probability for one trial is known.

High School

The student demonstrates understanding of statistics and probability concepts; that is, the student:

M4a Organizes, analyzes, and displays single-variable data, choosing appropriate frequency distribution, circle graphs, line plots, histograms, and summary statistics.

M4b Organizes, analyzes, and displays two-variable data using scatter plots, estimated regression lines, and computer generated regression lines and correlation coefficients.

M4c Uses sampling techniques to draw inferences about large populations.

M4d Understands that making an inference about a population from a sample always involves uncertainty and that the role of statistics is to estimate the size of that uncertainty.

M4e Formulates hypotheses to answer a question and uses data to test hypotheses.

M4f Interprets representations of data, compares distributions of data, and critiques conclusions and the use of statistics, both in school materials and in public documents.

M4g Explores questions of experimental design, use of control groups, and reliability.

M4h Creates and uses models of probabilistic situations and understands the role of assumptions in this process.

M4i Uses concepts such as equally likely, sample space, outcome, and event in analyzing situations involving chance.

M4j Constructs appropriate sample spaces, and applies the addition and multiplication principles for probabilities.

M4k Uses the concept of a probability distribution to discuss whether an event is rare or reasonably likely.

M4l Chooses an appropriate probability model and uses it to arrive at a theoretical probability for a chance event.

M4m Uses relative frequencies based on empirical data to arrive at an experimental probability for a chance event.

M4n Designs simulations including Monte Carlo simulations to estimate probabilities.

M4o Works with the normal distribution in some of its basic applications.

M5 Problem Solving and Mathematical Reasoning

Elementary School

The student demonstrates logical reasoning throughout work in mathematics, i.e., concepts and skills, problem solving, and projects; demonstrates problem solving by using mathematical concepts and skills to solve non-routine problems that do not lay out specific and detailed steps to follow; and solves problems that make demands on all three aspects of the solution process—formulation, implementation, and conclusion.

Formulation

M5a Given the basic statement of a problem situation, the student:

- makes the important decisions about the approach, materials, and strategies to use, i.e., does not merely fill in a given chart, use a pre-specified manipulative, or go through a predetermined set of steps;
- uses previously learned strategies, skills, knowledge, and concepts to make decisions;
- uses strategies, such as using manipulatives or drawing sketches, to model problems.

Implementation

M5b The student makes the basic choices involved in planning and carrying out a solution; that is, the student:

- makes up and uses a variety of strategies and approaches to solving problems and uses or learns approaches that other people use, as appropriate;
- makes connections among concepts in order to solve problems;
- solves problems in ways that make sense and explains why these ways make sense, e.g., defends the reasoning, explains the solution.

Conclusion

M5c The student moves beyond a particular problem by making connections, extensions, and/or generalizations; for example, the student:

- explains a pattern that can be used in similar situations;
- explains how the problem is similar to other problems he or she has solved;
- explains how the mathematics used in the problem is like other concepts in mathematics;
- explains how the problem solution can be applied to other school subjects and in real world situations;
- makes the solution into a general rule that applies to other circumstances.

Middle School

The student demonstrates problem solving by using mathematical concepts and skills to solve non-routine problems that do not lay out specific and detailed steps to follow, and solves problems that make demands on all three aspects of the solution process—formulation, implementation, and conclusion.

Formulation

M5a The student participates in the formulation of problems; that is, given the basic statement of a problem situation, the student:

- formulates and solves a variety of meaningful problems;
- extracts pertinent information from situations and figures out what additional information is needed.

Implementation

M5b The student makes the basic choices involved in planning and carrying out a solution; that is, the student:

- uses and invents a variety of approaches and understands and evaluates those of others;
- invokes problem solving strategies, such as illustrating with sense-making sketches to clarify situations or organizing information in a table;
- determines, where helpful, how to break a problem into simpler parts;
- solves for unknown or undecided quantities using algebra, graphing, sound reasoning, and other strategies;
- integrates concepts and techniques from different areas of mathematics;
- works effectively in teams when the nature of the task or the allotted time makes this an appropriate strategy.

Conclusion

M5c The student provides closure to the solution process through summary statements and general conclusions; that is, the student:

- verifies and interprets results with respect to the original problem situation;
- generalizes solutions and strategies to new problem situations.

High School

The student demonstrates problem solving by using mathematical concepts and skills to solve non-routine problems that do not lay out specific and detailed steps to follow, and solves problems that make demands on all three aspects of the solution process—formulation, implementation, and conclusion.

Formulation

M5a The student participates in the formulation of problems; that is, given the statement of a problem situation, the student:

- fills out the formulation of a definite problem that is to be solved;
- extracts pertinent information from the situation as a basis for working on the problem;
- asks and answers a series of appropriate questions in pursuit of a solution and does so with minimal "scaffolding" in the form of detailed guiding questions.

Implementation

M5b The student makes the basic choices involved in planning and carrying out a solution; that is, the student:

- chooses and employs effective problem solving strategies in dealing with non-routine and multi-step problems;
- selects appropriate mathematical concepts and techniques from different areas of mathematics and applies them to the solution of the problem;
- applies mathematical concepts to new situations within mathematics and uses mathematics to model real world situations involving basic applications of mathematics in the physical and biological sciences, the social sciences, and business.

Conclusion

M5c The student provides closure to the solution process through summary statements and general conclusions; that is, the student:

- concludes a solution process with a useful summary of results;
- evaluates the degree to which the results obtained represent a good response to the initial problem;
- formulates generalizations of the results obtained;
- carries out extensions of the given problem to related problems.

Mathematical reasoning

M5 d The student demonstrates mathematical reasoning by generalizing patterns, making conjectures and explaining why they seem true, and by making sensible, justifiable statements; that is, the student:

- formulates conjectures and argues why they must be or seem true;
- makes sensible, reasonable estimates;
- makes justified, logical statements.

Mathematical reasoning

M5 d The student demonstrates mathematical reasoning by using logic to prove specific conjectures, by explaining the logic inherent in a solution process, by making generalizations and showing that they are valid, and by revealing mathematical patterns inherent in a situation. The student not only makes observations and states results but also justifies or proves why the results hold in general; that is, the student:

- employs forms of mathematical reasoning and proof appropriate to the solution of the problem at hand, including deductive and inductive reasoning, making and testing conjectures, and using counterexamples and indirect proof;
- differentiates clearly between giving examples that support a conjecture and giving a proof of the conjecture.

M6 Mathematical Skills and Tools

Elementary School

The student demonstrates fluency with basic and important skills by using these skills accurately and automatically, and demonstrates practical competence and persistence with other skills by using them effectively to accomplish a task, perhaps referring to notes, books, or other students, perhaps working to reconstruct a method; that is, the student:

M6a Adds, subtracts, multiplies, and divides whole numbers correctly; that is:

- knows single digit addition, subtraction, multiplication, and division facts;
- adds and subtracts numbers with several digits;
- multiplies and divides numbers with one or two digits;
- multiplies and divides three digit numbers by one digit numbers.

M6b Estimates numerically and spatially.

M6c Measures length, area, perimeter, circumference, diameter, height, weight, and volume accurately in both the customary and metric systems.

M6d Computes time (in hours and minutes) and money (in dollars and cents).

M6e Refers to geometric shapes and terms correctly with concrete objects or drawings, including triangle, square, rectangle, side, edge, face, cube, point, line, perimeter, area, and circle; and refers with assistance to rhombus, parallelogram, quadrilateral, polygon, polyhedron, angle, vertex, volume, diameter, circumference, sphere, prism, and pyramid.

M6f Uses +, -, x, ÷, /, $\sqrt{}$, \$, ¢, %, and . (decimal point) correctly in number sentences and expressions.

M6g Reads, creates, and represents data on line plots, charts, tables, diagrams, bar graphs, simple circle graphs, and coordinate graphs.

M6h Uses recall, mental computations, pencil and paper, measuring devices, mathematics texts, manipulatives, calculators, computers, and advice from peers, as appropriate, to achieve solutions; that is, uses measuring devices, graded appropriately for given situations, such as rulers (customary to the ⅛ inch; metric to the millimeter), graph paper (customary to the inch or half-inch; metric to the centimeter), measuring cups (customary to the ounce; metric to the milliliter), and scales (customary to the pound or ounce; metric to the kilogram or gram).

Middle School

The student demonstrates fluency with basic and important skills by using these skills accurately and automatically, and demonstrates practical competence and persistence with other skills by using them effectively to accomplish a task (perhaps referring to notes, or books, perhaps working to reconstruct a method); that is, the student:

M6a Computes accurately with arithmetic operations on rational numbers.

M6b Knows and uses the correct order of operations for arithmetic computations.

M6c Estimates numerically and spatially.

M6d Measures length, area, volume, weight, time, and temperature accurately.

M6e Refers to geometric shapes and terms correctly.

M6f Uses equations, formulas, and simple algebraic notation appropriately.

M6g Reads and organizes data on charts and graphs, including scatter plots, bar, line, and circle graphs, and Venn diagrams; calculates mean and median.

M6h Uses recall, mental computations, pencil and paper, measuring devices, mathematics texts, manipulatives, calculators, computers, and advice from peers, as appropriate, to achieve solutions.

High School

The student demonstrates fluency with basic and important skills by using these skills accurately and automatically, and demonstrates practical competence and persistence with other skills by using them effectively to accomplish a task, perhaps referring to notes, or books, perhaps working to reconstruct a method; that is, the student:

M6a Carries out numerical calculations and symbol manipulations effectively, using mental computations, pencil and paper, or other technological aids, as appropriate.

M6b Uses a variety of methods to estimate the values, in appropriate units, of quantities met in applications, and rounds numbers used in applications to an appropriate degree of accuracy.

M6c Evaluates and analyzes formulas and functions of many kinds, using both pencil and paper and more advanced technology.

M6d Uses basic geometric terminology accurately, and deduces information about basic geometric figures in solving problems.

M6e Makes and uses rough sketches, schematic diagrams, or precise scale diagrams to enhance a solution.

M6f Uses the number line and Cartesian coordinates in the plane and in space.

M6g Creates and interprets graphs of many kinds, such as function graphs, circle graphs, scatter plots, regression lines, and histograms.

M6h Sets up and solves equations symbolically (when possible) and graphically.

M6i Knows how to use algorithms in mathematics, such as the Euclidean Algorithm.

M6j Uses technology to create graphs or spreadsheets that contribute to the understanding of a problem.

M6k Writes a simple computer program to carry out a computation or simulation to be repeated many times.

M6l Uses tools such as rulers, tapes, compasses, and protractors in solving problems.

M6m Knows standard methods to solve basic problems and uses these methods in approaching more complex problems.

M7 Mathematical Communication

Elementary School

The student uses the language of mathematics, its symbols, notation, graphs, and expressions, to communicate through reading, writing, speaking, and listening, and communicates about mathematics by describing mathematical ideas and concepts and explaining reasoning and results; that is, the student:

M7a Uses appropriate mathematical terms, vocabulary, and language, based on prior conceptual work.

M7b Shows mathematical ideas in a variety of ways, including words, numbers, symbols, pictures, charts, graphs, tables, diagrams, and models.

M7c Explains solutions to problems clearly and logically, and supports solutions with evidence, in both oral and written work.

M7d Considers purpose and audience when communicating about mathematics.

M7e Comprehends mathematics from reading assignments and from other sources.

Middle School

The student uses the language of mathematics, its symbols, notation, graphs, and expressions, to communicate through reading, writing, speaking, and listening, and communicates about mathematics by describing mathematical ideas and concepts and explaining reasoning and results; that is, the student:

M7a Uses mathematical language and representations with appropriate accuracy, including numerical tables and equations, simple algebraic equations and formulas, charts, graphs, and diagrams.

M7b Organizes work, explains facets of a solution orally and in writing, labels drawings, and uses other techniques to make meaning clear to the audience.

M7c Uses mathematical language to make complex situations easier to understand.

M7d Exhibits developing reasoning abilities by justifying statements and defending work.

M7e Shows understanding of concepts by explaining ideas not only to teachers and assessors but to fellow students or younger children.

M7f Comprehends mathematics from reading assignments and from other sources.

High School

The student uses the language of mathematics, its symbols, notation, graphs, and expressions, to communicate through reading, writing, speaking, and listening, and communicates about mathematics by describing mathematical ideas and concepts and explaining reasoning and results; that is, the student:

M7a Is familiar with basic mathematical terminology, standard notation and use of symbols, common conventions for graphing, and general features of effective mathematical communication styles.

M7b Uses mathematical representations with appropriate accuracy, including numerical tables, formulas, functions, equations, charts, graphs, and diagrams.

M7c Organizes work and presents mathematical procedures and results clearly, systematically, succinctly, and correctly.

M7d Communicates logical arguments clearly, showing why a result makes sense and why the reasoning is valid.

M7e Presents mathematical ideas effectively both orally and in writing.

M7f Explains mathematical concepts clearly enough to be of assistance to those who may be having difficulty with them.

M7g Writes narrative accounts of the history and process of work on a mathematical problem or extended project.

M7h Writes succinct accounts of the mathematical results obtained in a mathematical problem or extended project, with diagrams, graphs, tables, and formulas integrated into the text.

M7i Keeps narrative accounts of process separate from succinct accounts of results, and realizes that doing so can enhance the effectiveness of each.

M7j Reads mathematics texts and other writing about mathematics with understanding.

M8 Putting Mathematics to Work

Elementary School

The student conducts at least one large scale project each year, beginning in fourth grade, drawn from the following kinds and, over the course of elementary school, conducts projects drawn from at least two of the kinds.

A single project may draw on more than one kind.

M8 a Data study, in which the student:

- develops a question and a hypothesis in a situation where data could help make a decision or recommendation;
- decides on a group or groups to be sampled and makes predictions of the results, with specific percents, fractions, or numbers;
- collects, represents, and displays data in order to help make the decision or recommendation; compares the results with the predictions;
- writes a report that includes recommendations supported by diagrams, charts, and graphs, and acknowledges assistance received from parents, peers, and teachers.

M8 b Science study, in which the student:

- decides on a specific science question to study and identifies the mathematics that will be used, e.g., measurement;
- develops a prediction (a hypothesis) and develops procedures to test the hypothesis;
- collects and records data, represents and displays data, and compares results with predictions;
- writes a report that compares the results with the hypothesis; supports the results with diagrams, charts, and graphs; acknowledges assistance received from parents, peers, and teachers.

M8 c Design of a physical structure, in which the student:

- decides on a structure to design, the size and budget constraints, and the scale of design;
- makes a first draft of the design, and revises and improves the design in response to input from peers and teachers;
- makes a final draft and report of the design, drawn and written so that another person could make the structure; acknowledges assistance received from parents, peers, and teachers.

Middle School

The student conducts at least one large scale investigation or project each year drawn from the following kinds and, over the course of middle school, conducts investigations or projects drawn from three of the kinds.

A single investigation or project may draw on more than one kind.

M8 a Data study based on civic, economic, or social issues, in which the student:

- selects an issue to investigate;
- makes a hypothesis on an expected finding, if appropriate;
- gathers data;
- analyzes the data using concepts from Standard 4, e.g., considering mean and median, and the frequency and distribution of the data;
- shows how the study's results compare with the hypothesis;
- uses pertinent statistics to summarize;
- prepares a presentation or report that includes the question investigated, a detailed description of how the project was carried out, and an explanation of the findings.

M8 b Mathematical model of physical phenomena, often used in science studies, in which the student:

- carries out a study of a physical system using a mathematical representation of the structure;
- uses understanding from Standard 3, particularly with respect to the determination of the function governing behavior in the model;
- generalizes about the structure with a rule, i.e., a function, that clearly applies to the phenomenon and goes beyond statistical analysis of a pattern of numbers generated by the situation;
- prepares a presentation or report that includes the question investigated, a detailed description of how the project was carried out, and an explanation of the findings.

M8 c Design of a physical structure, in which the student:

- generates a plan to build something of value, not necessarily monetary value;
- uses mathematics from Standard 2 to make the design realistic or appropriate, e.g., areas and volumes in general and of specific geometric shapes;

High School

The student conducts at least one large scale investigation or project each year drawn from the following kinds and, over the course of high school, conducts investigations or projects drawn from at least three of the kinds.

A single investigation or project may draw on more than one kind.

M8 a Data study, in which the student:

- carries out a study of data relevant to current civic, economic, scientific, health, or social issues;
- uses methods of statistical inference to generalize from the data;
- prepares a report that explains the purpose of the project, the organizational plan, and conclusions, and uses an appropriate balance of different ways of presenting information.

M8 b Mathematical model of a physical system or phenomenon, in which the student:

- carries out a study of a physical system or phenomenon by constructing a mathematical model based on functions to make generalizations about the structure of the system;
- uses structural analysis (a direct analysis of the structure of the system) rather than numerical or statistical analysis (an analysis of data about the system);
- prepares a report that explains the purpose of the project, the organizational plan, and conclusions, and uses an appropriate balance of different ways of presenting information.

M8 c Design of a physical structure, in which the student:

- creates a design for a physical structure;
- uses general mathematical ideas and techniques to discuss specifications for building the structure;
- prepares a report that explains the purpose of the project, the organizational plan, and conclusions, and uses an appropriate balance of different ways of presenting information.

M8 d Management and planning analysis, in which the student:

- carries out a study of a business or public policy situation involving issues such as optimization, cost-benefit projections, and risks;
- uses decision rules and strategies both to analyze options and balance trade-offs; and brings

M8d Management and planning, in which the student:

- decides on what to manage or plan, and the criteria to be used to see if the plan worked;
- identifies unexpected events that could disrupt the plan and further plans for such contingencies;
- identifies resources needed, e.g., materials, money, time, space, and other people;
- writes a detailed plan and revises and improves the plan in response to feedback from peers and teachers;
- carries out the plan (optional);
- writes a report on the plan that includes resources, budget, and schedule, and acknowledges assistance received from parents, peers, and teachers.
- writes a report that includes recommendations supported by diagrams, charts, and graphs, and acknowledges assistance received from parents, peers, and teachers.

M8e Pure mathematics investigation, in which the student:

- decides on the area of mathematics to investigate, e.g., numbers, shapes, patterns;
- describes a question or concept to investigate;
- decides on representations that will be used, e.g., numbers, symbols, diagrams, shapes, or physical models;
- carries out the investigation;
- writes a report that includes any generalizations drawn from the investigation, and acknowledges assistance received from parents, peers, and teachers.
- summarizes the important features of the structure;
- prepares a presentation or report that includes the question investigated, a detailed description of how the project was carried out, and an explanation of the findings.

M8d Management and planning, in which the student:

- determines the needs of the event to be managed or planned, e.g., cost, supply, scheduling;
- notes any constraints that will affect the plan;
- determines a plan;
- uses concepts from any of Standards 1 to 4, depending on the nature of the project;
- considers the possibility of a more efficient solution;
- prepares a presentation or report that includes the question investigated, a detailed description of how the project was carried out, and an explanation of the plan.

M8e Pure mathematics investigation, in which the student:

- extends or "plays with," as with mathematical puzzles, some mathematical feature, e.g., properties and patterns in numbers;
- uses concepts from any of Standards 1 to 4, e.g., an investigation of Pascal's triangle would have roots in Standard 1 but could tie in concepts from geometry, algebra, and probability; investigations of derivations of geometric formulas would be rooted in Standard 2 but could require algebra;
- determines and expresses generalizations from patterns;
- makes conjectures on apparent properties and argues, short of formal proof, why they seem true;
- prepares a presentation or report that includes the question investigated, a detailed description of how the project was carried out, and an explanation of the findings.

in mathematical ideas that serve to generalize the analysis across different conditions;

- prepares a report that explains the purpose of the project, the organizational plan, and conclusions, and uses an appropriate balance of different ways of presenting information.

M8e Pure mathematics investigation, in which the student:

- carries out a mathematical investigation of a phenomenon or concept in pure mathematics;
- uses methods of mathematical reasoning and justification to make generalizations about the phenomenon;
- prepares a report that explains the purpose of the project, the organizational plan, and conclusions, and uses an appropriate balance of different ways of presenting information.

M8f History of a mathematical idea, in which the student:

- carries out a historical study tracing the development of a mathematical concept and the people who contributed to it;
- includes a discussion of the actual mathematical content and its place in the curriculum of the present day;
- prepares a report that explains the purpose of the project, the organizational plan, and conclusions, and uses an appropriate balance of different ways of presenting information.

S1 Physical Sciences Concepts

APPENDIX III

The elementary school standards are set at a level of performance approximately equivalent to the end of fourth grade. The middle school standards are set at a level of performance approximately equivalent to the end of eighth grade. The high school standards are set at a level of performance approximately equivalent to the end of tenth grade. It is expected that some students might achieve these levels earlier and others later than these grades.

The Science standards are founded upon both the National Research Council's *National Science Education Standards* and the American Association for the Advancement of Science's Project 2061 *Benchmarks for Science Literacy*. These documents, each of which runs to several hundred pages, contain detailed explication of the concepts identified here.

Elementary School

The student produces evidence that demonstrates understanding of:

S1 a Properties of objects and materials, such as similarities and differences in the size, weight, and color of objects; the ability of materials to react with other substances; and different states of materials.

S1 b Position and motion of objects, such as how the motion of an object can be described by tracing and measuring its position over time; and how sound is produced by vibrating objects.

S1 c Light, heat, electricity, and magnetism, such as the variation of heat and temperature; how light travels in a straight line until it strikes an object or how electrical circuits work.

Middle School

The student produces evidence that demonstrates understanding of:

S1 a Properties and changes of properties in matter, such as density and boiling point; chemical reactivity; and conservation of matter.

S1 b Motions and forces, such as inertia and the net effects of balanced and unbalanced forces.

S1 c Transfer of energy, such as transformation of energy as heat; light, mechanical motion, and sound; and the nature of a chemical reaction.

High School

The student produces evidence that demonstrates understanding of:

S1 a Structure of atoms, such as atomic composition, nuclear forces, and radioactivity.

S1 b Structure and properties of matter, such as elements and compounds; bonding and molecular interaction; and characteristics of phase changes.

S1 c Chemical reactions, such as everyday examples of chemical reactions; electrons, protons, and energy transfer; and factors that affect reaction rates such as catalysts.

S1 d Motions and forces, such as gravitational and electrical; net forces and magnetism.

S1 e Conservation of energy and increase in disorder, such as kinetic and potential energy; energy conduction, convection, and radiation; random motion; and effects of heat and pressure.

S1 f Interactions of energy and matter, such as waves, absorption and emission of light, and conductivity.

S2 Life Sciences Concepts

APPENDIX III

Elementary School

The student produces evidence that demonstrates understanding of:

S2a Characteristics of organisms, such as survival and environmental support; the relationship between structure and function; and variations in behavior.

S2b Life cycles of organisms, such as how inheritance and environment determine the characteristics of an organism; and that all plants and animals have life cycles.

S2c Organisms and environments, such as the interdependence of animals and plants in an ecosystem; and populations and their effects on the environment.

S2d Change over time, such as evolution and fossil evidence depicting the great diversity of organisms developed over geologic history.

Middle School

The student produces evidence that demonstrates understanding of:

S2a Structure and function in living systems, such as the complementary nature of structure and function in cells, organs, tissues, organ systems, whole organisms, and ecosystems.

S2b Reproduction and heredity, such as sexual and asexual reproduction; and the role of genes and environment on trait expression.

S2c Regulation and behavior, such as senses and behavior; and response to environmental stimuli.

S2d Populations and ecosystems, such as the roles of producers, consumers, and decomposers in a food web; and the effects of resources and energy transfer on populations.

S2e Evolution, diversity, and adaptation of organisms, such as common ancestry, speciation, adaptation, variation, and extinction.

High School

The student produces evidence that demonstrates understanding of:

S2a The cell, such as cell structure and function relationships; regulation and biochemistry; and energy and photosynthesis.

S2b Molecular basis of heredity, such as DNA, genes, chromosomes, and mutations.

S2c Biological evolution, such as speciation, biodiversity, natural selection, and biological classification.

S2d Interdependence of organisms, such as conservation of matter; cooperation and competition among organisms in ecosystems; and human effects on the environment.

S2e Matter, energy, and organization in living systems, such as matter and energy flow through different levels of organization; and environmental constraints.

S2f Behavior of organisms, such as nervous system regulation; behavioral responses; and connections with anthropology, sociology, and psychology.

S3 Earth and Space Sciences Concepts

Elementary School

The student produces evidence that demonstrates understanding of:

S3 a Properties of Earth materials, such as water and gases; and the properties of rocks and soils, such as texture, color, and ability to retain water.

S3 b Objects in the sky, such as Sun, Moon, planets, and other objects that can be observed and described; and the importance of the Sun to provide the light and heat necessary for survival.

S3 c Changes in Earth and sky, such as changes caused by weathering, volcanism, and earthquakes; and the patterns of movement of objects in the sky.

Middle School

The student produces evidence that demonstrates understanding of:

S3 a Structure of the Earth system, such as crustal plates and land forms; water and rock cycles; oceans, weather, and climate.

S3 b Earth's history, such as Earth processes including erosion and movement of plates; change over time and fossil evidence.

S3 c Earth in the Solar System, such as the predictable motion of planets, moons, and other objects in the Solar System including days, years, moon phases, and eclipses; and the role of the Sun as the major source of energy for phenomena on the Earth's surface.

S3 d Natural resource management.

High School

The student produces evidence that demonstrates understanding of:

S3 a Energy in the Earth system, such as radioactive decay, gravity, the Sun's energy, convection, and changes in global climate.

S3 b Geochemical cycles, such as conservation of matter; chemical resources and movement of matter between chemical reservoirs.

S3 c Origin and evolution of the Earth system, such as geologic time and the age of life forms; origin of life; and evolution of the Solar System.

S3 d Origin and evolution of the universe, such as the "big bang" theory; formation of stars and elements; and nuclear reactions.

S3 e Natural resource management.

S4 Scientific Connections and Applications

Elementary School

The student produces evidence that demonstrates understanding of:

S4a Big ideas and unifying concepts, such as order and organization; models, form and function; change and constancy; and cause and effect.

S4b The designed world, such as development of agricultural techniques; and the viability of technological designs.

S4c Personal health, such as nutrition, substance abuse, and exercise; germs and toxic substances; personal and environmental safety.

S4d Science as a human endeavor, such as communication, cooperation, and diverse input in scientific research; and the importance of reason, intellectual honesty, and skepticism.

Middle School

The student produces evidence that demonstrates understanding of:

S4a Big ideas and unifying concepts, such as order and organization; models, form, and function; change and constancy; and cause and effect.

S4b The designed world, such as the reciprocal nature of science and technology; the development of agricultural techniques; and the viability of technological designs.

S4c Health, such as nutrition, exercise, and disease; effects of drugs and toxic substances; personal and environmental safety; and resources and environmental stress.

S4d Impact of technology, such as constraints and trade-offs; feedback; benefits and risks; and problems and solutions.

S4e Impact of science, such as historical and contemporary contributions; and interactions between science and society.

High School

The student produces evidence that demonstrates understanding of:

S4a Big ideas and unifying concepts, such as order and organization; models, form and function; change and constancy; and cause and effect.

S4b The designed world, such as the reciprocal relationship between science and technology; the development of agricultural techniques; and the reasonableness of technological designs.

S4c Health, such as nutrition and exercise; disease and epidemiology; personal and environmental safety; and resources, environmental stress, and population growth.

S4d Impact of technology, such as constraints and trade-offs; feedback; benefits and risks; and problems and solutions.

S4e Impact of science, such as historical and contemporary contributions; and interactions between science and society.

S5 Scientific Thinking

Elementary School

The student demonstrates scientific inquiry and problem solving by using thoughtful questioning and reasoning strategies, common sense and conceptual understanding from Science Standards 1 to 4, and appropriate methods to investigate the natural world; that is, the student:

S5 a Asks questions about natural phenomena; objects and organisms; and events and discoveries.

S5 b Uses concepts from Science Standards 1 to 4 to explain a variety of observations and phenomena.

S5 c Uses evidence from reliable sources to construct explanations.

S5 d Evaluates different points of view using relevant experiences, observations, and knowledge; and distinguishes between fact and opinion.

S5 e Identifies problems; proposes and implements solutions; and evaluates the accuracy, design, and outcomes of investigations.

S5 f Works individually and in teams to collect and share information and ideas.

Middle School

The student demonstrates scientific inquiry and problem solving by using thoughtful questioning and reasoning strategies, common sense and conceptual understanding from Science Standards 1 to 4, and appropriate methods to investigate the natural world; that is, the student:

S5 a Frames questions to distinguish cause and effect; and identifies or controls variables in experimental and non-experimental research settings.

S5 b Uses concepts from Science Standards 1 to 4 to explain a variety of observations and phenomena.

S5 c Uses evidence from reliable sources to develop descriptions, explanations, and models.

S5 d Proposes, recognizes, analyzes, considers, and critiques alternative explanations; and distinguishes between fact and opinion.

S5 e Identifies problems; proposes and implements solutions; and evaluates the accuracy, design, and outcomes of investigations.

S5 f Works individually and in teams to collect and share information and ideas.

High School

The student demonstrates skill in scientific inquiry and problem solving by using thoughtful questioning and reasoning strategies, common sense and diverse conceptual understanding, and appropriate ideas and methods to investigate science; that is, the student:

S5 a Frames questions to distinguish cause and effect; and identifies or controls variables in experimental and non-experimental research settings.

S5 b Uses concepts from Science Standards 1 to 4 to explain a variety of observations and phenomena.

S5 c Uses evidence from reliable sources to develop descriptions, explanations, and models; and makes appropriate adjustments and improvements based on additional data or logical arguments.

S5 d Proposes, recognizes, analyzes, considers, and critiques alternative explanations; and distinguishes between fact and opinion.

S5 e Identifies problems; proposes and implements solutions; and evaluates the accuracy, design, and outcomes of investigations.

S5 f Works individually and in teams to collect and share information and ideas.

S6 Scientific Tools and Technologies

APPENDIX III

S6 makes explicit reference to using telecommunications to acquire and share information. A recent National Center on Education Statistics survey recently reported that only 50% of schools and fewer than 9% of instructional rooms currently have access to the Internet. We know this is an equity issue—that far more than 9% of the homes in the United States have access to the Internet and that schools must make sure that students' access to information and ideas does not depend on what they get at home—so we have crafted performance standards that would use the Internet so that people will make sure that all students have access to it. New Standards partners have made a commitment to create the learning environments where students can develop the knowledge and skills delineated here.

Elementary School

The student demonstrates competence with the tools and technologies of science by using them to collect data, make observations, analyze results, and accomplish tasks effectively; that is, the student:

S6a Uses technology and tools (such as rulers, computers, balances, thermometers, watches, magnifiers, and microscopes) to gather data and extend the senses.

S6b Collects and analyzes data using concepts and techniques in Mathematics Standard 4, such as average, data displays, graphing, variability, and sampling.

S6c Acquires information from multiple sources, such as experimentation and print and non-print sources.

Middle School

The student demonstrates competence with the tools and technologies of science by using them to collect data, make observations, analyze results, and accomplish tasks effectively; that is, the student:

S6a Uses technology and tools (such as traditional laboratory equipment, video, and computer aids) to observe and measure objects, organisms, and phenomena, directly, indirectly, and remotely.

S6b Records and stores data using a variety of formats, such as data bases, audiotapes, and videotapes.

S6c Collects and analyzes data using concepts and techniques in Mathematics Standard 4, such as mean, median, and mode; outcome probability and reliability; and appropriate data displays.

S6d Acquires information from multiple sources, such as print, the Internet, computer data bases, and experimentation.

S6e Recognizes sources of bias in data, such as observer and sampling biases.

High School

The student demonstrates competence with the tools and technologies of science by using them to collect data, make observations, analyze results, and accomplish tasks effectively; that is, the student:

S6a Uses technology and tools (such as traditional laboratory equipment, video, and computer aids) to observe and measure objects, organisms, and phenomena, directly, indirectly, and remotely, with appropriate consideration of accuracy and precision.

S6b Records and stores data using a variety of formats, such as data bases, audiotapes, and videotapes.

S6c Collects and analyzes data using concepts and techniques in Mathematics Standard 4, such as mean, median, and mode; outcome probability and reliability; and appropriate data displays.

S6d Acquires information from multiple sources, such as print, the Internet, computer data bases, and experimentation.

S6e Recognizes and limits sources of bias in data, such as observer and sample biases.

S7 Scientific Communication

Elementary School

The student demonstrates effective scientific communication by clearly describing aspects of the natural world using accurate data, graphs, or other appropriate media to convey depth of conceptual understanding in science; that is, the student:

S7 a Represents data and results in multiple ways, such as numbers, tables, and graphs; drawings, diagrams, and artwork; and technical and creative writing.

S7 b Uses facts to support conclusions.

S7 c Communicates in a form suited to the purpose and the audience, such as writing instructions that others can follow.

S7 d Critiques written and oral explanations, and uses data to resolve disagreements.

Middle School

The student demonstrates effective scientific communication by clearly describing aspects of the natural world using accurate data, graphs, or other appropriate media to convey depth of conceptual understanding in science; that is, the student:

S7 a Represents data and results in multiple ways, such as numbers, tables, and graphs; drawings, diagrams, and artwork; and technical and creative writing.

S7 b Argues from evidence, such as data produced through his or her own experimentation or by others.

S7 c Critiques published materials.

S7 d Explains a scientific concept or procedure to other students.

S7 e Communicates in a form suited to the purpose and the audience, such as by writing instructions that others can follow; critiquing written and oral explanations; and using data to resolve disagreements.

High School

The student demonstrates effective scientific communication by clearly describing aspects of the natural world using accurate data, graphs, or other appropriate media to convey depth of conceptual understanding in science; that is, the student:

S7 a Represents data and results in multiple ways, such as numbers, tables, and graphs; drawings, diagrams, and artwork; technical and creative writing; and selects the most effective way to convey the scientific information.

S7 b Argues from evidence, such as data produced through his or her own experimentation or data produced by others.

S7 c Critiques published materials, such as popular magazines and academic journals.

S7 d Explains a scientific concept or procedure to other students.

S7 e Communicates in a form suited to the purpose and the audience, such as by writing instructions that others can follow; critiquing written and oral explanations; and using data to resolve disagreements.

S8 Scientific Investigation

APPENDIX III

Best practice in science has always included extensive inquiry and investigation, but these are frequently given less emphasis at the elementary level in the face of competing demands form English language arts and mathematics. There are many opportunities to learn science outside of school, including Scouts, Boys and Girls Clubs, 4-H, and Future Farmers of America. The work done in these venues can and should be used to provide evidence of meeting the standards.

Elementary School

The student demonstrates scientific competence by completing projects drawn from the following kinds of investigations, including at least one full investigation each year and, over the course of elementary school, investigations that integrate several aspects of Science Standards 1 to 7 and represent all four of the kinds of investigation:

S8a An experiment, such as conducting a fair test.

S8b A systematic observation, such as a field study.

S8c A design, such as building a model or scientific apparatus.

S8d Non-experimental research using print and electronic information, such as journals, video, or computers.

A single project may draw on more than one kind of investigation.

A full investigation includes:

- Questions that can be studied using the resources available.
- Procedures that are safe, humane, and ethical; and that respect privacy and property rights.
- Data that have been collected and recorded (see also Science Standard 6) in ways that others can verify and analyze using skills expected at this grade level (see also Mathematics Standard 4).
- Data and results that have been represented (see also Science Standard 7) in ways that fit the context.
- Recommendations, decisions, and conclusions based on evidence.
- Acknowledgment of references and contributions of others.
- Results that are communicated appropriately to audiences.
- Reflection and defense of conclusions and recommendations from other sources and peer review.

Middle School

The student demonstrates scientific competence by completing projects drawn from the following kinds of investigations, including at least one full investigation each year and, over the course of middle school, investigations that integrate several aspects of Science Standards 1 to 7 and represent all four of the kinds of investigation:

S8a Controlled experiment.

S8b Fieldwork.

S8c Design.

S8d Secondary research, such as use of others' data.

A single project may draw on more than one type of investigation.

A full investigation includes:

- Questions that can be studied using the resources available.
- Procedures that are safe, humane, and ethical; and that respect privacy and property rights.
- Data that have been collected and recorded (see also Science Standard 6) in ways that others can verify, and analyzed using skills expected at this grade level (see also Mathematics Standard 4).
- Data and results that have been represented (see also Science Standard 7) in ways that fit the context.
- Recommendations, decisions, and conclusions based on evidence.
- Acknowledgment of references and contributions of others.
- Results that are communicated appropriately to audiences.
- Reflection and defense of conclusions and recommendations from other sources and peer review.

High School

The student demonstrates scientific competence by completing projects drawn from the following kinds of investigation, including at least one full investigation each year and, over the course of high school, investigations that integrate several aspects of Science Standards 1 to 7 and represent all four of the kinds of investigation:

S8a Controlled experiment.

S8b Fieldwork.

S8c Design.

S8d Secondary research.

A single project may draw on more than one type of investigation.

A full investigation includes:

- Questions that can be studied using the resources available.
- Procedures that are safe, humane, and ethical; and that respect privacy and property rights.
- Data that have been collected and recorded (see also Science Standard 6) in ways that others can verify, and analyzed using skills expected at this grade level (see also Mathematics Standard 4).
- Data and results that have been represented (see also Science Standard 7) in ways that fit the context.
- Recommendations, decisions, and conclusions based on evidence.
- Acknowledgment of references and contributions of others.
- Results that are communicated appropriately to audiences.
- Reflection and defense of conclusions and recommendations from other sources and peer review.

A1 Problem Solving

The elementary school standards are set at a level of performance approximately equivalent to the end of fourth grade. The middle school standards are set at a level of performance approximately equivalent to the end of eighth grade. The high school standards are set at a level of performance approximately equivalent to the end of tenth grade. It is expected that some students might achieve these levels earlier and others later than these grades.

Elementary School

The student conducts projects involving at least two of the following kinds of problem solving each year and, over the course of elementary school, conducts projects involving all three kinds of problem solving.

- Design a Product, Service, or System: Identify needs that could be met by new products, services, or systems and create solutions for meeting them.
- Improve a System: Develop an understanding of the way systems of people, machines, and processes work; troubleshoot problems in their operation and devise strategies for improving their effectiveness.
- Plan and Organize an Event or an Activity: Take responsibility for all aspects of planning and organizing an event or an activity from concept to completion, making good use of the resources of people, time, money, and materials and facilities.

Each project should involve subject matter related to the standards for English Language Arts, and/or Mathematics, and/or Science, and/or other appropriate subject content.

Design a Product, Service, or System

A1 a The student designs and creates a product, service, or system to meet an identified need; that is, the student:

- develops ideas for the design of the product, service, or system;
- chooses among the design ideas and justifies the choice;
- establishes criteria for judging the success of the design;
- uses an appropriate format to represent the design;
- plans and carries out the steps needed to turn the design into a reality;
- evaluates the design in terms of the criteria established for success.

Improve a System

A1 b The student troubleshoots problems in the operation of a system in need of repair or devises and tests ways of improving the effectiveness of a system in operation; that is, the student:

- identifies the parts of the system and the way the parts connect with each other;

Middle School

The student conducts projects involving at least two of the following kinds of problem solving each year and, over the course of middle school, conducts projects involving all three kinds of problem solving.

- Design a Product, Service, or System: Identify needs that could be met by new products, services, or systems and create solutions for meeting them.
- Improve a System: Develop an understanding of the way systems of people, machines, and processes work; troubleshoot problems in their operation and devise strategies for improving their effectiveness.
- Plan and Organize an Event or an Activity: Take responsibility for all aspects of planning and organizing an event or an activity from concept to completion, making good use of the resources of people, time, money, and materials and facilities.

Each project should involve subject matter related to the standards for English Language Arts, and/or Mathematics, and/or Science, and/or other appropriate subject content.

Design a Product, Service, or System

A1 a The student designs and creates a product, service, or system to meet an identified need; that is, the student:

- develops a range of ideas for design of the product, service, or system;
- selects one design option to pursue and justifies the choice with reference, for example, to functional, aesthetic, social, economic, or environmental considerations;
- establishes criteria for judging the success of the design;
- uses appropriate conventions to represent the design;
- plans and carries out the steps needed to create the product, service, or system;
- makes adjustments as needed to conform with specified standards or regulations regarding quality and safety;
- evaluates the quality of the design in terms of the criteria for success and by comparison with similar products, services, or systems.

High School

The student conducts projects involving at least two of the following kinds of problem solving each year and, over the course of high school, conducts projects involving all three kinds of problem solving.

- Design a Product, Service, or System: Identify needs that could be met by new products, services, or systems and create solutions for meeting them.
- Improve a System: Develop an understanding of the way systems of people, machines, and processes work; troubleshoot problems in their operation and devise strategies for improving their effectiveness.
- Plan and Organize an Event or an Activity: Take responsibility for all aspects of planning and organizing an event or activity from concept to completion, making good use of the resources of people, time, money, and materials and facilities.

Each project should involve subject matter related to the standards for English Language Arts, and/or Mathematics, and/or Science, and/or other appropriate subject content.

Design a Product, Service, or System

A1 a The student designs and creates a product, service, or system to meet an identified need; that is, the student:

- develops a design proposal that:
  - shows how the ideas for the design were developed;
  - reflects awareness of similar work done by others and of relevant design standards and regulations;
  - justifies the choices made in finalizing the design with reference, for example, to functional, aesthetic, social, economic, and environmental considerations;
  - establishes criteria for evaluating the product, service, or system;
  - uses appropriate conventions to represent the design;
- plans and implements the steps needed to create the product, service, or system;
- makes adjustments as needed to conform with specified standards or regulations regarding quality or safety;
- evaluates the product, service, or system in terms of the criteria established in the design

- identifies parts or connections in the system that have broken down or that could be made to work better;
- devises ways of making the system work again or making it work better;
- evaluates the effectiveness of the strategies for improving the system and supports the evaluation with evidence.

Plan and Organize an Event or an Activity

A1c The student plans and organizes an event or an activity; that is, the student:

- develops a plan for the event or activity that:
  - includes all the factors and variables that need to be considered;
  - shows the order in which things need to be done;
  - takes into account the resources available to put the plan into action, including people and time;
- implements the plan;
- evaluates the success of the event or activity by identifying the parts of the plan that worked best and the parts that could have been improved by better planning and organization;
- makes recommendations to others who might consider planning and organizing a similar event or activity.

Improve a System

A1b The student troubleshoots problems in the operation of a system in need of repair or devises and tests ways of improving the effectiveness of a system in operation; that is, the student:

- describes the structure and management of the system in terms of its logic, sequences, and control;
- identifies the operating principles underlying the system, i.e., mathematical, scientific, organizational;
- evaluates the way the system operates;
- devises strategies for putting the system back in operation or improving its performance;
- evaluates the effectiveness of the strategies for improving the system and supports the evaluation with evidence.

Plan and Organize an Event or an Activity

A1c The student plans and organizes an event or activity; that is, the student:

- develops a plan that:
  - reflects research into relevant precedents and regulations;
  - includes all the factors and variables that need to be considered;
  - shows the order in which things need to be done;
  - takes into account the resources available to put the plan into action, including people and time;
- implements the plan in ways that:
  - reflect the priorities established in the plan;
  - respond effectively to unforeseen circumstances;
- evaluates the success of the event or activity;
- makes recommendations to others who might consider planning and organizing a similar event or activity.

proposal, and with reference to:

  - information gathered from sources such as impact studies, product testing, or market research;
  - comparisons with similar work done by others.

Improve a System

A1b The student troubleshoots problems in the operation of a system in need of repair or devises and tests ways of improving the effectiveness of a system in operation; that is, the student:

- explains the structure of the system in terms of its:
  - logic, sequences, and control;
  - operating principles, that is, the mathematical, scientific, and/or organizational principles underlying the system;
- analyzes the way the system works, taking account of its functional, aesthetic, social, environmental, and commercial requirements, as appropriate, and using a relevant kind of modeling or systems analysis;
- evaluates the operation of the system, using qualitative methods and/or quantitative measurements of performance;
- develops and tests strategies to put the system back in operation and/or optimize its performance;
- evaluates the effectiveness of the strategies for improving the system and supports the evaluation with evidence.

Plan and Organize an Event or an Activity

A1c The student plans and organizes an event or an activity; that is, the student:

- develops a planning schedule that:
  - is sensible in terms of the goals of the event or activity;
  - is logical and achievable;
  - reflects research into relevant precedents and regulations;
  - takes account of all relevant factors;
  - communicates clearly so that a peer or colleague could use it;
- implements and adjusts the planning schedule in ways that:
  - make efficient use of time, money, people, resources, facilities;
  - reflect established priorities;
  - respond effectively to unforeseen circumstances;
- evaluates the success of the event or activity using qualitative and/or quantitative methods;
- makes recommendations for planning and organizing subsequent similar events or activities.

A2 Communication Tools and Techniques

Elementary School

A2 a The student makes an oral presentation of project plans or findings to an appropriate audience; that is, the student:

- organizes the presentation in a logical way appropriate to its purpose;
- speaks clearly and presents confidently;
- responds to questions from the audience;
- evaluates the effectiveness of the presentation.

A2 b The student composes and sends correspondence, such as thank-you letters and memoranda providing information; that is, the student:

- expresses the information or request clearly;
- writes in a style appropriate to the purpose of the correspondence.

A2 c The student writes and formats information for short publications, such as brochures or posters; that is, the student:

- organizes the information into an appropriate form for use in the publication;
- checks the information for accuracy;
- formats the publication so that it achieves its purpose.

Middle School

A2 a The student makes an oral presentation of project plans or findings to an audience beyond the school; that is, the student:

- organizes the presentation in a logical way appropriate to its purpose;
- adjusts the style of presentation to suit its purpose and audience;
- speaks clearly and presents confidently;
- responds appropriately to questions from the audience;
- evaluates the effectiveness of the presentation.

A2 b The student conducts formal written correspondence with an organization beyond the school; that is, the student:

- expresses the information or request clearly for the purpose and audience;
- writes in a style appropriate to the purpose and audience of the correspondence.

A2 c The student publishes information using several methods and formats, such as overhead transparencies, handouts, and computer generated graphs and charts; that is, the student:

- organizes the information into an appropriate form for use in the publication;
- checks the information for accuracy;
- formats the published material so that it achieves its purpose.

High School

A2 a The student makes an oral presentation of project plans or findings to an audience with expertise in the relevant subject matter; that is, the student:

- organizes the presentation in a logical way appropriate to its purpose;
- adjusts the style of presentation to suit its purpose and audience;
- speaks clearly and presents confidently;
- responds appropriately to questions from the audience;
- evaluates the effectiveness of the presentation and identifies appropriate revisions for a future presentation.

A2 b The student prepares a formal written proposal or report to an organization beyond the school; that is, the student:

- organizes the information in the proposal or report in a logical way appropriate to its purpose;
- produces the proposal or report in a format similar to that used in professionally produced documents for a similar purpose and audience.

A2 c The student develops a multi-media presentation, combining text, images, and/or sound; that is, the student:

- selects an appropriate medium for each element of the presentation;
- uses the selected media skillfully, including editing and monitoring for quality;
- achieves coherence in the presentation as a whole;
- communicates the information effectively, testing audience response and revising the presentation accordingly.

A3 Information Tools and Techniques

Elementary School

A3a The student gathers information to assist in completing project work; that is, the student:

- identifies potential sources of information to assist in completing the project;
- uses appropriate techniques to collect the information, e.g., considers sampling issues in conducting a survey;
- distinguishes relevant from irrelevant information;
- shows evidence of research in the completed project.

A3b The student uses information technology to assist in gathering, organizing, and presenting information; that is, the student:

- acquires information for specific purposes from on-line sources, such as the Internet, and other electronic data bases, such as an electronic encyclopedia;
- uses word-processing, drawing, and painting programs to produce project reports and related materials.

Middle School

A3a The student gathers information to assist in completing project work; that is, the student:

- identifies potential sources of information to assist in completing the project;
- uses appropriate techniques to collect the information, e.g., considers sampling issues in conducting a survey;
- interprets and analyzes the information;
- evaluates the information for completeness and relevance;
- shows evidence of research in the completed project.

A3b The student uses information technology to assist in gathering, analyzing, organizing, and presenting information; that is, the student:

- acquires information for specific purposes from on-line sources, such as the Internet, and other electronic data bases, such as a scientific data base on CD ROM;
- uses word-processing, graphics, data base, and spreadsheet programs to produce project reports and related materials.

High School

A3a The student gathers information to assist in completing project work; that is, the student:

- identifies potential sources of information to assist in completing the project;
- uses appropriate techniques to collect the information, e.g., considers sampling issues in conducting a survey;
- interprets and analyzes the information;
- evaluates the information in terms of completeness, relevance, and validity;
- shows evidence of research in the completed project.

A3b The student uses on-line sources to exchange information for specific purposes; that is, the student:

- uses E-mail to correspond with peers and specialists in the subject matter of their projects;
- incorporates into E-mail correspondence data of different file types and applications.

A3c The student uses word-processing software to produce a multi-page document; that is, the student:

- uses features of the software to create and edit the document;
- uses features of the software to format the document, including a table of contents, index, tabular columns, charts, and graphics;
- uses features of the software to create templates and style sheets for the document.

A3d The student writes, adds content to, and analyzes a data base program that uses a relational data base; that is, the student:

- writes a program capable of handling data with at least two files;
- creates macros to facilitate data entry, analysis, and manipulation;
- creates multiple report formats that include summary information;
- merges data from the data base with other files.

A3e The student creates, edits, and analyzes a spreadsheet of information that displays data in tabular, numeric format and includes multiple graphs; that is, the student:

- creates a spreadsheet that displays the use of formulas and functions;
- uses features of the software to sort, arrange, display, and extract data for specific purposes;
- uses features of the software to create multiple spreadsheets and to synthesize the spreadsheets into a single presentation.

A4 Learning and Self-management Tools and Techniques

Elementary School

A4 a The student learns from models; that is, the student:

- consults with or observes other students and adults at work, and identifies the main features of what they do and the way they go about their work;
- examines models for the results of project work, such as professionally produced publications, and analyzes their qualities;
- uses what he or she learns from models to assist in planning and conducting project activities.

A4 b The student keeps records of work activities in an orderly manner; that is, the student:

- sets up a system for storing records of work activities;
- maintains records of work activities in a way that makes it possible to find specific materials quickly and easily.

A4 c The student identifies strengths and weaknesses in his or her own work; that is, the student:

- understands and establishes criteria for judging the quality of work processes and products;
- assesses his or her own work processes and products.

Middle School

A4 a The student learns from models; that is, the student:

- consults with or observes other students and adults at work, and identifies the main features of what they do and the way they go about their work;
- identifies models for the results of project work, such as professionally produced publications, and analyzes their qualities;
- uses what he or she learns from models to assist in planning and conducting project activities.

A4 b The student develops and maintains a schedule of work activities; that is, the student:

- establishes a schedule of work activities that reflects priorities and deadlines;
- seeks advice on the management of conflicting priorities and deadlines;
- updates the schedule regularly.

A4 c The student sets goals for learning and reviews his or her progress; that is, the student:

- sets goals for learning;
- reviews his or her progress towards meeting the goals;
- seeks and responds to advice from others in setting goals and reviewing progress.

High School

A4 a The student learns from models; that is, the student:

- consults with and observes other students and adults at work and analyzes their roles to determine the critical demands, such as demands for knowledge and skills, judgment and decision making;
- identifies models for the results of project work, such as professionally produced publications, and analyzes their qualities;
- uses what he or she learns from models in planning and conducting project activities.

A4 b The student reviews his or her own progress in completing work activities and adjusts priorities as needed to meet deadlines; that is, the student:

- develops and maintains work schedules that reflect consideration of priorities;
- manages time;
- monitors progress towards meeting deadlines and adjusts priorities as necessary.

A4 c The student evaluates his or her performance; that is, the student:

- establishes expectations for his or her own achievement;
- critiques his or her work in light of the established expectations;
- seeks and responds to advice and criticism from others.

A5 Tools and Techniques for Working With Others

Elementary School

A5 a The student works with others to complete a task; that is, the student:

- reaches agreement with group members on what work needs to be done to complete the task and how the work will be tackled;
- takes a share of the responsibility for the work;
- consults with group members regularly during the task to check on progress in completing the task, to decide on any changes that are required, and to check that all parts have been completed at the end of the task.

A5 b The student shows or explains something clearly enough for someone else to be able to do it.

A5 c The student responds to a request from a client; that is, the student:

- interprets the client's request;
- asks questions to clarify the demands of a task.

Middle School

A5 a The student takes responsibility for a component of a team project; that is, the student:

- reaches agreement with team members on what work needs to be done to complete the task and how the work will be tackled;
- takes specific responsibility for a component of the project;
- takes all steps necessary to ensure appropriate completion of the specific component of the project within the agreed upon time frame.

A5 b The student coaches or tutors; that is, the student:

- assists one or more others to learn on the job;
- analyzes coaching or tutoring experience to identify more and less effective ways of providing assistance to support on-the-job learning;
- uses the analysis to inform subsequent coaching or tutoring activities.

A5 c The student responds to a request from a client; that is, the student:

- consults with a client to clarify the demands of a task;
- interprets the client's request and translates it into an initial plan for completing the task, taking account of available resources;
- negotiates with the client to arrive at an agreed upon plan.

High School

A5 a The student participates in the establishment and operation of self-directed work teams; that is, the student:

- defines roles and shares responsibilities among team members;
- sets objectives and time frames for the work to be completed;
- establishes processes for group decision making;
- reviews progress and makes adjustments as required.

A5 b The student plans and carries out a strategy for including at least one new member in a work program; that is, the student:

- plans and conducts an initial activity to introduce the new member to the work program;
- devises ways of providing continuing on-the-job support and advice;
- monitors the new member's progress in joining the program, and revises the kinds and ways of providing support and advice accordingly;
- reviews the success of the overall strategy.

A5 c The student completes a task in response to a commission from a client; that is, the student:

- negotiates with the client to arrive at a plan for meeting the client's needs that is acceptable to the client, achievable within available resources, and includes agreed-upon criteria for successful completion;
- monitors client satisfaction with the work in progress and makes adjustments accordingly;
- evaluates the result in terms of the negotiated plan and the client's evaluation of the result.

STANDARDS DEVELOPMENT STAFF

Harold Asturias, Academic Advancement, University of California Office of the President

Pam Beck, Academic Advancement, University of California Office of the President

Ann Borthwick, Learning Research and Development Center, University of Pittsburgh

Bill Calder, Fort Worth Independent School District, TX

Shannon C'de Baca, Thomas Jefferson High School, Council Bluffs, IA

Janet Coffey, Edmund Burke School, Washington, DC

Duane A. Cooper, Center for Mathematics Education and Department of Mathematics, University of Maryland

Phil Daro, Academic Advancement, University of California Office of the President

Mishaa DeGraw, Academic Advancement, University of California Office of the President

Diana Edwards, Learning Research and Development Center, University of Pittsburgh

Gary Eggan, Learning Research and Development Center, University of Pittsburgh

JoAnne Eresh, Learning Research and Development Center, University of Pittsburgh

Sally Hampton, Fort Worth Independent School District, TX

Drew Kravin, Cornell Elementary School, Albany, CA

Georgia Makris, Academic Advancement, University of California Office of the President

Mary Marsh, Fort Worth Independent School District, TX

Megan Martin, Academic Advancement, University of California Office of the President

Evy McPherson, Academic Advancement, University of California Office of the President

Kate Nolan, Learning Research and Development Center, University of Pittsburgh

Andy Plattner, National Center on Education and the Economy

Lonny Platzer, Learning Research and Development Center, University of Pittsburgh

Mark Rasmussen, Cornell Elementary School, Albany, CA

Jennifer Regen, Fort Worth Independent School District, TX

Christine Ross, Learning Research and Development Center, University of Pittsburgh

Annette Seitz, Learning Research and Development Center, University of Pittsburgh

Ann Shannon, Academic Advancement, University of California Office of the President

Liz Spalding, National Council of Teachers of English

Elizabeth Stage, Academic Advancement, University of California Office of the President

Dick Stanley, Dana Center, University of California at Berkeley

Cathy Sterling, Academic Advancement, University of California Office of the President

John Tanner, Fort Worth Independent School District,TX

Ginny Van Horne, Education and Human Resources, American Association for the Advancement of Science

ACKNOWLEDGMENTS

Peter Afflerbach, University of Maryland

Bob Anderson, California Department of Education

Laura Arndt, Eaglecrest High School, Aurora, CO

Rob Atterbury, San Diego City Schools, CA

Linda Ballenger, West Park Elementary, Fort Worth, TX

Jerry Bell, Education and Human Resources, American Association for the Advancement of Science

Neal Berkin, White Plains Schools, White Plains, NY

Victoria Bill, Institute for Learning, Learning Research and Development Center, University of Pittsburgh

Linda Block-Gandy, Mountainview Elementary, CO

Greg Bouljon, Bettendorf Middle School, IL

Rupi Boyd, Taft Junior High School, CA

Diane Briars, Pittsburgh Public Schools, PA

Melanie Broujos, Frick International Studies Academy, Pittsburgh, PA

Shirley Patton Brown, West Memphis High School, West Memphis, AR

Hugh Burkhardt, Shell Centre for Mathematics Education, Nottingham, England

Charlotte Burrell, Trimble Tech High School, Fort Worth, TX

Jill Calder, Wedgwood Sixth Grade School, Fort Worth, TX

Ruben Carriedo, San Diego City Schools, CA

Linda Carstens, San Diego City Schools, CA

Cynthia Carter, New York City Lab School, NY

Sharon Chambers, Forbes Elementary School, Penn Hills, PA

Miriam Chaplin, National Council of Teachers of English

Phyllis Chapman, Linden Elementary School, Pittsburgh, PA

Lynda Chittenden, Park Elementary, Mill Valley, CA

Fran Claggett, Forestville, CA

Doug Clarke, Australian Catholic University, Australia

Gill Close, King's College, University of London, England

Laurel Collins, Linton Middle School, Pittsburgh, PA

Kathy Comfort, California Department of Education

John Davis, Langley High School, Pittsburgh, PA

Marshé DeLain, Delaware Department of Public Instruction

Dot Down, Dublin High School, CA

Mark Driscoll, Education Development Center, Newton, MA

Xandra Williams Earlie, Aldine Independent School District, Houston, TX

Phyllis Eisen, National Association of Manufacturers

Marcia Elliott, Somers Public Schools, CT

Ed Esty, Independent Consultant, Chevy Chase, MD

Alan Farstrup, International Reading Association

Harry Featherstone, Featherstone & Associates, Wooster, OH

Susan Fineman, East Hill ISA, PA

Donna Foley, Parker School, Chelmsford, MA

Amanda Frohberg, PS 41, New York, NY

Karen Fujii, Bucher Middle School, Santa Clara, CA

Matt Gandal, American Federation of Teachers

Don Geary, Linton Middle School, Pittsburgh, PA

Roger Gehman, Linton Middle School, Pittsburgh, PA

Karrie Gengo, Meadowdale High School, Lynnwood, WA

Judy Goldfeder, PS 116, New York, NY

Amy Granatire, Penn Hebron Elementary School, Pittsburgh, PA

Eunice Greer, University of Illinois

Susan Halbert, National 4-H Council

Mike Hale, Council Bluffs Community Schools, Council Bluffs, IA

Jerry Halpern, Langley High School, Pittsburgh, PA

Shirley Brice Heath, Stanford University

Rae Ann Hirsh, Penn Hebron Elementary School, Pittsburgh, PA

Bonnie Hole, Princeton Institute for Research, New Haven, CT

Bill Honig, San Francisco State University

Kathy Howard, Reizenstein Middle School, Pittsburgh, PA

David Hughes, Linton Middle School, Pittsburgh, PA

Beth Hulbert, Barre City Elementary School, VT

Sharon Woods Hussey, Girl Scouts of the U.S.A.

Robin Ittigson, Minadeo Elementary School, Pittsburgh, PA

Tom Jones, National Alliance for Restructuring Education

Nancy Kellogg, CONNECT, Colorado Department of Education

Don King, Department of Mathematics, Northeastern University, Boston, MA

Denis Krysinski, Vann Elementary School, Pittsburgh, PA

Brian Lawler, Eaglecrest High School, Aurora, CO

Lyn Le Countryman, Price Lab School, IA

Steve Leinwand, Connecticut State Department of Education

Jane Lester, New York City Lab School, NY

Denise Levine, New York City Community District 2, NY

Linda Lewis, Fort Worth Independent School District, TX

Debra Liberman, Fells High School, Philadelphia, PA

Bob Livingston, Pennsylvania Department of Education

Anthony Lucas, Duquesne University, Pittsburgh, PA

Denise Lutz, Peabody High School, Pittsburgh, PA

Susan MacArthur, South Portland High School, South Portland, ME

Gary MacDonald, Junior High School, Greely, CO

Shirley Malcom, American Association for the Advancement of Science

Kelly Maloney-Fermoile, Carrie E. Tompkins School, Croton-on-Hudson, NY

Rich Matthews, Pittsburgh Public Schools, PA

Ken McCaffrey, Brattleboro Union High School, VT

Jim Meadows, Mountlake Terrace High School, Mountlake Terrace, WA

David Mintz, National Alliance for Restructuring Education

Harriet Mosatche, Girl Scouts of the U.S.A.

Jo Ann Mosier, Kentucky Department of Education

Tim Moynihan, Mountlake Terrace High School, Mountlake Terrace, WA

Monty Multanen, Edmonds School District, WA

Sandy Murphy, University of California at Davis

Martha Murray-Zinn, Wedgwood Middle School, Fort Worth, TX

Miles Myers, National Council of Teachers of English

Tienne Myers, Hancock Elementary School, Philadelphia, PA

Christina Myren, Acacia Elementary School, Thousand Oaks, CA

Joseph Newkirk, School for the Physical City, New York, NY

Lee Odell, Rensselaer Polytechnic Institute, Troy, NY

Gary Oden, Institute for Learning, Learning Research and Development Center, University of Pittsburgh

Alan Olds, Standley Lake High School, Westminster, CO

Marian Opest, Penn Hills Senior School, Pittsburgh, PA

Ann Osborne, Linton Middle School, Pittsburgh, PA

Jean O'Shell, Linton Middle School, Pittsburgh, PA

Kevin Padian, Department of Integrative Biology, University of California at Berkeley

Dennie Palmer Wolf, Harvard PACE

Tim Patterson, Mountlake Terrace High School, Mountlake Terrace, WA

Risa Payne, Wedgwood Middle School, Fort Worth, TX

David Pearson, University of Illinois

Charles Peters, Oakland Michigan Schools, MI

Marge Petit, Vermont Institute for Mathematics, Science, and Technology

Cindy Phillips, Tri City Elementary, Myrtle Creek, OR

Marcia Pink, Newport High School, WA

John Porter, National Alliance for Restructuring Education

Robert Probst, University of Georgia

Fred Quinonez, Overland Trail Middle School, Brighton, CO

Susan Radley, Teachers College Writing Project at Columbia University, NY

Donald Raintree, Universal Dynamics Inc., Woodbridge, VA

Lynn Raith, Pittsburgh Public Schools, PA

Ginny Redish, Redish & Associates, Inc.

Eeva Reeder, Mountlake Terrace High School, Mountlake Terrace, WA

Susan Rowe, Bonnieville School, CT

Don Rubin, University of Georgia

Carmen Rubino, Eaglecrest High School, Aurora, CO

Robert Rueda, University of Southern California

Marge Sable, National Alliance for Restructuring Education

Sandy Short, Hillview Crest Elementary School, New Haven Unified School District, CA

Cheryl Sims, School for the Physical City, New York, NY

Sandy Smith, Harrison High School, Aurora, CO

Dave Steward, John Evans Jr. High School, Greely, CO

John Swang, National Student Research Center, Mandeville, LA

Carol Tateishi, Bay Area Writing Project

Johnny Tolliver, Delaware State University

Cathy Topping-Wiese, U-32 Junior/Senior High School, Montpelier, VT

Lora Turner, A. Leo Weil School, Pittsburgh, PA

Ann Tweed, Eaglecrest High School, Aurora, CO

Zalman Usiskin, The University of Chicago School Mathematics Project

John Vibber, Mt. Abraham Union High School, Briston, VT

Dale Vigil, San Diego City Schools, CA

Rhonda Wagner, Cherry Creek Schools, Englewood, CO

Brenda Wallace, New York, NY

Anne Weinstock, PS 116, New York, NY

Eric Weiss, U-32 Junior/Senior High School, Montpelier, VT

Sandra Wilcox, Michigan State University

Arnold Willens, PS 41, New York, NY

Ann Marie Williams, PS 41, New York, NY

Darby Williams, Sacramento County Office of Education, CA

Scott J. Wolff, Davenport West High School, IA

Victoria Young, Texas Education Agency

Judi Zawojewski, National-Louis University, Evanston, IL

MATERIALS USED WITH PERMISSION

"Miss Sadie" student work. From *Student Essays Illustrating the CAP Rhetorical Effectiveness Scoring System.* Copyright 1992 by California Department of Education, 721 Capital Mall, 4th Floor, Sacramento, CA 95814.

"Candle Life" task. From *Algebra Experiments, Book 1: Exploring Linear Functions.* By Mary Jean Winter and Ronald Carlson. Copyright 1993 by Addison-Wesley Publishing Company.

"Light Reflection" research format and student work. From *The Student Researcher.* National Student Research Center, Dr. John I. Swang, Mandeville Middle School, 2525 Soult Street, Mandeville, LA 70448. Tel. 504-626-5980 or nsrcmms@aol.com.

"Spot Remover" task and student work. California Assessment Program. Copyright 1989 by California Department of Education, 721 Capital Mall, 4th Floor, Sacramento, CA 95814.

REFERENCES

American Association for the Advancement of Science. (1993). *Benchmarks for Science Literacy: Project 2061.* New York: Oxford University Press.

American Federation of Teachers. (1994). *Defining World Class Standards: A Publication Series.* Vol. 1-3. Washington, DC: Author.

American Federation of Teachers. (1995). *Making Standards Matter: A Fifty-State Progress Report on Efforts to Raise Academic Standards.* Washington, DC: Author.

Balanced Assessment Project. (In preparation). Schoenfeld, A.H., et al. *Twenty Plus Assessment Packages at Grades Four, Eight, Ten and Twelve.* Berkeley, CA: Graduate School of Education, University of CA at Berkeley.

Boy Scouts of America. (1990). *The Boy Scout Handbook.* Irving, TX: Author.

The Business Task Force on Student Standards. (1995). *The Challenge of Change: Standards To Make Education Work For All Our Children.* Washington, DC: Business Coalition for Education Reform.

Commission on Standards for School Mathematics. (1989). *Curriculum and Evaluation: Standards for School Mathematics.* Reston, VA: National Council of Teachers of Mathematics.

Fitzgerald. W., et al. (1986). *Middle Grades Mathematics Project: Factors and Multiples.* Menlo Park, CA: Addison-Wesley Publishing Company.

Girl Scouts of the U.S.A. (1995). *Cadette Girl Scout Handbook.* New York: Author.

Lappan, G., et al. (1986). *Middle Grades Mathematics Project: Similarity and Equivalent Fractions.* Menlo Park, CA: Addison-Wesley Publishing Company.

Lenchner, G. (1983). *Creative Problem Solving in School Mathematics.* Boston, MA: Houghton Mifflin Company.

National Council of Teachers of English & International Reading Association. (1996). *Standards for the English Language Arts.* Urbana, IL and Newark, DE: NCTE and IRA.

National Council of Teachers of Mathematics. (1994). *Mathematics Teaching in the Middle School.* Vol. 1. No. 1. Reston, VA: Author. pp. 53-54.

National Council of Teachers of Mathematics. (1994). *Mathematics Teaching in the Middle School.* Vol. 1. No. 3. Reston, VA: Author. p. 223.

National Education Goals Panel, Technical Planning Group. (1993). *Promises to Keep: Creating High Standards for American Students.* Washington, DC: Author.

National Research Council. (1996). *National Science Education Standards.* Washington, DC: National Academy Press.

New Standards Project. (1994). *The New Standards Framework for Applied Learning.* Discussion draft. Washington, DC: Author.

Phillips, E., et al. (1986). *Middle Grades Mathematics Project: Probability.* Menlo Park, CA: Addison-Wesley Publishing Company.

Sallee, G. T., et al. (In preparation). *College Preparatory Mathematics.* Davis, CA: CRESS Center, University of California at Davis.

Secretary's Commission on Achieving Necessary Skills. (1992). *Learning A Living: A Blueprint for High Performance—A SCANS Report For America 2000.* Washington, DC: U.S. Department of Labor.

Shroyer, J. and Fitzgerald, W. (1986). *Middle Grades Mathematics Project: Mouse and Elephant: Measuring Growth.* Menlo Park, CA: Addison-Wesley Publishing Company.

Usiskin, Z. (1990). *Transition Mathematics.* The University of Chicago School Mathematics Project (UCSMP). Glenview, IL: Scott, Foresman.

SELECT BIBLIOGRAPHY

Australian Education Council and Curriculum Corporation. (1991). *A National Statement on Mathematics for Australian Schools.* Carlton, Victoria: Curriculum Corporation.

California State Board of Education. (1987). *English-Language Arts Framework for California Public Schools.* Sacramento: Author.

California State Board of Education. (1985). *Mathematics Framework for California Public Schools.* Sacramento: Author.

California State Board of Education. (1990). *Science Framework for California Public Schools.* Sacramento: Author.

Colorado State Department of Education. (Draft). *Model Content Standards for Mathematics.* Denver: Author.

Colorado State Department of Education. (Draft). *Model Content Standards for Reading and Writing.* Denver: Author.

Colorado State Department of Education. (Draft). *Model Content Standards for Science.* Denver: Author.

Commission on Maine's Common Core of Learning. (1990). *Maine's Common Core of Learning: An investment in Maine's future.* Augusta, ME: Maine Department of Education.

Curriculum Corporation. (1994). *English—a curriculum profile for Australian schools.* Carlton, Victoria: Author.

Curriculum Corporation. (1994). *Mathematics—a curriculum profile for Australian schools.* Carlton, Victoria: Author.

Curriculum Corporation. (1994). *Science—a curriculum profile for Australian schools.* Carlton, Victoria: Author.

Der Kultusminister des Landes Nordrhein-Westfalen. (1989). *Grundschule in Nordrhein-Westfalen.* Köln, Bundesrepublik Deutschland: Greven Verlag Köln.

Dutch Ministry of Education and Science. (1993). *The Dutch National Curriculum for Primary School.* Typescript provided in translation by the Dutch Ministry of Education and Science.

Dutch Ministry of Education and Science. (1993). *Mathematics: General and Core Objectives.* Typescript provided in translation by the Dutch Ministry of Education and Science.

Educational and Cultural Exchange Division, UNESCO and International Affairs Department, Science and International Affairs Bureau, Ministry of Education, Science and Culture. (1983). *Course of Study for Elementary Schools in Japan.* (Notification No. 155 of Ministry of Education, Science and Culture.) Tokyo: Printing Bureau, Ministry of Finance.

Educational and Cultural Exchange Division, UNESCO and International Affairs Department, Science and International Affairs Bureau, Ministry of Education, Science and Culture. (1983). *Course of Study for Lower Secondary Schools in Japan.* (Notification No. 156 of Ministry of Education, Science and Culture.) Tokyo: Printing Bureau, Ministry of Finance.

Educational and Cultural Exchange Division, UNESCO and International Affairs Department, Science and International Affairs Bureau, Ministry of Education, Science and Culture. (1983). *Course of Study for Upper Secondary Schools in Japan.* (Notification No. 163 of Ministry of Education, Science and Culture.) Tokyo: Printing Bureau, Ministry of Finance.

Girl Scouts of the U.S.A. (1993). *Brownie Girl Scout Handbook.* New York: Author.

Girl Scouts of the U.S.A. (1995). *Cadette Girl Scout Handbook.* New York: Author.

Girl Scouts of the U.S.A. (1995). A *Resource Book for Senior Girl Scouts.* New York: Author.

Illinois Academic Standards Project of the Illinois State Board of Education. (Draft). *Illinois Academic Standards, State Goals 1-10: English Language Arts and Mathematics.* Springfield, IL: Author.

Illinois Academic Standards Project of the Illinois State Board of Education. (Draft). *Illinois Academic Standards, State Goals 11-18: Science and Social Studies.* Springfield, IL: Author.

Iowa Department of Education. (1994). *Education is Iowa's Future: The State Plan for Educational Excellence in the 21st Century.* Des Moines, IA: Author.

Kentucky Department of Education. (1993). *Transformations: Kentucky's Curriculum Framework.* Frankfort, KY: Author.

Maine Department of Education. (Draft). *Learning Results.* Augusta, ME: Author.

Ministère de l'Éducation Nationale. (1985). *Colléges: Programmes et Instructions.* Paris: Centre National de Documentation Pédagogique.

Ministère de l'Éducation Nationale. (1994). *Évaluation à l'entrée en seconde générale et technologique: Français.* Paris: Direction de l'Évaluation et de la Prospective.

Ministère de l'Éducation Nationale de la Jeunesse et des Sports, Direction des Écoles. (1991). *Les cycles à l'école primaire.* Paris: Centre National de Documentation Pédagogique & Hachette Écoles.

Ministère de l'Éducation Nationale. (1991). *Baccalauréat Professionel: Enseignements généraux.* Paris: Centre National de Documentation Pédagogique.

Ministry of Education, New Zealand. (1994). *English in the New Zealand Curriculum.* Wellington, New Zealand: Learning Media Ltd.

Ministry of Education, New Zealand. (1994). *Mathematics in the New Zealand Curriculum.* Wellington, New Zealand: Learning Media Ltd.

Ministry of Education, New Zealand. (1994). *Science in the New Zealand Curriculum.* Wellington, New Zealand: Learning Media Ltd.

Ministry of Education and Research. (1987). *Curriculum Guidelines for Compulsory Education in Norway.* W. Nygaard, Norge: H. Aschehoug & Co.

Ministry of Education of the Russian Federation and the General School Education Institute of the Russian Academy of Education. (1993). *The Provisional State Education Standards, General Secondary Education: Mathematics.* Moscow: Author.

Ministry of Education and Training, Canada. (1993). *Provincial Standards: Mathematics.* Toronto, Ontario: Queen's Printer for Ontario.

Ministry of Education and Training, Canada. (1993). *The Common Curriculum, Grades 1-9.* Toronto, Ontario: Queen's Printer for Ontario.

Missouri Department of Education. (Draft). *Academic Performance Standards and Curriculum Frameworks.* Jefferson City, MO: Author.

National Science Teachers Association. (1992). *Scope, Sequence, and Coordination Content Core.* Washington, DC: Author.

Nolan, Kate. (1994). *Mathematics in Five Countries.* Pittsburgh, PA: New Standards.

Oregon Department of Education. (1993). *21st Century Schools: Information Packet.* Salem, OR: Author.

Oregon Department of Education. (1986). *English Language Arts: Common Curriculum Goals.* Salem, OR: Author.

Oregon Department of Education. (1986). *Essential Learning Skills.* Salem, OR: Author.

Oregon Department of Education. (1987). *Mathematics: Common Curriculum Goals.* Salem, OR: Author.

Rhode Island Department of Education. (1994). *First Draft: Mathematics Framework for Grades K-12.* Providence, RI: Author.

School Curriculum and Assessment Authority. (1994). *Design & Technology in the National Curriculum.* Draft Proposals. London: Author and the Central Office of Information.

School Curriculum and Assessment Authority. (1994). *English in the National Curriculum.* Draft Proposals. London: Author and the Central Office of Information.

School Curriculum and Assessment Authority. (1994). *Science in the National Curriculum.* Draft Proposals. London: Author and the Central Office of Information.

School-to-Work Transition Team. (1994). *Education for Employment in Rhode Island: The Report of the School-to-Work Opportunities Transition Team.* Providence, RI: Author.

Scottish Office Education Department. (1991). *Curriculum and Assessment in Scotland, National Guidelines: English Language 5-14.* Edinburgh: Author.

Southern Examining Group. (1992). *English: General Certificate of Secondary Education, National Curriculum Syllabus, 1994 Examinations.* Surrey, England: Author.

Speech Communication Association. (1996). *Speaking, Listening, and Media Literacy Standards For K through 12 Education.* Annendale, VA: Author.

State of Delaware. (1995). *English Language Arts Curriculum Framework: Volumes One and Two.* Dover, DE: Author.

State of Delaware. (1995). *Mathematics Curriculum Framework: Volumes One and Two.* Dover, DE: Author.

State of Delaware. (1995). *Science Curriculum Framework: Volumes One and Two.* Dover, DE: Author.

The State of Vermont Department of Education. (1995). *Content Standards: Working Draft.* Montpelier, VT: Author.

The State of Vermont Department of Education. (1995). *Performance Standards: Working Draft.* Montpelier, VT: Author.

The State of Vermont Department of Education. (1995). *Vermont's Common Core Framework for Curriculum and Assessment: Draft.* Montpelier, VT: Author.

Stigler, J. and Stevenson, H. W. (1991). "How Asian Teachers Polish Each Lesson to Perfection." *American Educator.* Spring, 1991, 12-20, 43-47.

Texas Education Agency. (1995). *English Language Arts Essential Elements: Chapter 75, Texas Administrative Code.* Austin, TX: Author.

Texas Education Agency. (1995). Mathematics *Essential Elements: Chapter 75, Texas Administrative Code.* Austin, TX: Author.

Texas Education Agency. (1995). *Science Essential Elements: Chapter 75, Texas Administrative Code.* Austin, TX: Author.

The University of the State of New York and The State Education Department. (1995). Preliminary *Draft Framework for Career Development and Occupational Studies.* Albany, NY: Authors.

The University of the State of New York and The State Education Department. (1994). Preliminary *Draft Framework for English Language Arts.* Albany, NY: Authors.

The University of the State of New York and The State Education Department. (1995). *Preliminary Draft Framework for Mathematics, Science and Technology.* Albany, NY: Authors.

Utbildningsdepartmentet. (1993). *Kursplaner för Grundskolan.* Stockholm: Nordstedts Tryckeri AB.

NEW STANDARDS PRODUCTS AND SERVICES: WHERE TO FIND WHAT YOU NEED

These performance standards serve as the basis of design specifications for the New Standards reference examinations and portfolios, which in turn provide information about performance to students, teachers, and parents.

But the performance standards cannot by themselves provide all of the information students and teachers will need in order to improve student performance in the core subjects.

Therefore, we include here some of the common requests we encounter from people who have begun to use the performance standards, along with information about the New Standards resources available to answer those requests.

- **Where can I find samples of student work that do not yet meet the standards? What about rubrics and scoring guides?**

New Standards Released Tasks contain sample tasks, scoring rubrics, and samples of student work at all of the score points given in the rubrics. Released Tasks can be ordered from Harcourt Brace Educational Measurement (Tel. 800-228-0752).

- **Clearly, many parts of the performance standards can only be assessed through some kind of portfolio system. Does New Standards offer portfolios?**

Yes—the New Standards portfolios in Mathematics, Science, English Language Arts, and Applied Learning are constructed to link directly to the performance standards. Portfolios are available individually, in classroom sets, and in sampler packets. Portfolios can be ordered directly from New Standards (Tel. 888-361-6233).

- **Our school district is using the performance standards to improve teaching and learning. We want standardized tests that can tell us how our students are doing based on the standards. What does New Standards offer?**

The New Standards reference examinations are available in English Language Arts and Mathematics for grades 4, 8, and 10. The examinations are designed using the performance standards as their foundation. Score reports for the reference examinations tell teachers and students about the quality of student work by referring to the performance standards. To order reference examinations, call Harcourt Brace Educational Measurement (Tel. 800-228-0752).

- **In order to move to a standards-based district, we need professional development and consulting for teachers and central office staff. Can New Standards help us with this?**

New Standards consultants can provide on-site services in several areas, including professional development, public engagement, strategic planning, standards linking, and technical issues involved with performance assessment. To discuss services needed by your school or district, call the Office of State and Local Relations, located at the National Center on Education and the Economy (Tel. 202-783-3668).